COLLEGE OF MARIN LIBRARY
COLLEGE AVENUE
KENTFIELD, CA 94904

A GEORGE ELIOT DICTIONARY

A GEORGE ELIOT DICTIONARY

The Characters and Scenes of the Novels Stories and Poems Alphabetically Arranged

BY
ISADORE G. MUDGE
AND
M. E. SEARS
Authors of *A Thackeray Dictionary*

HASKELL HOUSE PUBLISHERS LTD.
Publishers of Scarce Scholarly Books
NEW YORK, N. Y. 10012
1972

HASKELL HOUSE PUBLISHERS LTD.
Publishers of Scarce Scholarly Books
280 LAFAYETTE STREET
NEW YORK, N. Y. 10012

```
Library of Congress Cataloging in Publication Data

Mudge, Isadore Gilbert, 1875-1957.
  A George Eliot dictionary.

   Bibliography: p.
   1.  Eliot, George, pseud., i. e. Marian Evans,
afterwards Cross, 1819-1880--Dictionaries, indexes, etc.
I.  Sears, Minnie Earl, 1873-1933, joint author.
II.  Title.
PR4695.M8  1972        823'.8      72-762
ISBN 0-8383-1350-7
```

Printed in the United States of America

CONTENTS

	PAGE
PREFACE	vii
CHRONOLOGICAL LIST OF NOVELS, STORIES, AND POEMS	xi
SYNOPSES	xiii
AUTHORITIES CITED IN DICTIONARY	xxxix
LIST OF ABBREVIATIONS	xliii
DICTIONARY	1
BOOKS MENTIONED IN THE NOVELS AND STORIES	245
INDEX TO ORIGINALS	255

PREFACE

THE present Dictionary was begun about ten years ago when the compilers made a tour of the George Eliot country for the purpose of visiting the scenes of the novels and stories. Interrupted necessarily during the war, it has since been resumed and completed, with such changes and additions as the passage of time has suggested. Like our earlier work, the *Thackeray Dictionary*, it is not an encyclopædia of everything connected with its subject, but merely a dictionary of the characters and scenes of the novels and short stories, and of the poems also, in so far as these latter contain fictitious names or characters. For the purpose of this work the *Impressions of Theophrastus Such* has been counted as fiction and the numerous fictitious characters in those papers indexed.

The aim has been to include in the Dictionary the names of all characters, either fictitious or historical, which have a definite part, however small, in the action of a story, or influence in any way the development of the plot. In the same way all place-names, either real or fictitious, which constitute a definite scene, are included. Historical characters are differentiated from fictitious, and real places from those which exist only in "literary geography". Personal or place-names which are mentioned merely as allusions are omitted, though it has not always been easy to decide just where this line excluding names as allusions should be drawn. *Middlemarch*, for example, with its background of medical education and medical reform, contains many references to the names of real physicians and scientists who are not themselves actual characters in the story. When these, however, are given as influencing the scientific ambition of the hero, Dr. Lydgate, they have been counted as influencing the development of the plot and have been included. *Romola*, again, is so crowded with references to historical persons and places that it has been described as an archæological mosaic. Its many references to classical authors have been excluded, but the poet Luigi Pulci, for example, is included on the ground that the frequent quoting of his poems by Nello, the barber, weaves him into the fabric of the novel. In general, it may be added, the work on names in *Romola* constitutes a very special feature of the Dictionary. The historical characters, some of them very obscure, have been identified and historical notes about them included, and all buildings and streets in Florence mentioned in the story have been identified and notes as to their location, present names, etc., added. The information of this sort is included with the idea of its usefulness in the libraries of schools and colleges where *Romola* is studied as an English text.

While the general plan of this Dictionary is similar to our *Thackeray Dictionary*, there are certain differences which have been indicated by differences in the works of the two writers. George Eliot, herself a good musician, introduced many musical references, names of songs, etc., into her stories, always taking care to make these appropriate to the character or story with which they are connected. This is such a marked feature of her literary method that a record of her musical references has interest, and accordingly all names of songs introduced into the action of the story have been included, with brief notes as to the authors, composers, etc. Another marked feature of her method is the extent to which she mentions books in connexion with her characters to indicate character or local colour. As such references possess a distinct interest, the books mentioned have been identified and included with brief explanations in a separate list at the end of the Dictionary.

Much has been written about the originals of characters and scenes in George Eliot's novels. "More than most writers of fiction," says Parkinson, in his *Scenes*, "George Eliot took her characters and incidents from actual life and set them amid scenes with which she herself was familiar and loved." In her first work of fiction, the *Scenes of Clerical Life*, so much was recognized as real that residents of her old home, Nuneaton, were able to compile lists of originals, sometimes possibly without much foundation for their identification. The fact that a favourite character in fiction had an original in real life is something which seems to interest nearly everyone, and, where identifications rest upon good authority, information about originals has been included. If, however, the authority is questionable, the identification has not been accepted, though it is sometimes mentioned with a caution. Where an original is so generally accepted as to admit of no possible question—for example, Chilvers Coton as the original of Shepperton—no authority is quoted, but in other cases, in view of the inaccurate identifications sometimes met with, authorities are given. For some originals many authorities might be quoted. Where there is such abundance of evidence, the authorities which seem on the whole the best have been chosen for citation. In most cases the references are to printed books or articles, but as the compilers are so fortunate as to have some of the Nuneaton lists mentioned above, some references are to this manuscript information and to other unpublished material. For the convenience of those who wish to work from the original to the fictitious name, an index of originals is given.

Our thanks and acknowledgements are due to many who have helped us during the progress of the work. To George Eliot's nephew, the Reverend Frederic Rawlins Evans, we are especially indebted for information given both at the beginning of our work and during its progress. Canon Evans has aided us on many points, both from his own information and from the relics of George Eliot's early life now in his possession. The novelist's husband, Mr. John W. Cross, has kindly answered an inquiry referred to him. We are much indebted to Dr. Guido Biagi, Chief Librarian of the Medicean-Laurentian Library, Florence, who has supplied us with special information on the history and topography of the Florence of Romola's time, in addition to that which he has made accessible to all in his edition of *Romola*. Mr. Charles Nowell, the City Librarian of Coventry, has kindly contributed items of information about George Eliot and Coventry. Finally, we wish to record our gratitude to the Reverend Hubert H. M. Bartleet, Vicar of Little Malvern, who has most generously placed at our disposal much information from the large collection of notes about prototypes of characters and scenes which he made both during his residence in the George Eliot country and at a later period. Much of the information which Mr. Bartleet has furnished has never been in print before, and his whole-hearted co-operation has made possible a comprehensive record of that aspect of George Eliot's work.

I. G. M.
M. E. S.

CHRONOLOGICAL LIST

BY DATE OF PUBLICATION

OF

GEORGE ELIOT'S NOVELS, SHORT STORIES AND POEMS INCLUDED IN THE DICTIONARY

1857.	**The Sad Fortunes of the Reverend Amos Barton.** (Scenes of Clerical Life.)
1857.	**Mr. Gilfil's Love Story.** (Scenes of Clerical Life.)
1857.	**Janet's Repentance.** (Scenes of Clerical Life.)
1859.	**Adam Bede.**
1859.	**The Lifted Veil.**
1860.	**The Mill on the Floss.**
1861.	**Silas Marner : the Weaver of Raveloe.**
1862–3.	**Romola.**
1864.	**Brother Jacob.**
1866.	**Felix Holt.**
1868.	**The Spanish Gypsy.**
1869.	**Agatha.** (Later included in The Legend of Jubal and Other Poems. 1874.)
1869.	**Brother and Sister.** (Later included in The Legend of Jubal and Other Poems. 1874.)
1869.	**How Lisa Loved the King.** (Later included in The Legend of Jubal and Other Poems. 1874.)
1870.	**The Legend of Jubal.** (Later included in The Legend of Jubal and Other Poems. 1874.)
1871.	**Armgart.** (Later included in The Legend of Jubal and Other Poems. 1874.)
1871–2.	**Middlemarch.**
1874.	**Arion.** (Included in The Legend of Jubal and Other Poems. 1874.)

1874.	**A Minor Prophet.** (Included in The Legend of Jubal and Other Poems. 1874.)	
1874.	**Stradivarius.** (Included in The Legend of Jubal and Other Poems. 1874.)	
1876.	**Daniel Deronda.**	
1878.	**A College Breakfast Party.** (Reprinted in The Legend of Jubal and Other Poems. 2nd edition. 1879.)	
1879.	**The Death of Moses.** (Included in The Legend of Jubal and Other Poems. 2nd edition. 1879.)	
1879.	**Impressions of Theophrastus Such.**	
1919.	**Early Essays.** (Dating from the period of about 1846. Three essays only included in the Dictionary.)	

SYNOPSES

Adam Bede. 1st edition, Edinburgh: William Blackwood and Sons, 1859. 3 vols.

SCENE: "Hayslope," "Broxton," and other villages in "Loamshire" (i.e. Ellastone, Roston, etc., in Staffordshire); "Snowfield" and "Stoniton", in "Stonyshire" (i.e. Wirksworth and Derby, in Derbyshire); points on the road from "Hayslope" to Windsor.

TIME: 18th June, 1799–November, 1801; Epilogue, June, 1807.

Adam Bede is a picture of English village life at the end of the eighteenth century, bringing into the canvas life-like portraits of artisan, village worthy, tenant farmer, Wesleyan preacher, rector, and squire. The outstanding figures are: Adam Bede, the honest craftsman; Mrs. Poyser, of keen eye and pungent, homely humour; Dinah Morris, the Methodist; and Hetty Sorrel, one of George Eliot's many studies in egoism. The climax of the plot—Hetty's crime and trial, and her confession to Dinah Morris—was suggested by an experience of the real Dinah, George Eliot's "Methodist Aunt Samuel", in which she had brought to confession an ignorant girl sentenced to death for child murder. Throughout, the book contains much in both characters and descriptions that is reminiscent of the early residence of Robert Evans and other members of his family in Staffordshire.

Adam Bede, a young carpenter of ability and force of character, has made his way against odds to the position of foreman of Jonathan Burge's timber yard, in Hayslope. He might even marry his employer's daughter, but he has eyes for no one except Hetty Sorrel, the shallow little beauty of Hayslope, who lives with her uncle, Martin Poyser, a substantial farmer. Mrs. Poyser's niece, Dinah Morris, a saintly young Methodist preacher, visits at the Poysers' and preaches on the village Green. Seth, Adam's brother, is in love with Dinah. Grieved at Hetty's worldliness, Dinah tries unsuccessfully to turn her thoughts to higher things. One of Adam Bede's warmest friends is Arthur Donnithorne, the old Squire's heir, a generous, impulsive young man, popular with the tenantry. Attracted by Hetty's beauty, Arthur visits Mrs. Poyser's dairy to talk with Hetty. Later they meet frequently in the woods of Donnithorne Chase, and Arthur, though he makes a feeble effort to break away from her attraction, ends by falling in love with her, ignorant of the fact that his friend Adam is courting her. Hetty, believing that he means to marry her and make her lady of the manor, yields entirely to his passion. Adam finds Arthur and Hetty together in the woods and forces Arthur to fight. Ignorant of how far matters have gone, Adam reproaches Arthur with putting wrong ideas into Hetty's head, and makes him promise to write a letter to Hetty breaking off the affair. Arthur allows Adam to believe that it has been merely a flirtation, and writes the letter to Hetty, giving her, however, an address at which she can find him, in case she needs his help, and then goes away to join his regiment. Hetty, miserable over the end of her day-dream, comes to think of Adam as the best that is left her, and eventually promises to marry him. The wedding is set for early spring, but the Poysers meanwhile are worrying over their own affairs, as the inimitable Mrs. Poyser has offended the stingy old Squire with her caustic statement of some home truths, and they fear that he will give them notice to quit the farm, which their family has held for generations. As the time of the wedding approaches, Hetty, realizing that she cannot much longer conceal her condition, thinks of suicide, but lacks the courage to kill herself. She leaves home on pretence of visiting Dinah Morris at Snowfield, but goes instead by a devious route to Windsor, the address which Arthur Donnithorne had given her. Finding that Arthur has gone with his regiment to Ireland, she turns back in despair with a vague idea of throwing herself on Dinah Morris, whose friendliness she remembers. On the way back her child is born in a strange house, where she has sought lodgings. Adam, meanwhile, believing that Hetty is visiting Dinah, is happily making preparations for their wedding. When he goes to Snowfield to bring Hetty back from her supposed visit, he finds that she has never been there, and after searching for her for a time returns to bring the news to the Poysers. Mr. Irwine, the rector, learns that Hetty has been arrested for child-murder and is awaiting trial in Stoniton jail. Hetty, terrified and dazed, maintains at her trial a sullen silence which alienates sympathy, and obstinately refuses to confess even after she has been found guilty and condemned to death. Dinah Morris goes to Stoniton to try to help Hetty, stays with her in her cell, softens her heart, and persuades her to confess. On the last day Dinah rides in the cart with Hetty to the place of execution, but at the last moment Hetty's sentence is commuted to transportation. Her reprieve has been brought by Arthur Donnithorne, who, overwhelmed on his return from Ireland by the news of Hetty's tragedy, has bent every effort to saving her life. The Poysers and Adam Bede plan to move away from the lands of the man who has deeply injured them, but finally agree to stay when Arthur, deeply repentant, exiles himself to the army on the Continent. After time has healed his feeling about Hetty, Adam finds that he loves Dinah Morris. Though she at first refuses him, she realizes later that her feeling for him is too strong for them to remain apart, and they are married.

Agatha. *See* **Poems—Agatha.**

Amos Barton. *See* **Scenes of clerical life. Sad fortunes of the Reverend Amos Barton.**

Arion. *See* **Poems—Arion.**

Armgart. *See* **Poems—Armgart.**

Brother and Sister. *See* **Poems—Brother and Sister.**

Brother Jacob. First published in the *Cornhill Magazine*, vol. x, pp. 1–32, July, 1864. Reprinted with *Silas Marner* and the *Lifted Veil* in a volume of the Cabinet edition of the Works, 1878.

SCENE : " Grimworth," a small market town.

Brother Jacob was originally written in 1860, under the title *Mr. David Faux, Confectioner*, but was not published till 1864, when George Eliot gave it to Smith & Elder to make up for the fact that *Romola*, for which that firm had paid a very high price, was not at that time selling quite as well as had been hoped.

David Faux, in order to go to the West Indies to make his fortune, steals his mother's hoard of twenty guineas, but before he can make way with it is seen by his idiot brother Jacob. To divert Jacob's attention, David tells him that guineas turn into yellow lozenges, and wins the idiot's inconvenient love by giving him the sweetmeats. After six years in Jamaica, where instead of making a fortune he works as a cook, David returns to England, and under the name of Edward Freely establishes himself as a confectioner in the little town of Grimworth, passing himself off as a scion of a good family, the nephew of a fictitious Admiral Freely. The convenience of his cooked food demoralizes the good housewives of Grimworth, and David prospers, gains quite a reputation as a great traveller of many adventures, and succeeds in becoming engaged to pretty Penny Palfrey, the young daughter of the richest farmer in the neighbourhood. He makes the mistake, however, of claiming a small legacy which his father had left him, and this recalls him to the mind of the idiot brother with the sweet tooth. When David is entertaining his fiancée and her family, brother Jacob appears, raids the supply of lozenges, and claims relationship with " Mr. Freely ". David's real name and his theft are discovered, and he loses his bride and has to leave Grimworth.

College Breakfast Party. *See* **Poems—College Breakfast Party.**

Daniel Deronda. First issued in eight monthly parts, beginning February, 1868, making four volumes. First book edition, Edinburgh : William Blackwood and Sons, 1868. 4 vols.

SCENE: "Wessex," "Topping Abbey," London and vicinity; "Leubronn," Frankfort, Mainz, Genoa, and other points on the Continent.

TIME: 1865–6.

Daniel Deronda is a novel of two distinct themes and stories, presenting on the one hand a picture of Jewish life and character and of the Jewish aspiration for the restoration of a separate national existence and culture, and on the other, a study of selfishness in the character of Gwendolen Harleth, who, through suffering and the consciousness of wrong doing, is saved " as by fire " and regenerated into the beginning of something better. The two stories touch in the character of Daniel Deronda, in whom Mordecai, the Jew, sees the restorer of his race, and in whom Gwendolen Harleth finds the saving force which changes her philosophy of life.

Gwendolen Harleth, a beauty, who has been spoiled by an adoring family, is ambitious for a distinguished position. She has no fortune, so she expects to marry someone who can give her the position and consideration to which she thinks that she is entitled, and at the same time appreciate her superiority enough to let her lead him in everything. Though selfish, she is not entirely heartless. When Sir Hugo Mallinger's nephew, the rich Henleigh Grandcourt, a blasé, middle-aged autocrat, first sees Gwendolen, he admires her beauty. Piqued by her aloofness, he pays her marked court and intends to marry her. Mrs. Glasher, Grandcourt's discarded mistress, tells Gwendolen that Grandcourt ought to marry her and legitimize her four children. Gwendolen promises Mrs. Glasher not to marry Grandcourt, and goes with friends to the Continent to avoid him. At Leubronn she gambles and begins to lose as soon as she sees that Daniel Deronda is watching her with disapproval instead of with the admiration which she excites in others. Deronda, a handsome man with many virtues and no vices, has been brought up by Sir Hugo Mallinger as his nephew, though he himself believes that he is Sir Hugo's natural son. This belief, though it does not lessen in any way his affection for Sir Hugo, has made him somewhat detached and aloof. From Leubronn Gwendolen is called home suddenly by the loss of her mother's small fortune, and finds that she must do something to earn money. The thought of a position as governess is so distasteful to her that she breaks her promise to Mrs. Glasher, and, when Grandcourt renews his suit, accepts him, assuring herself that she does it for her mother's sake, and feeling sure that Grandcourt will always be led by her. On the day of her wedding she receives a bitter letter from Mrs. Glasher which throws her into hysterics. Unwilling to injure Mrs. Glasher still further, she conceals from Grandcourt the reason for her agitation, and their married life starts with irritation on his side and unhappiness on hers. While visiting at Sir Hugo Mallinger's, Gwendolen meets Deronda again, and, anxious to justify herself in his eyes, makes opportunities of talking to him, gradually coming under the influence of his higher idealism, taking him as a sort of spiritual guide. Grandcourt, a selfish tyrant who has never permitted the slightest opposition on the part of any of his dependents, objects to his wife's evident interest in Deronda, and tells her so unpleasantly. Deronda, however, has only a friendly interest in Gwendolen, as he has now found interests in London which absorb him. While boating on the Thames he rescues Mirah Cohen (or Lapidoth), a beautiful and friendless Jewess, from suicide, and takes her to the home of his friends, the Meyricks, until her lost brother Ezra can be found. While seeking this Ezra Cohen, Deronda meets Mordecai, a consumptive Hebrew dreamer, whose idealism and evident liking for Deronda draw Deronda to him. From Mordecai, Deronda learns much about Jewish history and ideals, especially about Mordecai's own dream of a restored Jewish nationality. Eventually a chance remark shows that Mordecai is Mirah's lost brother, Ezra Mordecai Cohen, and Deronda brings together Mordecai, for whom he now feels a strong friendship, and Mirah, whom he is beginning to love. Gwendolen, meantime, is finding only unhappiness in her married life. Instead of the indulgent husband that she expected, Grandcourt has shown himself a tyrant, and, his irritation once aroused, is thwarting her in all her desires and treating her with cruelty. Her unhappiness awakens her conscience, and she feels the need of the spiritual help which Deronda means to her. At times she fancies that she could even kill her husband. Grandcourt starts on a yachting trip on the Mediterranean, forcing Gwendolen to accompany him. At Genoa, Grandcourt's irritation is increased by finding Deronda there. Deronda's presence at Genoa is due to the fact that he had been summoned there to meet his hitherto unknown mother. She proves to be the Princess Halm-Eberstein (formerly a great prima donna, the Alcharisi), a Jewess who hated her race and who had sent her little son to England to be brought up as a Christian, ignorant of his race. Grandcourt takes Gwendolen, against her will, out in a small sail boat and accidently falls overboard and drowns before Gwendolen throws him a rope. Gwendolen, who had delayed for a moment in throwing the rope, believes herself guilty of his death and jumps in after him, but is rescued. To Deronda she accuses herself of Grandcourt's murder, and finds her only comfort, both then, and after her return to England, in the counsel which he gives her. Grandcourt's will makes Mrs. Glasher's son his heir, and leaves only a small provision for Gwendolen. Deronda, returning to England with the news that he is a Jew, is welcomed with joy by Mordecai and Mirah. He and Mirah marry, and after Mordecai's death, go to Palestine to try to make true his dream of a restored Jewish nation.

Early Essays. Privately printed, 1919.

A small volume containing five essays written during George Eliot's stay in Coventry, probably about 1846, while she was still feeling her way in literary form, and not published until 1919, the year of the centenary of her birth. The five essays are : From the note-book of an eccentric ; How to avoid disappointment ; The wisdom of the child ; A little fable with a great moral ; Hints on snubbing. The first, second, and fourth of these, which contain fictitious names, have been included in the Dictionary.

Felix Holt, the Radical. 1st edition, Edinburgh : William Blackwood and Sons, 1866. 3 vols.

SCENE : " Treby Magna," " Little Treby," " Duffield," " Loamford," all in " North Loamshire ".

TIME : Principal action, 1832–3 ; retrospective narratives, 1729, 1812–25.

Felix Holt is a study in the Radicalism of the time of the Reform Bill, contrasting the ideal radicalism of Felix Holt, who, with talent which might command material success, prefers to spend himself in social service, and the political radicalism of the good business man, Harold Transome, who breaks away from the Tory traditions of his family because he sees that " Radical sticks are growing while Tory oaks are rotting ". While Radicalism furnishes the theme of the story, the plot is woven around an intricate point of inheritance, and involves two contrasted cases of concealed parentage, that of Esther Lyon, where the concealment has been prompted by affection, and that of Harold Transome, where the secret has sprung from sin and the revelation brings further unhappiness. Contrasted with various types of worldliness is the unworldly, eccentric, lovable Rufus Lyon, one of the finest representations in fiction of English Dissent.

Retrospective.—The Transomes, of Transome Court, hold their estate in base fee. In 1729 John Justus Transome entailed his estate on his son Thomas and Thomas's heirs, with remainder to the Bycliffes. Thomas, a spendthrift, disposed of his and his descendants' rights to his lawyer cousin Durfey, who became Durfey-Transome. On the extinction of Thomas's line, the property must pass from Durfey's descendants to the Bycliffes. By 1832 the only descendant of Thomas left is old Tommy Trounsem, the bill-sticker. The Transomes feel quite safe, however, as the Bycliffes are supposed to have died out in 1812 with Maurice Christian Bycliffe, who started suit for the estate that year, but died in prison, into which he had been thrown on a trumped-up charge. Bycliffe had, however, married secretly a young French girl, Annette Ledru, and, shortly after her husband's death, Annette and her baby were rescued from starvation by the Independent minister, Rufus Lyon, who married Annette and after her death brought up her child as his own daughter, Esther. Esther Lyon is, therefore, a Bycliffe, though she is ignorant of her parentage and her step-father is ignorant of her legal rights. Lawsuits and mismanagement have made the Transomes poorer. As Mr. Transome is a weak-minded invalid, the estate has been managed by his handsome imperious wife. With no affection for her husband, Mrs. Transome had turned to the sharp lawyer, Jermyn, who first made love to her and then used his hold over her to fleece the estate. Avoided by her neighbours because of scandal, she had centred all her affection on her second son, Harold, who went East to make his fortune.

The Story.—At the beginning of the story, in 1832, Harold Transome returns to England to take his place as heir after the death of his elder brother. He treats his mother generously, but does not defer to her, and his announcement that he will stand for Parliament as a Radical shocks her and his Tory neighbours. His canvass soon brings him into contact with Felix Holt, a Radical with ideals of social service which will always keep him poor, who lives in Treby Magna where he follows the trade of a watchmaker, although his parents had planned to have him rise socially by becoming a physician. As a matter of principle, he makes his mother give up the profitable sale of some worthless medicines. She asks her minister, Rufus Lyon, to remonstrate with Felix, and Felix thus meets Mr. Lyon's beautiful and fastidious daughter, Esther, who has a natural taste for the refinements of life. While antagonized by Esther's standards, Felix is interested in her, and continues the acquaintance, though at first only to lecture her, and she, while offended by his disregard for appearances, is attracted and wants to justify herself in his eyes. Felix finds a lost pocket-book, which he leaves with Mr. Lyon to be restored to its owner. Mr. Lyon sees in this some articles which must have belonged to Bycliffe, Esther's real father. When Maurice Christian (really Henry Scaddon, once a fellow prisoner of Bycliffe's in France) claims the wallet and refuses to answer questions, Mr. Lyon, distressed and believing that Christian may be Esther's father, whom he supposed dead, consults Mr. Jermyn, telling him Esther's story. As Jermyn knows the Bycliffe claims he realizes Esther's importance, but keeps the knowledge to himself to use as a weapon against Harold Transome. He secures Christian's silence by threats, but the latter, though ignorant of the Bycliffe claims, begins to piece bits of information together, and when he sees Esther as Mr. Lyon's daughter he recognizes her likeness to Bycliffe, and guesses the truth and eventually puts together the whole story. Though he fears it may cost him her affection, Rufus Lyon tells Esther her true story, and finds that the revelation touches her and draws her closer to him. Meantime, Felix and Esther have been gradually falling in love, though Felix believes that the difference in their attitude towards life makes marriage impossible, and Esther, while her ambition to be a great lady is changing, is not quite ready to give up all for Felix. In his political work Felix had found that the Transome agents, unknown to Harold Transome, were using means which he thinks will lead to riot. When election day comes trouble starts at once and the Riot Act is read. Felix, realizing the danger of serious disturbance, joins the crowd with the idea of leading it away from trouble. He is partly successful, but accidentally kills a constable and is arrested. In the riot old Tommy Trounsem is trampled to death. Losing the election, Harold Transome takes up business matters, and, having already suspected Jermyn of dishonesty, starts suit against him. Jermyn appeals to Mrs. Transome to save him by telling Harold the truth about himself and their past relations. After she refuses, he tells Harold that there is a Bycliffe, known only to him, whose claim has matured now that Tommy Trounsem is dead, and threatens Harold with the loss of the estate unless he stops proceedings against him. While Harold is still undecided what course to take, Christian offers to sell him the same information. He honourably refuses to suppress evidence, but learns from Christian that Esther Lyon is the heir. With his mother he invites Esther to Transome Court to try to reach some amicable adjustment, and ends by falling in love with her. Esther sees Mrs. Transome's unhappiness and her embittered life, and that, with the recognition of her love for Felix, who is now awaiting trial for manslaughter, makes her realize that the wealth and rank which once seemed so attractive do not bring happiness. At the trial Esther volunteers testimony in his behalf, but he is sentenced to imprisonment. At a meeting organized to petition for his pardon, Jermyn, who has just learned that Harold has resumed proceedings against him, threatens Harold, and at last tells him publicly that he is his father. Harold offers to relinquish the whole estate to Esther, but as the trial has shown her that she loves Felix, she resigns her claims and returns to her father. Felix is pardoned and he and Esther are married.

Note.—In her desire to be quite accurate on points of law, George Eliot several times consulted Frederic Harrison about the details of the legal part of the plot of *Felix Holt*. For an account of the help which he gave her in this matter, *see* the note under Bycliffe versus Transome in the main part of the Dictionary.

How Lisa loved the King. *See* **Poems—How Lisa loved the King.**

Janet's Repentance. *See* **Scenes of Clerical Life. Janet's Repentance.**

Legend of Jubal. *See* **Poems—Legend of Jubal.**

Impressions of Theophrastus Such. 1st edition, Edinburgh: William Blackwood and Sons, 1879.

Theophrastus Such, a whimsical, humorous, middle-aged bachelor, observes life as he sees it in the society about him and records his observations in a series of satirical character sketches. Chapter ii, "Looking Backward," in which the supposed author gives his recollections of his boyhood in the Midlands, is largely autobiographic, containing some of George Eliot's own recollections of her childhood in Warwickshire.

Contents.—I, Looking inward; II, Looking backward; III, How we encourage research; IV, A man surprised at his originality; V, A too deferential man; VI, Only temper; VII, A political molecule; VIII, The watch-dog of knowledge; IX, A half-breed; X, Debasing the moral currency; XI, The wasp credited with the honeycomb; XII, "So young"; XIII, How we come to give ourselves false testimonials and believe in them; XIV, The too ready writer; XV, Diseases of small authorship; XVI, Moral swindlers; XVII, Shadows of the coming race; XVIII, The modern Hep! Hep! Hep!

The Lifted Veil. Published, anonymously, in *Blackwood's Edinburgh Magazine*, July, 1859. Reprinted with *Silas Marner* and *Brother Jacob* in a volume of the Cabinet edition of the Works, 1878.

SCENE: Geneva, Basle, Prague, Vienna, England.

TIME: *circa* 1830–20th September, 1850.

The Lifted Veil is a mystical story of clairvoyance, the central idea of which—that superhuman gifts do not make for happiness—is best expressed in the motto which George Eliot added to it later:—

"Give me no light, great heaven, but such as turns
To energy of human fellowship;
No powers beyond the human heritage
That makes completer manhood."

That the story was a favourite with its author is indicated by her comment to William Blackwood: "I care for the idea which it embodies and which justifies its painfulness . . . There are many things in it which I would willingly say over again, and I shall never put them in any other form."

Latimer, a frail, sensitive lad, is neglected at home because his father prefers his healthy elder brother, Alfred. At sixteen he is sent to study at Geneva, where he forms a warm friendship for Charles Meunier and passes the happiest years of his life. After a severe illness he finds that he has acquired a strange power of clairvoyance, which enables him, at times, to see distant scenes and events and to read the thoughts of others. When he meets Bertha Grant, a beautiful, cold girl, who is betrothed to Alfred, he is fascinated by her, and his new gift tells him that she is heartless and that he is destined to marry her. At first, however, she is the only one whose thoughts he cannot read. Alfred's death in a hunting accident makes Latimer the heir and he marries Bertha. The marriage is unhappy, as Bertha is dissatisfied because it does not give her all the social success she craves, and Latimer, when his wife's cruel heart and barren mind are eventually open to his insight, finds only misery in the union. At the end of seven years Charles Meunier, now a distinguished physician, visits Latimer. Bertha's maid, Archer, is taken ill and Bertha watches over her anxiously as though afraid to leave her. When Archer is apparently dead an experiment of Dr. Meunier's revives her for a few moments, and she reveals the fact that Bertha means to poison Latimer. Bertha and Latimer separate, and he eventually secludes himself in the country to await the death which his unhappy insight tells him will occur from heart disease on 20th September, 1850.

Middlemarch, A Study of Provincial Life. First issued in eight parts, forming four volumes, December, 1871–December, 1872. 1st edition, Edinburgh: William Blackwood and Sons, 1871-2. 4 vols.

SCENE: "Middlemarch" (Coventry) and vicinity; Rome; London.

TIME: 1829-32.

Middlemarch tells two separate stories, that of Dorothea Brooke and her two marriages, and that of Dr. Lydgate and the Vincy family, loosely knit together by the fact that they are acted on the same stage and before the same detailed background of middle-class life in and near an English provincial town. It was originally begun as two separate novels, *Miss Brooke*, Dorothea's story, and *Middlemarch*, which was to picture the Lydgate-Vincy-Garth scenes, but the two, when partly finished, were combined under the second title. The main theme, failure through pressure of circumstances to realize an ideal aim, is the same in both stories, though its development is different. Dorothea, with the ideals and aspirations of a modern Saint Theresa, blocks the channels of her aspiration by a marriage of which her friends cannot approve, and Lydgate, fired by ambition for the highest service in his profession, is dragged from his ideal by the fact that he has tied himself to a selfish wife. There is a minor story in the love affairs of Fred Vincy and Mary Garth, and the picture of medical men and medical practice in the early nineteenth century is keen and true social satire.

Dorothea Brooke and her younger sister, Celia, are orphans who live with their bachelor uncle at his estate of Tipton Grange, near Middlemarch. Young and ardent, with ideas of self-sacrifice, Dorothea longs for some great vocation in which she can spend herself. She is being courted by Sir James Chettam, a young baronet whose estate adjoins her uncle's, but when she meets the Rev. Mr. Casaubon, a narrow, elderly pedant engaged in an endless work of arid research, she thinks him a great soul and marries him, believing that devotion to his work will realize her ideal of service. They go to Rome on their wedding trip, and there Dorothea sees something of her husband's cousin, Will Ladislaw, a mercurial young man with artistic tastes and no fortune, who is attracted to Dorothea. After her return to England Dorothea soon realizes the futility of her husband's great work, and, though she loyally adapts herself to him, she unconsciously irritates him by seeming to espouse the cause of Will Ladislaw, whom Mr. Casaubon dislikes, although he has educated him out of a sense of responsibility, as Ladislaw's grandmother (Casaubon's aunt) had been disinherited. Mr. Casaubon's estate is near Middlemarch, and there Dorothea meets again Dr. Lydgate, a promising young physician, with ideas about medical reform. Mr. Casaubon has a heart attack and Lydgate, called in to attend him, tells him and Dorothea that the disease may end fatally at any time. About eighteen months after their marriage, Mr. Casaubon, a disappointed man, dies before obtaining from Dorothea a promise that in the event of his death she will carry out his wishes. His will leaves his property to Dorothea, but with the insulting provision that she shall forfeit it all if she marries Ladislaw. Sir James Chettam, now Dorothea's brother-in-law, as he has married Celia, would like to have Ladislaw discreetly removed from the neighbourhood, but he remains to help Mr. Brooke, who is standing for Parliament and has found Ladislaw useful as his factotum.

Dr. Lydgate, in whose work Dorothea had become interested through her husband's illness, is a promising young physician of skill and education but no fortune, who, since he came to Middlemarch some two years before, has been building up a practice and has received from Mr. Bulstrode, a rich man who is trying by philanthropy to ease his conscience about past sharp practices, the appointment as physician to the New Hospital. Lydgate's modern ideas have made enemies among the old school physicians and their supporters. When Lydgate meets Rosamond Vincy, the Mayor's beautiful daughter, he finds her so attractive that he is blind to her selfishness. Rosamond, ambitious to rise socially, and impressed by the fact that Lydgate is nephew to a baronet, decides to marry him and they are married before Lydgate has established himself sufficiently to meet the expense of the style of living that Rosamond considers necessary. The Vincys are connected by marriage with old Peter Featherstone, the miser, as are also the Garths. Fred Vincy, Rosamond's brother, and Mary Garth, the sensible, good-humoured daughter of Caleb Garth, builder and agent, have been in love since childhood. When Peter Featherstone dies without providing for him, Fred, to please Mary, gives up the idea of entering the Church, for which he is not fitted, and Caleb takes him into his business. Eventually Fred and Mary are married and he becomes a successful and respected farmer. In the meantime, as Rosamond will not adapt herself in any way, the Lydgates have lived beyond their means, and

Dr. Lydgate, in serious money difficulties, is hampered by the unsympathetic attitude and stubborn opposition of his wife. When Mr. Bulstrode, his patron at the New Hospital, becomes involved in scandal caused by dishonourable acts in his past, Lydgate is unjustly involved in his disgrace because some financial aid which he has had from Bulstrode at an unfortunate time is wrongly interpreted as a bribe. Almost the only one who stands by him and believes in his integrity is Dorothea Casaubon. Since her husband's death Dorothea has not been happy. She has not been able to find any service which satisfies her idea of self-devotion, and she is increasingly conscious of her love for Ladislaw, although she feels that circumstances have made it impossible for them ever to come together. In her efforts to find ways of spending herself she has given generously to Lydgate's hospital. When she learns that he intends to solve his difficulties by leaving Middlemarch and the work which represents the higher part of himself, she lends him the money to pay Bulstrode, and visits Rosamond to try to persuade her to stand by her husband. At Rosamond's she finds Will Ladislaw, and believing that he is flirting with Rosamond, suffers greatly from the thought, until Rosamond later, touched by Dorothea's generous friendliness, explains the mistake. Realizing her love for Ladislaw, and seeing no satisfaction except in devotion to him, Dorothea decides to marry him and relinquish her property. In this marriage, although for a time it separates her from her family, Dorothea finds the kind of happiness which her nature demands. Lydgate is less fortunate, as Rosamond never sympathizes with his ideals. To meet her demands he has to give up his idea of scientific distinction, and cultivate rich patients, and he dies comparatively young, feeling that his life has been a failure.

Mill on the Floss. 1st edition, Edinburgh : William Blackwood and Sons, 1860. 3 vols.

SCENE : " St. Ogg's " (Gainsborough) and vicinity.

TIME : *circa* 1830–40 (see note).

Mill on the Floss is an " autobiographic novel ", recording much of the author's recollection of her own childhood and of the people and scenes of her Warwickshire days. According to her husband, John Walter Cross, " the early part of Maggie's portraiture is the best representation we can have of George Eliot's own feelings in her childhood, and many of the incidents in the book are based on real experiences of family life, but so mixed with fictitious elements and situations that it would be absolutely misleading to trust to it as history." The title originally selected was *Sister Maggie*, but after the book was about one-third finished, this was changed, at the suggestion of William Blackwood, to *Mill on the Floss*.

As children, Tom and Maggie Tulliver live happily in their home at Dorlcote Mill, the " Mill on the Floss ", which has been in their father's family for five generations. Maggie, a passionate, undisciplined, impulsive, imaginative girl of nine, is devoted to her practical, unimaginative brother, who is three years older. Her fondness for Tom, her devotion to her father, whose favourite child she is, and her instinctive revolt against the standards of the overpoweringly respectable Dodsons, her mother's family—especially Mrs. Glegg, the eldest Dodson aunt—are the forces which mould Maggie's childhood. She is fond of her gentle cousin, Lucy Deane, a neat blond girl who is held up as a model Dodson, but once, in a fit of jealousy at Tom's preference for Lucy, Maggie runs away to join the Gypsies. After an unhappy experience with lawyers through his addiction to lawsuits, Mr. Tulliver determines to educate Tom to be a match for " Old Harry and the raskills ", and places him with the Reverend Walter Stelling, who gives him an entirely unsuitable education. The only other pupil is Philip Wakem, a sensitive, deformed lad, the son of Lawyer Wakem, Mr. Tulliver's enemy. The boys never become real friends, but Philip develops a devoted friendship for Maggie. Mr. Tulliver involves himself in an expensive lawsuit with a neighbour, which is decided against him. The expense bankrupts him, and after an encounter with Wakem he has a stroke which nearly proves fatal. Tom is called back from school, and he and Maggie find the bailiffs in possession of the Mill. The well-to-do Dodsons lament the family disgrace, but give no practical help, and Tom, now sixteen years old, goes to work in a minor position with Guest & Co., his Uncle Deane's firm. To humiliate his fallen enemy, Mr. Wakem buys the Tulliver property and offers to keep Mr. Tulliver on as his employee at the Mill. Mr. Tulliver, recovering, accepts the humiliation, but makes Tom swear eternal enmity against the Wakems. For three years all live a drab, narrow existence. Mr. Tulliver and Tom are straining every nerve to save enough to pay the creditors in full and thus rehabilitate the family honour, and Maggie, with a passionate longing for a fuller-life, finds her only safety in self-sacrifice. Philip Wakem renews their friendship, and he and Maggie meet in the Red Deeps. To Maggie, now in her seventeenth year, it has been merely a tender friendship which brightens her sad life, and when Philip tells her of his love, she does not realize that her affection is not love. The friendship had been concealed from her family, but Tom discovers it and forces Maggie to dismiss Philip. Tom, through Bob Jakin, the packman, learns how to trade on his own account, and with capital borrowed from Aunt Glegg makes enough to complete the sum needed to pay his father's creditors. After the formal payment, Mr. Tulliver, excited by his triumph, has an altercation with Wakem, and suffers another stroke, from which he dies. After her father's death Maggie teaches until, at nineteen, she visits her cousin Lucy Deane, the belle of St. Ogg's, a gentle, sweet-natured girl, who is being courted by the rich Stephen Guest. At Lucy's, Maggie, who has now developed from a plain child into a beautiful woman, tastes for the first time the social pleasures natural to girls of her age. Stephen Guest falls in love with her and she returns his feeling. In Lucy's circle is Philip Wakem, whose love for Maggie is unchanged, and Lucy, knowing the old affection between the two, is blind to Stephen's infatuation and thinks only of bringing Philip and Maggie together. Meanwhile, Guest & Co. buy back the old Mill, and Tom, who has made himself valuable to Mr. Deane's firm, is put in charge as manager. Maggie fights against her feeling for Stephen, but he selfishly forces her to admit her love. They go boating on the Floss and are accidentally carried by the tide too far to return. He persuades her to elope with him, but after they have gone some distance her sense of duty to Lucy asserts itself, and she insists upon returning. Tom, now established at the Mill, proves unforgiving and turns her off. She resists Stephen's importunities to marry him, and tries to find occupation, but public opinion is against her. The fall rains swell the Floss, and a heavy flood comes. Maggie, realizing Tom's danger, rows to the Mill to rescue him. The sudden danger wipes out all their misunderstanding, and they face the peril with a renewal of their childish affection. When they have nearly reached safety they are overwhelmed and drowned together.

Note.—The time of the story is somewhat confused. It opens about 1830—Catholic emancipation, and the burning of York Minster, both events of 1829, and the " Swing " outrages, 1830, are mentioned in the early chapters—and it covers ten years, as Maggie is nine at the beginning and nineteen when she dies. The flood in which Maggie perishes should therefore have taken place about 1840. The historic great flood mentioned in the last chapter as having taken place sixty years before that in which Maggie and Tom perish actually occurred in 1770, seventy years before. Possibly the " sixty years " was reckoned from the beginning rather than the end of the novel.

Minor Prophet. *See* **Poems—Minor Prophet.**

Mr. Gilfil's Love Story. *See* **Scenes of Clerical Life. Mr. Gilfil's Love Story.**

Poems. George Eliot's published poetry consisted of one long dramatic poem, the " Spanish Gypsy ", and fourteen shorter poems. Of these, **all which contain** anything in the way of a story or names of **characters have been included in the Dictionary and are described below. Four poems not included in the Dictionary are** : " O may I join the choir invisible " ; " **Self and Life** " ; " Sweet evenings come and go, Love " ; and " **Two Lovers** ".

Agatha, a poem. First published in the *Atlantic Monthly*, 1869, and issued in separate form the same year. Reprinted in *Jubal and other poems*. Edinburgh : William Blackwood and Sons, 1874.

Agatha, a saintly peasant woman, beloved by her neighbours, is visited by the fair young Countess Linda, to whom she talks of her simple philosophy of life and of a pilgrimage which she once made.

Arion. First published in the *Legend of Jubal and other poems*. Edinburgh : William Blackwood and Sons, 1874.

Arion, the sweet singer, captured by wicked men, pours forth his soul in song before leaping to his death in the waves.

Armgart, a poem. First published in *Macmillan's Magazine*, July, 1871. In book form first reprinted in *The Legend of Jubal and other poems*. Edinburgh : William Blackwood and Sons, 1874.

Armgart, a beautiful young singer with a glorious voice, has been watched over by her old music teacher, Leo, and her cousin, Walpurga, both of whom have made the perfecting of her talent their one aim in life. At her first appearance as a *prima donna* she wins a great triumph. Graf Dornberg, a rich noble, wishes her to marry him, but she refuses, declaring that she must be artist first before she is woman. After a year of unbroken success, she loses her voice as a result of an illness. She would accept the Graf now, but he does not renew his offer, now that her fame, part of her charm in his eyes, is gone. In her despair she thinks that life is ended for her, but from Leo and Walpurga she learns " to bury her dead joy " and live for others.

Brother and Sister: Sonnets. By Marian Lewes. London, 1869. For private circulation only. Reprinted in *The Legend of Jubal and other poems*. Edinburgh : William Blackwood and Sons, 1874.

Brother and Sister is a series of eleven sonnets describing the happy childhood experiences and adventures of two children, a boy—" little man, of forty inches, bound to show no dread "—and his adoring younger sister, who tells the story. Written when the author had reached middle age, they are a true picture of a real sister and brother, George Eliot herself and her older brother Isaac, to whom she was devotedly attached, and form a poetical version of the brother and sister part of *Mill on the Floss*, even mentioning some of the same incidents, the fishing expedition, for example, and the little sister's luck. The poem gives a charming picture of a relationship which actual separation in later life was powerless to break entirely, as the touching last lines show :—

" But were another childhood world my share,
I would be born a little sister there."

A College Breakfast Party, a poem. First published in *Macmillan's Magazine*, 1878. In book form first reprinted in *The Legend of Jubal and other poems*, 2nd edition. Edinburgh : William Blackwood and Sons, 1879.

Death of Moses. First published in *The Legend of Jubal and other poems.* 2nd edition. Edinburgh : William Blackwood and Sons, 1879.

How Lisa loved the King. First published in *Blackwood's Edinburgh Magazine*, May, 1869. In book form first published in *The Legend of Jubal and other poems.* Edinburgh : William Blackwood and Sons, 1874.

SCENE : Palermo.

TIME : *circa* 1282.

Lisa, the beautiful young daughter of Bernardo, a rich Florentine settled at Palermo, is wooed by Perdicone, a noble youth of little fortune. Lisa's parents favour his suit, but she herself thinks only of King Pedro, with whom she has fallen deeply in love when she saw him at a tournament. Wasting away with her hopeless and innocent love, she expects to die and thinks that the worst pang of death is that the king will never know how she loved him. Thinking of ways to reach him, she sends for Minuccio, the great singer, tells him of her love, and begs him to sing it to the king. Minuccio has his friend, the poet Mico, put the tale in verse, and then sings it before the king. Touched by the song and by Minuccio's explanation, King Pedro visits Lisa and bids her live, and he and Queen Constance take both Lisa and Perdicone under their protection. Lisa marries Perdicone happily, and King Pedro always wears Lisa's favour, and calls himself her knight.

Note.—In the concluding stanza of the poem George Eliot indicated the source of Lisa's story when she said :—

" Reader, this story pleased me long ago
In the bright pages of Boccaccio."

It is a poetical version of the story told in the *Decamerone*, tenth day novel seven. The poem follows Boccaccio closely, with very slight changes in form of names and a few other minor details.

Legend of Jubal, a poem. First published in *Macmillan's Magazine*, May, 1870. In book form first published in *The Legend of Jubal and other poems.* Edinburgh : William Blackwood and Sons, 1874.

For the outline of the poem see note under Jubal in the Dictionary.

A Minor Prophet. Written 1865. First published in *The Legend of Jubal and other poems.* Edinburgh : William Blackwood and Sons, 1874.

Elias Baptist Butterworth, an American " vegetarian seer ", discourses enthusiastically on the millennium which will come when men shall have ceased to eat flesh.

Spanish Gypsy. See below, under **Spanish Gypsy.**

Stradivarius. First published in *The Legend of Jubal and other poems.* Edinburgh : William Blackwood and Sons, 1874.

Antonio Stradivari, the great maker of violins, talks with the idle painter Naldo about his gospel of honest work, insisting on the craftsman's responsibility to turn out perfect work, and the dignity of work.

> " 'Tis God gives skill,
> But not without men's hands : He could not make
> Antonio Stradivari's violins
> Without Antonio Stradivari."

Romola. First published in the *Cornhill Magazine* in fourteen instalments, July, 1862–August, 1863. 1st edition in book form, London : Smith, Elder and Co., 1863. 3 vols. Both magazine and books were illustrated.

SCENE : Florence and vicinity ; an Italian village on the Mediterranean.

TIME : 1492–8 ; Epilogue, 22nd May, 1509.

Romola is the story of the spiritual history of a beautiful, high-minded young Florentine, married to a consummate egoist, who struggles to preserve the ideal of her love until forced to realize her husband's baseness, and then, under Savonarola's influence, reconstructs upon the wreck of her personal happiness a life of unselfish service to her community. Aside from the fictitious characters, Romola and Tito, the outstanding figure is Savonarola, whose triumph and downfall are interwoven in the plot, and many minor historical characters throng the scene. The tragedy of Romola's love and Tito's deterioration is played out before a rich historical background of the popular, literary, religious, and political life of Florence at the end of the fifteenth century.

Tito Melema is the adopted son of Baldassarre Calvo, a rich scholar, who had brought Tito up with all the love and care that he would have given his own child. On a voyage to Delos they were shipwrecked and Baldassarre was captured by pirates, while Tito, carrying their fortune in gems, saved himself by swimming. As a shipwrecked stranger, he makes his way to Florence to seek his fortune. In the Mercato Vecchio his charm wins a breakfast for love from Tessa, the pretty contadina, and Nello, the barber, who knows everyone in Florence, takes him under his protection. Nello introduces him to the *eruditi* who patronize his shop, and later presents him to the blind scholar, Bardo de' Bardi, and Bardo's beautiful daughter, Romola. His charm and gentleness win both, and he is soon installed as Bardo's helper. His talents and tact quickly win him a recognized position, he sells his father's gems and has money enough to begin a search for his father. Arguing, however, that as he does not know definitely that his father is alive, he is not bound to search for him, he puts the money aside for his own use. After a few months, at the time of the San Giovanni celebration, a monk brings him a letter from his father telling that he has been sold into slavery and begging him to use his gems to ransom him. Although he has no idea of sacrificing himself to seek his father, he is alarmed at the thought that the news may become known, especially when he learns that the returned monk is Romola's brother. The monk falls ill, and Tito, relieved for a time, temporizes, and he and Romola become engaged. At the Peasants' Fair, Tito meets Tessa again, and goes through a mock marriage ceremony, which she takes seriously. Romola's brother dies without revealing his knowledge that Baldassarre Calvo is alive, and Tito and Romola are married. Tito prospers steadily, and when, in 1494, the French king, Charles VIII, enters Florence, he is one of those prominent in his reception. Some prisoners of the French escape, and one of them clutches Tito in his flight. Terrified, Tito recognizes his injured father, but refuses to acknowledge him, and the old man disappears. Though his sufferings have affected his mind, he recognizes Tito and concentrates all his remaining powers on the thought of vengeance. In spite of the fact that he is in love with Romola only, Tito has kept up relations with Tessa. Visiting her one evening, he finds that she has given shelter to his father. Baldassarre tries to stab Tito, but the chain armour that he is wearing protects him. Shortly before this Romola's father had died, leaving to Romola the task of seeing that his treasured library, which he had spent a lifetime in collecting, is preserved for the people of Florence. This library, which Romola regards as a sacred trust, Tito sells in order to raise money. Romola, whose eyes have now been opened to her husband's baseness, decides to leave him, and starts for Bologna, but is turned back by Savonarola, the great Dominican preacher, whose sermons are stirring Florence. He appeals to her to rise above the wreck of her own happiness and to return to Florence to work for the community. Romola becomes one of Savonarola's devoted adherents, and for two years spends herself in work for his ideals. During that time Tito prospers steadily. He is in the confidence of both parties, Savonarola's and the Medicean. Baldassarre's mind returns temporarily, and he makes a public charge against Tito, but on Tito's denial the old man is thrown into prison and kept there for two years. Much enfeebled, he still holds to his idea of vengeance, but all that he accomplishes is to tell Romola of the existence of Tessa and her children. Tito slips from treachery to treachery. When a Medicean plot is discovered, in 1497, one of those arrested is Bernardo del Nero, Romola's godfather, to whom she is much attached. Tito cleverly makes himself safe, but Bernardo is condemned and executed after Romola has made an urgent but vain appeal in his behalf to Savonarola, now at the height of his power. Sick at heart, Romola leaves Florence and recovers her hold on life only after she has worked as an angel of mercy in a plague-stricken village. During her absence Savonarola is arrested, and riot rages in the city. Some of Tito's double-dealing is at last suspected, and he is pursued by a mob as he is about to leave the city. He leaps into the Arno and escapes the mob by swimming, but at the end, exhausted, is found by Baldassarre Calvo, who strangles him and then dies himself. Romola, returning to Florence, learns of her husband's death, and is present at the execution of Savonarola. She finds Tessa and her children deserted and in misery, and takes them to live with her. Years after she still keeps sacred the memory of Savonarola who had helped her at the great crisis of her life.

Sad Fortunes of the Reverend Amos Barton. *See* **Scenes of Clerical Life. Sad Fortunes of the Reverend Amos Barton.**

Scenes of Clerical Life. I : The Sad Fortunes of the Reverend Amos Barton ; II : Mr. Gilfil's Love Story ; III : Janet's Repentance. First published in *Blackwood's Edinburgh Magazine*, January-November, 1857. 1st edition, Edinburgh : William Blackwood and Sons, 1857. 2 vols.

The Scenes of Clerical Life, George Eliot's first work of fiction, consist of three simple and touching stories, each of which was based upon some occurrence or real story well known in the neighbourhood of the Warwickshire home in which she spent her childhood.

I. *Sad Fortunes of the Reverend Amos Barton. Blackwood's,* January-February, 1857.

SCENE : " Shepperton " (Chilvers Coton) and " Milby " (Nuneaton).

TIME : *circa* 1837–8.

The *Sad Fortunes of the Reverend Amos Barton* is the story of a commonplace, rather stupid man, whose capacity for suffering under his " sad fortunes " is as great as that of any tragic hero.

Amos Barton, at 40, is curate of Shepperton Church, with a stipend of £80 a year on which he has to support a wife and six children and keep up a respectable clerical appearance. Without the aid of his wife's cleverness he would be quite unable to make both ends meet, and, as it is, he owes money and has to borrow £20 from the Squire. His wife, Milly Barton, is a beautiful, gracious woman, devoted to her husband and children and beloved by all the parishioners, who for her sake overlook Mr. Barton's blunders and aid the family with occasional gifts. The Countess Czerlaski, a pretty widow with no fortune, who has come to the parish to look for a second husband with money, cultivates the Bartons, and they, in spite of the suspicions of the parish, accept her at her face value, and Mr. Barton believes that she is going to make his fortune by recommending him to someone who has the presentation of a good living. When the Countess quarrels with her brother and leaves his house, the Bartons good-naturedly take her in for a short time only, as they think, but she quarters herself on them for six months, running them into debt, wearing out poor Milly's strength, and alienating Mr. Barton's parishioners, who regard the matter as scandalous. She is driven away by some home truths which an irate housemaid tells her, and for awhile the Barton fortunes seem brighter. But Milly's strength has been too deeply undermined, and when her seventh child is born she dies, leaving a heartbroken husband who for the first time realizes her full worth. For her sake the parish restores Amos to its favour, but just as he is beginning to feel that he is really surrounded by friends his rector withdraws his curacy, and he sorrowfully goes to a distant parish, finding his only consolation in the reflection of Milly's love which he sees in his daughter Patty.

II. *Mr. Gilfil's Love Story.* *Blackwood's,* March–June,

SCENE : " Cheverel Manor " (Arbury) ; " Shepperton " (Chilvers Coton).

TIME : Principal action, 1788–90.

Sir Christopher Cheverel, a fine old English baronet with a passion for architecture, has spent nearly fifteen years in making over his old Manor House into a beautiful Gothic building. Though he is childless, Cheverel Manor is not without young people. Sir Christopher's ward, Maynard Gilfil, a young man who has just entered the Church, lives there, as does also Lady Cheverel's protégée, Caterina Sarti. Caterina is a young Italian girl with a beautiful voice, who has been a member of the family ever since Lady Cheverel rescued her, when, as a child of only three, she had been left destitute in Milan by her father's death. Sir Christopher intends that Maynard Gilfil and Caterina shall marry, but though Maynard has loved the beautiful Italian from childhood Caterina feels for him only the affection of a sister. Her passionate love has been won by the attentions of Captain Anthony Wybrow, Sir Christopher's nephew and heir, who has amused himself by flirting with Caterina. Following Sir Christopher's wishes, Captain Wybrow courts Beatrice Assher, a rich heiress, and Beatrice, after accepting him, comes to visit at Cheverel Manor. Caterina, jealous and unhappy, cannot altogether conceal her feelings, and Miss Assher soon begins to suspect some relation between her lover and Caterina. To excuse himself Captain Wybrow leads Beatrice to think that Caterina has given him her love unsought, and Miss Assher reproaches her for such conduct. Frenzied by the unjust accusation, Caterina, who is going to meet Anthony in a part of the grounds called the Rookery, seizes a dagger and takes it with her, thinking that she will kill him. When she reaches the Rookery she finds him lying dead, where he had fallen from an attack of heart disease. The shock makes her forget everything except her former love, and when she faints, after carrying the news to Sir Christopher, Maynard finds the dagger in her possession. Distraught and self-reproachful, Caterina wanders from home the next day, and is eventually found to have sought refuge, worn-out and ill, with her former nurse. The Manor has too many sad associations for her to return there, but after she has spent some months with Mr. Gilfil's sister she recovers sufficiently to return from her unhappy passion to the refuge of Maynard's strong and considerate love. Caterina and Maynard are married, and have a short time of happiness, but she dies within a year, and Maynard's love goes "with her into deep silence for evermore". A part of Mr. Gilfil's life closes entirely with her death, and he always shows the effect of the tragedy of his youth, though he lives on for years, the eccentric and whimsical, but always upright and beloved, old vicar of Shepperton.

Janet's Repentance. Blackwood's, July–November, 1857.

SCENE: " Milby " (Nuneaton).

TIME: *circa* 1830-2.[1]

In the town of Milby sentiment is divided over the work of the new Evangelical curate, Mr. Tryan. His own adherents recognize the earnestness and spiritual force of his labours, but the friends of the snuffy old curate, Mr. Crewe, regard Mr. Tryan as a dangerous innovation, to be suppressed at any cost. One of the most vociferous enemies of Mr. Tryan is Robert Dempster, a lawyer of violent character who has taken to drink. Janet, Dempster's beautiful wife, aids the lawyer in his persecution of the curate, helping him prepare a scurrilous poster against Mr. Tryan deriding his Sunday evening lecture, and Mr. Tryan on his way to church is jeered and hissed by a hostile crowd. His persecution of Mr. Tryan costs Dempster some of his good clients, and this still further inflames his rage. Janet has meanwhile met Mr. Tryan at the home of a sick woman whom both were aiding, and has been impressed with his nobility of character, though she still supports her husband. Janet, who is a woman of noble possibilities, is far from happy. She is often ill-treated, and even beaten, by her brutal husband, and her unhappiness has driven her to seek forgetfulness in drink. In his last fit of anger Dempster turns her out of doors in her nightdress, at midnight, and she seeks refuge with an old friend, Mrs. Pettifer, who is one of Mr. Tryan's adherents. Her unhappiness and despair lead her to remember the impression she has retained of Mr. Tryan's nobility, and she talks with him, and through his aid determines to take up her struggle again and break herself of her habit

---

[1] The exact date is open to question, as some of the books mentioned early in the story were published as late as 1832-3.

of drink. Dempster is thrown from his cart when drunk and badly injured, so that he dies from delirium tremens, watched over by Janet, who for the short time that he lives forgets her injuries and remembers only that they once loved each other. After his death Janet has one more period of terrible temptation to return to her habit of drink, but resists it, and, becoming one of Mr. Tryan's most loyal supporters, spends herself in good works. A deep affection develops between her and the curate, but his health fails under his heavy labours, and he dies, beloved and regretted even by those who had once persecuted him. His living monument in Milby is Janet Dempster, restored to noble womanhood.

Note.—The *Scenes of Clerical Life* were brought to an end with the third story. A fourth story, to be called the " Clerical Tutor ", had been projected, but was never written.

Silas Marner, the Weaver of Raveloe. 1st edition, Edinburgh : William Blackwood and Sons, 1861.

SCENE : " Raveloe," a village in a Midland county (i.e. Warwickshire) ; " Lantern Yard," a street in a manufacturing town in the North.

TIME : Principal action, *circa* 1806-22.

Silas Marner, " a story of old-fashioned village life," was the last of George Eliot's novels which owed much to the influences of her childhood and girlhood in Warwickshire. She herself best describes its theme in a letter to her publisher, William Blackwood, in which she says that the story " is intended to set in a strong light the remedial influences of pure, natural, human relations ". The principal agency through which these remedial influences were to work is expressed in the quotation from Wordsworth given on the title page of the first edition :—

" A child more than all other gifts
That earth can offer to declining man,
Brings hope with it and forward-looking thoughts."

The same letter to William Blackwood says that the story " came to me first of all quite suddenly as a legendary tale suggested by my recollection of having once in early childhood seen a linen weaver with a bag on his back ".

Silas Marner, a handloom weaver, is living a lonely life in Raveloe. Fifteen years before, when he was an ardent, devoted member of an Independent church in Lantern Yard, in a northern manufacturing town, he had been unjustly accused of theft by his best friend, the real thief, had been tried according to the casting of lots, found guilty, and cast off both by his church and by his sweetheart. With all faith in both God and man utterly shattered, he had wandered to Raveloe, where he had settled near some deserted stone pits. Though awed by his cataleptic attacks, the villagers would have taken him into their life, but his numbed mind and soul were incapable of responding. His one emotion is love of the gold in which his unremitting toil is paid, and his one pleasure is handling this gold after his work is done. One stormy November evening when he returns to his cottage he finds that his gold has been stolen. In trembling despair he rushes with the news of his loss to the circle of village worthies at the Rainbow Inn. The theft, which remains unexplained, has been committed by Dunstan, or Dunsey, Cass, the worthless second son of the village Squire. Godfrey Cass, the Squire's eldest son, is in love with good and pretty Nancy Lammeter, but two years before he had married secretly a barmaid in a neighbouring town. Godfrey's secret, and the fact that he has a child, are known to Dunsey, who uses his hold over Godfrey to extort money from him. Dunsey, knowing of Silas's rumoured hoard, enters Silas's cottage, steals the gold, and disappears entirely. On New Year's Eve, Godfrey's wife is on her way to Raveloe to reveal her marriage to Godfrey's father. She yields to her addiction to opium, and, overcome by the drug, dies in the snow near Silas Marner's cottage, while her little golden-haired child slips from her arms and crawls into the cottage, unseen by Silas, who has fallen into one of his cataleptic fits. When he comes to he sees only the gleam of golden hair, and thinks for a moment that his gold has come back. Godfrey, desiring to marry Nancy, refrains from identifying the woman or claiming the child from Silas. The child touches Silas's heart, and he, feeling vaguely that she has been sent to him instead of the lost treasure, clings to her in spite of his neighbours' protests, adopts her, and with the help of good Dolly Winthrop brings her up, calling her Eppie. The task of caring for her, the relations with his neighbours which the child's needs bring about, and the child's love gradually restore Silas to the normal cheerful creature that he had been before his misfortune at Lantern Yard. Godfrey has married Nancy, but, in spite of their love, is not entirely happy, as he has no children, and he has a guilty feeling because he has not acknowledged Eppie. Silas's money has never been found, but he, happy in the new life with Eppie, has ceased to regret it. After sixteen years, the draining of the stone pits reveals Dunstan's skeleton and the lost money. Stirred by this discovery, Godfrey tells Nancy that Eppie is his daughter, and Nancy agrees to welcome her. She and Godfrey tell Eppie and Silas the truth, expecting Eppie to turn to them. Eppie, however, refuses to leave Silas, whom she regards as her real father, and Godfrey realizes that he cannot escape the penalties of his early deceit. With his restored money Silas takes Eppie to visit Lantern Yard, but can find no trace of his former life. Eppie marries Aaron Winthrop, her old playmate, and with Silas continues to live the humble life of a villager.

Note.—*Jermola the Potter*, a novel by the Polish writer, Kraszewski, has a theme so like that of *Silas Marner* that it has been frequently pointed out as the source of the central idea of George Eliot's story. Up to a certain point the resemblance is striking. Jermola, an old family servant, is turned adrift after a lifetime of devoted service, with no provision for his old age. He is sinking into a state of isolation and misery when he rescues a deserted infant left near his cottage. He keeps the boy, and their mutual affection and the child's needs restore him to normal activity and happiness. At the age of twelve the boy is claimed by his real parents, but refuses to desert his foster-father. He is taken from the old man, pines in his new home, and escapes to return to Jermola. Eventually the child dies from an illness contracted while the two are fleeing to a place of safety, and the old man sinks into misery and idiocy. Richard Garnett points out, in his edition of *Silas Marner*, that while the resemblance is too close to be merely accidental, it is difficult to account for it, as the Polish story, though published ten years before *Silas Marner*, was not translated until several years after the publication of that story. The resemblance, while interesting, is not important, as George Eliot's genius has made a totally different story from the same theme.

Spanish Gypsy, a poem. 1st edition, Edinburgh : William Blackwood and Sons, 1868.

SCENE : Fortress and town of Bedmár, in Andalusia, Spain ; the desert near by, and the Mediterranean coast.

TIME : *circa* 1487.

The *Spanish Gypsy* is the tragic story of two lovers, one of whom, Fedalma, renounces her happiness before the call of what she feels is duty to her race, while the other, Silva, places his love ahead of the obligations of honour and inheritance. George Eliot herself stated plainly the theme of the poem : " The subject of the Spanish Gypsy was originally suggested to me by a picture which hangs in the Scuola di San Rocco at Venice . . . It is an Annunciation, said to be by Titian . . . here was a great dramatic motive . . . A young maiden, believing herself on the eve of the chief event of her life—marriage—about to share in the ordinary lot of womanhood, full of young hope, has suddenly announced to her that she is chosen to fulfil a great destiny, entailing a terribly different experience from that ordinary womanhood . . . as a result of foregoing hereditary conditions : she obeys." " In Silva is presented the claim of fidelity to social pledges ; in Fedalma the claim constituted by an hereditary lot less consciously shared." *See* Cross, *George Eliot's Life*, vol. iii, pp. 42, 49.

Fedalma, a Gypsy by birth, stolen from her tribe when an infant, has been educated as a high-born Spanish girl in the family of the Duchess Diana, Duke Silva's mother. Silva, the commandant of the fortress of Bedmár, is deeply in love with Fedalma, and the two are betrothed, but their marriage is opposed by the Prior Isidor, the Inquisitor, on the ground that Fedalma is both a Gypsy and a heretic.

In order to stop the marriage the Prior means to hand Fedalma over to the Inquisition. A band of Gypsy prisoners are in the town, and the chief of these, Zarca, learns Fedalma's story. Fedalma, dancing in pure light-heartedness and joy of life before the people in the Plaça Santiago, is seen by Zarca, who recognizes her as his lost daughter. Zarca gains access to Fedalma, tells her that he is her father, and exhorts her to place her duty to her people before her personal happiness. Fedalma, though deeply in love with Silva, feels the call of her blood, and after at first trying to reconcile duty and happiness, sacrifices her hopes of happiness with Silva and joins her father in escaping from Bedmár. Silva, stricken by her loss, broods over it for a while, relaxing his hold on the thought of duty, and eventually deserts his post at Bedmár to follow her to the Gypsy camp. Zarca, confident of Fedalma's strength of purpose, offers her her choice, but she elects to abide by her duty to her people, and Silva, seeing no other way of winning her, declares that he will become a Gypsy and take the Gypsy oath. Zarca has patriotic dreams of leading his people to Africa and establishing a Gypsy nation there, but meantime he allies himself with the Moor, El Zagal, against the Spaniards. While Silva is kept in the Gypsy camp, Zarca and El Zagal attack Bedmár, capture it, and kill Silva's friends. The Prior Isidor is condemned to death. As he is being led to execution, Silva arrives. The Prior curses him as a traitor, and Silva, desperate at the reproaches and at the thought of the evil which his desertion of his post has wrought, stabs Zarca. When his people would kill Silva in return, Zarca magnanimously saves his life, and dies after laying upon Fedalma the duty of taking his place as leader of the Gypsies. Fedalma takes up the burden and leads her people to Africa after one farewell interview with Silva. Silva takes the habit of a pilgrim and goes to Rome to seek pardon and the right to use his sword again in the service of his country.

Stradivarius. *See* **Poems—Stradivarius.**

Theophrastus Such. *See* **Impressions of Theophrastus Such.**

LIST OF AUTHORITIES CITED

THE following list includes only the books which are definitely referred to in the notes in the body of the Dictionary, and does not include the many others, notably numerous volumes on Florentine history and topography, which were consulted in connexion with *Romola*. For information about the streets of Florence, for example, the excellent *Stradario Storico*, published by the City of Florence in 1913, was consulted throughout, and a complete list of the books used in compiling the Dictionary would include many additional titles.

ACTON, JOHN EMERICH EDWARD DALBERG, 1st Baron. *Historical Essays and other Studies.* London: Macmillan, 1907.

ADEMOLLO, AGOSTINO. *Marietta de' Ricci.* 2a ed. per cura di Luigi Passerini. Firenze: Stabilimento Chiari, 1845. 6 v.

ANDREWS, WILLIAM, ed. *Bygone Warwickshire.* Hull: Andrews, 1893.

AXON, WILLIAM EDWARD ARMYTAGE. *George Eliot's Use of Dialect.* London: Trübner, 1880.

BARTHOLOMEW, JOHN GEORGE. *Literary and Historical Atlas of Europe.* London: Dent, 1912.

BEACONSFIELD, BENJAMIN DISRAELI, 1st Earl of. *Life and Writings of Mr. Disraeli.* (In *Curiosities of Literature*, by Isaac Disraeli. New ed., with memoir and notes by his son, B. Disraeli. London: Warne, 1866.)

BLIND, MATHILDE. *George Eliot.* New ed. Boston: Little, 1904.

BONNELL, HENRY HOUSTON. *Charlotte Bronte, George Eliot, Jane Austin.* London: Longmans, 1902.

BROWNING, OSCAR. *Life of George Eliot.* London: W. Scott, 1890.

—— *Memories of Sixty Years.* London: Lane, 1910.

COLLINS, JOHN CHURTON. *Studies in Poetry and Criticism.* London: Bell, 1905.

COOKE, GEORGE WILLIS. *George Eliot: a Critical Study of her Life, Writings, and Philosophy.* Boston: Osgood, 1883.

COVENTRY LIBRARIES COMMITTEE. *George Eliot Centenary, November, 1919. Catalogue.* Coventry, 1919.

DEAKIN, MARY HANNAH. *The Early Life of George Eliot.* Manchester: University Press, 1913.

Dictionary of National Biography. Edited by Leslie Stephen and Sidney Lee. London, 1885–1901. 66 v.

DILKE, EMILIA FRANCIS (STRONG), Lady. *Book of the Spiritual Life,* by the late Lady Dilke, with a memoir of the author by the Rt. Hon. Sir Charles Dilke. London: Murray; New York: Dutton, 1905.

DRYDEN, ALICE, ed. *Memorials of Old Warwickshire.* London: Bemrose, 1908.

ELIOT, GEORGE, pseud. *George Eliot's Life as Related in her Letters and Journals,* arranged and edited by her husband, J. W. Cross. Edinburgh: Blackwood, 1885.

ELIOT, GEORGE, pseud. *Romola.* Edited, with introduction and notes, by Dr. Guido Biagi. London: Unwin, 1907. 2 v.

EVANS, ARTHUR BENONI. *Leicestershire Words, Phrases, and Proverbs,* edited with additions by Sebastian Evans. London: Trübner, 1881.

GARRISON, FIELDING HUDSON. *An Introduction to the History of Medicine.* 3rd ed. Philadelphia: Saunders, 1921.

HARRISON, FREDERIC. *Memories and Thoughts.* London: Macmillan, 1906.

—— *Studies in Early Victorian Literature.* London: Arnold, 1910.

JACOBS, JOSEPH. *George Eliot, Matthew Arnold, Browning, Newman: Essays and Reviews from the " Athenæum ".* London: Nutt, 1891.

KRASZEWSKI, JOZEF IGNACY. *Jermola.* Tr. by Mrs. M. Carey. New York: Dodd, 1891.

MASEFIELD, CHARLES. *Staffordshire.* 2nd ed. London: Methuen, 1918.

MOTTRAM, WILLIAM. *The True Story of George Eliot in Relation to " Adam Bede ".* London: Griffiths, 1905.

MUIRHEAD, FINDLAY. *England.* London: Macmillan, 1920.

NEGRI, GAETANO. *George Eliot, la sua Vita e i suoi Romanzi.* Milano: Fratelli Treves, 1891. 2 v.

NERLI, FILIPPO DE'. *Commentarj de' fatti civili occorsi dentro la città di Firenze dall' anno 1215 al 1537.* Augusta, 1728.

NEWDIGATE-NEWDEGATE, ANNE EMILY (GARNIER), Lady. *The Cheverels of Cheverel Manor.* London: Longmans, 1898.

OLCOTT, CHARLES SUMNER. *George Eliot, Scenes and People in her Novels.* London: Cassell, 1910.

PARKINSON, S. *Scenes from the George Eliot Country.* Leeds: Jackson, 1888.

POOLE, BENJAMIN. *Coventry, its History and Antiquities. Illustrated by W. F. Taunton.* London: J. R. Smith, 1870.

Roslyn, Guy, pseud. *George Eliot in Derbyshire: a Volume of Gossip about Passages and People in the Novels of George Eliot.* London: Ward, Lock & Tyler, 1876.

Skeat, Walter William, ed. *A Bibliographical List of the Works that have been published . . . illustrative of the various Dialects of England.* London: Trübner, 1877.

Staley, Edgcumbe. *The Guilds of Florence.* London: Methuen, 1906.

Stark, Adam. *History and Antiquities of Gainsburgh.* 2nd ed. London: Longmans, 1843.

Stephen, Sir Leslie. *George Eliot.* London: Macmillan, 1902.

Timmins, Samuel. *A History of Warwickshire.* London: E. Stock, 1889.

Vasari, Giorgio. *Lives of the most Eminent Painters, Sculptors, and Architects*; tr. from the Italian . . . by Mrs. Jonathan Foster. London: Bell, 1895–1901. 6 v.

Villari, Pasquale. *Life and Times of Girolamo Savonarola*; tr. by Linda Villari. London: Unwin, 1889.

Women Novelists of Queen Victoria's Reign. London: Hurst, 1897.

Manuscript Information

Where the authority for a note is given as " manuscript information " the reference is generally to the many notes on George Eliot prototypes collected by the Reverend Hubert H. M. Bartleet and by him generously placed at the disposal of the authors of the Dictionary. In a few cases the reference is to unpublished lists of prototypes in the possession of the authors.

LIST OF ABBREVIATIONS

ABBREVIATIONS	TITLE
Adam B.	Adam Bede.
Amos B.	Sad fortunes of the Reverend Amos Barton.
B. J.	Brother Jacob.
D. D.	Daniel Deronda.
E. E. 1	Early essays:— From the note-book of an eccentric.
E. E. 2	How to avoid disappointment.
E. E. 3	A little fable with a great moral.
F. H.	Felix Holt.
J. R.	Janet's Repentance.
L. V.	Lifted Veil.
M. F.	Mill on the Floss.
Mid.	Middlemarch.
Mr. G.'s L. S.	Mr. Gilfil's Love Story.
P.—Agatha	Poems:— Agatha.
P.—Arion.	Arion.
P.—Armg.	Armgart.
P.—B. S.	Brother and Sister.
P.—C. B. P.	College Breakfast Party.
P.—D. M.	Death of Moses.
P.—L. J.	Legend of Jubal.
P.—Lisa	How Lisa loved the King.
P.—M. P.	Minor Prophet.
P.—Strad.	Stradivarius.
Rom.	Romola.
S. M.	Silas Marner.
Sp. G.	Spanish Gypsy.
T. S.	Theophrastus Such.

THE GEORGE ELIOT DICTIONARY

A

ABBEY. The name of the Donnithorne mansion, at Donnithorne Chase. *Adam B.* xxvii, xxxii, xliv. For description, etc., *see* Donnithorne Chase.

ABBEY (TOPPING ABBEY). *See* TOPPING ABBEY.

ABBOTT. Cousin of the Dodsons, whose decease is always expected. *M. F.* Bk. 1, vii, ix ; Bk. 7, iii.

ABDERAHMAN'S TOWER. Tower in the Castle of Bedmár where the astrologer Sephardo has his study. *Sp. G.* ii.

ABEL. Farmer at Stone Court. *Mid.* lxix–lxx.

ABEL, MRS. Mr. Bulstrode's housekeeper at Stone Court. *Mid.* lxix–lxxi, lxxvi.

When Mr. Bulstrode has her watch the invalid Raffles, his tormentor, he allows her to give the patient brandy and an overdose of opium, which the doctor has said would be fatal.

ACCIAJOLI (*Hist.*). A Florentine scholar who was " minded to take the cowl and join the community of San Marco ". *Rom.* xxv.

Note.—Zanobi Acciajoli (1461–1519 or 1520), who, influenced by Savonarola, entered San Marco in 1495. In 1518 he was made prefect of the Vatican, at Rome, and devoted himself to its library. The Acciajoli were a prominent Florentine family, many of whose members were Piagnoni, or followers of Savonarola.

ACCIAJOLI, DIANORA. A Piagnone who marries the young Albizzi. *Rom.* xii.

Monna Brigida attends the wedding and considers the bride's dress plain and the wedding solemn.

ACER. *T. S.* viii.

ADAM, MRS. Mordecai Cohen's landlady. *D. D.* lxiii, lxvi–lxvii.

ADELAIDE. Ship. *M. F.* Bk. 5, v.

ADIMARI, CORSO DEGLI (*Real*). A street in Florence where Tito Melema is walking before he meets Tessa on the day of San Giovanni. *Rom.* ix, xvi.

Note.—The Corso degli Adimari, named from the houses of the Adimari family which occupied its whole length, was a short street extending south from the Piazza del Duomo to the Via degli Speciali. It is now part of the Via Calzaioli.

B

ADOLPHE. An artist who, disappointed in love, consoles himself by love of his work. *E. E.* 2.

ADRASTUS. A busy essayist who writes on many subjects. *T. S.* xiv.

AGATHA. A saintly peasant woman, beloved by her neighbours. *P.—Agatha.*

AGLI (*Hist.*). A Florentine family whose houses were in Ognissanti. *Rom.* xxii.

"AH, PERCHÈ NON POSSO ODIARTI" (I LOVE THEE STILL) (*Real*). A song from the "Somnambula" [*sic*], which Philip Wakem sings. *M. F.* Bk. 6, vii.
Note. — "La Sonnambula," an opera by Bellini (1801–35), first produced in 1831.

AJACCIO (*Real*). One of the Mediterranean towns where the Grandcourts touch on their yachting trip. *D. D.* liv.
Note.—The capital of Corsica, on the west coast of that island.

ALBANI, MAESTRO. Lady Cheverel's music master in Milan. *Mr. G.'s L. S.* iii.

ALBERGO DELL' ITALIA (*Real*). Hotel in Genoa where Daniel Deronda and his mother meet. *D. D.* l–li, liv–lv, lix.

ALBERTI (*Hist.*). Member of the Arrabbiati. *Rom.* xxxix.
Note.—Piero Alberti, probably, who was a member of the Arrabbiati, and Gonfaloniere in 1497.

ALBERTI, LEON BATTISTA (*Hist.*). *Rom.* xxxix.
Note.—A famous writer, architect, sculptor and painter, born at Genoa 1404, died at Rome 1472.

ALBIZZI (*Hist.*). A prominent Florentine family, adherents of Savonarola. *Rom.* lxiii.

ALBIZZI, LUCA ANTONIO. A young Piagnone who marries Dianora Acciajoli. *Rom.* xii.

ALBIZZI, BORGO DEGLI. *See* BORGO DEGLI ALBIZZI.

ALCHARISI. Stage name of Daniel Deronda's mother, the Princess Halm - Eberstein. *See* Halm-Eberstein, Leonora, Princess.

ALDA. *Sp. G.* i.

ALDO MANUZIO (*Hist.*). A printer who wishes Bardo de' Bardi to give him the aid of his annotated manuscripts. *Rom.* v.
Note.—Aldus Manutius (1450–1515), the great Venetian printer and humanist, who established himself in Venice in 1490 and began printing not long after that date.

ALEXANDER VI, POPE (*Hist.*). The Pope, opposed to Savonarola. *Rom.* xiii–xiv, xvi, xxi, xlv, lv, lxii, lxiv, lxxi.
"A lustful, greedy, lying, and murderous old man, once called Rodrigo Borgia, and now lifted to the pinnacle of infamy as Pope Alexander the Sixth." *Ch.* lv.
Note.—Rodrigo Borgia, 1431–1503 ; made cardinal 1455, pope 1492–1503 ; father of Cæsar and Lucretia Borgia.

ALFONSO, CROWN PRINCE OF NAPLES (*Hist.*). *Rom.* xxi.
Note.—Son of King Ferdinand, whom he succeeded on the throne of Naples in 1494.

ALFONSO, DUKE. Hans Meyrick's name for Mr. Grandcourt. *See* GRANDCOURT, HENLEIGH MALLINGER.

ALFRED. Latimer's elder half-brother and rival, a "handsome, self-confident man", who loses his life on the hunting-field. *L. V.* i–ii.

ALICE. The Countess Czerlaski's buxom maid, who marries Mr. Bridmain, brother of the Countess. *Amos B.* iii, v.

ALICE. The Deanes' maid. *M. F.* Bk. 7, iv.

ALICK. Mr. Poyser's shepherd and head man. *Adam B.* vi–vii, xviii, xx, xxii, xl, lii–liii.
"Alick, indeed, was not by any means a honeyed man; his speech had usually something of a snarl in it, and his broad-shouldered aspect something of the bull-dog expression . . . but he was honest even to the splitting of an oat-grain . . . and as 'close-fisted' with his master's property as if it had been his own." *Ch.* liii.

ALIQUIS, "who lets no attack on himself pass unnoticed." *T. S.* xiii.

"ALL THINGS JOURNEY, SUN AND MOON." One of the songs of Juan, the minstrel, in the *Spanish Gipsy*. *Sp. G.* iii.

"ALL WE LIKE SHEEP" (*Real*). A chorus from Handel's *Messiah* which Caterina Sarti plays. *Mr. G.'s L. S.* xiii.

ALLEN, SISTER. *Adam B.* iii.

ALTHORPE. *Mid.* li.

ALVAR, DON. Duke Silva's friend, who is killed when the Moors and Gypsies take Bedmár. *Sp. G.* i–ii, iv.

AMADOR, DON. A gaunt grey-haired soldier, Master of Duke Silva's retinue. *Sp. G.* ii.

AMBROGIO, SAN. *See* SAN AMBROGIO.

"ANCHOR TAVERN." Tavern in St. Ogg's, frequented by sailors. *M. F.* Bk. 5, iii.
Note.—This is the "Crown and Anchor", a small tavern in Bridge Street, Gainsborough. (*See* article by John Foster Fraser in *Bookman* (London), vol. 9, p. 55.)

ANCONA (*Real*). Place near which Tito Melema had been shipwrecked. *Rom.* vi.
Note.—An Italian port on the Adriatic.

ANDRÈS. A young Spaniard, Pepita's suitor. *Sp. G.* i.

ANGELO, MESSER. *See* POLIZIANO, ANGELO.

ANGUS. Servant. *D. D.* liv.

ANN. Mrs. Raynor's small servant. *J. R.* xxi.

ANNA, AUNT. Janet Dempster's sick aunt who lives at Thurston. *J.R.* xxv.

ANNIBAL. Roldan's monkey, "a misanthropic monkey, grey and grim." *Sp. G.* i–ii.

ANNUNZIATA, CHURCH OF THE (*Real*). Church in Florence, where Tito Melema finds Tessa on the day of the Fierucola. *Rom.* xiv.
Note.—Church of the Santissima Annunziata on the north-

east side of the Piazza dell' Annunziata, founded 1250.

ANNUNZIATA, PIAZZA DELL' (*Real*). Square in Florence, where the Fierucola (Peasants' Fair) is held. *Rom.* xiii–xiv.

Note.—The Piazza dell' Annunziata is the square in front of the Church of the Annunziata, from which it takes its name.

ANTELLA, LAMBERTO DELL' (*Hist.*). A renegade Medicean whose arrest " with a tell-tale letter on his person and a bitter rancour against the Medici in his heart " leads to the discovery of the Medicean conspiracy. *Rom.* lvi-lvii.

Note.—For an historical account of Lamberto dell' Antella's part in the discovery of the plot *see* Villari, *Savonarola*.

ANTIGONE, MADONNA. Name by which the painter Piero di Cosimo sometimes addresses Romola; *see* BARDI, ROMOLA DE'.

ANTIOCH (*Real*). City where Baldassarre Calvo was held in slavery. *Rom.* x–xi, xxx.

Note.—The ancient capital of Syria.

"APOLLO AND THE RAZOR." Nello's barber-shop which serves as a meeting-place for literary and artistic Florentines. *Rom.* iii–iv, viii, xiii, xvi, xxii, xxix, xlv–xlvii.

" Ah, Messer Greco, if you want to know the flavour of our scholarship, you must frequent my shop: it is the focus of Florentine intellect, and in that sense the navel of the earth—as my great predecessor, Burchiello, said of *his* shop, on the more frivolous pretension that his street of the Calimara was the centre of our city. And here we are at the sign of 'Apollo and the Razor'. Apollo, you see, is bestowing the razor on the Triptolemus of our craft, the first reaper of beards, the sublime *Anonimo*, whose mysterious identity is indicated by a shadowy hand." Ch. iii.

Note.—The original of Nello's shop was the shop of Burchiello, the barber-poet of Florence. *See also* note under NELLO.

APOLLOS, MR. " The eloquent Congregational preacher who had studied in Germany and had advanced liberal views." *T. S.* ix.

AQUILA. A conversational bird of prey who instinctively appropriates from others morsels of information to use in his brilliant conversations. *T. S.* xi.

" AR HYD Y NOS " (*Real*). An air which Fred Vincy practises on his flute. *Mid.* xi.

Note.—" Ar hyd y nos " (All through the night), a Welsh air.

ARBUES, MASTER (*Real*). Grand Inquisitor in Aragon. *Sp. G.* i.

Note.—Maestre Pedro Arbues, a canon of the cathedral of Saragasso, who was appointed Inquisitor by Torquemada in 1484. September 15, 1485, he was attacked as he was praying in the cathedral, and died a few days later as a result of his injuries. He was regarded as a martyr, and was canonized in 1867.

ARCHER, MRS. Latimer's wife's maid, who, when unconscious and apparently dead, is brought back to life by Dr. Meunier's experiment long enough to reveal the fact that her mistress means to poison Latimer. *L. V.* ii.

ARCHERY CLUB. *See* BRACKENSHAW ARCHERY CLUB.

ARCHERY MEETING. A meeting of the Brackenshaw Archery Club, at which Grandcourt first sees Gwendolen Harleth. *D. D.* x.

AREZZO (*Real*). Town, Baldassarre's pretended destination when he leaves the hospital. *Rom.* viii, xvi, xxii, xxix–xxx, xlii.

Note.—A town 54 miles south-east of Florence.

ARGIROPULO, GIOVANNI (*Hist.*). A Greek scholar under whom Bardo de' Bardi studied. *Rom.* iii, v.

Note.—Giovanni Argiropolo, or Argyropulo, was a Greek who came to Italy about 1434; about 1456 he was teaching Greek in Florence. He died at Rome 1489.

ARIAS. A stripling of fifteen, in Duke Silva's retinue, who is killed when the Moors take Bedmár. *Sp. G.* ii, iv.

ARION. Singer " whose melodic soul, taught the dithyramb to roll ". *P.*—*Arion.*

ARKWRIGHT'S MILLS, CROMFORD (*Real*). *Adam B.* i.

Note.—The mills established at Cromford, Derbyshire, in 1771 by Sir Richard Arkwright, cotton spinning inventor.

ARMGART. A great prima donna. *P.*—*Armg.* i–iv.

In the first flush of her success as a singer, she means to give up all for her art, and refuses the offer of marriage of Graf Dornberg. A year later after a serious illness she loses her voice, but the Graf does not renew his offer. Without her art Armgart is at first in despair, but takes up her life anew, resolved to live for others.

ARMSTRONG, MR. A wealthy client of Lawyer Dempster's. *J. R.* vii, xiii.

ARMYN, MISS. Mrs. Gascoigne's maiden name. *See* GASCOIGNE, MRS. NANCY.

ARNO (*Real*). The river which flows through Florence, into which Tito Melema leaps when pursued by the mob. *Rom.* Proem, viii, x, xx, xxxiii, xxxvi, xliii–xliv, liv, lxvii, lxx.

ARRABBIATI (*Hist.*). The aristocratic party in Florence, bitter enemies of Savonarola and his party. *Rom.* xxxix, lvii, lxiii.

ARROWPOINT, MR. Owner of Quetcham Hall. *D. D.* iii, v, ix–x, xxii, xxxv.

" A perfect gentleman, of whom no one had anything to say but that he had married Miss Cuttler, and imported the best cigars." Ch. v.

ARROWPOINT, MRS. Wife of the above; a woman noted for her oddities, who is much disappointed when her daughter does not make a brilliant marriage. *D. D.* iii, v, ix–x, xiv, xxii, xxxv, xliv–xlv.

"It was occasionally recalled that she had been the heiress of a fortune gained by some moist or dry business in the city, in order fully to account for her having a squat figure, a harsh parrot-like voice, and a systematically high head-dress; and since these points made her externally rather ridiculous, it appeared to many only natural that she should have what are called literary tendencies." Ch. v.

ARROWPOINT, MISS CATHERINE. The amiable daughter of the above; a great heiress and an accomplished musician, who marries Herr Klesmer, in opposition to her parents' wishes. *D. D.* iii, v–vi, ix–xii, xiv, xxi–xxii, xxxv, xxxix, lii, lxx.

"Miss Arrowpoint, unfortunately also dressed in white, immediately resembled a *carte-de-visite* in which one would fancy the skirt alone to have been charged for. . . Miss Arrowpoint was generally liked for the amiable unpretending way in which she wore her fortunes, and made a softening screen for the oddities of her mother." Ch. v.

ARROWPOINT, OLD ADMIRAL. *D. D.* xxxv.

ART OF THE BUTCHERS (*Real*). A Florentine guild. *Rom.* i.

Note.—The Arte di Beccai, one of the fourteen Lesser Arts or Guilds. *See below* under ARTS.

ART OF THE MONEY-CHANGERS (*Real*). A Florentine guild. *Rom.* viii.

Note.—The Arte del Cambio, one of the seven Greater Arts. *See below* under ARTS.

ARTE DI CALIMARA. *See* CALIMARA, CORPORATION OF THE.

ARTS OF FLORENCE (*Real*). The 21 Guilds of Florence, described as taking part in the San Giovanni and Impruneta processions. *Rom.* viii, xxv, xliii.

Note.—Every Florentine citizen who wished to take any part in public life had to enroll in one of the Arti (Companies or Guilds). There were twenty-one of the guilds, divided into the Greater Arts, seven in number, and the fourteen Lesser Arts (at one time divided as the five Intermediate and the nine Lesser Arts). The seven Greater Arts were: the lawyers and notaries, the Calimala or dealers in foreign cloth, the guild of wool, the bankers and money-changers, the guild of silk or "Por Santa Maria", the doctors and apothecaries, and the furriers and skinners. The Lesser Arts included the butchers, blacksmiths, shoemakers, builders, retailers of cloths, wine merchants, innkeepers, tanners, provision dealers, saddlers, locksmiths, armourers, carpenters, and bakers. For a detailed account of the various guilds *see* Staley, *Guilds of Florence.*

ASHBY (*Real*). *Adam B.* xxxvi. The town for which Hetty Sorrel starts when she leaves Stoniton to go to Windsor.

Note.—Probably Ashby de la Zouch, a town about 16¼ miles south of Derby ("Stoniton").

ASSHER, LADY. Beatrice's mother, an uninteresting, middle-aged widow who had been Sir Christopher Cheverel's earliest love. *Mr. G.'s L. S.* iv–v, ix–xi, xiii–xiv.

Note.—The original of Lady Assher was Lady Anstruther. (*See* Olcott, *George Eliot*, p. 15.)

ASSHER, MISS BEATRICE. The dazzling beauty to whom Captain Wybrow is engaged; a selfish, cold-hearted and jealous young woman. *Mr. G.'s L. S.* ii, iv–xiii, xv–xvi.

"Miss Assher was tall, and gracefully though substantially formed, carrying herself with an air of mingled graciousness and self-confidence; her dark-brown hair, untouched by powder, hanging in bushy curls round her face, and falling behind in long thick ringlets nearly to her waist. The brilliant carmine tint of her well-rounded cheeks, and the finely cut outline of her straight nose, produced an impression of splendid beauty, in spite of commonplace brown eyes, a narrow forehead, and thin lips." Ch. v.

Note.—The original of Miss Assher was Jane (always called Jessy) Anstruther, who married Charles Parker, the original of Captain Wybrow. (*See* Olcott, *George Eliot*, pp. 15, 33; Newdigate, *The Cheverels*, p. 67.)

ASSHER, SIR JOHN. Beatrice's dead father. *Mr. G.'s L. S.* vi, xi.

ASSOCIATION FOR THE PROSECUTION OF FELONS. *Mr. G.'s L. S.* i.

"AT THE BATTLE OF CLAVIJO." Song in the *Spanish Gypsy* sung by Arias, the page. *Sp. G.* ii.

ATHENS (*Real*). Greek city which Baldassarre Calvo and Tito Melema visited to study Greek inscriptions. *Rom.* vi.

Note.—At the time of *Romola* Athens was in the possession of the Turks, who had captured it in 1458. For a long time after its capture it almost disappeared from the knowledge of the western world.

AUGUSTINIAN MONK. A monk who advised Tito to go to Florence instead of Rome. *Rom.* iii.

AUGUSTINIAN MONK, OF SAN SPIRITO. Bernardo del Nero's confessor. *Rom.* lx, lxx.

He conducts Romola from the scene of her godfather's execution and later gives her the news of Tito's death.

AUGUSTINIANS (*Hist.*). A monastic order, called also the Frati Neri, or Black Brethren. *Rom.* xliii, lxx.

"Augustinians of San Spirito, with more cultured human faces . . . men who had inherited the library of Boccaccio, and had made the most learned company in Florence when learning was rarer." Ch. xliii.

Note.—The Augustinian Canons or Austin Canons, also called from the colour of their habit the Black Canons, or Black Brethren, who in the eleventh century adopted the Rule of St. Augustine. Their convent in Florence was the Convent and Church of Santo Spirito.

"AULD LANG SYNE" (*Real*). Tune played by the Tory band at the Treby election. *F. H.* xxxi.
Note.—A Scottish popular song which Robert Burns set originally to an older tune which was displaced in 1799 by the present tune; an air popular in Scotland during the second half of the eighteenth century. There is some question whether Burns wrote all the words or adapted some stanzas from an older song.

AURISPA (*Hist.*). A scholar who brought back manuscripts from Greece. *Rom.* vi.
Note.—Giovanni Aurispa (*c.* 1369–1460), a distinguished Italian humanist, at one time professor of Greek at Florence. He went to Greece and brought back more than 200 manuscripts of classical authors.

AVIGNON (*Real*). The French city where Lydgate found Madame Laure when he followed her from Paris. *Mid.* xv.
Note.—A picturesque town on the Rhone, about 400 miles south of Paris.

AVIS. A man giving to "saccharine excesses". *T. S.* xii.

B

BACCIO (*Hist.*). Painter, who assisted at the Bonfire of Vanities. *Rom.* xxv, xlix.
"That young painter who had lately surpassed himself in his fresco of the Divine child on the wall of the Frate's bare cell—unconscious yet that he would one day himself wear the tonsure and the cowl, and be called Fra Bartolommeo." Ch. xxv.
Note. — Fra Bartolommeo (Baccio della Porta, 1475–1517). A distinguished Florentine painter, and an adherent of Savonarola, after whose death he assumed the Dominican habit. He painted the well-known portrait of Savonarola.

BADEN-BADEN (*Real*). German spa. *D. D.* ii, xv.
Note.—A beautifully situated watering-place at the entrance to the Black Forest.

BADGERS, OF HILLBURY. *F. H.* xl.

BADIA, CHURCH OF THE (*Real*). Church in Florence, where Romola meets Baldassarre Calvo. *Rom.* Proem, i, viii, x, lii, liv.
Note.—The Church of La Badia, originally a Benedictine convent (abbatia) founded in the tenth century by Willa, mother of the Margrave Hugo; the present church was largely reconstructed in the seventeenth century.

BAGSHAWE. A clergyman. *Amos B.* vi.

BAGSTER. The Whig Member for Middlemarch. *Mid.* xxxviii, li.

BAIRD, MR. A young clergyman present at the clerical meeting held at Milby Vicarage. *Amos B.* vi.
"Mr. Baird has since gained considerable celebrity as an original writer and metropolitan lecturer, but at that time he used to preach in a little church something like a barn, to a congregation consisting of three rich farmers and their servants, about fifteen labourers, and the due proportion of women and children. The rich farmers understood him to be 'very high learnt'; but if you had interrogated them for a more precise description, they would have said that he was 'a thinnish-faced man, with a sort o' cast in his eye, like'." Ch. vi.

Note.—In the lists of originals which were made in Nuneaton after the publication of *Scenes of Clerical Life* the original of Mr. Baird was said to be the Rev. George William Sanford, Vicar of Weddington.

BAKER, WILL. One of Bartle Massey's neighbours. *Adam B.* xxi.

BALDASSARRE. *See* CALVO, BALDASSARRE.

BALDWIN, MR. Tax-gatherer. *Mid.* lxxi.

BALE, KESTER. Aged worker on Mr. Poyser's farm, "one of those invaluable labourers who can not only turn their hand to everything, but excel in everything they turn their hand to." *Adam B.* liii.

BALLARD, MRS. Mistress of a school. *Mid.* xl.

BAMBRIDGE, MR. Horse-dealer in Middlemarch, who lends money to Fred Vincy. *Mid.* xxiii, lx, lxvi, lxxi.

BANKS. Bailiff at Transome Court. *F. H.* i, viii, xxxi, xxxix.

BANKS. Sir Hugo Mallinger's bailiff. *D. D.* xvi.

BANKS, MRS. The bailiff's wife. *D. D.* xvi.

"BANNOCKBURN" (*Real*). A tune which Felix Holt is whistling when he finds Christian's lost pocketbook. *F. H.* xiii.

Note.—*Bannockburn*, or *Scot's, wha hae wi' Wallace bled*, a song by Robert Burns, set to the old Scotch tune called *Hey tutti taitie*.

BANTAM. A small, feebly crowing individual who attempts to correct the brilliant Aquila. *T. S.* xi.

BANTAM, SIR HONG KONG. One of Mixtus's fashionable acquaintances. *T. S.* ix.

BAPTISTERY (*Real*). *Rom.* Proem, iii, viii, xxii, xxv, xxix, xxxix, xlv, lix.

"The quaint octagon of San Giovanni in front of them, showing its unique gates of storied bronze, which still bore the somewhat dimmed glory of their original gilding. The inlaid marbles were then fresher in their pink, and white, and purple, than they are now, when the winters of four centuries have turned their white to the rich ochre of well-mellowed meerschaum." Ch. iii.

Note.—The Battistero, or Church of San Giovanni Battista, probably founded in the seventh or eighth century and remodelled about 1200, which, until the twelfth century, was the cathedral of Florence. It still is the church in which all children born in Florence are baptized.

BARABBAS, MR. A swindler whose morals are such a contrast to those of that excellent family man, Sir Gavial Mantrap. *T. S.* xvi.

BARDI (*Hist.*). The famous Florentine family to which Romola de' Bardi belongs. *Rom.* v.

"They were a proud and energetic stock, these Bardi; conspicuous among those who clutched the sword in the earliest world-famous quarrels of Florentines with Florentines . . . But the Bardi hands were of the sort that not only clutch the sword-hilt with vigour, but love the more delicate pleasure of fingering minted metal . . . and by the middle of the fourteenth century we find them risen from their original condition of *popolani* to be possessors, by purchase, of lands and strongholds, and the feudal dignity of Counts of Vernio . . . disastrously signalized only a few years later as standing in the very front of European commerce . . . undertaking to furnish specie for the wars of our Edward the Third, and having revenues 'in kind' made over to them; especially in wool, most precious of freights for Florentine galleys. Their august debtor left them with an august deficit . . . But an old Florentine family was many-rooted, and we find the Bardi maintaining importance and rising again and again to the surface of Florentine affairs in a more or less creditable manner, implying an untold family history that would have included even more vicissitudes . . . than are usually seen on the background of wide kinship." Ch. v.

Note.—Accounts of the Bardi, especially of the battle which ended in the destruction of their house, and the expulsion of some members from the city, are found in various historical works. The text of *Romola* refers to Villani's history, and Dr. Guido Biagi points out that the source from which George Eliot probably obtained her first knowledge of the family was Ademollo's *Marietta dei Ricci*. (*See* Ademollo, vol. iii, p. 1135–52.)

BARDI, BARDO DE'. Romola's father, a blind scholar, whose consuming desire is to be assured that his library and art collection will be kept together under his name, after his death. *Rom.* iii, v–vii, xi–xiii, xv, xvii, xix–xx, xxvii, xxxi.

"The blind father sat with head uplifted and turned a little aside towards his daughter, as if he were looking at her. His delicate paleness, set off by the black velvet cap which surmounted his drooping white hair, made all the more perceptible the likeness between his aged features and those of the young maiden . . . There was the same refinement of brow and nostril in both, counterbalanced by a full though firm mouth and powerful chin, which gave an expression of proud tenacity and latent impetuousness." Ch. v.

He had spent his fortune collecting rare manuscripts, books and art treasures, upon which he planned to base great works of scholarship. When his blindness interfered with his writing these himself, he depended on his son, who, however, left him to become a monk. Embittered by his son's desertion, he trained his daughter to help in his work, and when Tito appears welcomes him as a substitute for his son. He encourages Romola's marriage to Tito, and dies believing that Tito will carry out his wishes about his library.

BARDI, BERNARDINO DE', *called* DINO. Romola's brother who had left home to become a monk. *See* LUCA, FRA.

BARDI, ROMOLA DE'. Bardo de' Bardi's daughter, later Tito Melema's wife; a beautiful and noble girl who makes a disastrous marriage, but, under Savonarola's influence, subordinates her personal unhappiness to the service of others. *Rom.* v–vi, x–xiii, xv, xvii, xix–xxi, xxiv, xxvii–xxviii, xxxi–xxxii, xxxv–xxxvii, xl–xliv, xlvi–lvi, lviii, lxi, lxviii–lxxii, Epilogue.

"The only spot of bright colour in the room was made by the hair of a tall maiden of seventeen or eighteen . . . The hair was of a reddish-gold colour, enriched by an unbroken small ripple, such as may be seen in sunset clouds on grandest autumnal evenings. It was confined by a black fillet above her small ears, from which it rippled forward again and made a natural veil for her neck above her square-cut gown of black . . .

"The blind father sat with head uplifted . . . His delicate paleness . . . made all the more perceptible the likeness between his aged features and those of the young maiden . . . There was the same refinement of brow and nostril in both, counterbalanced by a full though firm mouth and powerful chin, which gave an expression of proud tenacity and latent impetuousness . . . It was a type of face of which one could not venture to say whether it would inspire love or only that unwilling admiration which is mixed with dread; the question must be decided by the eyes . . . as she approached her father . . . her hazel eyes filled with pity . . . At that moment the doubtful attractiveness of Romola's face, in which pride and passion seemed to be quivering in the balance with native refinement and intelligence, was transfigured to the most lovable womanliness by mingled pity and affection." Ch. v.

She has led a secluded life, devoted entirely to her blind father, whose secretary she is. She falls in love with Tito Melema almost at first sight, gives him her entire trust as well as her love, and marries him, believing that he has the same high ideals as herself. Aside from her love for Tito, her devotion to her father is the strongest feeling in her life, and after his death she feels it a sacred obligation to carry out his wish to have his library preserved for the city of Florence. Although several things disturb her confidence in Tito, her eyes are not opened to his real character until he sells her father's library to the Duke of Milan in violation of what she considers a sacred trust. Believing that this shattering of her love releases her from her marriage vows, she decides to leave her husband, and is leaving Florence in disguise when she is stopped by Savonarola, who tells her that she can not thus break a sacred bond, and exhorts her to return and take up work for others if her personal happiness is gone. She yields to his influence, becomes one of his devoted followers, even though she does not accept all of his religious beliefs, and for several years spends herself in good works, staying with Tito, although their real separation in character and ideals becomes constantly more evident as Tito drifts from one treachery to another. When her godfather, Bernardo del Nero, is arrested, as she fears through Tito's treachery, and is executed in spite of her efforts to persuade Savonarola to save him, the limit of her endurance is reached. Disappointed in Savonarola and grief-stricken at her godfather's death, she flees from Florence. By chance she reaches a plague-stricken village, and wins back peace and spiritual health by working among the sufferers. She returns to Florence just after Tito's death, and finds and cares for his two natural children and their mother. She is present at Savonarola's execution, and both then and during the rest of her life reveres him as a great religious leader who had helped her at a critical moment of her life.

Note.—Romola, though nominally an Italian of the Renaissance, is so essentially an English Puritan that the suggestion has been made that some things in her character represent experiences of George Eliot's spiritual life. There is probably no ground for tracing a general resemblance, but in one respect, Romola's devotion to her father, there is, perhaps, a suggestion of a picture of George Eliot's affection for her father.

BARDI, VIA DE' (*Real*). Street in Florence where Romola de' Bardi lived. *Rom.* v, x–xi, xviii, xx, xxxiii, xli, xliii–xliv, xlvi–xlvii, xlix, lviii, lxiv, lxvi–lxvii.

"The Via de' Bardi, a street noted in the history of Florence, lies in Oltrarno . . . It extends from the Ponte Vecchio to the Piazza de' Mozzi at the head of the Ponte alle Grazie; its right-hand line of houses and walls being backed by the rather steep ascent which in the fifteenth century was known as the hill of Bogoli . . . its left-hand buildings flanking the river and making on their northern side a length of quaint, irregularly-pierced façade, of which the waters give a softened loving reflection as the sun begins to decline towards the western heights. But quaint as these buildings are, some of them seem to the historical memory a too modern substitute for the famous houses of the Bardi family, destroyed by popular rage in the middle of the fourteenth century." Ch. v.

Note.—The picturesque Via de' Bardi, one of the oldest streets in Florence, extends from the Piazza de' Mozzi to the Via Guicciardini. Some parts of it were altered in the nineteenth century, in the making of the quay of Lung Arno Torrigiani.

BARDI HOUSE. A house on the Via de' Bardi, belonging to the Neri, in which Romola and her blind father lived. *Rom*. v, and later chapters.

"The house in which Bardo lived was situated on the side of the street nearest the hill, and was one of those large sombre masses of stone building pierced by comparatively small windows, and surmounted by what may be called a roofed terrace or loggia, of which there are many examples still to be seen in the venerable city. Grim doors, with conspicuous scrolled hinges, having high up on each side of them a small window defended by iron bars, opened on a groined entrance court." Ch. v.

Note.—A house on the Via de' Bardi, which, like Romola's, has a loggia on the roof, has been pointed out as the one which George Eliot may have had in mind in describing Romola's house.

BARGELLO, THE (*Real*). Public building in Florence; within its court Bernardo del Nero and the other Mediceans were executed. *Rom*. viii, lx.

Note.—The Palazza del Podestà, on the Via del Proconsolo, commonly known as the Bargello, was from about 1261 the residence of the Podestà or chief magistrate of Florence; from 1574 it was a prison and office of the chief of police. Now it is a National Museum.

BARI (*Real*). Tito Melema's birthplace. *Rom*. iii, vi.

Note.—An Italian seaport, on the Adriatic, in Apulia.

BARNES, JOHN. A Methodist. *Adam B*. xxx.

BARTOLOMMEO, FRA. *See* BACCIO.

BARTON, MRS. AMELIA *called* MILLY. Amos Barton's beautiful and lovable wife, the mother of a large family of children. *Amos B*. i–ix.

"She was a lovely woman— Mrs. Amos Barton; a large, fair, gentle Madonna, with thick, close, chestnut curls beside her well-rounded cheeks, and with large, tender, short-sighted eyes. The flowing lines of her tall figure made the limpest dress look graceful, and her old frayed black silk seemed to repose on her bust and limbs with a placid elegance and sense of distinction . . . The caps she wore would have been pronounced, when off her head, utterly heavy and hideous—for in those days even fashionable caps were large and floppy; but surmounting her long arched neck, and mingling their borders of cheap lace and ribbon with her chestnut curls, they seemed miracles of successful millinery. Among strangers she was shy and tremulous as a girl of fifteen; she blushed crimson if any one appealed to her opinion; yet that tall, graceful, substantial presence was so imposing in its mildness, that men spoke to her with an agreeable sensation of timidity." Ch. ii.

She is loved by all her husband's parishioners, who for her sake modify their criticism of the less popular Amos. With entirely inadequate means she cheerfully and skilfully contrives to meet the needs of her large family, and her whole life is given in loving service to Amos and her children. Entirely honest and guileless herself, she does not see through the shallow pretence of the Countess Czerlaski, and when the Countess quarters herself on the Barton household Milly loads herself with extra burdens to make the visitor comfortable. The strain proves too much, and after the birth of her seventh child she dies, thinking to the last of the welfare of her children and husband.

Note.—The original of Milly Barton was Mrs. Emma Gwyther, *née* Wilson, wife of the Reverend John Gwyther. They had six children. Mrs. Evans, George Eliot's mother (the original of Mrs. Hackit), was her intimate friend, but was not with her in her last illness, as Mrs. Evans died shortly before Mrs. Gwyther. The name Milly Barton was probably suggested by that of "Mrs. Milly Barton", a sister of Lady Newdigate, second wife of Sir Roger Newdigate. (*See* Deakin, *Early Life of George Eliot*, p. 126–7; Newdigate, *The Cheverels*, p. 66; also references under Barton, Amos.)

BARTON, REV. AMOS. Curate of Shepperton; a commonplace man with a large family and insufficient means. *Amos B.* i–x, Conclusion; mentioned *Mr. G.'s L. S.* i.

"As Mr. Barton hangs up his hat in the passage, you see that a narrow face of no particular complexion—even the small-pox that has attacked it seems to have been of a mongrel, indefinite kind—with features of no particular shape, and an eye of no particular expression, is surmounted by a slope of baldness gently rising from brow to crown. You judge him, rightly, to be about forty." Ch. ii.

"The Rev. Amos Barton, whose sad fortunes I have undertaken to relate, was . . . in no respect an ideal or exceptional character, and perhaps I am doing a bold thing to bespeak your sympathy on behalf of a man who was so very far from remarkable—a man whose virtues were not heroic, and who had no undetected crime within his breast; who had not the slightest mystery hanging about him, but was palpably and unmistakably commonplace . . . His very faults were middling—he was not *very* ungrammatical. It was not in his nature to be superlative in anything; unless, indeed, he was superlatively middling, the quintessential extract of mediocrity. If there was any one point on which he showed an inclination to be excessive, it was confidence in his own shrewdness and ability in practical matters, so that he was very full of plans which were something like his moves in chess—admirably well calculated, supposing the state of the case were otherwise." Ch. v.

In his mediocre way he tries to attend to all parish duties, but with a small stipend can never make both ends meet, and has to be helped by his parishioners and his squire. Dazzled by the Countess Czerlaski's pretended gentility, he receives her into his family when she quarrels with her brother, and thus increases the existing gossip and alienates his parishioners. He regains their regard only when crushed under the grief of Milly's death.

Note. — The original of Amos Barton was the Rev. John Gwyther, B.A., curate of Chilvers Coton during George Eliot's girlhood and, later, vicar of Fewston, Yorkshire, where he died in 1873. (Browning, *Life of George Eliot*, p. 47; Cooke, *George Eliot*, p. 282; Parkinson, *Scenes*, p. 37; manuscript list.)

BARTON, CHUBBY. The Barton's youngest girl. *Amos B.* ii, viii–ix.

BARTON, DICKEY. The Barton's second boy, an affectionate little fellow, "a boisterous boy of five, with large pink cheeks and sturdy legs"; in later life a talented engineer. He is Mrs. Hackit's favourite. *Amos B.* ii, v, viii–ix, Conclusion.

BARTON, FRED. The Barton's eldest son. *Amos B.* ii, v, viii–ix.

BARTON, PATTY. The Barton's eldest child; a sweet, serious girl who takes her mother's place after Milly's death, and remains her father's devoted companion. *Amos B.* ii, viii–ix, Conclusion.

BARTON, SOPHY. One of the Barton children. *Amos B.* ii, v, viii–ix.

BARTON, WALTER. Milly's year-old baby. *Amos B.* ii, v, vii–ix.

BASLE (*Real*). One of the cities visited by Latimer and his family. *L. V.* i.

Note.—Basle, or Basel, one of the principal Swiss cities, capital of the half canton of Basel-Stadt.

BASS, TRAPPING. Poacher. *Mid.* lxxxiv.

BASSET. Parish in which the Mosses live. *M. F.* Bk. 1, viii; Bk. 6, x.

"Basset had a poor soil, poor roads, a poor non-resident landlord, a poor non-resident vicar, and rather less than half a curate, also poor." Bk. 1, viii.

BATES, MR. Gardener at Cheverel Manor; a great friend of Caterina. *Mr. G.'s L. S.* ii, iv–v, vii, xiv–xv, xvii, xxi.

"He was a sturdy Yorkshireman, approaching forty, whose face Nature seemed to have coloured when she was in a hurry, and had no time to attend to *nuances*, for every inch of him visible above his neckcloth was of one impartial redness; so that when he was at some distance your imagination was at liberty to place his lips anywhere between his nose and chin. Seen closer, his lips were discerned to be of a peculiar cut, and I fancy this had something to do with the peculiarity of his dialect, which, as we shall see, was individual rather than provincial. Mr. Bates was further distinguished from the common herd by a perpetual blinking of the eyes; and this, together with the red-rose tint of his complexion, and a way he had of hanging his head forward, and rolling it from side to side as he walked, gave him the air of a Bacchus in a blue apron, who, in the present reduced circumstances of Olympus, had taken to the management of his own vines. Yet, as gluttons are often thin, so sober men are often rubicund; and Mr. Bates was sober, with that manly, British, churchman-like sobriety which can carry a few glasses of grog without any perceptible clarification of ideas." Ch. iv.

Note.—In the lists of originals which were made in Nuneaton after the publication of *Scenes of Clerical Life*, the original of Mr. Bates was said to be Baines, the gardener at Arbury. (*See* Olcott, *George Eliot*, p. 15.)

BATH (*Real*). The town to which Captain Wybrow goes to court Miss Assher. *Mr. G.'s L. S.* ii, iv–v; mentioned *Mid.* xxviii.
Note.—A noted English watering-place in Somerset, fashionable in the eighteenth century.

BATHERLEY. Market town near Raveloe where Molly Farren lived. *S. M.* iii–iv, viii, xiv.

BATT AND COWLEY. Lawyers of the Bycliffes. *F. H.* xxi, xxxvii.

"BATTI, BATTI" (*Real*). One of the songs which Rosamond Vincy sings. *Mid.* xvi.
Note.—"Batti batti, o bel Masetto," an aria by Mozart.

BAVIECA. Duke Silva's black charger. *Sp. G.* i.

BAZLEY. Lord Brackenshaw's agent. *D. D.* xxi, xxv.

BEALE, MOLLY. "A brawny old virago." *J. R.* iv.

"BEAR AND RAGGED STAFF." Public house in Milby. *J. R.* iv.
Note.—As the scene of the story is laid in Warwickshire, the name of this inn is one of the touches of local colour, a bear and ragged staff being the coat of arms of the Earls of Warwick.

BEATON, MARGARET. Mr. Tulliver's mother's name. *M. F.* Bk. 3, viii.

BEAUCAIRE, SENESCHAL DE (*Hist.*). Great favourite of the French king, for whom he purchases Bardo de' Bardi's art treasures. *Rom.* xxxi–xxxii.

Note.—Etienne de Vers, originally a lackey and later Seneschal Beaucaire.

BECK, MRS. Lodging-house keeper. *Mid.* xxv.

BECKY. Maid. *Mr. G.'s L. S.* xix.

BEDE, ADAM. An honourable, independent and able carpenter, the hero of the novel *Adam Bede.* *Adam B.* i, iii–v, viii–xi, xiv, xvi–xxx, xxxiii–xxxv, xxxviii–xliii, xlvi, xlviii–lv, Epilogue.

"A large-boned muscular man nearly six feet high, with a back so flat, and a head so well poised that when he drew himself up to take a more distant survey of his work, he had the air of a soldier standing at ease. The sleeve rolled up above the elbow showed an arm that was likely to win the prize for feats of strength; yet the long supple hand, with its broad fingertips, looked ready for works of skill. In his tall stalwartness Adam Bede was a Saxon, and justified his name; but the jet-black hair, made the more noticeable by its contrast with the light paper cap, and the keen glance of the dark eyes that shone from under strongly marked, prominent and mobile eyebrows, indicated a mixture of Celtic blood. The face was large and roughly hewn, and when in repose had no other beauty than such as belongs to an expression of good-humoured honest intelligence." Ch. i.

Poverty and his father's bad habits had given him much to contend against, but with a strong will he had overcome obstacles, gained an education in Bartle Massey's night school, and made himself a capable artisan, respected by his neighbours for his ability and upright character. At the beginning of the story he is chief workman in Jonathan Burge's timber yard, with prospects of a partnership some day, especially if he is willing to marry gentle Mary Burge. He has ideas about timber, and his friend Arthur Donnithorne, the heir of the manor, for whom Adam entertains a strong friendship dating from their boyhood, intends to put Adam in charge of the Donnithorne woods whenever the old squire dies. He is deeply in love with shallow Hetty Sorrel, the village beauty, who, however, ignores him, as her head has been turned by attentions from Arthur Donnithorne. When Adam finds that Arthur has been making love to Hetty, he fights Arthur, in spite of his strong affection for him, and forces him to break with Hetty, not knowing how far the relations between the two had gone. Later Adam becomes engaged to Hetty, but she runs away just before the date set for the wedding. When he learns that she has been arrested and is to be tried for child-murder Adam is overwhelmed with despair, and with rage against Arthur. He stands by Hetty in court, but is implacable against Arthur for a time, although later, won over by Arthur's genuine remorse, he consents to remain on the estate. Eventually he marries Dinah Morris.

Note.—It is generally agreed that the character of Adam Bede and some of the incidents of his career are drawn from Robert Evans, George Eliot's father. There are many points of resemblance in character and circumstances, and George Eliot herself admitted this, although she said that Adam was not a portrait of her father. There was the same kind of friendship between Robert Evans and young Francis Newdigate as between Adam Bede and Arthur Donnithorne. (*See* Browning, *Life of George Eliot*, pp. 14, 58, 63 ; Cross, *George Eliot's Life*, vol. i, p. 2 ; vol. ii, pp. 67–8 ; Dictionary of National Biography, article *Cross, Mary Ann* ; Mottram, *True Story of George Eliot*, ch. iv.)

BEDE, ADAM, *called* ADDY. Two-year-old son of Adam and Dinah. *Adam B.* Epilogue.

BEDE, LISBETH. Mother of Adam Bede, an affectionate and querulous woman. *Adam B.* iv–v, viii, x–xi, xiv, xviii, xx, xxiii, xxvi, xxx, xxxv, xl, l.

"She is an anxious, spare, yet vigorous old woman, clean as a snowdrop. Her grey hair is turned neatly back under a pure linen cap with a black band round it ; her broad chest is covered with a buff neckerchief, and below this you see a sort of short bed-gown made of blue-checkered linen, tied round the waist and descending to the hips, from whence there is a considerable length of linsey-wolsey petticoat. For Lisbeth is tall, and in other points too there is a strong likeness between her and her son Adam. Her dark eyes are somewhat dim now—perhaps from too much crying—but her broadly marked eyebrows are still black, her teeth are sound, and as she stands knitting rapidly and unconsciously with her work-hardened hands, she has as firmly-upright an attitude as when she is carrying a pail of water on her head from the spring." Ch. iv.

She is almost idolatrously devoted to her eldest son, Adam. Desiring him to make a sensible marriage, she is at first opposed to his marrying Hetty Sorrel. She had grown fond of Dinah Morris, when the latter came to comfort her at the time of her husband's death, and it is her desire to bring about a marriage between Adam and Dinah which eventually reveals to Adam his own affection for Dinah.

Note.—It has been suggested that Mary Evans, mother of Robert Evans ("Adam Bede") was the original of Lisbeth, but there is little evidence on which to base such a statement.

BEDE, LISBETH. Four-year-old daughter of Adam and Dinah. *Adam B.* Epilogue.

BEDE, MATTHIAS, *called* THIAS. Adam's father. *Adam B.* ii, iv–v, viii, x, xvi, xviii.

He had been a good carpenter and an affectionate father, but had taken to drink, and had caused much unhappiness to his wife and sons. At the opening of the story he is drowned in Willow Brook while coming home drunk from Treddleston.

Note.—George Evans, father of Robert Evans ("Adam Bede"), has been suggested as the original of Thias Bede, but there is no evidence to bear this out, as George Evans was a man of steady character, not a drunkard. An uncle of George Eliot's was drowned in the same way as Thias Bede, and that probably furnished the suggestion for Thias's death.

BEDE, SETH. A Methodist carpenter, Adam Bede's younger brother; a gentle and unselfish man, devoted to Adam. *Adam B.* i–v, viii, x–xi, xiv, xviii, xxiii, xxv–xxvii, xxx, xxxv, xxxviii, xl, l–li, lv, Epilogue.

"The next workman is Adam's brother. He is nearly as tall; he has the same type of features, the same hue of hair and complexion; but the strength of the family likeness seems only to render more conspicuous the remarkable difference of expression both in form and face. Seth's broad shoulders have a slight stoop; his eyes are grey; his eyebrows have less prominence and more repose than his brother's; and his glance, instead of being keen, is confiding and benignant. He has thrown off his paper cap, and you see that his hair is not thick and straight, like Adam's, but thin and wavy, allowing you to discern the exact contour of a coronal arch that predominates very decidedly over the brow." Ch. i.

Less able and ambitious than his energetic elder brother, he is characterized chiefly by his strong religious convictions and his capacity for loyal affection. From the beginning he is in love with Dinah Morris, and more than once asks her to marry him. When he finds that Adam himself is in love with Dinah, he does what he can to help his brother's suit, and later finds his chief happiness in his affection for Dinah and Adam and their children.

Note.—It was universally recognized that the original of Seth Bede was George Eliot's uncle, Samuel Evans. He was a zealous Methodist, and married Elizabeth Tomlinson, the original of Dinah Morris.

BEDFORD ROW (*Real*). The street in London where Mr. Johnson lives. *F. H.* xvii, xxx, Epilogue.

Note.—A street in Holborn, at the north end of Brownlow Street.

BEDMÁR. Town in Spain, the principal scene of the *Spanish Gypsy. Sp. G.* i–ii.

Note.—There is a small town of Bedmar in the province of Jaen, in Andalusia, Spain, which has a ruined fortress, dating from Moorish times, with the remains of a secret passage somewhat like the one described in the poem.

BEEVOR, CAPTAIN. *Mid.* lv.

BEEVOR, MRS. The captain's wife, step-daughter to Lord Grinsell. *Mid.* lv.

"BEGGAR'S OPERA" (*Real*). *Adam B.* xii; *M. F.* Bk. 6, vii.
Note.—An opera, with libretto by John Gay, written 1727.

"BEGONE, DULL CARE" (*Real*). *M. F.* Bk. 6, ii.
Note.—A popular song, the words of which were suggested by a sixteenth century song, while the music was derived from the "Queen's Jigg".

BELLAMY, MR. Butler at Cheverel Manor. *Mr. G.'s L. S.* ii, iv.

BELLAMY, MRS. Housekeeper at Cheverel Manor. *Mr. G.'s L. S.* ii, iv, xvi.

"BELLE SAUVAGE" (*Real*). London inn, where Annette Ledru goes with her baby, expecting to meet her husband. *F. H.* vi.

BELLINI, ARIA FROM (*Real*). Song sung by Gwendolen Harleth. *D. D.* v.
Note.—Vincenzo Bellini (1801–35), a famous Italian operatic composer.

BELVEDERE GALLERY, VIENNA (*Real*). An art gallery, on the terrace of which Latimer has one of his experiences of clairvoyance. *L. V.* i.
Note.—The Belvedere, an imperial chateau erected for Prince Eugene of Savoy, formerly contained the picture gallery which was later moved to the Imperial Art Museum.

BEN. *M. F.* Bk. 3, ix.

BENCI, VIA DE' (*Real*). Street in Florence along which Tito Melema sometimes passes on his way to or from the Via de' Bardi. *Rom.* xx, xxvi.
Note.—The Via de' Benci which leads from the Piazza Santa Croce towards the Ponte alle Grazie is named after the Benci family. At the time of *Romola* the part of the present Via de' Benci from the Borgo Santa Croce to the bridge was called Via del Fosso.

BENEDETTO. A Jewish baby rescued by Romola in the plague-stricken village. *Rom.* lxviii–lxix.

BENEDICTINES (*Hist.*). Monastic order. *Rom.* xliii.
Note.—The term Benedictines, or Black Monks, is the general name given to the monks living under the rule of St. Benedict, who himself founded the first Benedictine monastery.

"BENEFIT CLUB." An association in Middlemarch which considers taking Dr. Lydgate as its medical man. *Mid.* xlv, lxxi; Benefit Clubs are mentioned also in *Amos B.* i, *F. H.* xxxi.
Note.—Benefit Clubs were clubs for mutual insurance against illness, unemployment, death, etc.

BENEVIENI, ANTONIO (*Hist.*). "The greatest master of the chirurgic art," one of Nello's patrons. *Rom.* xvi.
Note.—An Italian physician and professor of medicine, who was born at Florence, and died there 1502.

BENEVIENI, GIROLAMO (*Hist.*). A mystic poet, an adherent of Savonarola. *Rom.* xxv.
Note.—Girolamo Benevieni (1453–1542) was a religious and lyrical poet, whose poems voiced the ideas and aspirations of Savonarola.

BEORL. The father of Ogg, the patron saint of St. Ogg's. *M. F.* Bk. 1, xii.

BERENICE (*Hist.*). The character in which Hans Meyrick paints a series of sketches of Mirah Cohen. *D. D.* xxxvii, xxxix.
Note.—The Jewess, Berenice, daughter of Herod Agrippa.

BERNARDO. A rich Florentine; Lisa's father. *P.—Lisa.*

BERTA, MONNA. A friend of Monna Brigida's. *Rom.* xii, li.

BERTUCCE, or BABOONS, HOSTELRY OF THE. Tavern in Florence near which Tito rescues Tessa from the *cerretano* or conjurer on Midsummer Day. *Rom.* x.

BEST, MRS. Housekeeper at Donnithorne Chase. *Adam B.* vii, xii, xxii, xxvi, lv.

BETHELL. Servant at Donnithorne Chase. *Adam B.* xxxii.

BETHESDA SPA. Proposed name for the baths, by means of which Mr. Jermyn hoped to turn Treby Magna into a fashionable watering place. *F. H.* iii.

BETTY. Dairymaid. *Adam B.* vi.

BETTY. The Dempster's middle-aged cook. *J. R.* v, vii, xvii, xxi.

BETTY. Mrs. Patten's dairymaid. *Amos B.* i.

BIBBIENA, CARDINAL DA. *See* DOVIZI, BERNARDO.

BIBBIENA, SER PIERO DA. *See* DOVIZI, SER PIERO.

BICHAT (*Hist.*). A great French scientist whose work had inspired Dr. Lydgate. *Mid.* xv.
Note.—Marie François Xavier Bichat (1771–1802), a French anatomist and physiologist.

BILKLEY. A town forty miles from Middlemarch. *Mid.* lxx–lxxi.

BINCOME. Former owner of Pivart's farm. *M. F.* Bk. 2, ii.

BINTON COPPICE. *Adam B.* xxxiv.

BINTON HILLS. The hills near Hayslope. *Adam B.* ii, v, xxxv, xliv, liii.
"High up against the horizon were the huge conical masses of hill, like giant mounds intended to fortify this region of corn and grass against the keen and hungry winds of the north." Ch. ii.
Note.—The originals of the Binton Hills are the Weaver Hills in the parish of Ellastone ("Hayslope"), in Staffordshire. (*See* Mottram, *True Story of George Eliot,* p. 41.)

BISHOP, THE. *J. R.* v–vi.
"The Bishop was an old man, and probably venerable (for though he was not an eminent Grecian, he was the brother of a Whig lord)." Ch. vi.

BISHOP (*Hist.*). The church dignitary who performs the ceremony of degradation on Savonarola, just before his execution. *Rom.* lxxii.
Note.—Benedetto Cristoforo de' Pagagnotti, Bishop of Vaison and Vicar-General of Florence.

BLACK BRETHREN (FRATI NERI).
See AUGUSTINIANS.
"BLACK-EYED MONKEY." Sir Christopher Cheverel's name for Caterina. See SARTI, CATERINA.
"BLACK-EYED SUSAN" (*Real*). One of the songs which Rosamond Vincy sings. *Mid.* xvi.
 Note.—A song composed by Richard Leveridge (c. 1670–1758), said to have been arranged by him from a still older melody.
"BLACK SWAN." Public-house at King's Lorton frequented by Mr. Poulter. *M. F.* Bk. 2, iv.
BLACKBIRD. Daniel Knott's horse. *Mr. G.'s L. S.* xix.
BLACKFRIARS BRIDGE (*Real*). A bridge over the Thames. *D. D.* xx, xxxviii, xl.
BLACKSMITH, POPISH. *Amos B.* i.
 Note.—Original: Bull, of Griff.
BLACKHEATH (*Real*). Henry Scaddon's birthplace. *F. H.* xxi.
 Note.—A suburb of London.
BLAKESLEY, JUSTICE. *Mid.* lvi.
BLARNEY, LORD. An acquaintance mentioned by the Countess Czerlaski. *Amos B.* iii.
BLAS. *Sp. G.* i.
BLASCO. A prosperous silversmith from Aragon. *Sp. G.* i–ii.
BLENNY. A former tenant of Offendene. *D. D.* xv.
BLETHERS, VISCOUNT. *Mr. G.'s L. S.* i.
BLICK, DR., OF FLITTON. *S. M.* xi.
BLICK, MR. Mr. Irwine's predecessor. *Adam B.* v.
BLINDMAN'S COURT. *Mid.* lxix.

BLOUGH, LORD. An acquaintance of Mr. Vandernoodt's. *D. D.* xxxv.
BLUCHER. Mr. Bulstrode's dog. *Mid.* lxi.
"BLUE BULL." Inn in Middlemarch. *Mid.* xxxix, lx.
"BLUE COW." Public-house, Sproxton. *F. H.* xi.
BLYTHE. One of Mr. Irwine's parishes. *Adam B.* v.
BODKIN, BROTHER. A member of Mr. Lyon's congregation. *F. H.* v.
BOGOLI, HILL OF (*Real*). Hill back of the Via de' Bardi, from which stone was quarried. *Rom.* Proem. v, xvii, xxxiii.
 Note.—The Bogoli, now the Boboli Hill, was named after an old family, the Borgoli, that formerly held property there. The Boboli Garden is on the hill.
BOLOGNA (*Real*). Italian city; Romola plans to go there when she starts to leave her husband Tito Melema. *Rom.* xiv, xxi, xxxvi–xxxvii, xlv.
 Note.—Bologna, in the province of Bologna, in the old Romagna, north of Florence.
BOMBUS. A loud buzzing, bouncing writer. *T. S.* xiv.
BOND, MISS. *Amos B.* v.
BOND, MR.[1] Churchwarden at Shepperton. *Amos B.* v; mentioned *Mr. G.'s L. S.* i.
BOND, MRS. The churchwarden's wife, who takes charge of the Barton children during their mother's last illness. *Amos B.* ii, viii; mentioned *J. R.* xi.

---

[1] The originals of Mr. and Mrs. Bond were Mr. and Mrs. Hollick. (MS. notes.)

BOND, TOMMY, called "LITTLE CORDUROYS". A favourite of Mr. Gilfil's, "a saucy boy, impervious to all impressions of reverence." *Mr. G.'s L. S.* i.

BONFIRE OF VANITIES (*Hist.*). *Rom.* xlix, l, lxii.

"On this last day of the festival, at evening, the pile of vanities was to be set ablaze to the sound of trumpets, and the ugly old Carnival was to tumble into the flames amid the songs of reforming triumph." Ch. xlix.

Note.—The first Bonfire of Vanities took place the 7th of February, 1497. A second one took place on 27th February, 1498.

BONI. A druggist in whose shop Monna Brigida tries to take refuge from the collectors of Vanities. *Rom.* li.

BONSI, DOMENICO (*Hist.*). A learned doctor of law; one of the four syndics or commissioners charged with the effecting of the treaty between Charles VIII of France and the people of Florence. *Rom.* xxix.

Note.—Domenico Bonsi (1430-1501) was a Florentine diplomat of distinction and a partisan of Savonarola.

BOOTS, of the Red Lion, Milby. *J. R.* i, iv.

BORGIA, RODRIGO. *See* ALEXANDER VI, POPE.

BORGO DE' GRECI (*Real*). Street in Florence near which Romola and Tito meet a funeral Carnival procession while returning from their betrothal in Santa Croce. *Rom.* xx.

Note.—The Borgo de' Greci, a street leading from the Piazza di Santa Croce, has been said mistakenly to take its name from the fact that the Byzantine Emperor and his brother, the Greek Patriarch, were there in 1436. The name is, however, of earlier date, and may be derived from the Greci family.

BORGO DEGLI ALBIZZI (*Real*). Street in Florence where Monna Brigida lives. *Rom.* xlix, lxx, lxxi. In Ch. xlix called *Corso* degli Albizzi.

Note.—The Borgo degli Albizzi (now Albizi) is an old street of Florence, continuing the Via del Corso and extending to the Via Giuseppe Verdi. It was named after the Albizzi family, which had many houses there.

BORGO DI SAN LORENZO (*Real*). Street in Florence up which one of Baldassarre Calvo's fellow-prisoners turns when he escapes. *Rom.* xxii.

Note.—The Borgo San Lorenzo leads from near the Baptistery to the Piazza San Lorenzo.

BORGO LA CROCE (*Real*). Street in Florence where Romola finds the runaway Lillo. *Rom.* lvi.

Note.—The Borgo La Croce extends from the Piazza San Ambrogio to the Piazza Beccaria (Porta alla Croce).

BORGO PINTI (*Real*). Street in Florence where Tito Melema meets Romola when she is hastening

to see her dying brother. *Rom.*
xiii, xxxvii, Epilogue.
   Note.—The Borgo Pinti is a long street running to the Porta Pinti (Piazzale Donatello).

BORGO SANTA CROCE (*Real*). Street in Florence near which Tito Melema hears the sound of Niccolò Caparra's forge. *Rom.* xxvi.
   Note.—The Borgo Santa Croce extends from the Church of Santa Croce to the Via de' Benci.

BOTT'S CORNER. *Mid.* xl.

BOULOGNE (*Real*). Place where Raffles had known Will Ladislaw's father. *Mid.* lx.
   Note.—Boulogne, in the *département* of Pas-de-Calais, a French seaport on the English Channel.

BOVIS. A gentleman who is horrified at the saccharine excesses of Avis, not realizing that he himself takes twenty-six lumps of sugar each day. *T. S.* xiii.

BOVIS, MRS. Mr. Bovis's watchful wife, who counts his lumps of sugar. *T. S.* xiii.

BOWYER, MR. An idle bachelor addicted to comic songs and ventriloquism. *Mid.* xvi, xxv, li, lx.

BRACCIO, SER. *Rom.* xx.

BRACKENSHAW, LADY. Lord Brackenshaw's gracious wife. *D. D.* iii, x–xi, xlviii.

BRACKENSHAW, LORD. Mrs. Davilow's kind landlord and Mr. Gascoigne's friend, a "middle-aged peer of aristocratic seediness in stained pink, with easy-going manners which would have made the threatened deluge seem of no consequence." *D. D.* iii, vii, x–xi, xiv, xxi, xliv, lxiv, lxix.

BRACKENSHAW, LADY BEATRICE AND LADY MARIA. Lord and Lady Brackenshaw's young daughters. *D. D.* vii.

BRACKENSHAW ARCHERY CLUB. A select club where Gwendolen Harleth and Grandcourt first met. *D. D.* iii, x–xi, xiii–xiv.

BRACKENSHAW CASTLE. Home of Lord Brackenshaw. *D. D.* v–vi, x, xxxv, lxix.

BRADWELL. *Adam B.* xvi.

BRADY'S. *J. R.* xvii.

BRAMCOTE. *S. M.* iii.

BRAMHILL. A living of Lord Watling's. *Amos B.* vi.

BRAND, MR. The Shepperton doctor, "obnoxious to Mr. Pilgrim." *Amos B.* v, vii–ix.
   Note.—In the lists of originals which were made in Nuneaton after the publication of the *Scenes of Clerical Life*, the original of Mr. Brand was said to be a Mr. Harris. (*See* Olcott, *George Eliot*, p. 14.)

BRASENOSE (*Real*). The college to which Mr. Casaubon's dreaded critic, Mr. Carp, belongs. *Mid.* xxix, xxxvii.
   Note.—A college at Oxford, founded 1509 by William Smith, Bishop of Lincoln, and Sir Richard Sutton.

BRASSING. Town near Middlemarch. *Mid.* xiii, xxxii, xxxv–xxxvi, xl, xlv–xlvi, li, lvi, lviii, lxi, lxvi, lxxvii.

BRATTI FERRAVECCHI. A loquacious pedlar and dealer in second-hand goods who is fond of bargaining. *Rom.* i–iii, xiv, xvi, xxx, l–li, lix–lxx.

"He was a grey-haired, broad-shouldered man, of the type which, in Tuscan phrase, is moulded with the fist and polished with the pickaxe; but the self-important gravity which had written itself out in the deep lines about his brow and mouth seemed intended to correct any contemptuous inferences from the hasty workmanship which Nature had bestowed on his exterior." Ch. i.

He is the first person to see Tito when the latter comes to Florence, and he introduces him to Nello, the barber, and later sells his onyx ring for him. After Tito's death Romola is able to find Tessa through Bratti, who has taken Tessa's necklace in pawn.

BRECON. A student who became a superior expensive kind of idiot after obtaining a Double First. *D. D.* xvi.

BRENDALL, HARRY. A relative of the Arrowpoints', who would have the property if Catherine were disinherited. *D. D.* xxii.

BRENT. Gardener at Treby Manor. *F. H.* vii.

BRETTON, MRS. Former owner of the house in which the Lydgates live. *Mid.* xxxvi.

BREWITT. Blacksmith, fond of his trade. *D. D.* lviii.

BRICK, MRS. An inmate of Shepperton workhouse, an old woman much given to snuff. *Amos B.* ii.

"Mrs. Brick, one of those hard undying old women, to whom age seems to have given a network of wrinkles, as a coat of magic armour against the attacks of winters, warm or cold. The point on which Mrs. Brick was still sensitive — the theme on which you might possibly excite her hope and fear — was snuff. It seemed to be an embalming powder, helping her soul to do the office of salt."

BRIDE STREET. An insignificant street in Middlemarch, where the rooms are like cages. *Mid.* lxiv.

BRIDGE WAY. Street in Milby where Mr. Dempster meets with a fatal accident. *J. R.* iv, xvii, xxii.

"One of those dismal wide streets where dirt and misery have no long shadows thrown on them to soften their ugliness." Ch. iv.

BRIDGEPORT. *Amos B.* ii.

BRIDGET. The Irwines' servant. *Adam B.* v.

BRIDMAIN, MR. EDMUND. Countess Czerlaski's half-brother, a retired silk manufacturer, who marries his sister's maid. *Amos B.* ii–v, vii.

"Mr. Bridmain . . . by unimpeached integrity and industry, had won a partnership in a silk manufactory, and thereby a moderate fortune, that enabled him to retire . . . to study politics, the weather, and the art of conversation, at his leisure . . . Every man who is not a monster, a mathematician, or a mad philosopher, is the slave of some woman or other. Mr. Bridmain had put his neck under the yoke of his handsome sister, and though his soul was a very little one—of the smallest description indeed—he would not have ventured to call it his own." Ch. iv.

Note.—In the lists of originals which were made in Nuneaton after the publication of *Scenes of Clerical Life* the original of Mr. Bridmain was said to be Sir John Waldron. (*See* Olcott, *George Eliot*, p. 14.)

BRIGFORD. Village. *B. J.* i.

BRIGGS. Sir James Chettam's coachman. *Mid.* lxxxiv.

BRIGIDA, MONNA. Romola's cousin; a garrulous but good-hearted old woman fond of dress. *Rom.* v, xii–xiii, xv, xx, xxxi, xlix, li–lii, lviii, lxx, Epilogue.

"A short, stout, black-eyed woman about fifty, wearing a black velvet berretta, or close cap, embroidered with pearls, under which surprisingly massive black braids surmounted the little bulging forehead, and fell in rich plaited curves over the ears, while an equally surprising carmine tint on the upper region of the fat cheeks contrasted with the surrounding sallowness. Three rows of pearls and a lower necklace of gold reposed on the horizontal cushion of her neck; the embroidered border of her trailing black velvet gown and her embroidered long-drooping sleeves of rose-coloured damask, were slightly faded." Ch. xii.

She disapproves of the sober dress of the Piagnoni, but is persuaded unwillingly to give up her false hair and finery to be burned in the Bonfire of Vanities. After Tito's death Romola lives with her and she becomes attached to Tessa's children.

"BRIMSTONE." A Methodist brickmaker and converted poacher. Pupil in Bartle Massey's night school. *Adam B.* xxi.

BRINCEY, MICHAEL. *See* BRINDLE, MIKE.

BRINDLE, MIKE. A head miner, whose real name is Michael Brincey; one of the witnesses for Felix Holt at his trial. *F. H.* xi, xlvi.

BRINLEY, MRS. Carpenter's wife. *J. R.* xiii.

BRITTON, MRS. The farmer's wife. *Adam B.* xxvi.

BRITTON, LUKE. The largest Broxton farmer. *Adam B.* v, ix, xiv, xxiii, xxvi.

BRITTON, YOUNG LUKE. The farmer's son, an admirer of Hetty Sorrel's. *Adam B.* ix.

BROMPTON (*Real*). The part of London in which Modecai Cohen and his sister live after they find each other. *D. D.* xlvi, lxii, lxvi–lxvii.

Note.—A section in the west part of London, including the South Kensington Museums.

BROOKE, MR. ARTHUR. Bachelor uncle and guardian of Dorothea and Celia. *Mid.* i–x, xviii, xxviii, xxx, xxxiv, xxxvii–xl, xlv–xlvii, xlix–li, liv, lxii–lxiii, lxxi–lxxii, lxxvi–lxxvii, lxxxi, lxxxiv, Finale.

"A man nearly sixty, of acquiescent temper, miscellaneous opinions, and uncertain vote. He had travelled in his younger years, and was held in this part of the county to have contracted a too rambling habit of mind. Mr. Brooke's conclusions were as difficult to predict as the weather; it was only safe to say that he would act with benevolent intentions, and that he would spend as little money as possible in carrying them out." Ch. i.

He takes his responsibilities towards his nieces very lightly, and, although disapproving of the elderly Mr. Casaubon as a husband for Dorothea, makes only a ridiculously inadequate remonstrance when she announces her intention of marrying him. Later, when he plunges into politics and wishes to run for Parliament, he engages the services of Will Ladislaw and retains him in the neighbourhood to the displeasure of jealous Mr. Casaubon. When Dorothea, then a young widow, marries Will Ladislaw, he is unable to manifest any serious displeasure and, although he at first talks of cutting the entail, her eldest son eventually inherits his estates.

BROOKE, CELIA. Dorothea's pretty and proper younger sister. *Mid.* i–x, xxiii, xxviii–xxx, xxxiv, xxxviii, xlviii–l, liv–lv, lxii, lxvii, lxxii, lxxvii, lxxxiv, Finale.

"The rural opinion about the new young ladies, even among the cottagers, was generally in favour of Celia, as being so amiable and innocent-looking . . . Since they could remember, there had been a mixture of criticism and awe in the attitude of Celia's mind towards her elder sister. The younger had always worn a yoke; but is there any yoked creature without its private opinions?" Ch. i.

"But on safe opportunities she had an indirect mode of making her negative wisdom tell upon Dorothea, and calling her down from her rhapsodic mood by reminding her that people were staring, not listening. Celia was not impulsive; what she had to say could wait, and came from her always with the same quiet staccato evenness." Ch. iii.

Her sense of propriety is often shocked by Dorothea's unconventional views and deeds, and she occasionally has courage to utter her criticisms. She dislikes Mr. Casaubon, to whose blinking and moles she strongly objects. After Dorothea marries Mr. Casaubon, Celia makes a very happy marriage with the correct Sir James Chettam, and feels an affectionate superiority to her sister, as one who has managed her life less well. Her real affection for Dorothea does not allow her to be parted from her, even when she greatly disapproves of her second marriage.

Note.—The original of Celia Brooke was George Eliot's elder sister, Christiana Evans, later Mrs. Edward Clarke, although the character of Celia is not an exact portrait of her sister. (*See* Cross, *George Eliot's Life*, vol. 1, p. 31.)

BROOKE, DOROTHEA. A beautiful, noble-minded and ardent girl, with an intense longing for goodness and a great desire to be helpful to others. *Mid.* i–xi, xix–xxii, xxviii–xxxi, xxxiv, xxxvii–xxxix, xlii–xliv, xlvi–lii, liv–lvi, lix, lxii–lxiii, lxvii, lxxi–lxxii, lxxvi–lxxxiv, Finale.

"Miss Brooke had that kind of beauty which seems to be thrown into relief by poor dress. Her hand and wrist were so finely formed that she could wear sleeves not less bare of style than those in which the Blessed Virgin appeared to Italian painters; and her profile as well as her stature and bearing seemed to gain the more dignity from her plain garments, which by the side of provincial fashion gave her the impressiveness of a fine quotation from the Bible—or from one of our elder poets—in a paragraph of to-day's newspaper. She was usually spoken of as being remarkably clever, but with the addition that her sister Celia had more common-sense." Ch. i.

"She came into the drawing-room in her silver-grey dress—the simple lines of her dark-brown hair parted over her brow and coiled massively behind, in keeping with the entire absence from her manner and expression of all search after mere effect. Sometimes when Dorothea was in company there seemed to be as complete an air of repose about her as if she had been a picture of Santa Barbara." Ch. x.

"The intensity of her religious disposition, the coercion it exercised over her life, was but one aspect of a nature altogether ardent, theoretic and intellectually consequent; and with such a nature struggling in the bands of a narrow teaching, hemmed in by a social life which seemed nothing but a labyrinth of petty courses, a walled-in maze of small paths that led no whither, the outcome was sure to strike others as at once exaggeration and inconsistency." Ch. iii.

Dorothea at nineteen marries the middle-aged and pedantic Mr. Casaubon because she is in love with the idea of being a helpmate to him in his great work. She soon realizes that she has idealized her husband, who is a cold, jealous, and selfish man, engaged in a work of no real value. Although the shock of the disillusion is great and her intense nature at times rebels, she loyally devotes herself to Mr. Casaubon while he lives. She is on the point of sacrificing her future happiness by making him a promise, which, though she does not know its nature, would have separated her from Will Ladislaw, his young cousin, when Mr. Casaubon dies. Eventually she gives up her social position and Mr. Casaubon's money in order to marry Will Ladislaw.

Note.—Dorothea's religious side was drawn, recognizably, from letters to George Eliot from Emilia Strong, who became first Mrs. Mark Pattison and later Lady Dilke. (Dilke, *Book of*

Spiritual Life, p. 16.) There are points in her character—her opinions and her relation to her sister—which were suggested by things in George Eliot's own life.

BROOKS, OLD. *Mr. G.'s L. S.* vii.

BROTHER. The elder of the two children in the poem *Brother and Sister*. *P.—B. S.*
He is the hero and leader in the childish adventures and explorations, and is followed with puppy-like affection by his little sister of four or five years of age.
Note.—The poem *Brother and Sister* is autobiographic, and describes the relation between George Eliot and her brother Isaac Evans, the "Brother" of the poem.

"BROTHER, HEAR, AND TAKE THE CURSE." The Zincali's song in the *Spanish Gypsy*. *Sp. G.* iii.

BROUNSELL AFFAIR. *Amos B.* vi.

BROUSSAIS (*Hist.*). A French physician whom Lydgate knew when he was a student in Paris. *Mid.* x.
Note. — François Joseph Victor Broussais (1772–1838), a French physician whose lectures in Paris were attended by great numbers of students.

BROWNIE. Mongrel belonging to the Garths. *Mid.* lvii, lxxxvi.

BROXTON. Village near Hayslope, where Mr. Irwine is rector. *Adam B.* ii, iv–v, xxii, xxvii, xxxix.
Note.—The original of Broxton was the hamlet of Roston, near Norbury.

BROXTON RECTORY. Mr. Irwine's home. *Adam B.* iv–v, xiii, xvi, xxxix, xl.

BRUIN. An epicure who found and tasted a honeycomb. *T. S.* xi.

BRUMBY, DICK. *M. F.* Bk. 3, vi.

BRUMLEY. *M. F.* Bk. 2, ii.

BRUSSELS (*Real*). *D. D.* ii, xx.

BRYCE. The gentleman fond of hunting, who purchases Godfrey Cass's hunter Wildfire. *S. M.* iii–iv, viii.

BUCHAN. Saddler, member of the Philosophers' Club. A cool Scotchman. *D. D.* xlii.

BUCKS. One of Bob Jakin's imaginary acquaintances; a lady with a cork leg. *M. F.* Bk. 5, ii.

BUDD, MR. Churchwarden at Milby; a satellite of Lawyer Dempster's. *J. R.* i–ii, iv, vi, viii, x, xiv, xvii, xxv–xxvi.
"Mr. Budd was a small, sleek-headed bachelor of five and forty, whose scandalous life had long furnished his more moral neighbours with an after-dinner joke. He had no other striking characteristic, except that he was a currier of choleric temperament, so that you might wonder why he had been chosen as clergyman's churchwarden, if I did not tell you that he had recently been elected through Mr. Dempster's exertions, in order that his zeal against the threatened evening lecture might be backed by the dignity of office." Ch. i.
Note —The original of Mr. Budd was said to have been a Mr. Burton. (*See* Olcott, *George Eliot*, p. 16.)

BUGLE. Lady's maid in Mrs. Davilow's family. *D. D.* iii, vii.

BULSTRODE, ELLEN. Mr. and Mrs. Bulstrode's daughter. *Mid.* xxvi, lxxiv, lxxxv.

BULSTRODE, MRS. HARRIET. The banker's handsome and loyal wife, and Mr. Vincy's sister. *Mid.* xi–xiv, xvi, xviii, xxvii, xxxi, xxxvi, xlvi, liii, lx–lxi, lxiv, lxviii, lxix–lxxi, lxxiii–lxxiv, lxxxv–lxxxvi.

"But this imperfectly taught woman, whose phrases and habits were an odd patchwork, had a loyal spirit within her. The man whose prosperity she had shared through nearly half a life, and who had unvaryingly cherished her— now that punishment had befallen him, it was not possible to her in any sense to forsake him. There is a forsaking which still sits at the same board and lies on the same couch with the forsaken soul, withering it the more by unloving proximity. She knew when she locked her door, that she should unlock it ready to go down to her unhappy husband and espouse his sorrow, and say of his guilt, I will mourn and not reproach. But she needed time to gather up her strength; she needed to sob out her farewell to all the gladness and pride of her life." Ch. lxxiv.

Of a wholesome worldly nature she frankly enjoys her husband's wealth and position before scandal touches him. When she learns of his unworthiness her loyalty to him never wavers, although she suffers greatly.

BULSTRODE, KATE. Mr. and Mrs. Bulstrode's daughter. *Mid.* xxxi, lxxiv, lxxxv.

BULSTRODE, MR. NICHOLAS. Banker in Middlemarch; a man whose marked piety covers a dishonourable past. *Mid.* x–xiv, xvi–xviii, xxvi–xxvii, xxxi, xxxvi, xxxviii, xl–xli, xliv–xlvi, li, liii, lx–lxi, lxiii–lxiv, lxvii–lxxi, lxxiii–lxxiv, lxxvi, lxxix, lxxxi–lxxxii, lxxxv.

"He had a pale blonde skin, thin grey besprinkled brown hair, light-grey eyes, and a large forehead. Loud men called his subdued tone an undertone, and sometimes implied that it was inconsistent with openness . . . Mr. Bulstrode had also a deferential bending attitude in listening and an apparently fixed attentiveness in his eyes which made those persons who thought themselves worth hearing infer that he was seeking the utmost improvement from their discourse." Ch. xiii.

"Strange, piteous conflict in the soul of this unhappy man, who had longed for years to be better than he was—who had taken his selfish passions into discipline and clad them in severe robes, so that he had walked with them as a devout choir." Ch. lxx.

He had been connected with a London pawnshop, which dealt with thieves, had married his employer's rich widow, after concealing from her the fact that her daughter, Will Ladislaw's mother, for whom she was searching, was alive, had inherited her money on her death, and settled in Middlemarch. Here he married Mr. Vincy's sister, and made a place for himself as a prosperous man interested in philanthropy. When Raffles, who knows of his early life, appears in Middlemarch, Mr. Bulstrode bribes him to keep silent. He tries to atone for his action about his first wife's daughter by offering money to her son, Will Ladislaw, when he learns of the relationship, only to have his offer refused. During Raffles' last illness Mr. Bulstrode knowingly allows Dr. Lydgate's orders to be disobeyed, and Raffles dies, but Mr. Bulstrode's secret has become known, and he leaves Middlemarch a disgraced man, involving Lydgate, who had accepted a loan from him, in his disgrace.

BULT, MR. A political man who aspires to marry Miss Arrowpoint, the heiress. *D. D.* xxii.
" The expectant peer, Mr. Bult, an esteemed party man, who, rather neutral in private life, had strong opinions concerning the districts of the Niger . . . was studious of his Parliamentary and itinerant speeches, and had the general solidity and suffusive pinkness of a healthy Briton on the central table-land of life." Ch. xxii.

BUNCH. Sheepstealer. *Mid.* iv.

BUNNEY, OLD MASTER. *Mid.* lxxx.

BUONDELMONTI (*Hist.*). " High house of Buondelmonti, patrons of the church," guardians of the image of the Madonna dell' Impruneta. *Rom.* xlii.

Note. — The Church of the Impruneta was founded by the Buondelmonti family.

BUONOMINI DI SAN MARTINO (GOOD MEN OF ST. MARTIN). *See* GOOD MEN OF ST. MARTIN.

BURCHIELLO (*Hist.*). A barber, Nello's great predecessor, often mentioned by him, whose shop was on the Calimara. *Rom.* iii.
" Now a barber can be dispassionate ; the only thing he necessarily stands by is the razor, always providing he is not an author. That was the flaw in my great predecessor Burchiello : he was a poet, and had consequently a prejudice about his own poetry." Ch. iii.

Note.—Domenico di Giovanni, called Il Burchiello, poet and barber in Florence, who was born in Florence about 1404 and died at Rome 1448. His sonnets (first edition Bologna, 1474) were very popular, and were frequently reprinted.

BURDETT, SIR FRANCIS (*Hist.*) A radical. *F. H.* i.
Note.—Sir Francis Burdett (1770–1844), the most popular liberal politician of his time ; an advocate of many reforms and radical measures.

BURGE, JONATHAN. Carpenter and builder in the village of Hayslope. He is the employer of Adam and Seth Bede and later takes Adam into partnership. *Adam B.* i, iii–iv, xviii–xix, xxiv, xxvii, xxxiii–xxxiv, xl, lv.

BURGE, MARY. Jonathan Burge's plain and gentle daughter, who is in love with Adam Bede. *Adam B.* i, iv, ix, xxiii, xxvi, xxxiv, lv.

BURNING OF VANITIES. *See* BONFIRE OF VANITIES.

BUTCHER'S LANE, MILBY. *J. R.* iii, xxiii.

BUTTERWORTH, ELIAS BAPTIST. A vegetarian, who believes that a millenium will come when flesh-eating ceases. He and his beliefs furnish a text for the poem. *P.—Minor prophet.*

BUTTON, PEGGY. An inhabitant of Sproxton. *F. H.* xi.

BUTTS, SALLY. *J. R.* xxvi.

BUTZKOPF. A German scholar. *T. S.* iii.

BUXTON. *M. F.* Bk. 1, vii.

BYCLIFFE, EDWARD. The ancestor of Esther Lyon, who lived at the time when the base-fee to the Transome estates was created. *F. H.* xxxvii.

BYCLIFFE, ESTHER. *See* LYON, ESTHER.

BYCLIFFE, MAURICE CHRISTIAN. The representative of the family which claimed the Transome estate; Esther Lyon's father. *F. H.* xiv, xviii, xxi, xxv, xxix, xxxv.

When a prisoner of war in France he had married Annette Ledru. By exchanging names with Henry Scaddon, a fellow-prisoner whose exchange had been effected, he was able to return to England, leaving his wife to follow him. In England he instituted a suit against the Transomes, believing that the estate was legally his. During the progress of the suit he had been imprisoned as Henry Scaddon, and had died in prison, before his wife and infant daughter could reach him.

BYCLIFFE, MRS. MAURICE CHRISTIAN. *See* LEDRU, ANNETTE.

BYCLIFFE *versus* TRANSOME. Lawsuit instituted by Maurice Christian Bycliffe, Esther Lyon's father, to obtain possession of the Transome estate. *F. H.* xxi, xxviii–xxix, xxxv.

John Justus Transome in 1729 had made a settlement of his estates entailing them on his son Thomas and his heirs-male, with remainder to the Bycliffes in fee. Thomas, a prodigal, had sold his own and his descendants' rights to a lawyer-cousin named Durfey, whose descendants, the Durfey-Transomes (the Transomes of the story), are the rightful holders of the estate as long as there exists a male descendant of Thomas Transome. In the absence of such male descendant the right to the estate would pass to the Bycliffes. The complicated legal plot of the story rests upon this Durfey-Transome-Bycliffe situation and the fact that Esther Lyon's claim (as the last Bycliffe) becomes valid on the death of old Tommy Trounsem, the last descendant of Thomas Transome.

Note.—In order to be sure that she was right in her handling of a plot based upon a question of law, George Eliot consulted Frederic Harrison, who suggested the legal scheme of the story and wrote the lawyer's " opinion on the case ", which was incorporated in the novel. Frederic Harrison said later: "I remember telling her, when she inserted these lines in the book, that I had written at least a sentence which was embodied in English literature." (*See* Harrison, *Studies in Early Victorian Literature*, p. 218; *also* his *Memories and Thoughts*, p. 137–140; *also* Cross, *George Eliot's Life*, vol. 2, p. 420, 423.)

BYGATE, MR. Squire Donnithorne's lawyer. *Adam B.* xliv.

BYLES, MR. Butcher in Middlemarch, to whom Lydgate owed money. *Mid.* lxxi.

BYLES, MR. LUKE. An inhabitant of Milby, "who piqued himself on his reading and was in the habit of asking casual acquaintances if they knew anything of Hobbes." *J. R.* i, xvii.

Note.—Mr. Byles' original was a Tom Payne. (MS. notes.)

C

CACHALOT, MONSIEUR. A French scholar, who comments on the Merman-Grampus dispute. *T. S.* iii.

CADWALLADER, MRS. ELINOR. The rector's managing wife; a high-born, sharp-tongued lady fond of a joke. *Mid.* i, v, vi–viii, x, xxviii–xxxiv, xxxviii, l, liv–lv, lxii, lxxvii, lxxxiv.

" A lady of immeasurably high birth, descended, as it were, from unknown earls, dim as the crowd of heroic shades — who pleaded poverty, pared down prices, and cut jokes in the most companionable manner, though with a turn of tongue that let you know who she was. Such a lady gave a neighbourliness to both rank and religion, and mitigated the bitterness of uncommuted tithe. A much more exemplary character with an infusion of sour dignity would not have furthered their comprehension of the Thirty-nine Articles, and would have been less socially uniting." Ch. vi.

CADWALLADER, MR. HUMPHREY. Rector of Tipton and Freshitt; an easy-going man, noted for his devotion to fishing. *Mid.* vi, viii, x, xxxiv, xxxviii, liv–lv, lxxxiv.

" Mr. Cadwallader was a large man, with full lips and a sweet smile; very plain and rough in his exterior, but with that solid imperturbable ease and good-humour which is infectious, and like great grassy hills in the sunshine, quiets even an irritated egoism, and makes it rather ashamed of itself . . . He always saw the joke of any satire against himself. His conscience was large and easy, like the rest of him; it did only what it could do without any trouble." Ch. viii.

CÆSAR. An old Newfoundland belonging to Latimer. *L. V.* ii.

CALCONDILA, DEMETRIO (*Hist.*). A Greek scholar to whose professorship of Greek in Florence Tito Melema succeeds. *Rom.* ii–vi, ix.

Note.—Demetrius Chalcondylas or Demetrio Calcondila, a Greek, who was brought to Florence by Lorenzo de' Medici, was

D

for more than twenty years professor of Greek in that city. He left Florence for Milan in 1492; died c. 1510 or 1513.

CALDERINO (*Hist.*). "Men like Calderino who, as Poliziano has well shown, have recourse to impudent falsities of citation to serve the ends of their vanity and secure a triumph to their own mistakes." *Rom.* xii.
> *Note.*—Domizio Calderino (1446–1478), famous philologist, philosopher, and mathematician.

CALEB, SILLY. An idiot. *J. R.* iv.

CALIBUT, MR. A Tory who made his fortune in trade. *F. H.* xx.

CALIMARA, THE (*Real*). Street in Florence where Burchiello's barber shop was located. *Rom.* Proem, i, iii.
> *Note.* — The Via Calimara (or Calimala), one of the most ancient of Florentine streets, leads from the site of the former Mercato Vecchio, now the modern Piazza Vittorio Emanuele, to the Via Porta Rossa. The residence and offices of the Guild of the Calimala (workers of foreign cloth) were in this street.

CALIMARA, CORPORATION OF (*Hist.*). Dealers in foreign cloths to which a Florentine finish had been given; one of the corporations included in the San Giovanni procession. *Rom.* viii.
> *Note.*—The Calimala, or dealers in foreign cloth, one of the seven Greater Arts (or Guilds) of Florence.

CALLAM. Village. *Mr. G.'s L. S.* xix.

CALLISTA. An imaginative person, who frequently gives false testimonials. *T. S.* xiii.

CALLUM. Mr. Garth's clerk. *Mid.* lvi.

CALVO, BALDASSARRE. Tito Melema's adoptive father, a deserted and deeply injured old man, whose sufferings and wrongs affect his mind and leave him only one idea, that of vengeance. *Rom.* ix, xxii–xxv, xxvii–xxx, xxxiii, xxxviii, xlii, xlviii, l, lii–liii, lv, lxvii.

" He was very different in aspect from his two fellow-prisoners . . . he had passed the boundary of old age, and could hardly be less than four or five and sixty. His beard which had grown long in neglect, and the hair which fell thick and straight round his baldness, were nearly white. His thickset figure was still firm and upright, though emaciated, and seemed to express energy in spite of age — an expression that was partly carried out in the dark eyes and strong dark eyebrows, which had a strangely isolated intensity of colour in the midst of his yellow, bloodless, deep-wrinkled face with its lank grey hairs. And yet there was something fitful in the eyes, which contradicted the occasional flash of energy; after looking round with quick fierceness at windows and faces, they fell again with a lost and wandering look." Ch. xxii.

A great scholar and of ample means, he had adopted Tito Melema as a child and had brought him up as his own son. While journeying to Delos he is captured by pirates, though Tito, who carries their fortune in gems, escapes. Carried into captivity, he believes that his son will find and ransom him, and succeeds in sending Tito word of his whereabouts. After desertion and illness have broken him down, he is sent back to Italy, and, as a prisoner of the French, is brought to Florence, where Tito has been prospering since their separation. Near the Duomo he escapes from his guards and runs into Tito, who knows him, but denies him. Brooding over this treachery, he attempts to kill Tito when they meet again, and later, when his mental powers have returned temporarily, makes charges against Tito at the great supper in the Rucellai Gardens, but is again denied by Tito and again breaks down, and is cast into prison, where he languishes for two years, until released during the famine. Romola succours him and he seeks to enlist her aid against Tito, by telling her of Tito's "other wife", Tessa. Reduced to a pitiable condition by mental and physical suffering and forced to beg, he is kept alive only by the hope of vengeance. Eventually he finds Tito again, when the latter, worn out by his long swim to escape the mob, is cast ashore on the river bank, and he strangles Tito, dying himself immediately after.

Note.—While Baldassarre Calvo is a fictitious character, there is an historical original for one of the events of his career. Villari, in his *Life of Savonarola*, tells of the escape of three prisoners at the time of the French entry into Florence who were liberated by the crowd just as in *Romola*. As this is the only printed source for this story, George Eliot undoubtedly took this incident from Villari, as Guido Biagi points out. (*See* Villari, *Savonarola*, p. 231; also Biagi edition of *Romola*, Introd. p. xxxiv.)

CAMARALZAMAN, PRINCE. Nickname given to Deronda by the Meyricks. See DERONDA, DANIEL.

CAMBINI, ANDREA (*Hist.*). "A well-known satellite of Francesco Valori." *Rom.* lix.

Note.—Andrea Cambini, historian and translator, who lived during the second half of the fifteenth century. He was a zealous follower of Savonarola.

CAMBRIDGE (*Real*). English university where Daniel Deronda and Hans Meyrick are fellow-students. *D. D* xvi ; mentioned *Amos B.* ii, vi ; *Mid.* ii.

"CAME A PRETTY MAID." One of the songs of Juan, the minstrel. *Sp. G.* i.

CAMP VILLA. Residence of the Countess Czerlaski and her brother, situated half a mile from Milby. *Amos B.* iii–v.

Note.—The original of Camp Villa was a house near Nuneaton called the Briars. (Manuscript information; also Olcott, *George Eliot*, p. 15.)

CAMPAGNA (*Real*). One of Dorothea Brooke's favourite drives while she was in Rome. *Mid.* xx.

Note.—A large plain surrounding Rome which offers opportunity for many excursions.

CANCER CURE. One of the quack medicines to which Felix Holt is heir. *F. H.* iv–v.

"CANDELABRUM." A journal which prints an unfavourable notice of Vorticella's one book. *T. S.* xv.

CANTO DI PAGLIA (*Real*). Place in Florence where Maestro Tacca, the doctor, lives. *Rom.* xvi.

Note. — The Canto alla Paglia ("Straw Corner") at a corner of the Borgo S. Lorenzo and Via dei Cerretani took this name from the fact that until comparatively recent years the market for hay and straw was held there daily.

CAPARRA, NICCOLÒ (*Hist.*). Armourer; a famous worker in iron. *Rom.* i, xvi, xxvi, xliv.

"He was one of those figures for whom all the world instinctively makes way, as it would for a battering-ram. He was not much above the middle height, but the impression of enormous force which was conveyed by his capacious chest, and brawny arms bared to the shoulder, was deepened by the keen sense and quiet resolution expressed in his glance and in every furrow of his cheek and brow. He had often been an unconscious model to Domenico Ghirlandajo, when that great painter was making the walls of the churches reflect the life of Florence." Ch. i.

Tito Melema buys from him the coat of mail which he wears after the return of Baldassarre Calvo, and Baldassarre buys there the hunting knife with which he hopes to kill Tito.

Note.—Niccolò Grosso, called Caparra from his habit of insisting on earnest money in any bargain.

CAPPONI, PIERO (*Hist.*). One of the four syndics charged with effecting the treaty between Charles VIII and the people of Florence, who at the critical moment spoke out and opposed the king. *Rom.* xxv, xxix.

Note.—Piero di Gino di Neri Capponi (1446–1496), a member of an illustrious family and gonfaloniere of Florence, who was especially celebrated for the courageous stand he took in the negotiations with Charles VIII.

CARDELL CHASE. A meeting place of the Brackenshaw Archery Club, where Gwendolen Harleth encounters Mrs. Glasher and learns of her relations with Grandcourt. *D. D.* xi, xiii–xiv.

CAREGGI (*Real*). The country house of the Medici near Florence, where Lorenzo de' Medici died. *Rom.* Proem, i, xxxix.

Note.—The Villa Medicea di Careggi bought by Cosimo the Elder and reconstructed for him after 1433. It was set on fire, but not destroyed, in 1529, and still retains practically its original form.

CARMELITES (*Hist.*). Monks who take part in the procession of L'Impruneta in Florence. *Rom.* xliii.
Note.—One of the four great orders of mendicants; founded 1156 by the Crusader Berthold, at Mt. Carmel, in Palestine.

CARP. An old acquaintance whose criticism Mr. Casaubon resents. *Mid.* xxix, xlii.

CARPE, MR. The non-resident Vicar of Shepperton, who comes to reside at Shepperton as a pretext for removing Amos Barton, in order ultimately to give the curacy to his own brother-in-law. *Amos B.* vi, ix.

CARR, MR. An invalid who became childish, and was fed with a spoon for three years. *M. F.* Bk. 3, iii.

CARROLL. Mr. Irwine's butler. *Adam B.* v, xxi, xxxix, xl.

CARTER, MRS. Mr. Brooke's cook. *Mid.* vi.

CARTWRIGHT (*Hist.*). A gentleman at whose house Mr. Brooke had once dined with Sir Humphrey Davy and Wordsworth. *Mid.* ii.
Note.—Edmund Cartwright (1743-1823), the inventor of the power-loom. His interest in agriculture led him into a correspondence with Sir Humphrey Davy. He was also the author of some published poems.

CASA GHERARDESCA. *See* SCALA PALACE.

CASAUBON, DOROTHEA. *See* BROOKE, DOROTHEA.

CASAUBON, REVEREND EDWARD. A pedantic, middle-aged scholar, intensely self-centred and jealous. *Mid.* i-xi, xix-xxii, xxviii-xxx, xxiv, xxxvii-xxxix, xlii-xliv, xlvi-l, lix.

"Mr. Casaubon had never had a strong bodily frame, and his soul was sensitive without being enthusiastic; it was too languid to thrill out of self-consciousness into passionate delight; it went on fluttering in the swampy ground where it was hatched, thinking of its wings and never flying. His experience was of that pitiable kind which shrinks from pity, and fears most of all that it should be known; it was that proud, narrow sensitiveness which has not mass enough to spare for transformation into sympathy, and quivers thread-like in small currents of self-preoccupation or at best of an egoistic scrupulosity. And Mr. Casaubon had many scruples; he was capable of severe self-restraint; resolute he was in being a man of honour according to the code; he would be unimpeachable by any recognized opinion . . . the difficulty of making his Key to all Mythologies unimpeachable weighed like lead upon his mind . . . even his religious faith wavered with his wavering trust in his own authorship, and the consolations of the Christian hope in immortality seemed to lean on the immortality of the still unwritten Key to all Mythologies." Ch. xxix.

He marries Dorothea Brooke, who has idealized him, and soon proves himself selfishly blind to her claims, and incapable of responding to her devotion. His ambition is centred in his projected masterpiece, "Key to all Mythologies," but he lacks the ability necessary to carry it to completion. Because Dorothea manifests a friendly interest in his young kinsman, Will Ladislaw, he becomes unreasonably jealous, and when he dies some two years after his marriage, he leaves a codicil to his will depriving Dorothea of his property in case she marries Ladislaw.

Note.—It has been claimed by some that the Reverend Mark Pattison, Rector of Lincoln, was the original of Mr. Casaubon, while others have indignantly denied this. Mark Pattison was a visitor at George Eliot's home, and it is possible that she may, unconsciously, have copied some of his superficial characteristics. This, together with the name—Mark Pattison's best known work was his life of Isaac Casaubon—may have given rise to the report that he was the original. (*See* article by Lord Acton in *Nineteenth Century*, vol. 17, p. 480; Morley, *Critical Miscellanies*, vol. 3, p. 165; chapter by Mrs. Lynn Lynton, in *Women Novelists of Queen Victoria's Reign*, p. 100; article in *Academy*, 9th August, 1884.)

CASENTINO, THE (*Real*). A region from which the country people come to the fairs in Florence. *Rom.* viii, xiii.

Note.—The Casentino is the district of the upper valley of the Arno.

CASS, SQUIRE. The greatest man in Raveloe; a proud, violent man who has allowed his sons to grow up without proper discipline. *S. M.* i, iii, v, viii–xi, xiii, xvi.

"The old Squire was an implacable man; he made resolutions in violent anger, and he was not to be moved from them after his anger had subsided—as fiery volcanic matters cool and harden into rock. Like many violent and implacable men, he allowed evils to grow under favour of his own heedlessness, till they pressed upon him with exasperating force, and then he turned round with fierce severity and became unrelentingly hard." Ch. viii.

CASS, BOB. The squire's third son, his father's favourite. *S. M.* iii, xi, xiii.

CASS, DUNSTAN, *called* DUNSEY. Squire Cass's second son, "a thick-set, heavy looking young man," fond of drink and betting. *S. M.* iii, iv, viii–x, xv, xviii.

"People shook their heads at the courses of the second son, Dunstan, commonly called Dunsey Cass, whose taste for swopping and betting might turn out to be a sowing of something worse than wild oats. To be sure, the neighbours said, it was no matter what became of Dunsey—a spiteful, jeering fellow, who seemed to enjoy his drink the more when other people went dry." Ch. iii.

He takes advantage of his knowledge of his brother Godfrey's secret marriage to extort money from him. Moved by a sudden impulse, he enters Silas Marner's unprotected cottage to borrow money, steals the weaver's savings, and disappears from Raveloe. Years later his skeleton and the money are found in a pit into which he had fallen after the robbery.

CASS, GODFREY. Squire Cass's eldest son and Eppie's real father; an amiable and affectionate, but irresolute and morally weak, young man. *S. M.* iii, v, viii–xiii, xv–xx, Conclusion.

"That big muscular frame of his held plenty of animal courage, but helped him to no decision when the dangers to be braved were such as could neither be knocked down nor throttled. His natural irresolution and moral cowardice were exaggerated by a position in which dreaded consequences seemed to press equally on all sides." Ch. iii.

Although he is in love with pretty Nancy Lammeter, he had, in a weak moment, contracted a secret marriage with Molly Farren, a barmaid. When his wife, who is bringing their little child to Raveloe to expose him, dies at Silas Marner's door, he does not acknowledge the little girl, but allows Silas to keep her. This death removes the only obstacle to his marriage to Nancy. Years later, unhappy because they have no children, he wishes to acknowledge Eppie as his daughter, but she refuses to leave Silas.

CASS, MRS. GODFREY (first wife). *See* FARREN, MOLLY.

CASS, MRS. GODFREY (second wife). *See* LAMMETER, NANCY.

CASSON, MR. Landlord of the "Donnithorne Arms", an ex-butler, who has a scorn for those who speak the "dileck". *Adam B.* ii, xviii, xxiii, xxxii.

"Mr. Casson's person . . . appeared to consist principally of two spheres, bearing about the same relation to each other as the earth and the moon; that is to say, the lower sphere might be said, at a rough guess, to be thirteen times larger than the upper . . . no head and face could look more sleek and healthy, and its expression, which was chiefly confined to a pair of round and ruddy cheeks, the slight knot and interruptions forming the nose and eyes being scarcely worth mention, was one of jolly contentment." Ch. ii.

CATERINA. *See* SARTI, CATERINA.

CATHEDRAL OF SANTA MARIA DEL FIORE. *See* DUOMO.

CATTLETON. Market town near Grimworth. *B. J.* ii–iii.

CATULUS, S. A younger member of Shark's remarkable family. *T. S.* iii.

CECCA (*Hist.*). Engineer, who had provided the huge drapery in the Piazza del Duomo for the Midsummer Day celebration. *Rom.* viii.

Note.—Francesco d'Angelo, called La Cecca (1447–1488), a

famous Florentine engineer who devised ingenious machinery and elaborate decorations for the Midsummer Day and other great festivals and processions. For the description of these, from which George Eliot took her account, *see* Vasari, *Lives*.

CECCO. A hungry man who helps Romola to succour Baldassarre when she finds the latter starving. *Rom*. xlij, xliv.

"Cecco was a wild-looking figure; a very ragged tunic, made shaggy and variegated by cloth-dust and clinging fragments of wool, gave relief to a pair of bare bony arms and a long sinewy neck; his square jaw shaded by a bristly black beard, his bridgeless nose and low forehead, made his face look as if it had been crushed down for purposes of packing." Ch. xlii.

CECCONE, SER, *or* SER FRANCESCO DI SER BARONE (*Hist*.). A "sharp-nosed notary of evil repute". *Rom*. xlv, xlvii, lvii, lxiii, lxvi, lxxi.

While apparently a member of Savonarola's party he is secretly an agent of the Mediceans. When the Mediceans are arrested he tries to buy his own safety by betraying them, and hates Tito Melema as a more successful traitor than himself. Later he attaches himself to the Arrabbiati and Dolfo Spini, becomes a bitter enemy of Savonarola, and, at Savonarola's trial and torture, tampers with and perverts the evidence and confession.

Note.—Ser Ceccone, or Ser Ceccone di Ser Barone, the infamous notary who falsified Savonarola's depositions.

CEI, FRANCESCO (*Hist*.). Popular poet; a frequenter of Nello's barber shop. He is an opponent of Savonarola. *Rom*. viii, xiii, xvi, xxix, xlv, lxvi.

Note.—Francesco Cei was a Florentine poet of the second half of the fifteenth century, of a considerable reputation among his contemporaries. His only published work was a collection entitled: *Sonecti, capitoli, canzoni, sextine stanze e strambatti, composti in laude di Clitia*. Florence, 1503. This was reprinted several times under different titles.

CENNINI, DOMENICO (*Hist*.). Son of Bernardo Cennini, the first printer of Florence; a goldsmith and printer with whom Tito Melema banks the money which he obtains from the sale of his rings. *Rom*. iv, vi, ix, xvi, xlv, lx.

Note.—Domenico Cennini, goldsmith, born 1452, who in 1470–71 co-operated with his father, Bernar doCennini, in the printing of the Commentary on Virgil. George Eliot describes him as the elder brother, but he was seven years younger than Pietro.

CENNINI, PIETRO (*Hist*.). Goldsmith and printer, the younger brother of Domenico; an "erudite corrector of proof-sheets", who employs Tito Melema to help in

editing his classical texts. *Rom.* iv, vi, viii, xxix, lxii.
Note. — Pietro Cennini, writer, humanist, and printer, born 1445, who in 1470–71 worked as "emendator" on his father's edition of the Commentary on Virgil. George Eliot makes him the younger of the two brothers, but he was seven years older than Domenico (*see above*).

CERRETANI, VIA DE' (*Real*). Street in Florence along which Tito Melema and a French dignitary proceed to the Duomo when preparing for the French king's entry into Florence. *Rom.* xxii.
Note.—The Via de' Cerretani, named after an old family, extends from the Piazza di San Giovanni toward the Piazza Santa Maria Novella, as far as the Via Panzani.

CERRETANO, THE. *See* VAIANO, MAESTRO.

CERTALDO (*Real*). A place on the Siena Road, where Tito Melema receives a message from Piero de' Medici. *Rom.* xlv.
Note.—This is the small town of Certaldo on the Elsa, in Tuscany, 18 miles south-west of Florence.

CHAD'S BESS. *See* CRANAGE, BESSY.

CHALKY FLATS. Place where Mrs. Cranch resides. *Mid.* xxxii, xxxiv, liii.

CHALONER, MR. Rector at Grimworth. *B. J.* ii–iii.

CHALONER, MRS. The rector's wife, who patronizes Mr. Edward Freely's shop. *B. J.* ii.

"CHANNEL ISLANDS, WITH NOTES AND AN APPENDIX." The title of Vorticella's one book. *T. S.* xv.

CHAPLAIN OF THE JAIL, STONITON. *Adam B.* xlii, xlv.

CHARISI, DANIEL. Daniel Deronda's grandfather; a learned Jew with an iron will, and a heart set on Judaism, who had greatly desired a grandson to carry on his work and had forced his daughter to marry her cousin. *D. D.* li, liii, lx, lxiii.

CHARISI, EPHRAIM. Daniel Deronda's father, who made it the labour of his life to devote himself to his wife, the prima donna. *D. D.* li.

CHARLES VIII (*Hist.*). The French king, who enters Florence in 1494. *Rom.* xxi, xxvi–xxix, xxxi.
"If the young monarch under the canopy, seated on his charger with his lance upon his thigh, had looked more like a Charlemagne and less like a hastily modelled grotesque, the imagination of his admirers would have been much assisted. It might have been wished that the scourge of Italian wickedness and 'Champion of the honour of women' had had a less miserable leg, and only the normal sum of toes; that his mouth had been of a less reptilian width of slit, his nose and head of a less exorbitant outline." Ch. xxvi.
Note. — Charles VIII (1470–98), king of France 1483–98. In 1494 Lodovico Il Moro asked Charles for help against Naples, and Charles went to Italy and conquered Naples.

CHA 42 CHE

George Eliot's account of the events of his entry into Florence follows history closely.

CHASE, THE. See DONNITHORNE CHASE.

CHASE FARM. *Adam B.* xxvii, xxxii.

CHE FARÒ SENZA EURIDICE (*Real*). One of Sir Christopher Cheverel's favourite airs, which Caterina sings to him. *Mr. G.'s L. S.* ii.
Note.—A song from Gluck's opera *Orfeo*, act 3.

CHELSEA (*Real*). Part of London where the Meyricks live. *D. D.* xvii, xxxvii, xxxix–xl, xliii, xlvii.
Note.—A residential part of London on the north bank of the Thames. George Eliot herself dwelt there during the last few weeks of her life.

CHELTENHAM (*Real*). *Mid.* liv, lxxi.
Note.—A fashionable resort and watering-place in Gloucestershire, seven miles north-east of Gloucester.

CHERRY, MRS. Lady's maid at Treby Manor. *F. H.* xii.

"CHERRY RIPE" (*Real*). Song which Fred Vincy strums on the piano. *Mid.* xvi.
Note.—The words of the song are by Herrick, the music by Charles E. Horn.

CHESHIRE, MR. (*Hist.*). A medical man who used "irons, trying to make people straight". *Mid.* xlv.
Note.—Robert Chessher (1750–1831) a surgeon of Hinckley, Leicestershire, who had devised a special apparatus for weak spines. (*See* Garrison, *History of Medicine*, p. 518.)

CHESTER. Servant. *Adam B.* xviii.

CHETTAM, DOWAGER LADY. Mother of Sir James; a stately, affable woman. *Mid.* vi, x, xxviii–xxix, xxxiv, liv–lv, lxxxiv.

CHETTAM, ARTHUR. Sir James and Lady Chettam's little son, named after Mr. Brooke. *Mid.* xlix–l, liv–lv, lxxvii, lxxxiv, Finale.

CHETTAM, CELIA, LADY. See BROOKE, CELIA.

CHETTAM, SIR JAMES. An amiable, prosperous and handsome baronet, with a great dislike for the unconventional. *Mid.* i–vi, viii–x, xxvii–xxix, xxxiv, xxxvii–xl, xlix–li, liv–lvi, lxii, lxvii, lxxii, lxxvi–lxxvii, lxxxi, lxxxiv, Finale.

"He was made of excellent human dough, and had the rare merit of knowing that his talents, even if let loose, would not set the smallest stream in the country on fire; hence he liked the prospect of a wife to whom he could say: 'What shall we do?' about this or that; who could help her husband out with reasons, and would also have the property qualification for doing so." Ch. ii.

He is in love with Dorothea Brooke, whose superiority he recognizes, and he is much shocked when she marries the elderly Mr. Casaubon. He soon transfers his affections to her sister Celia, and becomes an affectionate and indulgent husband. He loyally retains an admiration for Dorothea and opposes her second marriage, which he considers unworthy of her.

CHEVEREL, LADY. Sir Anthony's handsome wife. *Mr. G.'s L. S.* ii, xi.

CHEVEREL, SIR ANTHONY. An imposing ancestor of Sir Christopher's, the renovator of the family splendour in the reign of Charles II. *Mr. G.'s L. S.* ii.

Note.—The original of Sir Anthony Cheverel was Sir Richard Newdegate, first baronet.

CHEVEREL, SIR CHRISTOPHER. The proud, strong-willed, but kind-hearted, owner of Cheverel Manor. *Mr. G.'s L. S.* ii–xix, xxi.

" As fine a specimen of the old English gentleman as could well have been found in those venerable days of cocked-hats and pigtails. His dark eyes sparkled under projecting brows, made more prominent by bushy grizzled eyebrows; but any apprehension of severity excited by these penetrating eyes, and by a somewhat aquiline nose, was allayed by the good-natured lines about the mouth, which retained all its teeth and its vigour of expression in spite of sixty winters. The forehead sloped a little from the projecting brows, and its peaked outline was made conspicuous by the arrangement of the profusely-powdered hair, drawn backward and gathered into a pigtail." Ch. ii.

His pride and ambition are centred in his beautiful house, which he is rebuilding, and in his nephew and heir, Captain Wybrow, whose marriage to Miss Assher he uses every effort to further. He is fond also of his protegée, Caterina Sarti, and, quite blind to her passion for Captain Wybrow, is anxious to have her marry Mr. Gilfil, his ward. He is deeply affected by the death of his nephew and Caterina's unhappiness.

Note. — The original of Sir Christopher was Sir Roger Newdigate, fifth baronet. (*See* Newdigate, *The Cheverels*, pp. 229–31; Stephen, *George Eliot*, pp. 56–7.)

CHEVEREL, HENRIETTA, LADY. Sir Christopher's stately wife; an unsympathetic, awe-inspiring but kind woman. *Mr. G.'s L. S.* ii–xv, xviii, xxi.

" She is tall, and looks the taller because her powdered hair is turned backward over a toupee, and surmounted by lace and ribbons. She is nearly fifty, but her complexion is still fresh and beautiful, with the beauty of an auburn blonde; her proud pouting lips, and her head thrown a little backward as she walks, give an expression of hauteur which is not contradicted by the cold grey eye. The tucked-in kerchief, rising full over the low tight bodice of her blue dress, sets off the majestic form of her bust, and she treads the lawn as if she were one of Sir Joshua Reynolds's stately ladies, who had suddenly stepped from her frame to enjoy the evening cool." Ch. ii.

" Lady Cheverel, though not very tender-hearted, still less sentimental, was essentially kind, and liked to dispense benefits like a goddess, who looks down benignly on the halt, the maimed, and the blind that approach her shrine." Ch. ii.

Note. — The original of Lady Cheverel was Hester Margaretta (Mundy), Lady Newdigate, Sir Roger Newdigate's second wife. (See Newdigate, *The Cheverels*, p. 229.)

CHEVEREL MANOR. Home of Sir Christopher and Lady Cheverel, which Sir Christopher rebuilds in the Gothic style. *Mr. G.'s L. S.* ii–vi, viii–xix.

" The castellated house of grey-tinted stone, with the flickering sunbeams sending dashes of golden light across the many-shaped panes in the mullioned windows, and a great beech leaning athwart one of the flanking towers, and breaking, with its dark flattened boughs, the too formal symmetry of the front; the broad gravel-walk winding on the right, by a row of tall pines, alongside the pool—on the left branching out among swelling grassy mounds, surmounted by clumps of trees, where the red trunk of the Scotch fir glows in the descending sunlight against the bright green of limes and acacias." Ch. ii.

Note.—The original of Cheverel Manor was Arbury Hall, the seat of the Newdigate family near Nuneaton, which was rebuilt in the Gothic style by Sir Roger Newdigate just as Cheverel Manor was rebuilt by Sir Christopher. George Eliot was frequently at Arbury during her childhood. (*See* Newdigate, *The Cheverels*, passim; Bartholomew, *Literary and Historical Atlas*, p. 135.)

CHICHELY, MR. Coroner in Middlemarch. *Mid.* x, xvi, lxiii, lxxi, lxxv.

" A middle-aged bachelor and coursing celebrity, who had a complexion something like an Easter egg, a few hairs carefully arranged, and a carriage implying the consciousness of a distinguished appearance." Ch. x.

CHOWNE. Farmer. *Adam B.* xviii, xxiii.

CHOWNE, MRS. The farmer's wife, " a poor soft thing, wi' no more head-piece nor a sparrow." *Adam B.* xviii.

CHOYCE. Farmer. *Adam B.* vi.

CHRISTIAN, MAURICE. Assumed name of Henry Scaddon. A clever but not very successful adventurer. *F. H.* vii, xii, xiv, xix–xxi, xxiv–xxvi, xxviii–xxx, xxxvi, xli, Epilogue.

In his youth he had been wild, dissipating his fortune and committing forgery. Later he had been a fellow prisoner-of-war in France with Maurice Christian Bycliffe, and by exchanging names with him had helped Bycliffe to escape to England. He kept the name of Maurice Christian and much later enters the service of Philip Debarry, which brings him to Treby. There he sees Esther Lyon, learns from Mr. Lyon that she is Bycliffe's daughter, and then sells this information to Harold Transome.

CHRISTIAN OBSERVER (*Real*). A periodical which Amos Barton

would have taken in if he had been able to afford it. *Amos B.* ii.

Note.—A monthly magazine, published 1802–74; continued as the *Christian Observer and Advocate*, 1875–1877.

CHRIST'S HOSPITAL (*Real*). School from which Hans Meyrick enters Cambridge as an exhibitioner. *D. D.* xvi. In *Felix Holt*, Mr. Jermyn " had got his Latin there for nothing ". *F. H.* ii.

Note. — Christ's Hospital, the famous " Blue Coat School " founded by Edward VI, was in London at the period of *Daniel Deronda*. It has since been moved to the country.

CHUBB, WILLIAM. Landlord of the Sugar Loaf, Sproxton, where Felix Holt goes to talk with the miners. *F. H.* xi, xvii, xxx–xxxi.

" Mr. Chubb was a remarkable publican ; none of your stock Bonifaces, red, bloated, jolly, and joking. He was thin and sallow, and was never, as his constant guests observed, seen to be the worse (or the better) for liquor . . . Mr. Chubb's reasons for becoming landlord of the Sugar Loaf were founded on the severest calculation. Having an active mind, and being averse to bodily labour, he had thoroughly considered what calling would yield him the best livelihood with the least possible exertion, and in that sort of line he had seen that a ' public ' amongst miners who earned high wages was a fine opening." Ch. xi.

" CHURCH CLOCK." An organ of Pumpiter opinion which reviews Vorticella's one book. *T. S.* xv.

CHURCH LANE, Stoniton. Street where Sarah Stone lived. *Adam B.* xliii.

CHURCHYARD LANE. Street in Middlemarch. *Mid.* xlv.

CIONI, SER (*Hist.*). A thin notary, member of Savonarola's party. *Rom.* i, xxii.

Note.—Filippo Cioni, a notary who in 1496 wrote an Epistle in defence of Savonarola.

CLEMENT, SIR JAMES. The ministerial candidate for Parliament in North Loamshire, " a poor baronet, hoping for an appointment," who retires before the election. *F. H.* ii, vii, xi.

CLEMENTINA, LADY. Lady Pentreath's daughter. *D. D.* xxxvi.

CLEMMENS. Solicitor in Brassing, who drew up Peter Featherstone's last will. *Mid.* xxxv.

" CLERICAL GAZETTE." A church paper read by Mr. Gascoigne. *D. D.* vii.

CLERICAL MEETING AND BOOK SOCIETY, MILBY. *Amos. B.* ii–iii, vi.

CLEVE, MRS. Owner of the shop which Mr. Freely rents. *B. J.* ii.

CLEVES, REV. MARTIN. Rector of Tripplegate, Amos Barton's neighbour and kind friend. *Amos B.* vi, ix.

" A man about forty, middle-sized, broad-shouldered, with a negligently-tied cravat, large irregular features, and a large head, thickly covered with lanky brown hair . . . *there* is the true parish priest, the pastor beloved, consulted, relied on by his flock; a clergyman who is not associated with the undertaker, but thought of as the surest helper under a difficulty, as a monitor who is encouraging rather than severe. Mr. Cleves has the wonderful art of preaching sermons which the wheelwright and the blacksmith can understand, not because he talks condescending twaddle, but because he can call a spade a spade, and knows how to disencumber words of their wordy frippery." Ch. vi.

Note.—In lists of originals which were made in Nuneaton after the publication of *Scenes of Clerical Life*, the prototype of the Reverend Mr. Cleves was given as the Reverend John Fisher.[1] (*See* Olcott, *George Eliot*, p. 14.)

CLIFF, MR. A retired tailor, former owner of the Warrens, who built the big stables there. *S. M.* vi.

CLIFF'S HOLIDAY. The name given to the ghostly manifestations at the stables built by Mr. Cliff. *S. M.* vi.

CLINT, MISS. Maiden name of Mr. Wakem's wife. *M. F.* Bk. 3, vii.

CLINTOCK, ARCHDEACON. *D. D.* v, xi.

CLINTOCK, MR. The archdeacon's classical son, who admires Gwendolen Harleth. *D. D.* v, x-xi.

CLINTUP, MR. "A diffident though distinguished nurseryman." *Mid.* lx.

COACHMAN FROM OAKBOURNE. A jolly old man who tries to joke with Hetty on her journey. *Adam B.* xxxvi.

COBURG, THE. London theatre where Mirah's father Lapidoth had worked. *D. D.* xx.

Note.—This may be a reference to the real Cobourg Theatre, Waterloo Bridge Road, Lambeth (opened 1818), although before the period of *Daniel Deronda* its name had been changed, in 1833, to the Victoria Theatre.

COCK-FIGHTING JACK. Name given to Mr. Lingon, in older and less serious days. *F. H.* xix.

"COCKALEEKIE ADVERTISER." A journal which reviews Vorticella's one book. *T. S.* xv.

COCOMERO, VIA DEL (*Real*). Street in Florence near San Marco, where Fra Domenico preaches Lenten sermons to the women in 1498. *Rom.* xi, lxiii.

Note.—The street formerly called Via del Cocomero is now the Via Ricasoli, extending from the Piazza San Marco to the Piazza del Duomo.

COHEN, *known as* LAPIDOTH. *See* LAPIDOTH.

COHEN, MRS. The pawnbroker's good-humoured mother. *D. D.* xxxiii-xxxiv, xl, xlii, xlvi, l, lxx.

"Not that there was anything very repulsive about her: the worst that could be said was that she had that look of having made her toilet with little water, and by twilight, which is common to unyouthful people of her class,

---

[1] Rector of Caldecot and of Higham-on-the-Hill, near Nuneaton.

and of having presumably slept in her large ear-rings, if not in her rings and necklace." Ch. xxxiii.

COHEN, MRS. ADDY. Ezra's wife. *D. D.* xxxiii–xxxiv, xlii, xlvi, lxx.

"A black-eyed young woman ... a sort of paroquet in a bright blue dress, with coral necklace and ear-rings, her hair set up in a huge bush—looked as complacently lively and unrefined as her husband." Ch. xxxiii.

COHEN, ADELAIDE REBEKAH. The Cohen's black-eyed little daughter. *D. D.* xxxiii–xxxiv, xxxviii, xlii, xlvi, lxx.

COHEN, EUGENIE ESTHER. The Cohen baby; "a black-eyed little one, its head already well covered with black curls." *D. D.* xxxiii–xxxiv, xlii, xlvi, lxx.

COHEN, EZRA. A pawnbroker, proud of his vocation. *D. D.* xxxiii–xxxiv, xlii, xlvi, lxx.

"If an amiable self-satisfaction is the mark of earthly bliss, Solomon in all his glory was a pitiable mortal compared with Mr. Cohen—clearly one of those persons who, being in excellent spirits about themselves, are willing to cheer strangers by letting them know it ... Deronda, not in a cheerful mood, was rashly pronouncing this Ezra Cohen to be the most unpoetic Jew he had ever met with in books or life; his phraseology was as little as possible like that of the Old Testament; and no shadow of a Suffering Race distinguished his vulgarity of soul from that of a prosperous pink-and-white huckster of the purest English lineage." Ch. xxxiii.

Daniel Deronda at first mistakes him for Mirah's brother, Ezra, for whom he is searching, and so introduces himself to the Cohen family. He and his family are kind-hearted, commonplace Jews, who care for Mordecai (the other Ezra Cohen) in his illness and poverty.

COHEN, EZRA MORDECAI, *called* MORDECAI. Mirah's brother and Daniel Deronda's friend and mentor, a consumptive idealistic Hebrew who dreams of a renewed national existence for his race. *D. D.* xxxiii–xxxiv, xxxviii, xl–xliii, xlvi–xlviii, l, lii, lxi–lxiii, lxvi–lxx.

"A man in threadbare clothing, whose age was difficult to guess—from the dead yellowish flatness of the flesh, something like an old ivory carving ... precisely such a physiognomy as that might possibly have been seen in a prophet of the Exile, or in some New Hebrew poet of the mediæval time. It was a finely typical Jewish face, wrought into intensity of expression apparently by a strenuous eager experience in which all the satisfaction had been indirect and far off, and perhaps by some bodily suffering also, which involved that absence of ease in the present. The features were clear-cut, not large; the brow not high, but broad, and fully defined by the crisp black hair. It might never have been a particularly handsome face, but it must always have been forcible." Ch. xxxiii.

"A man steeped in poverty and obscurity, weakened by disease, consciously within the shadow of advancing death, but living an intense life in an invisible past and future, careless of his personal lot, except for its possibly making some obstruction to a conceived good which he would never share except as a brief inward vision—a day afar off, whose sun would never warm him, but into which he threw his soul's desire, with a passion often wanting to the personal motives of healthy youth." Ch. xlii.

His whole life is wrapped up in his belief in the regeneration of a great Jewish nationality in Palestine if only the right leader of the race can be found. As a young man he had started east to work in Palestine, when he was recalled because his mother needed his help after her husband had deserted her. The need of caring for his mother and the consumption which he develops from exposure make him give up the idea of his own leadership, and when Daniel Deronda meets him he is living in semi-poverty as a watch mender in the Cohen pawnshop and an off-hour attendant in Mr. Ram's book shop, constantly hoping to find the leader on whom his mantle can descend. He sees in Deronda this destined leader, introduces Deronda to the Philosophers' Club at the " Hand and Banner ", and rouses his keen interest both in the Jewish race and in the thought that he may be a Jew himself. Through Deronda's instru-mentality, his relationship to Mirah is discovered, and after Deronda and Mirah are married he dies happy in the belief that they will realize his dream.

Note.—The original of Mordecai was a Jewish journeyman watchmaker, named Cohn, or Kohn, who was president of a philosophical club in Red Lion Square, which G. H. Lewes frequented in his youth, and which he describes in the *Fortnightly Review*, vol. 4, p. 386. To the personal characteristics of this Cohn, as Lewes described him, George Eliot added the belief in a renewed Jewish nationality, which she is said to have taken from a Moldavian Jew possessed of the same idea whom she met in Munich. (*See Dictionary of National Biography*, article Lewes ; Acton, *Historical Essays*, p. 300.)

COHEN, JACOB ALEXANDER. Ezra's six-year-old son, to whom Mordecai is devoted ; a precocious child, with a keen eye for a bargain. *D. D.* xxxiii–xxxiv, xxxviii, xlii, xlvi, l, lii, lxx.

COHEN, MIRAH. The pretty little Jewess whom Daniel Deronda rescues from suicide and later marries. *D. D.* xvii–xx, xxxii–xxxiii, xxxvi–xxxvii, xxxix, xlii, xlv–xlviii, l, lii, lxi–lxiii, lxvi–lxx.

" Imagine her with her dark hair brushed from her temples, but yet showing certain tiny rings there which had cunningly found their own way back, the mass of it hanging behind just to the nape of the little neck in curly fibres, such as renew themselves at their own will after being bathed into straightness like that of water-grasses. Then see the perfect cameo her profile makes, cut in a duskish shell where by some happy fortune there pierced a gem-like darkness for the eye and eyebrow; the delicate nostrils defined enough to be ready for sensitive movements, the finished ear, the firm curves of the chin and neck entering into the expression of a refinement which was not feebleness." Ch. xxxii.

When she was a young child her father, an actor, had taken her away from her mother and brother, and for many years they led a Bohemian life distasteful to Mirah, who was strongly attached to the Jewish faith. In order to escape the dishonourable attentions of a man seconded by her father, she runs away from her father and comes to London to seek her mother and brother. Unsuccessful in her search, worn out and penniless, she attempts to drown herself in the Thames, but is rescued by Daniel Deronda, and taken to Mrs. Meyrick. Here her voice, which has been carefully trained, supports her, and when her brother Ezra, or Mordecai, is found she cares for him tenderly until his death. Shortly before Mordecai's death she and Daniel Deronda are married.

COHEN, SARA. Mother of Mirah and Mordecai. *D. D.* xx, xxxii, lxiii, lxii.

COLEMAN. *Mid.* lxxxi.

"COLLEGE." Name given to Shepperton workhouse, "a huge square stone building," where Amos Barton reads prayers. *Amos B.* ii, v.

Note. — The original of the "College" was the Chilvers Coton workhouse or "College for the Poor, 1800", as it was inscribed.

COLLEGE OF PHYSICIANS (*Real*). *Mid.* xv.

Note.—The Royal College of Physicians, London.

COLMAN STREET. Street in London where Mirah Cohen had lived as a child. *D. D.* xx.

COLOGNE (*Real*). *D. D.* xx.

COLUMBA. *T. S.* xi.

COMINES, PHILIPPE DE (*Hist.*). A French statesman in the train of Charles VIII. *Rom.* lxiv.

Note.—Philippe de Comines, Sieur d'Argenton (1445-1509).

COMPAGNACCI, or EVIL COMPANIONS (*Hist.*). *Rom.* xlv-xlvi, xlviii, lxiii, lxv-lxvii.

"Compagnacci, or Evil Companions . . . all the dissolute young men belonging to the old aristocratic party, enemies of the Mediceans, enemies of the popular government, but still more bitter enemies of Savonarola. Dolfo Spini, heir of the great house with the loggia, over the bridge of the Santa Trintà, had organized these young men into an armed band, as sworn champions of extravagant suppers and all the pleasant sins of the flesh, against reforming pietists." Ch. xlv.

E

COMPANIES OF DISCIPLINE (*Real*). Participants in the procession of the Madonna de L'Impruneta, in Florence. *Rom.* xliii.
" The mysterious-looking Companies of Discipline, bound by secret rules to self-chastisement, and devout praise, and special acts of piety ; all wearing a garb which concealed the whole head and face except the eyes. Every one knew that these mysterious forms were Florentine citizens of various ranks . . . the garb of all was a complete shroud, and left no expression but that of fellowship." Ch. xliii.
Note. — These were companies called Compagnie dei Disciplinati, or di Disciplina. They were thirty-eight in number, and drew their members from all ranks, high and low. Their duties included works of charity, marching in processions, and burial services.

CONSTABLE. The man who arrests Hetty Sorrel. *Adam B.* xxxix.

CONSTANCE, QUEEN (*Hist.*). King Pedro's gentle queen, who is touched by Lisa's story and takes her under her protection. *P.—Lisa.*
Note.—Constance, daughter of Manfred of Beneventum, wife of Pedro III of Aragon; it was through her that Pedro acquired his rights over Sicily.

CONSTANTINOPLE (*Real*). *F. H.* i; *Rom.* iii, vi.
In *Felix Holt* Harold Transome goes to Constantinople as an attaché of the British Embassy; in *Romola* Constantinople is one of the places where Tito Melema had lived.
Note.—Constantinople, the capital of the Eastern Empire, was captured by the Turks in 1453, and after that date many Greek scholars made their way from there to Italy.

COOK, PHIB. An inhabitant of Bridge Way, Milby. *J. R.* iv.

COOPER, TIMOTHY. Farm labourer. *Mid.* lvi.

COPPLETON CHURCH. *Amos B.* vi.

CORINTH (*Real*). A city where Baldassarre Calvo is held in slavery ; from which he sends to Tito Melema his appeal for aid. *Rom.* x, xxx.
Note.—Corinth, an ancient city in Greece ; in the Middle Ages it had belonged to Venice but at the time of *Romola* was in the possession of the Turks.

CORSINI, LUCA (*Hist.*). Doctor of Law, an adherent of Savonarola, who was to have delivered an oration in Latin at the entrance of Charles VIII into Florence. *Rom.* xxi, xxv–xxvii.
Note.—Luca Corsini, a wealthy and influential member of a powerful family. In 1494 he refused to admit Piero de' Medici to the palace.

CORSO DEGLI ADIMARI. See ADIMARI, CORSO DEGLI.

CORSO DEGLI ALBIZZI. See under BORGO DEGLI ALBIZZI.

CORVUS. An inconsistent person who takes a mild view of Mordax's fierceness when it is directed against someone else. *T. S.* viii.

CORYDON. A chestnut horse belonging to Sir James Chettam. *Mid.* ii.

COSIMO, PIERO DI (*Hist.*). An eccentric painter, one of the patrons of Nello's shop, who does not share Nello's admiration for Tito Melema. *Rom.* iii-iv, viii, xvi, xviii, xx, xxii-xxiii, xxv, xxviii-xxix, xxxi, xxxviii, xlix, lxvii, Epilogue.

From the beginning he dislikes Tito Melema, suspecting him of concealing a cowardly and treacherous nature behind his bright face. He paints a picture of Bardo and Romola as "Oedipus and Antigone", and at Tito's request he paints the triptych decorated with the story of Bacchus and Ariadne, in which Tito has Romola lock up her brother's crucifix. For himself he paints a picture of Tito struck by fear, completing it by adding the picture of Baldassarre Calvo after he has seen the latter clutch Tito on the steps of the Duomo.

Note.—Piero di Lorenzo, called Cosimo from his master, Cosimo Rosselli (1441-1521); a Florentine painter of an eccentric and cynical nature, who painted many fanciful paintings. For the account of him which George Eliot evidently used *see* Vasari, *Lives.* Vasari gives his date of birth as 1441, but some other authorities give 1462.

COULTER, ANN. Mother of an idiot child. *S. M.* ii.

COUNT, THE. The man who pursues Mirah with dishonourable intentions and is the cause of her flight from her father. *D. D.* xx.

COURT ROOM, STONITON. Scene of Hetty Sorrel's trial. *Adam B.* xliii.

"The place fitted up that day as a court of justice was a grand old hall, now destroyed by fire. The mid-day light that fell on the close pavement of human heads, was shed through a line of high pointed windows, variegated with the mellow tints of old painted glass. Grim dusty armour hung in high relief in front of the dark oaken gallery at the farther end; and under the broad arch of the great mullioned window opposite was spread a curtain of old tapestry, covered with dim melancholy figures, like a dozing indistinct dream of the past. It was a place that through the rest of the year was haunted with the shadowy memories of old kings and queens, unhappy, discrowned, imprisoned." Ch. xliii.

Note.—The scene of Hetty's trial was Derby ("Stoniton"), but the original described in the Court Room was St. Mary's Hall, Coventry, which, at the time of George Eliot's residence in Coventry, was used for trials. A description of St. Mary's Hall, given in Poole's *Coventry*, agrees in many details with the description in *Adam Bede*. The detail of destruction by fire was taken from another original, the town hall of

Derby, which was destroyed by fire in 1841. (*See* "Coventry in relation to George Eliot's fiction", by F. W. Humberstone, in the *Coventry Herald*, 14th–15th November, 1919; Poole, *Coventry*, pp. 117–128; Mottram, *True Story of George Eliot*, p. 39.)

COWLEY. Member of the legal firm of Batt & Cowley. *F. H.* xxi, xxxvii.

COX. *S. M.* iii, ix.

COZEN, MR. GERMAN. Name given to Mr. Jermyn because of his clever shuffling. *F. H.* xxix.

CRAB-TREE MEADOW. *Adam B.* xxxii.

CRABBE, MR. "Glazier who gathered much news," a frequenter of the "Tankard". *Mid.* lxxi.

CRABSLEY. Town near Middlemarch. *Mid.* xlv.

CRACKENTHORP, MR. Rector at Raveloe. *S. M.* vi, viii, x, xi, xiii–xiv, Conclusion.

"He was not in the least lofty or aristocratic, but simply a merry-eyed, small-featured, grey-haired man, with his chin propped by an ample, many-creased white neckcloth, which seemed to predominate over every other point in his person, and somehow to impress its peculiar character on his remarks; so that to have considered his amenities apart from his cravat, would have been a severe, and perhaps a dangerous, effort of abstraction." Ch. xi.

CRACKENTHORP, MRS. The rector's wife. *S. M.* xi.

"A small blinking woman, who fidgeted incessantly with her lace, ribbons, and gold chain, turning her head about and making subdued noises, very much like a guinea-pig, that twitches its nose and soliloquizes in all company indiscriminately." Ch. xi.

CRAGSTONE, LADY. A gambler. *D. D.* xxviii.

CRAIG, MR. The gardener at Donnithorne Chase, a middle-aged Scotchman, who is one of Hetty Sorrel's suitors. *Adam B.* iv, xviii–xix, xxiii, xxvi–xxvii, xliv, liii, lv.

"Martin Poyser held Mr. Craig in honour, as a man who 'knew his business' . . . but he was less of a favourite with Mrs. Poyser, who had more than once said . . . 'for my part, I think he's welly like a cock as thinks the sun's rose o' purpose to hear him crow' . . . Mr. Craig had always been full of civilities to the family at the Hall Farm, and Mrs. Poyser was scrupulous in declaring that she had 'nothing to say again' him, on'y it was a pity he couldna be hatched o'er again, an' hatched different'." Ch. xviii.

CRAKE, SIR JOHN. Master of the harriers. *M. F.* Bk. 2, iii.

CRAMP, MRS. Charwoman who helps at Shepperton Vicarage. *Amos B.* x.

CRANAGE, BEN, *called* WIRY BEN. Carpenter in Jonathan Burge's shop, who performs a rustic dance at the coming-of-age festival. *Adam B.* i–ii, xxv, lv.

CRANAGE, BESSY. The blacksmith's buxom daughter, called Chad's

Bess, who is fond of finery. *Adam B.* ii–iii, viii, xxv, xlix, lv.

She is worked upon by Dinah Morris's preaching to give up some of her vanities, but when she wins the sack race at the birthday celebration she is bitterly disappointed that the prize is not a piece of finery.

CRANAGE, CHAD. Blacksmith, a brawny fellow, fond of laughing at his own jokes. *Adam B.* ii, xviii.

CRANCH, MRS. MARTHA. Peter Featherstone's poor sister; a wheezy old woman anxious to inherit some of her brother's riches. *Mid.* xxxii, xxxiv–xxxv, liii.

CRANCH, TOM. Mrs. Cranch's unattractive son, who is sent to watch during his uncle's last illness. *Mid.* xxxii–xxxiii, xxxv.

" Young Cranch was not exactly the balancing point between the wit and the idiot—verging slightly toward the latter type, and squinting so as to leave everything in doubt about his sentiments except that they were not of a forcible character." Ch. xxxii.

CRANE. Servant. *D. D.* xxxv.

" CREATION." (*Real*). Lucy Deane and Stephen Guest sing several of the songs from the " Creation ". *M. F.* Bk. 6, i.

Note.—An oratorio by Haydn (1732–1809).

CREDI, LORENZO DI (*Hist.*). Painter, who assisted at the Bonfire of Vanities. *Rom.* xlix.

Note.—Lorenzo di Credi (1459–1537), Florentine painter, and lifelong friend of Leonardo da Vinci, who came under the influence of Savonarola.

CREWE, MR. The inefficient old curate in Milby. *J. R.* i–ii, iv–vi, x, xii, xx, xxv.

" There was almost always something funny about old Mr. Crewe. His brown wig was hardly ever put on quite right, and he had a way of raising his voice for three or four words, and lowering it again to a mumble . . . It was clear he must be a learned man, for he had once had a large private school in connection with the grammar school, and had even numbered a young nobleman or two among his pupils. The fact that he read nothing at all now, and that his mind seemed absorbed in the commonest matters, was doubtless due to his having exhausted the resources of erudition earlier in life." Ch. ii.

Note.—In the lists of originals prepared in Nuneaton after the publication of *Scenes of Clerical Life,* the prototype of Mr. Crewe was the Rev. Hugh Hughes, (d. 1830), for 52 years curate of Nuneaton and for 30 years head master of the Grammar School. He married Sarah Warden.

CREWE, MRS. The curate's wife; a little, deaf old lady, who " would carry half her own spare dinner to the sick and hungry." *J. R.* ii–iii, v–vi, xii–xiii, xxi, xxiii, xxv.

CRICHLEY, MR. The old rector of Cumbermoor. *Mr. G.'s L. S.* xii, xxi.

CRINITO, PIETRO (*Hist.*). A "scholar of the more polished sort". *Rom.* iii, ix, xiii.
  Note.—Pietro Riccio, *called* Crinito or Crinitus (1465–1505), a Florentine poet and biographer.

CRISOLORA (THE YOUNGER) (*Hist.*). A Greek scholar, under whom Bardo de' Bardi had once studied. *Rom.* v.
  Note.—This was John Crisolora (died about 1427), who accompanied his uncle to Italy and became a professor of Greek. His uncle Manuel Crisolora (*ca.* 1350–1415), who came from Constantinople, and taught Greek in Florence and other Italian cities, is also mentioned by Bardo in Chapter vi of *Romola*.

CRISPI. An artist, one of Scintilla's fashionable circle. *T. S.* ix.

CRISTIANISSIMO, THE. *See* CHARLES VIII, KING OF FRANCE.

CRISTOFORO, FRA. Monna Brigida's Franciscan confessor at Santa Croce, an opponent of Savonarola. *Rom.* xii, li.

CRITERION. A saddle-horse belonging to Grandcourt which Gwendolen Harleth rides. *D. D.* xiii, xxvii–xxix.

CROCE, BORGO LA. *See* BORGO LA CROCE.

CROCE, SANTA (BORGO). *See* BORGO SANTA CROCE.

CROCE, SANTA (CHURCH). *See* SANTA CROCE, CHURCH OF.

CROCE, SANTA (PIAZZA). *See* SANTA CROCE, PIAZZA DI.

CROCE, SANTA (PORTA). *See* PORTA SANTA CROCE.

CROLY, MRS. A celebrated beauty in 1790. *Mid.* lxiv.

CROMFORD (*Real*). Place where Arkwright's mills, spoken of by Adam Bede, are located. *Adam B.* i.
  Note.—Cromford is about 15 miles from Derby.

CROMLECK, LORD. *S. M.* iv.

"CROMPTON ARGUS." Newspaper. *J. R.* iii.

CRONACA (*Hist.*). An architect, who is a devoted adherent of Savonarola; one of the patrons of Nello the barber. *Rom.* viii, xiii, xvi, xxix, xlvii.
  Note.—Simone Pollajuola, called Il Cronaca (1457–1508), a celebrated Florentine architect.

CROOP. Shoemaker; member of the Philosophers' Club. *D. D.* xlii.

CROSS FARM. Mrs. Patten's farm at Shepperton. *Amos B.* i, vi.

"CROSS KEYS." Inn at Sloppeter. *Mr. G.'s L. S.* xix.

"CROSS-KEYS." A venerable public-house in Treby, frequented by old Tommy Trounsem. *F. H.* xxviii, xxxi.

CROW, MR. High constable of Treby, an unpopular man who fails to quiet the Treby mob at the time of the election riot. *F. H.* xxxi, xxxiii.

CROWDER, MR. An old tenant of the Debarrys, "much in arrear as to his rent." *F. H.* vii, xx, xxxi.

CROWE, WIDOW. Macarthy's landlady. *E. E.* i.

"CROWN." A Duffield hotel. Debarry's headquarters. *F. H.* xxx.

CROWSE, MR. Curate, "with empty face and neat umbrella and mincing little speeches." *Mid.* xiv, lii.

CROWSFOOT COTTAGE. A cottage on the Cheverel estate. *Mr. G.'s L. S.* ii.

CRYPT, MR. ZEPHANIAH. A man who leaves money for the Yellow Coat School, Grimworth. *B. J.* i.

CRYSTAL PALACE, LONDON (*Real*). The place where Ezra Cohen and his mother once saw the Emperor and Empress. *D. D.* xxxiv.

Note.—The Crystal Palace, at Sydenham, 6 miles south of London Bridge, is a huge exhibition hall, a reconstruction of the one designed by Sir Joseph Paxton for the Exhibition of 1851, in Hyde Park. Napoleon III and Eugénie visited the Crystal Palace at Sydenham in 1855.

CUFF, JACOB. A charity-man. *F. H.* xxxi.

"CULTIVATION OF GREEN CROPS AND THE ECONOMY OF CATTLE FEEDING." Book written by Fred Vincy after he becomes a successful farmer. *Mid.* Finale.

CUMBERMOOR. Parish in which Cheverel Manor is situated. *Mr. G.'s L. S.* iv, xxi.

CUMBERMOOR CHURCH. *Mr. G.'s L. S.* xi.

CUSHAT, MR. and MRS. *D. D.* xii.

CUTLER, MISS. Mrs. Arrowpoint's maiden name. *See* ARROWPOINT, MRS.

"CZARINA." Hotel at Leubronn where Daniel Deronda stays. *D. D.* ii, xv.

CZERLASKI, COUNT. A foreign nobleman with small fortune who had earned his living by giving dancing lessons. *Amos B.* iv.

CZERLASKI, CAROLINE, COUNTESS. A pretty, selfish widow with small means, anxious to find a second husband with money. *Amos B.* ii–vii.

"The Countess Czerlaski was undeniably beautiful . . . small hands and feet, a tall lithe figure, large dark eyes, and dark silken braided hair. All these the Countess possessed, and she had, moreover, a delicately formed nose, the least bit curved, and a clear brunette complexion. Her mouth, it must be admitted, receded too much from her nose and chin, and to a prophetic eye threatened 'nut-crackers' in advanced age. But by the light of fire and wax-candles that age seemed very far off indeed, and you would have said that the Countess was not more than thirty." Ch. iii.

After settling near Shepperton with her brother, Mr. Bridmain, she cultivates the acquaintance of the Bartons. When her brother marries her maid she quarters herself on the Bartons for many months, thus heavily taxing their small means, arousing gossip and bringing down on Mr. Barton's head the wrath of his parish.

Note. — The prototype of the Countess Czerlaski was the " Countess Isabel ". (Manuscript information ; *also* Olcott, *George Eliot*, p. 15.)

D

DACEY, LADY. Lord Dacey's wife. *Adam B.* v–vi, xiv.

DACEY, LORD. A neighbour of the Irwines. *Adam B.* v–vi.

DAGGE, JOEL. A blacksmith's son who sets Rex Gascoigne's injured shoulder. *D. D.* vii.

DAGGE, SALLY. *D. D.* vii.

DAGLEY, MR. Farmer on Mr. Brooke's estate. *Mid.* xxxviii–xxxix.

DAGLEY, MRS. The farmer's overworked wife from whose life pleasure had entirely vanished. *Mid.* xxxix.

DAGLEY, JACOB. The farmer's little son, caught by Mr. Brooke killing a leveret. *Mid.* xxxix.

DALTON. Coachman at Donnithorne Chase. *Adam B.* xii.

DANE, WILLIAM. Silas Marner's false friend in Lantern Yard, a thief who robs Silas of his good name and his sweetheart, by causing a false accusation of theft to be made against him. *S. M.* i.

DANISH STREET. Street in St. Ogg's where Mr. Hyndmarsh has his grocery. *M. F.* Bk. 3, vii.

DANTE'S HOUSE (*Real*). *Rom.* mentioned i.

Note.—This house, which, rebuilt, is still standing in the Via Dante Alighieri, is said to have been the birthplace of Dante.

DARLEIGH, SQUIRE. *M. F.* Bk. 3, vii; Bk. 5, ii.

DAUPHIN. *See* IRWINE, REVEREND ADOLPHUS.

DAVID. Labourer on Mr. Poyser's farm. *Adam B.* liii.

DAVID. Mr. Gilfil's man. *Mr. G.'s L. S.* i.

DAVILOW, CAPTAIN. Gwendolen Harleth's step-father who, before his death, " joined his family only in a brief and fitful manner enough to reconcile them to his long absences." *D. D.* iii.

DAVILOW, ALICE. Gwendolen Harleth's oldest half-sister ; an uninteresting girl of fifteen, with high shoulders. *D. D.* iii–iv, vi–vii, xxi, xxviii, xliv, lviii.

DAVILOW, BERTHA. One of Mrs. Davilow's uninteresting daughters; a girl fond of whispering and tittering. *D. D.* iii, xxi, xxviii, xliv, lviii.

DAVILOW, FANNY. Daughter of Mrs. Davilow, given to whispering with her sister, Bertha. *D. D.* iii, xxi, xxviii, xliv, lviii.

DAVILOW, MRS. FANNY. Gwendolen Harleth's mother, whose beauty is worn by the troubles of her two unfortunate marriages and " whose motherly tenderness clung chiefly to her eldest girl ", Gwendolen. *D. D.* ii–vii, ix–xi, xiii–xv, xxi, xxiii–xxiv, xxvi–xxix, xxxi, xxxv, xliv, lviii–lix, lxiv–lxv, lxix.

DAVILOW, ISABEL. Mrs. Davilow's youngest daughter, " a plain and altogether inconvenient child with an alarming memory." *D. D.* iii–iv, vi, xxi, xxiii, xxviii, xliv, lviii.

DAVY, SIR HUMPHRY (*Hist.*). A chemist and poet with whom Mr. Brooke had once dined. *Mid.* ii, mentioned *F. H.* i.

Note.—Sir Humphry Davy (1778–1829) chemist and author.

DAWES. Mr. Dempster's man. *J. R.* xvii, xxi.

"DAY IS DYING, FLOAT, O SONG." One of the songs of Juan, the minstrel. *Sp. G.* i.

DEANE, MR. Lucy's father; a junior member of the firm of Guest & Co. *M. F.* Bk. 1, vi–vii; Bk. 3, iii, v, vii–viii; Bk. 5, ii, v–vii; Bk. 6, i, iv–viii, xiii; Bk. 7, iii.

"A large but alert-looking man, with a type of physique to be seen in all ranks of English society—bald crown, red whiskers, full forehead, and general solidity without heaviness. You may see noblemen like Mr. Deane, and you may see grocers or day-labourers like him; but the keenness of his brown eyes was less common than his contour." Bk. 1, vii.

Starting life as a poor boy, he had made himself valuable to the firm of Guest & Co., had been given a share in the business and advanced rapidly. When the Tullivers lose their property he is kindly disposed towards them and finds a place in the warehouse for Tom Tulliver, and is pleased with Tom's success in business.

DEANE, LUCY. Maggie Tulliver's good, pretty, and affectionate cousin, the favourite of the Dodson aunts. *M. F.* Bk. 1, ii, v, vii, ix–x; Bk. 2, vii; Bk. 3, vii; Bk. 5, iv–v; Bk. 6, i–iv, vi–x, xii–xiii; Bk. 7, i–iv.

"Certainly the contrast between the cousins was conspicuous, and, to superficial eyes, was very much to the disadvantage of Maggie, though a connoisseur might have seen 'points' in her which had a higher promise for maturity than Lucy's natty completeness. It was like the contrast between a rough, dark, overgrown puppy and a white kitten. Lucy put up the neatest little rosebud mouth to be kissed: everything about her was neat—her little round neck, with the row of coral beads; her little straight nose, not at all snubby; her little clear eyebrows, rather darker than her curls, to match her hazel eyes, which looked up with shy pleasure at Maggie." Bk. 1, vii.

When she is grown up, Lucy, the belle of St. Ogg's, still retains her childhood affection for her cousin Maggie whom she admires, and she delights in playing fairy-godmother to Maggie. When Lucy's fiancé, Stephen Guest, and Maggie go away together, Lucy suffers greatly, but does not blame Maggie for her unhappiness. Years later she and Stephen are married.

Note.—The original of Lucy Deane, in the part of the story in which she is still a child, was George Eliot's sister, Crissy.

DEANE, MRS. SUSAN. Mrs. Tulliver's sister, and Lucy's mother; "the thinnest and sallowest of all the

Miss Dodsons." *M. F.* Bk. 1, ii, v–vii, xiii ; Bk. 3, iii ; Bk. 5, v–vi ; Bk. 6, i.

"Mrs. Deane was a thin-lipped woman, who made small well-considered speeches on peculiar occasions, repeating them afterwards to her husband, and asking him if she had not spoken very properly." Bk. 3, iii.

Note.—For the original of Mrs. Deane, as one of the Dodson sisters, *see* note under Dodsons.

DEBARRY, LADY. Wife of Sir Maximus. *F. H.* i, vii, xl.

" A blue-eyed, well-featured lady, fat and middle-aged, a mountain of satin, lace, and exquisite muslin embroidery." Ch. vii.

DEBARRY, REV. AUGUSTUS. Rector of Treby Magna ; brother of Sir Maximus. *F. H.* iii, vii, xii, xiv–xv, xxii–xxiv, xxxi, xxxiii, xlvii.

" A fine specimen of the old-fashioned aristocratic clergyman, preaching short sermons, understanding business, and acting liberally about his tithe." Ch. iii.

DEBARRY, HARRIET. One of the elegant daughters of Sir Maximus and Lady Debarry. *F. H.* vii.

DEBARRY, SIR MAXIMUS. The head of the leading family in Treby Magna ; an open-handed, quick-tempered man of sixty. *F. H.* i–iii, vii, xiv, xx, xxiv, xlvii, Epilogue.

An aristocratic old Tory, he is prepared to welcome Harold Transome cordially until he finds that the latter has declared himself a Radical. He does not resume friendly relations with Harold until the scene of Mr. Jermyn's revelation to Harold.

DEBARRY, PHILIP. Son of Sir Maximus ; the successful Tory candidate for North Loamshire. *F. H.* i–ii, v, vii, xi–xii, xiv–xvi, xx, xxii–xxiv, xxx–xxxi, xxxvi, xli, xlvii.

" There is a portrait of Mr. Philip Debarry still to be seen at Treby Manor, and a very fine bust of him at Rome, where he died fifteen years later, a convert to Catholicism. His face would have been plain but for the exquisite setting of his hazel eyes, which fascinated even the dogs of the household. The other features, though slight and irregular, were redeemed from triviality by the stamp of gravity and intellectual preoccupation in his face and bearing." Ch. xiv.

DEBARRY, SELINA. The younger daughter of Sir Maximus and Lady Debarry, " a radiant girl of twenty who had given much time to the harp." *F. H.* vii, xiv.

DE BRACYS. Mrs. Cadwallader's aristocratic family. *Mid.* vi.

"DECOURCY, or the Rash Promise, a Tale for Youth." One of Miss Pratt's literary productions. *J. R.* iii.

DELOS (*Real*). Place to which Baldassarre Calvo and Tito Melema had been journeying when they were attacked by pirates. *Rom.* vi, ix.

Note.—A Greek island, one of the Cyclades, famous for its ancient ruins.

DEMPSTER, OLD MRS. Lawyer Dempster's mother; a quiet, meek old lady who always believed that her son would not have gone wrong if he had married the right woman. *J. R.* v, vii, xiii.

"A very little old lady she was, with a pale, scarcely wrinkled face, hair of that peculiar white which tells that the locks have once been blond, a natty pure white cap on her head, and a white shawl pinned over her shoulders. You saw at a glance that she had been a mignonne blonde." Ch. vii.

DEMPSTER, MRS. JANET. The lawyer's unhappy wife; a woman of noble beauty, marked by traces of suffering. *J. R.* iii-x, xii-xvi, xviii-xxviii.

"Her grandly-cut features, pale with the natural paleness of a brunette, have premature lines about them telling that the years have been lengthened by sorrow, and the delicately-curved nostril, which seems made to quiver, with the proud consciousness of power and beauty, must have quivered to the heart-piercing griefs which have given that worn look to the corners of the mouth." Ch. iv.

"No other woman in Milby has those searching black eyes, that tall graceful unconstrained figure, set off by her simple muslin dress and black lace shawl, that massy black hair now so neatly braided in glossy contrast with the white satin ribbons of her modest cap and bonnet. No other woman has that sweet speaking smile." Ch. v.

She had married Mr. Dempster for love but, after much ill-treatment, had yielded to the temptation to dull her suffering by drinking. As a climax to her unhappiness, her husband turns her out of the house in her nightgown at midnight. To please her husband she had joined in his persecution of Mr. Tryan, but in desperation she turns to that clergyman and his influence rescues her from her self-despair and gives her faith and strength to reform and lead a noble life.

Note.—The original of Janet Dempster was a Mrs. Buchanan (Nancy Wallington) whose story, similar to Janet's as far as the treatment by her husband was concerned, was well known in Nuneaton when George Eliot lived there. Her grave and those of her husband and mother can still be seen at Nuneaton. (See references under Dempster, Robert.)

DEMPSTER, MR. ROBERT. Lawyer in Milby; a prosperous, overbearing and unscrupulous man who is brutal toward his beautiful wife and intolerant toward Mr. Tryan. *J. R.* i-x, xiii-xiv, xvii-xviii, xxi-xxv.

"He was a tall and rather massive man, and the front half of his large surface was . . . well dredged with snuff. . . . Mr. Dempster habitually held his chin tucked in, and his head hanging forward, weighed down, perhaps, by a preponderant occiput and a bulging forehead, between which his closely-clipped coronal surface lay like a flat and new-mown table-land. The only other observable features were puffy cheeks and a protruding yet lipless mouth. Of his nose I can only say that it was snuffy, and as Mr. Dempster was never caught in the act of looking at anything in particular it would have been difficult to swear to the colour of his eyes." Ch. i.

Although a man of much native ability, he yields more and more to his evil propensities, and beats his wife when he is drunk. He is the mainstay of the persecution of Mr. Tryan, turns his wife, Janet, out of the house at midnight and shortly after is thrown from his cart, receiving injuries which result in his death in delirium tremens.

Note.—The original of Robert Dempster was a Mr. J. W. Buchanan, a lawyer of Nuneaton. The original of the Dempster house in "Orchard Street" still stands in Church Street, Nuneaton. (Manuscript and personal information; also Andrews, *Bygone Warwickshire*, p. 275; Browning, *Life of George Eliot*, pp. 52–3.)

DENNER. Mrs. Transome's devoted maid; wife of Mr. Hicks the butler, but always called by her maiden name. *F. H.* i–ii, vii–viii, xxxv, xxxix, xliii, xlv, l, Epilogue.

"Denner's feeling towards her mistress . . . was of that worshipful sort paid to a goddess in ages when it was not thought necessary or likely that a goddess should be very moral. . . . There was a tacit understanding that Denner knew all her mistress's secrets, and her speech was plain and unflattering; yet with wonderful subtlety of instinct she never said anything which Mrs. Transome could feel humiliated by . . . She was a hard-headed godless little woman, but with a character to be reckoned on as you reckon on the qualities of iron." Ch. i.

DENT. *Adam B.* xvi.

DERONDA, DANIEL. The Jewish hero of the story; Sir Hugo Mallinger's ward, a handsome and gifted young man who passes as Sir Hugo's nephew but is mistakenly believed by many to be his son. *D. D.* i–ii, xv–xx, xxv, xxviii–xxix, xxxii–xxxviii, xl–xliii, xlv–lvii, lix–lxi, lxiii–lxv, lxvii–lxx.

"Rowing in his dark-blue shirt and skull-cap, his curls closely clipped, his mouth beset with abundant soft waves of beard, he bore only disguised traces of the seraphic boy 'trailing clouds of glory' . . . Look at his hands . . . they are long, flexible, firmly grasping hands, such as Titian has painted in a picture where he wanted to show the combination of refinement with force. And there is something of a likeness, too, between the faces belonging to the hands—in both the uniform pale-brown skin, the perpendicular brow, the calmly penetrating eyes." Ch. xvii.

"His eyes had a peculiarity which has drawn many men into trouble; they were of a dark yet mild intensity, which seemed to express a special interest in every one on whom he fixed them, and might easily help to bring on him those claims which ardently sympathetic people are often creating in the minds of those who need help." Ch. xxix.

"To say that Deronda was romantic would be to misrepresent him; but under his calm and somewhat self-repressed exterior there was a fervour which made him easily find poetry and romance among the events of every-day life." Ch. xix.

As a child he had been brought to England by Sir Hugo and educated as one of his own family. He is sensitive about his ignorance of his parentage, though much attached to Sir Hugo whom he believes to be his father, and his equivocal position makes him restless and unsettled. At the opening of the story he sees Gwendolen Harleth gambling at Leubronn, and his disapproval disturbs her then and influences her later, when, after her return to England, she marries Grandcourt, Sir Hugo's nephew, and she and Deronda are thus thrown together in the same social circle. While rowing on the Thames Deronda saves Mirah Cohen, a beautiful Jewess who is attempting suicide, finding a refuge for her with his friends the Meyricks and continuing to watch over her. In his efforts to trace Mirah's lost brother, Ezra, he forms a strong friendship with Mordecai Cohen, becomes interested in Jewish questions through him, and eventually discovers that Mordecai is Mirah's brother Ezra and falls in love with Mirah. Meanwhile he feels a different kind of interest in Gwendolen who, in the unhappiness of her marriage, appeals to him for advice and guidance. When his acquaintance with Mordecai and Mirah has thoroughly aroused his interest in the Jews, he is summoned to Genoa to meet his hitherto unknown mother, the Princess Halm-Eberstein, learns from her that he is a Jew, and rejoices in the information. While he is still at Genoa, Grandcourt is drowned in the Mediterranean, and Deronda supports Gwendolen in her remorse and despair, and later she turns to him as her one source of help. On his return to England he devotes himself to work for the Jews, marries Mirah, and with her goes to Palestine to try to realize Mordecai's dream of a revival of Jewish nationalism.

Note.—According to Sir Leslie Stephen, Edmund Gurney (1847-1888) may have been, in some respects at least, the original of Daniel Deronda. Deronda's personal appearance was taken from the Christ in Titian's picture, the "Tribute Money", which haunted George Eliot for years after she had seen it in the Dresden gallery. (*See* Stephen, *George Eliot*, p. 191; Acton, *Historical Essays*, p. 299.)

DIAMOND. A hunter in which Fred Vincy invests with the ill-founded hope of making a little money. *Mid.* xxiii-xxiv.

DIANA, DUCHESS. Duke Silva's dead mother. *Sp. G.* i.

DIBBITTS. Druggist. *Mid.* xlv.

DIBBS, MR. A prosperous farmer who holds that if the Radicals are dangerous it is safer to be on their side. *F. H.* xx, xxxi.

DICKISON, MR. Landlord of the public-house in Basset; a man " with a melancholy pimpled face, looking as irrelevant to the day light as a last night's guttered candle ". *M. F.* Bk. 1, viii.

DIEGO, DON. A fiery don, Duke Silva's lieutenant to whom the Duke transfers the command when he is ill. *S. G.* i–ii.
" Don Diego, a most valiant man,
  More Catholic than the Holy Father's self,
  Half chiding God that he will tolerate,
  A Jew or Arab; though 'tis plain they're made
  For profit of."

" DILECK." Mr. Casson's word for the speech of Loamshire. *Adam B.* ii.
" They're cur'ous talkers i' this country, sir; the gentry's hard work to hunderstand 'em. I was brought hup among the gentry, sir, an' got the turn o' their tongue when I was a bye. Why, what do you think the folks here says for ' hevn't you ? '—the gentry, you know, says, ' hevn't you '—well, the people about here says ' hanna yey '. It's what they call the dileck as is spoke hereabout, sir. That's what I've heard Squire Donnithorne say many a time; it's the dileck, says he." Ch. ii.

George Eliot's use of dialect is both accurate and artistic. While all dialect words and phrases used are scrupulously correct, they are introduced only in so far as is needed to give the right local colour, and not in such numbers as to affect the intelligibility for the ordinary reader. The dialects used in the various novels are : *Adam Bede*, the dialect of North Staffordshire and the neighbouring part of Derbyshire; *Scenes of Clerical life*, *Silas Marner*, and, in general, the other provincial novels, the dialect of North Warwickshire. The above dialects do not differ greatly from the Leicestershire dialect and practically all of George Eliot's dialect words are given in Evans' *Leicestershire words*. (See Axon, *Dialect in George Eliot*; Letter from George Eliot to W. W. Skeat printed in English Dialect Society, *Bibliographical lists*, No. 1, p. viii; Cross, *George Eliot's Life*, vol. iii, p. 304.)

DILL, MR. Barber in Middlemarch; a frequenter of the " Tankard ", who feels himself a little above the company there. *Mid.* lxxi.

DINAH. *See* MORRIS, DINAH.

DINGALL, MR. The Treddleston grocer. *Adam. B.* xviii, xxxii.

DINGLEY. Parish near Milby. *J. R.* xiii, xxv.

DINO. Bernardino de'Bardi; Romola's brother who has left his family to become a monk. *See* LUCA, FRA.

DIPLOW. Hamlet. *D. D.* ix.

DIPLOW HALL. Sir Hugo Mallinger's place in Wessex where Grandcourt is residing when he first meets Gwendolen Harleth. *D. D.* ix, xi, xiii, xv, xxv, xxvii–xxix, xxxv, xliv, xlviii, lxix.

DIPPLEY. Place belonging to the Porters. *Amos. B.* iii.

DISCIPLINE, COMPANIES OF. *See* COMPANIES OF DISCIPLINE.

"DISPUTE." A picture painted by Naumann, in which Mr. Casaubon is the model for St. Thomas Aquinas. *Mid.* xxii, xxx.

DIX. A miller whose dispute with Mr. Tulliver about a dam is settled by arbitration. *M. F.* Bk. 1, iii; Bk. 2, ii; Bk. 3, viii.

DOBBIN. Mr. Lammeter's horse. *S. M.* xi.

DODO. Celia Brooke's name for her sister Dorothea. *See* BROOKE, DOROTHEA.

DODSONS, THE. Mrs. Tulliver's family, whose superiority is felt by all its members. *M. F.* Bk. 1, vi–vii, ix, xii; Bk. 2, ii; Bk. 3, i, iii, vii; Bk. 4, i; Bk. 6, xii; Bk. 7, iii.

"The Dodsons were a very respectable family indeed—as much looked up to as any in their own parish, or the next to it. . . . There were particular ways of doing everything in that family: particular ways of bleaching the linen, of making the cowslip wine, curing the hams, and keeping the bottled gooseberries; so that no daughter of that house could be indifferent to the privilege of having been born a Dodson rather than a Gibson or a Watson. . . . When one of the family was in trouble or sickness, all the rest went to visit the unfortunate member, usually at the same time, and did not shrink from uttering the most disagreeable truths that correct family feeling dictated." Bk. 1, vi.

"A conspicuous quality in the Dodson character was its genuineness: its vices and virtues alike were phases of a proud, honest egoism, which had a hearty dislike to whatever made against its own credit and interest, and would be frankly hard of speech to inconvenient 'kin', but would never forsake or ignore them—would not let them want bread, but only require them to eat it with bitter herbs." Bk. 4, i.

Note.—George Eliot's mother, Mrs. Robert Evans, was a Pearson, and it is admitted that her family, the Pearsons, were the originals of the Dodsons. There were three other sisters married and living near Mrs. Evans—Mrs. Everard, Mrs. Johnson, and Mrs. Garner, the originals of Aunt Glegg, Aunt Pullet, and Aunt Deane. (*See* Cross, *George Eliot's Life*, vol. i, pp. 13–14.)

DOG LANE. Street in Milby. *J. R.* iv.

DOLBY. Architect. *Amos. B.* vi.

DOLLOP, MRS. The spirited landlady of the "Tankard", Middlemarch. *Mid.* xlv, lxxi.

DOLLY. Jonathan Burge's old servant. *Adam. B.* i, iv, x.

DOLLY. Servant of the Gleggs. *M. F.* Bk. 1, xii.

DOMENICO, FRA (*Hist.*). A Dominican brother of San Marco, Savonarola's lieutenant. *Rom.* xii, xlix, lxiii–lxvi, lxxii.

When the Franciscan Fra Francesco challenges Savonarola to the Trial by Fire, Fra Domenico enthusiastically takes up the challenge. He is the Dominican representative in the Trial by Fire and later is one of the Dominicans arrested with Savonarola and executed with him.

Note.—Fra Domenico Bonvicini da Pescia, the loyal friend and coadjutor of Savonarola, who was executed with Savonarola.

DOMINGO, FRAY. *Sp. G.* ii.

DOMINI CANES. "Hounds of the Lord"; name applied to the Dominicans; a play upon the name of the Order. *Rom.* viii.

DOMINIC. Harold Transome's man. *F. H.* i–ii, xix, xxxiv, xxxvi, xxxviii–xl, xliii, xlviii–xlix.

"One of those wonderful southern fellows that make one's life easy. He's of no country in particular. I don't know whether he's most of a Jew, a Greek, an Italian, or a Spaniard. He speaks five or six languages, one as well as another. He's cook, valet, major-domo, and secretary all in one; and what's more, he's an affectionate fellow." Ch. ii.

DOMINICANS, OR, FRATI PREDICATORI (*Hist.*). The monastic order to which Savonarola belongs. *Rom.* viii, xii, xliii, lxii, lxiv–lxvi.

Savonarola is a Dominican, as also Fra Domenico who takes up the Franciscan challenge to the Trial by Fire, and Fra Salvestro who is Romola's confessor. It was the Dominicans that Romola's brother Bernardino de' Bardi joined when he left home, he goes to their monastery at Fiesole when he is ill, and dies at the Dominican convent of San Marco in Florence, of which Savonarola is Prior.

Note.—The Dominicans, or Order of Preachers (Ordo Predicatorum) founded by St. Dominic in 1215.

DONNITHORNE, SQUIRE. The "Old Squire"—Arthur Donnithorne's grandfather, "the delicately clean, finely-scented, withered old man . . . with his air of punctilious, acid politeness," who is the penurious owner of Donnithorne Chase. *Adam B.* ii, v, xviii, xxi, xxiv–xxvii, xxxii, xl.

He is disliked by his tenants as a stingy landlord who will not afford a proper steward, mismanages his woods and refuses to make repairs. He dislikes Adam Bede for his independence, but eventually puts him in charge of the woods. In order to strike a better bargain with a prospective tenant, he tries to deprive the Poysers of some needed land, but is fairly driven from the field by Mrs. Poyser, who "has her say out".

Note.—The original of Squire Donnithorne is said to have been Mr. Francis Parker Newdigate, the patron of Robert Evans, George Eliot's father. In 1806 when Mr. Newdigate succeeded to the Arbury Hall estates in Warwickshire, Robert Evans went with him to Warwickshire. (*See* Olcott, *George Eliot*, p. 24.)

DONNITHORNE, CAPTAIN (LATER COLONEL) ARTHUR. The Old Squire's grandson, a handsome, warm-hearted, thoughtless and impressionable young man, just coming of age. *Adam B.* v–ix, xii–xiii, xvi, xviii, xxii, xxiv–xxxi, xxxvi, xliv, xlvii–xlviii, Epilogue.

" But to the Hayslope tenants he was more intensely a captain than all the young gentlemen of the same rank in his Majesty's regulars. . . . If you want to know more particularly how he looked, call to your remembrance some tawny-whiskered, brown-locked, clear-complexioned young Englishman . . . well-washed, high-bred, white-handed, yet looking as if he could deliver well from the left shoulder, and floor his man : I will not be so much of a tailor as to trouble your imagination with the difference of costume, and insist on the striped waistcoat, long-tailed coat, and low top-boots." Ch. v.

"His own approbation was necessary to him, and it was not an approbation to be enjoyed quite gratuitously ; it must be won by a fair amount of merit. He had never yet forfeited that approbation, and he had considerable reliance on his own virtues. No young man could confess his faults more candidly ; candour was one of his favourite virtues ; and how can a man's candour be seen in all its lustre unless he has a few failings to talk of ? But he had an agreeable confidence that his faults were all of a generous kind—impetuous, warm-blooded, leonine ; never crawling, crafty, reptilian. It was not possible for Arthur Donnithorne to do anything mean, dastardly, or cruel." Ch. xii.

He is much liked by his grandfather's tenantry, who look forward to the time when he will be the Squire. As a boy he was much attached to Adam Bede, and this friendship continues after Arthur is grown up, causing him to plan the many things which he will do for Adam when he inherits the estate. At the opening of the story he is invalided home from his regiment with a broken arm, and beguiles the tedium of his inaction by noticing pretty Hetty Sorrel, not knowing that Adam Bede is courting her. Finding that her attraction is becoming too strong, he resolves to break away, but cannot keep his good resolution and ends by really falling in love with her, without any idea on his part of marriage, although Hetty believes that he will marry her. When Adam finds Hetty and Arthur together, he and Arthur fight, and the latter, forced to it by Adam who does not know how far things have gone, writes a letter to Hetty breaking off their relationship, but telling her how to reach him if she needs him, and then joins his regiment. When he learns that Adam and Hetty are to be married he is relieved that the affair has ended so well, and salves his conscience with the thought of the kind things that he means to do for

F

them. His remorse is great when, called home by his grandfather's death, he learns that Hetty is being tried on the charge of murdering his child and hers. At the very last minute he succeeds in having her sentence of death commuted to transportation, and then exiles himself from home, to the army on the Continent.

DONNITHORNE, MISS LYDIA. Squire Donnithorne's spinster daughter who presides over his household and is tyrannized over by her father. *Adam B.* ix, xii, xviii, xxi, xxv–xxvi, xliv.

DONNITHORNE ARMS. Inn at Hayslope. *Adam B.* ii, xxxii.

"The Donnithorne Arms stood at the entrance of the village, and a small farmyard and stackyard which flanked it, indicating that there was a pretty take of land attached to the inn, gave the traveller a promise of good feed for himself and his horse, which might well console him for the ignorance in which the weather-beaten sign left him as to the heraldic bearings of that ancient family, the Donnithornes." Ch. ii.

Note.—The original of the "Donnithorne Arms" was the Bromley Davenport Arms at Ellastone ("Hayslope"). It was at one time kept by a Mr. Evans, a cousin of George Eliot. (*See* Browning, *Life of George Eliot*, p. 64 ; Mottram, *True Story of George Eliot*, pp. 136, 141.)

DONNITHORNE CHASE. The Donnithorne estate at Hayslope, noted for its fine woods. The house is called the "Abbey". *Adam B.* ii, vii, ix, xii–xiii, xxii–xxix, xliv, xlviii.

"The house would have been nothing but a plain square mansion of Queen Anne's time, but for the remnant of an old abbey to which it was united at one end, in much the same way as one may sometimes see a new farmhouse rising high and prim at the end of older and lower farm-offices. The fine old remnant stood a little backward and under the shadow of tall beeches." Ch. xxii.

The house and the woods of the Chase are the scene of several of the main events of the story. Arthur Donnithorne's coming-of-age festivities are held there, Arthur and Hetty meet in the woods and the little Hermitage, the fight between Arthur and Adam Bede takes place there, and after Hetty's trial it is in the Chase and the Hermitage that Arthur and Adam meet again and are reconciled.

Note.—The original of Donnithorne Chase was Wooton Hall, near Ellastone, the estate of Francis Parker Newdigate, on which George Eliot's father, Robert Evans ("Adam Bede") began his career as land agent. Another house near Ellastone, Calwich Abbey, has sometimes been suggested as the original, possibly merely because of its name. Wooton Hall is a low stone mansion built about 1730. In 1766 J. J. Rousseau stayed there.

DORCAS. *See* KNOTT, DORCAS.

DORLCOTE MILL. The "Mill on the Floss", *M. F.* Bk. 1, i, and throughout.

"And this is Dorlcote Mill . . . Even in this leafless time of departing February it is pleasant to look at—perhaps the chill damp season adds a charm to the trimly kept, comfortable dwelling-house, as old as the elms and chestnuts that shelter it from the northern blast. The stream is brimful now, and lies high in this little withy plantation, and half drowns the grassy fringe of the croft in front of the house." Bk. 1, i.

It had been the property of the Tullivers for five generations, but Mr. Tulliver loses it as a result of his many law-suits. When it then passes into the hands of Lawyer Wakem, his enemy, Mr. Tulliver continues as manager. When it is purchased by Guest & Co. some years after Mr. Tulliver's death, Tom Tulliver becomes its manager and it is from the Mill that Maggie rescues Tom in her row boat before both are drowned in the swollen Floss.

Note.—A mill on the Trent (the "Floss") a short distance north of Gainsborough has been claimed as the original of Dorlcote Mill, but the description does not fit this, although it does fit, with considerable exactness, an old mill near George Eliot's childhood home at Griff. It is probable that she had this second mill in mind and moved it, in the novel, to the Trent, i.e. the "Floss". (*See* Olcott, *George Eliot*, pp. 76–7.) The description of some parts of the house, the attic, at least, was taken from George Eliot's childhood home, Griff House. (*See* Andrews, *Bygone Warwickshire*, p. 266.)

DORNBERG, GRAF. A noble in love with Armgart, who asks her to marry him and give up her career when she is at the height of her success, but does not renew his offer after her voice fails her. *Armgart*, i, ii, v.

DOUBLE OAK. A well-known point in Cardell Chase. *D. D.* xiv.

DOVER, MR. Silversmith, Lydgate's chief creditor, who is willing to take back a portion of the plate and jewellery. *Mid.* lviii, lxiv–lxv, lxvii, lxix.

DOVER (*Real*). *D. D.* xiv, xx–xxi.
Note.—An English port on the strait of Dover, a principal port for the packet service to the Continent.

DOVIZI, BERNARDO, OF BIBBIENA (*Hist.*). An acquaintance of Tito Melema's. *Rom.* xiii, xx.
Note. — Bernardo Dovizi da Bibbiena, later Cardinal da Bibbiena (1470–1520), an Italian ecclesiastic and poet, created Cardinal 1513, author of *La Calandria*.

DOVIZI, SER PIERO, *also called* SER PIERO DA BIBBIENA (*Hist.*). "The weasel that Piero de' Medici keeps at his beck to slip through small holes for him." Brother of Bernardo Dovizi. *Rom.* xiii, xvi.

Note. — Piero da Bibbiena, secretary to Piero de' Medici, who had previously held the same office under Piero's father, Lorenzo de' Medici. He was hated by the people and was forced to flee from Florence at the same time as Piero de' Medici.

Dow. Printer in Treby Magna. *F. H.* xxviii.

Dowlas, Mr. Farrier, a defiant fellow, "intensely opposed to compromise," and fond of an argument; the "negative spirit" at the Rainbow inn gatherings. *S. M.* vi–vii, Conclusion.

Downes, Bill. Stone-sawyer, a pupil in Bartle Massey's night school who wins the donkey race at the birthday games. *Adam B.* xxi, xxv.

Downes, Kit. Farmer on Mr. Brooke's land. *Mid.* xxxviii.

D'Oyley. A former inhabitant of Treddleston. *Adam B.* xvi.

Dredge. Miner in Sproxton; "a big, red-whiskered man." *F. H.* xi, xxxiii, xlvi.

He takes part in the election riot at Treby and is sentenced to a year's imprisonment.

Dresden (*Real*). *D. D.* xx, lxii; *L. V.* i.

Note.—A German city, capital of Saxony.

Drumlow, Mr. Former rector at Raveloe. *S. M.* vi.

Dudley. Town. *D. D.* xxx.

Duffield. Town near Treby Magna. *F. H.* ii, viii, xx–xxi, xxvi, xxviii, xxx–xxxi, xxxiii, xlvi.

"Duffield Watchman." Liberal newspaper. *F. H.* vii–viii, xliv.

Dugong. A German scholar. *T. S.* iii.

Duke, Rev. Archibald. One of the clergymen present at the Clerical meeting at Milby Vicarage. *Amos B.* vi.

"A very small man with a sallow and somewhat puffy face, whose hair is brushed straight up, evidently with the intention of giving him a height somewhat less disproportionate to his sense of his own importance than the measure of five feet three accorded him by an oversight of nature. This is the Rev. Archibald Duke, a very dyspeptic and evangelical man, who takes the gloomiest view of mankind and their prospects, and thinks the immense sale of the *Pickwick Papers*, recently completed, one of the strongest proofs of original sin. Unfortunately, though Mr. Duke was not burdened with a family, his yearly expenditure was apt considerably to exceed his income; and the unpleasant circumstances resulting from this, together with heavy meat breakfasts, may probably have contributed to his desponding views of the world generally." Ch. vi.

Note.—In the lists of orginals made in Nuneaton after the publication of *Scenes of Clerical Life*, the original of the Reverend Archibald Duke was the Reverend

Mr. Hoke. (*See* Olcott, *George Eliot*, p. 14.)

DUMMILOW, JOB. A poor old man in Broxton village. *Adam B.* v.

DUNCAN, ARCHIE. A spiteful admirer of Sarah Dunkirk's, who had told her of her parent's disreputable business. *Mid.* lx.

DUNKIRK, MR. A rich London pawnbroker, Mr. Bulstrode's early patron, who made his fortune by conducting a receiving house for stolen goods. *Mid.* lxi.

DUNKIRK, MRS. The pawnbroker's wife, "a simple pious woman"; later Mr. Bulstrode's first wife. *Mid.* lxi.

On her husband's death she inherited his wealth, never having realized the nature of his business. She refused to marry Mr. Bulstrode until efforts had been made to find her lost daughter. Mr. Bulstrode concealed his knowledge of the daughter's whereabouts, and Mrs. Dunkirk married him and left him her fortune without reservation.

DUNKIRK, SARAH. Will Ladislaw's mother; Mr. and Mrs. Dunkirk's proud-spirited daughter. *Mid.* xxxvii, lx-lxi.

When she learned the dishonourable nature of her father's business, she ran away from home, went on the stage and later married Mr. Ladislaw, a Polish refugee.

DUNLOW COMMON. The place where Maggie Tulliver hopes to find the gypsies when she runs away to them. *M. F.* Bk. 1, xi.

DUNN, MR. Draper in Milby; an adherent of Mr. Tryan's. *J. R.* ix-x.

DUNN, MRS. The draper's wife. *J. R.* v, x.

DUNN, MARY. The draper's daughter, a rather unattractive young girl. *J. R.* v.

DUOMO, OR, SANTA MARIA DEL FIORE (*Real*). The Cathedral of Florence; the church in which Savonarola preaches. *Rom.* Proem, i, iii, viii, xii, xvi, xxi-xxvii, xxix, xlii-xliv, xlvii, xlix, lii, lv, lxii, lxvi.

When Baldassarre Calvo escapes from the French soldiers it is on the steps of the Duomo that he clutches Tito Melema, who thus becomes aware of his foster father's presence in Florence. Later, within the Duomo, Baldassarre hears Savonarola preach and is seen by Romola.

Note.—The Duomo, or Cathedral of Santa Maria del Fiore (so called from the lily which figures on the arms of Florence) is the present Cathedral of Florence. It was begun in the last decade of the thirteenth century by Arnolfo di Cambio. Giotto, the architect from 1332–6, began the tower. The dome was added by Brunelleschi during the first half of the fifteenth century and the church was finally consecrated 1436. The present façade was erected 1875–87.

DUOMO, PIAZZA DEL (*Real*). The square in Florence around the Duomo, where several important events in *Romola* take place. *Rom.* ii, viii, xxii, xxv, xxix–xxxi, xlv, xlvii.

Note.—The Piazza del Duomo takes its name from the Duomo or Cathedral which it surrounds.

DURFEYS. Ancestors of the Transomes of the time of Felix Holt, and cousins of the original Transomes; they came into possession of the Transome estate through purchase, and were then known as the Durfey-Transomes. *F. H.* xxix.

DYMICK and Halliwell. Lawyers. *F. H.* xxxv.

DYMOCK. Mr. Gascoigne's curate. *D. D.* lviii.

E

EAGLEDALE. A wild, lonely place to which Arthur Donnithorne goes on a fishing trip. *Adam B.* xii, xvi, xviii, xx.

"It's a wonderful sight—rocks and caves such as you never saw in your life. I never had a right notion o' rocks till I went there ... there's nothing but a bit of a inn i' that part where he's gone to fish." Ch. xx.

Note.—The original of Eagledale is Dovedale, a picturesque ravine some 20 or 30 miles north of Norbury, on the River Dove, the stream which divides the counties of Derby ("Stonyshire") and Stafford ("Loamshire"). The region was a favourite resort of Isaac Walton.

EAGRE. The tidal wave on the River Floss, "the rushing spring-tide, the awful Eagre, come up like a hungry monster." *M. F.* Bk. 1, v.

Note.—The eagre, hygre, or bore, is a curious tidal wave found on the Trent (the "Floss") and noticeable on that river as far up as the town of Gainsborough ("St. Ogg's"). Stark in his *History and Antiquities of Gainsburgh*, p. 522, says of it: "A curious phenomenon is observed in the Trent called the Eagre or Hygre. At spring tide the water rises on the surface of the river to a height of from seven to eight feet and rolls on in a large mass from the mouth of the Trent, considerably above the bridge. On account of the obstructions it meets with before it gets to Gainsburgh, the Eagre is somewhat diminished in size, but a few miles below the town it has a grand appearance." At the time of the fall equinox the Eagre is sometimes unusually high. For a description and picture of the Eagre during a very high equinoctial tide, *see* W. H. Wheeler, *Aeger in the Rivers Trent and Ouse*, in Nature, vol. 73, pp. 29–30.

EAST RETFORD (*Real*). A place where there was much bribery at elections. *Mid.* xxxviii.

Note.—In 1828, one year before the time of *Middlemarch*, the borough of East Retford in Nottinghamshire was disfranchised for repeated and incurable bribery.

EDINBURGH (*Real*). One of the places where Lydgate had carried on his medical studies. *Mid.* xv, xviii.

Note.—At the time of *Middlemarch*, in the early nineteenth century, Edinburgh was an important centre of medical study, which was carried on both at the University and in private medical classes.

EIGHT, THE (*Hist.*). Florentine officials who "attended to home discipline" and "presided over the administration of criminal justice". *Rom.* Proem, xvi, xxxix, xlii, xlv, lviii, lx, lxxi–lxxii.

Note.—This was the Eight of Guard and Custody (Otto di guardia e bália), a body elected every four months, which acted as a tribunal for criminal and political cases. It could inflict capital punishment by a vote of six out of its eight members. As the vote was taken by beans being placed in a bag the Court became known as the Sei Fave or Six Beans.

ELMSTOKE RECTORY. Residence of Mr. Prendergast. *J. R.* i, iii.

ELY, MR. The agreeable bachelor clergyman of Milby. *Amos B.* i–iv, vi.

"Mr. Ely was a tall, dark-haired, distinguished-looking man of three-and-thirty. By the laity of Milby and its neighbourhood he was regarded as a man of quite remarkable powers and learning, who must make a considerable sensation in London pulpits and drawing rooms on his occasional visits to the metropolis; and by his brother clergy he was regarded as a discreet and agreeable fellow. Mr. Ely never got into a warm discussion; he suggested what might be thought, but rarely said what he thought himself; he never let either men or women see that he was laughing at them, and he never gave anyone an opportunity of laughing at *him*. In one thing only he was injudicious. He parted his dark wavy hair down the middle; and as his head was rather flat than otherwise, that style of coiffure was not advantageous to him." Ch. iii.

Note.—The original of Mr. Ely was the Rev. William H. King, curate of Nuneaton. (Manuscript information.)

ENRIQUEZ. A member of Duke Silva's retinue.

EOCENE MINES. Sir Gavial Mantrap's swindling company. *T. S.* xvi.

EPPIE (HEPHZIBAH). The golden-haired child found by Silas Marner on his hearth in the place of his lost gold, who brings a new interest in life to the lonely old man. *S. M.* xii–xxi, Conclusion.

"A blond dimpled girl of eighteen, who has vainly tried to chastise her curly auburn hair into smoothness under her brown bonnet: the hair ripples as obstinately as a brooklet under the March breeze, and the little ringlets burst away from the restraining comb behind and show themselves below the bonnet-crown. Eppie cannot help being rather vexed about her hair, for there is no other girl in Raveloe who has hair at all like it, and she thinks hair ought to be smooth. She does not like to be blameworthy even in small things: you see how neatly her prayer-book is folded in her spotted handkerchief. . . ."

"The tender and peculiar love with which Silas had reared her in almost inseparable companionship with himself, aided by the seclusion of their dwelling, had preserved her from the lowering influences of the village talk and habits, and had kept her mind in that freshness which is sometimes falsely supposed to be an invariable attribute of rusticity. Perfect love has a breath of poetry which can exalt the relations of the least-instructed human beings; and this breath of poetry had surrounded Eppie from the time when she had followed the bright gleam that beckoned her to Silas's hearth; so that it is not surprising if, in other things besides her delicate prettiness, she was not quite a common village maiden, but had a touch of refinement and fervour which came from no other teaching than that of tenderly - nurtured unvitiated feeling." Ch. xvi.

When her mother, Molly Farren, Godfrey Cass's deserted wife, is trudging to Raveloe with her child, to denounce Godfrey, she sinks exhausted in the snow, and the child slips from the dead woman's arms and crawls to Silas Marner's hearth, where he finds her later, in place of his lost gold. Ignorant of her parentage, she is adopted and reared by the unhappy old weaver who, through her needs and companionship, is restored to happiness and a normal relation to his fellows. She grows into a good and charming young woman, and when her real father, Godfrey Cass, wishes to acknowledge her and take her home, she loyally refuses to leave the old man who has been a father to her. When she and Aaron Winthrop are married, the old weaver lives with them.

ETON (*Real*). The public school where Daniel Deronda was educated before he went to Cambridge. In *Felix Holt*, Harold Transome had been educated at Eton and in the *Lifted Veil* Latimer's elder brother had been at that school. *D. D.* xvi. *F. H.* i, viii; *L. V.* i. *Note.*—Eton College, at Eton, near Windsor, founded in 1440 by Henry VI.

EUPHEMIA. *T. S.* xiii.

EUPHORION. A plagiarist who freely acknowledges the source of his ideas when the citation of great names of the past will show his scholarship, but who passes off other borrowings as his own, and "is disposed to treat the distinction between mine and thine in original authorship as egoistic, narrowing, and low". *T. S.* xi.

"EVANGELICAL MAGAZINE" (*Real*). The magazine which the Muscats took in. *F. H.* vi.

Note.—The *Evangelical Magazine and Missionary Chronicle,* London, first established 1793.

EVIL COMPANIONS. *See* COMPAGNACCI.

F

FABIAN. A member of Duke Silva's retinue. *Sp. G.* ii.

FAG. Mr. Dagley's sheep-dog. *Mid.* xxxix.

"FAMILY TEA-TABLE." Periodical for which Kate Meyrick makes illustrations. *D. D.* xxxix.

FANTONI, GIAN. A Piagnone shopkeeper. *Rom.* xliii.

FAREBROTHER, MRS. The vicar's mother, a formal and precise old lady. *Mid.* xvii, xxvi, lii, liv, lvii, lix, lxiii, lxxx.

"The vicar's white-haired mother, befrilled and kerchiefed with dainty cleanliness, upright, quick-eyed, and still under seventy. . . . The old lady was evidently accustomed to tell her company what they ought to think, and to regard no subject as quite safe without her steering. She was afforded leisure for this function by having all her little wants attended to by Miss Winifred." Ch. xvii.

FAREBROTHER, REVEREND CAMDEN. Vicar of St. Botolph's, Middlemarch; a generous, honourable man with a gift for good preaching, and a liking for natural science. *Mid.* xiii-xiv, xvi-xviii, xxvi, xxxi, xxxvi, xxxviii, xl, xlv-xlvi, l, lii-liv, lvi-lvii, lix, lxiii-lxiv, lxvi, lxx-lxxii, lxxv-lxxvii, lxxx-lxxxi.

"It went along with other points of conduct in Mr. Farebrother which were exceptionally fine, and made his character resemble those southern landscapes which seem divided between natural grandeur and social slovenliness. Very few men could have been as filial and chivalrous as he was to the mother, aunt, and sister, whose dependence on him had in many ways shaped his life rather uneasily for himself. . . . Then, his preaching was ingenious and pithy, like the preaching of the English Church in its robust age, and his sermons were delivered without book. People outside his parish went to hear him; and since to fill the church was always the most difficult part of a clergyman's function, here was another ground for a careless sense of superiority. Besides, he was a likeable man; sweet-tempered, ready-witted, frank, without grins of suppressed bitterness or other conversational flavours which make half of us an affliction to our friends." Ch. xviii.

On an insufficient income he has to support his mother, aunt, and sister, and so is led into card-playing for money. For the same reason he would like to obtain the salaried chaplaincy of Bulstrode's new hospital, but from a sense of delicacy refrains from asking Lydgate, who has the deciding vote, to aid his candidacy against Bulstrode's candidate, Mr. Tyke. He is in love with Mary Garth, but renounces his own hopes in that direction in order to help Fred Vincy win Mary. Through Lydgate Mrs. Casaubon becomes interested in him and gives him the desirable Lowick living.

FAREBROTHER, MISS WINIFRED. The vicar's elder sister, "well-looking like himself, but nipped and subdued, as single women are apt to be who spend their lives in uninterrupted subjection to their elders." *Mid.* xvii, lii, lvii, lix.

FARLEIGH. Home of the Asshers. *Mr. G.'s L. S.* v, x–xi.

FARQUHAR, MR. The secondary squire in Shepperton parish. *Amos B.* ii–iii.
Note.—The original of Mr. Farquhar was a Mr. Harper. (Manuscript information; *also* Olcott, *George Eliot*, p. 14.)

FARQUHAR, MRS. Mr. Farquhar's wife, one of Mrs. Barton's kind neighbours. *Amos B.* ii–iii, v–vi, ix.

FARQUHAR, MISS ARABELLA. The squire's daughter, who sets her cap at Mr. Ely. *Amos B.* ii, ix.

FARQUHAR, MISS JULIA. One of the squire's two daughters. *Amos B.* ii, ix.

FARREN, MOLLY. Eppie's mother, a barmaid, addicted to drink and opium, whom Godfrey Cass married secretly. *S. M.* iii, xii–xiv.
On New Year's Eve, enraged at her husband's refusal to acknowledge her, she starts to walk to Raveloe with their child in her arms to disclose herself to Godfrey's father. On the way she yields to her slavery to opium, and as a result dies in the snow near Silas Marner's cottage, and is buried in a pauper's grave, unacknowledged by her husband.

FAULKNER. A gentleman to whom Mr. Bambridge had sold some horses. *Mid.* lxxi.

FAUX, MRS. David's forgiving mother. *B. J.* i, iii.

FAUX, DAVID. The ill-favoured pastry-cook who, under the name of Edward Freely, runs a successful confectioner's business at Grimworth until he is brought to grief by Brother Jacob, his idiot brother. *B. J.* i–iii.

Not satisfied with his modest prospects at home he steals his mother's small hoard of twenty guineas, goes to the West Indies, and later returns to England with an *alias* and a picturesque background of imaginary adventures and fictitious rich relatives. As Edward Freely he sets up in business as a confectioner at Grimworth, corrupts the good housewives of the town who had previously made their own pastry and is on the point of crowning his success by marrying pretty Penelope Palfrey, the daughter of the richest farmer in Grimworth, when his idiot brother Jacob finds him, and his real name and career are revealed.

FAUX, JACOB. David's idiot brother, who is a witness of David's theft of his mother's guineas and, later, the means of his discovery and disgrace. *B. J.* i, iii.

FAUX, JONATHAN. David's father, at whose death David inherits eighty-two pounds. *B. J.* i–iii.

FAUX, JONATHAN. David's eldest brother. *B. J.* iii.

FAWKES, BESSY. A sick woman whom Dolly Winthrop takes care of in her last illness; while sitting up with her, Dolly thinks out the puzzling question of Silas Marner and the drawing of lots. *S. M.* xvi.

FAWKS, BILL. A boy who gives Bob Jakin a terrier pup instead of drowning it. *M. F.* Bk. 3, vi.

FEATHERSTONE, JONAH. Peter's poor brother, the wit of the family, who had come down in the world, and is one of those who are on the watch lest Peter's money be left out of the family. *Mid.* xxxii–xxxiii, xxxv.

FEATHERSTONE, MR. PETER. A rich and miserly old widower, owner of Stone Court. *Mid.* xi–xiv, xvii, xxiii, xxv, xxvii, xxxi–xxxv, xl, liii.

"Old Featherstone had not been a Harpagon whose passions had all been devoured by the ever-lean and ever-hungry passion of saving, and who would drive a bargain with his undertaker beforehand. He loved money, but he also loved to spend it in gratifying his peculiar tastes, and perhaps he loved it best of all as a means of making others feel his power more or less uncomfortably. If anyone will here contend that there must have been traits of goodness in old Featherstone, I will not presume to deny this; but I must observe that goodness is of a modest nature, easily discouraged, and, when much elbowed in early life by unabashed vices, is apt to retire into extreme privacy, so that it is more easily believed in by those who construct a selfish old gentleman theoretically, than by those who form the narrower judgments based on his personal acquaintance." Ch. xxxiv.

He is connected with the Garths through his first wife and with the Vincys through his second wife, and has a host of relatives of his own who are anxious that he shall not leave his money outside his family. He enjoys arousing speculation as to his intentions, and leads Fred Vincy to expect a bequest, but disappoints him, as well as all his own greedy and scheming relatives, by leaving his property to a hitherto unheard-of natural son, Joshua Rigg. He has made many wills and at the end, when dying and helpless, he wants this will destroyed so that an earlier one providing for Fred will be operative, but cannot carry out his wishes.

FEATHERSTONE, RIGG, *otherwise known as* MR. JOSHUA RIGG. Peter Featherstone's frog-faced natural son. *Mid.* xxxv, xl–xli, xlvii, liii, lxix–lxx.

"Socially speaking, Joshua Rigg would have been generally pronounced a superfluity . . . Mr. Rigg Featherstone's low characteristics were all of the sober, water-drinking kind. From the earliest to the latest hour of the day he was always as sleek, neat, and cool as the frog he resembled, and old Peter had secretly chuckled over this offshoot almost more calculating, and far more imperturbable, than himself." Ch. xli.

His existence is unknown to the Featherstones until, at his father's death, he appears at Stone Court and inherits Peter's land, to the rage and disappointment of the Featherstone family. As his chief ambition is to be a money-changer, he sells his property to Mr. Bulstrode and departs from Middlemarch. His disreputable stepfather, Raffles, follows him to Stone Court, and this leads eventually to the discovery of Mr. Bulstrode's early life.

FEATHERSTONE, SOLOMON. Peter's rich and greedy brother, also on the watch for Peter's money. *Mid.* xii, xxxii–xxxiii, xxxv, lii–liii, lvi.

"He was a large-cheeked man, nearly seventy, with small furtive eyes, and was not only of much blander temper, but thought himself much deeper than his brother Peter; indeed, not likely to be deceived in any of his fellow-men, inasmuch as they could not well be more greedy and deceitful than he suspected them of being. Even the invisible powers, he thought, were likely to be soothed by a bland parenthesis here and there—coming from a man of property, who might have been as impious as others." Ch. xxxii.

FEATHERSTONE'S ALMS - HOUSES. Alms-houses for old men, for the erection of which Peter Featherstone bequeaths the residue of his property, after leaving his land to Joshua Rigg. *Mid.* xxxv.

FEBBRAI, VIA DE' (*Real*). A street in Florence, near the narrow entrance to which some apprentices engage in stone throwing during the Fierucola. *Rom.* xiv.
  Note.—This is the short Via Fibbiai, or Fivviai, which leads out of the Piazza dell' Annunziata past the Spedale degl' Innocenti.

FEDALMA. Zarca's daughter, betrothed to Duke Silva; a beautiful, gifted, high-minded Gypsy, who finds herself called upon to make a great renunciation for the sake of her people. *Sp. G.* i–vi.

Stolen from her people when a mere infant, she had been taken into the family of the Duchess Diana and brought up there with all love and tenderness. She and the young Duke Silva are betrothed, and when their marriage is near, Fedalma, deeply in love and looking forward to a happy future, learns from the prisoner Zarca that he is her father. When Zarca, a patriot and a visionary, points out to her the needs of her people and all that she can do for them if she will cast in her lot with them, she at first tries to reconcile love and duty, but later makes the sacrifice of her personal happiness, gives up Silva, and joins her father in his escape. When Silva, desperate at her loss, follows her and joins the Gypsy band to win her, she cannot rejoice entirely, as she feels that he is defying inherited obligations which will later become insistent. After Zarca captures Silva's town of Bedmár, and Silva, desperate with shame, kills Zarca, Fedalma finds herself separated for ever from her lover. She has one farewell interview with Silva, and then, renouncing all thought of self, leads her people to Africa.

FEDELE, CASSANDRA (*Hist.*). "The most learned woman in the world " to whom Romola, when she plans to leave Tito, intends to appeal for aid to make herself self-supporting. *Rom.* v, xxxvi.
   Note.—Cassandra Fedele Mapelli (1465–1558), scholar and writer.

FELICIA. A clever woman whose opinions are eagerly sought by Mr. Hintze, the too deferential man. *T. S.* v.

FELICITA, SANTA. See SANTA FELICITA, CHURCH OF.

FELLOWES, MR. Rector and magistrate, a man with a persuasive tongue. *Amos B.* vi.
   " A man of imposing appearance, with a mellifluous voice and the readiest of tongues. Mr. Fellowes once obtained a living by the persuasive charms of his conversation, and the fluency with which he interpreted the opinions of an obese and stammering baronet, so as to give that elderly gentleman a very pleasing perception of his own wisdom. Mr. Fellowes is a very successful man, and has the highest character everywhere except in his own parish, where, doubtless because his parishioners happen to be quarrelsome people, he is always at fierce feud with a farmer or two, a colliery proprietor, a grocer who was once churchwarden, and a tailor who formerly officiated as clerk." Ch. vi.
   Note.—In the lists of originals made in Nuneaton after the publication of the *Scenes of Clerical Life*, the original of Mr. Fellowes was given as the Rev. Henry Bellairs (1790–1872), rector of Bedworth 1830–64.

FENN, MR. Member of Parliament for West Orchards; a guest of the Mallingers. *D. D.* xxxv.

FENN, JULIET. Mr. Fenn's daughter who wins a gold arrow at the Brackenshaw Archery Club. *D. D.* x–xi, xxxv–xxxvi.
   " Juliet Fenn, a girl as middling as midday market in everything but her archery and plainness, in which last she was noticeably like her father: underhung and with receding brow resembling that of the more intelligent fishes." Ch. xi.

FENSHORE. *F. H.* xl.

FERDINAND, KING OF NAPLES (*Hist.*). *Rom.* xxi.
   Note.—Ferdinand, natural son of Alfonso of Aragon, King of Naples 1458–94.

FERRARA (*Real*). Savonarola's birthplace and early home were in " brilliant Ferrara ". *Rom.* xxii.
   Note.—Ferrara, thirty miles northeast of Bologna, was the capital of the House of Este.

In Savonarola's time it was a powerful city of about 100,000 inhabitants, and its court was one of the most famous and magnificent in Italy.

FERRAVECCHI (*Real*). Street in Florence where Bratti Ferravecchi had his second-hand shop. *Rom.* i–ii, xvi, xxx.
Note.—The Via de' (or tra') Ferravecchi was a street leading out of the Mercato Vecchio, which took its name from the fact that the dealers in old iron lived there. At the time when the Mercato Vecchio was swept away, the Ferravecchi became part of the Via degli Strozzi.

FERRAVECCHI, BRATTI. *See* BRATTI FERRAVECCHI.

FETCH. Mr. Grandcourt's jealous liver-coloured water-spaniel. *D. D.* xii–xiii.

FIBB'S END. *M. F.* Bk. 5, ii.

FICINO, MARSILIO (*Hist.*). A scholar, one of the men of mark in Florence who reverenced Savonarola. *Rom.* v, vii, xvi–xvii, xxxix.
Note.—Marsilio Ficino (1433–99) an Italian philosopher and writer on Plato, chosen by Cosimo de' Medici to preside over the Platonic Academy.

FIDO. Miss Lydia Donnithorne's pet dog. *Adam B.* xliv.

FIERUCOLA (*Real*). The "Little Fair"; a fair or festival held by the peasants on the seventh of September, the eve of the Nativity of the Virgin, in the Piazza dell' Annunziata. *Rom.* xiii–xiv.

Tito Melema, whose interest has been aroused by Nello's description of the Fierucola, goes to see the celebration, finds Tessa in the church of the Annunziata, wanders through the fair with her, and ends by going through a mock marriage ceremony which she ignorantly believes to be real.
Note.—Guido Biagi, in his edition of *Romola*, points out that it is not certain that the Fierucola was celebrated as early as the time of *Romola*, as, according to one tradition, the festival commemorates the taking of Siena in 1555.

FIERUCOLONI. Peasants. *Rom.* xiii–xiv.
"The contadine who came from the mountains of Pistoia, and the Casentino, and heaven knows where, to keep their vigil in the church of the Nunziata, and sell their yarn and dried mushrooms at the Fierucola (petty fair), as we call it. They make a queer show, with their paper lanterns, howling their hymns to the Virgin on this eve of her nativity." Ch. xiii.

FIESOLE (*Real*). "Fiesole with its crown of monastic walls and cypresses." *Rom.* mentioned in Proem, xliii.
Note.—Town about three miles north-east of Florence.

FIESOLE, DOMINICAN MONASTERY AT (*Real*). Place to which the sick monk, Fra Luca, is carried from San Marco. *Rom.* xi, xiii.
Note.—This is the Dominican monastery at San Domenico

di Fiesole, founded 1405, where Fra Angelico da Fiesole lived before his removal to San Marco, Florence.

FILELFO, FRANCESCO (*Hist.*). A scholar under whom Bardo de' Bardi once studied Greek. *Rom.* Proem (mentioned as the "fiery philosopher"), iv–vi.

Note.—Francesco Filelfo (1398–1481), an Italian humanist, and expositor of Virgil and Cicero. He taught Greek in various Italian cities—Bologna, Florence, and Siena, 1427–40; in 1481 he was called to the chair of Greek at Florence.

FILMORE, MR. A surgeon's assistant, "whose whiskers and shirt-pin were quite above the average." *F. H.* viii.

FILMORE, MR. A neighbour of Latimer's family. *L. V.* i.

FILMORE, MRS. Mr. Filmore's wife and Bertha Grant's aunt; "a commonplace, middle-aged woman." *L. V.* i.

FILMORE OF CORPUS. *F. H.* xxiii.

FINSBURY (*Real*). *Mid.* xli.

FIR TREE GROVE. The part of Donnithorne Chase where Arthur's "Hermitage" stands; he and Hetty Sorrel meet there. *Adam B.* xii–xiii, xxvii–xxviii, xlviii. "The delicious labyrinthine wood which skirted one side of the Chase, and which was called Fir-tree Grove, not because the firs were many, but because they were few. It was a wood of beeches and limes, with here and there a light, silver-stemmed birch—just the sort of wood most haunted by the nymphs. . . . It was not a grove with measured grass or rolled gravel for you to tread upon, but with narrow, hollow-shaped, earthy paths, edged with faint dashes of delicate moss—paths which look as if they were made by the freewill of the trees and underwood, moving reverently aside to look at the tall queen of the white-footed nymphs." Ch. xii.

FIRNISS, MISS. Mistress of a boarding school attended by Maggie Tulliver and Lucy Deane. *M. F.* Bk. 6, ix.

FIRNISS'S (MISS) BOARDING SCHOOL. The school in Laceham which Maggie Tulliver and her cousin Lucy attend. *M. F.* Bk. 2, vii; Bk. 3, i, viii.

FIRS, THE. Home of Mr. Quallon, the banker at Wanchester. *D. D.* v–vi.

FITCHETT, MASTER. The husband of the lodge-keeper at Tipton Grange. *Mid.* vi.

FITCHETT, MR. An inmate of the Shepperton workhouse who had once been a footman in the Oldinport family. *Amos B.* ii.

Note.—An old verger named Baker was said to have been the original of Mr. Fitchett. (*See* Olcott, *George Eliot*, pp. 15, 23.)

FITCHETT, MRS. Lodge-keeper at Tipton Grange. *Mid.* vi.

FITZADAM, MR. AND MRS. Guests of the Mallingers at the Abbey. *D. D.* xxxv.

FIVIZZANO (*Real*). Town near which the French soldiers had taken Baldassarre Calvo prisoner. *Rom.* xxiii.
   Note.—A small town 34 miles north-west of Lucca, Italy.

FLAVELL. A Methodist preacher who knocked down a hare that came across his path, pleading that he thought the Lord had sent him and his wife a good dinner. *Mid.* xxxix.

"FLAXEN-HEADED PLOUGHBOY" (*Real*). Squire Cass's favourite tune, which Solomon Macey plays at the New Year's dance. *S. M.* xi.
   Note.—This is the once popular song "The Ploughboy", beginning: "The flaxen-headed cow-boy, as simple as may be.... And next a merry ploughboy," etc. The words, by John O'Keefe, are included in his ballad-opera "The Farmer"; the music is by William Shield.

FLEET. Squire Cass's deer-hound. *S. M.* ix.

FLETCHER. Mr. Hawley's clerk. *Mid.* lxxi.

FLETCHER. One of the lessees of the collieries near Gadsmere, Grandcourt's place. *D. D.* xxx.

FLETCHER. Bertha Grant's maid. *L. V.* ii.

FLETCHER, MRS. (*Hist.*). One of the women preachers among the Methodists, of whom Dinah Morris talks. *Adam B.* viii.
   Note.—Mary Bosanquet (1739–1815), who in 1781 married John William Fletcher (or, de la Flechere), vicar of Madely. Of a wealthy family, she early entered into the work of the Methodists, and preached, before her marriage and also later, in Madely and vicinity, both during her husband's life-time and for thirty years after his death.

FLITTON. Town in the neighbourhood of Raveloe. *S. M.* iv, viii, xi.

FLORENCE (*Real*). Scene of the principal events in *Romola*. *Rom.* Proem; i–lxviii, lxx–lxxii, Epilogue.
   Many Florentine localities and buildings are mentioned in the novel. All of these which have any part, however small, in the plot of the story, are entered separately in their alphabetical places in the *Dictionary*, and the fuller information, including the historical notes, is given under these separate entries. The following list will show at a glance what localities in Florence and the immediate vicinity are mentioned. For fuller information, consult the separate entries in the main alphabet. As the form of name given in the following list is in every case that used by George Eliot, some places are given under their English names, others under the Italian.

ARNO. River. *Rom.* Proem, viii, x, xxxvi, lxvii, lxx.

BARDI HOUSE. *Rom.* v, xvii, xx, xxvii, xxxii, xlvi.

BOGOLI, HILL OF. *Rom.* Proem, v.

BRIDGES.
  PONTE ALLA CARRAJA. *Rom.* x, lxvii.
  PONTE RUBACONTE, *or,* PONTE ALLE GRAZIE. *Rom.* v, xx, xxvi, xxxvi, xliv, lxvii,
  PONTE SANTA TRINITÀ. *Rom.* xlv, lxvii.
  PONTE VECCHIO. *Rom.* Proem, v, x, xxi, xlii–xliii, xlvii, lxvii.

CANTO DI PAGLIA. *Rom.* xvi.

CHURCHES AND CONVENTS.
  ANNUNZIATA. *Rom.* xiv.
  BADIA. *Rom.* Proem, i, viii, x, lii, liv.
  BAPTISTERY, *or,* SAN GIOVANNI BATTISTA. *Rom.* iii, viii, xlv, lix.
  DUOMO, *or,* SANTA MARIA DEL FIORE. *Rom.* Proem, iii, viii, xxii–xxv, xlii, lii, lv, lxvi.
  OGNISSANTI. *Rom.* xliii.
  SAN AMBROGIO. *Rom.* lvi.
  SAN GAGGIO (outside the Porta Romana). *Rom.* xlii.
  SAN GIOVANNI. See above BAPTISTERY.
  SAN LORENZO. *Rom.* Proem, xii.
  SAN MARCO. *Rom.* Proem, x–xi, xv, xlvi, lix, lxii–lxiv, lxvi.
  SAN MINIATO. *Rom.* lxvii.
  SAN PULINARI. *Rom.* x.
  SAN SPIRITO. *Rom.* xliii, lxx.
  SAN STEFANO. *Rom.* xlii–xliv.
  SANTA CROCE. *Rom.* Proem, xii, xxvii, lxiii.
  SANTA FELICITÀ. *Rom.* xi.
  SANTA LUCIA. *Rom.* xx.
  SANTA MARIA DEL FIORE. *See above* DUOMO.
  SANTA MARIA NOVELLA. *Rom.* xxxviii.

DANTE'S HOUSE. *Rom.* i.

FIESOLE (three miles north-east of Florence). *Rom.* mentioned Proem, xliii.

FIESOLE, DOMINICAN MONASTERY AT. (SAN DOMENICO DI FIESOLE.) *Rom.* xi.

GATES.
  POR' DEL PRATO. *Rom.* viii (Porta al Prato), x, xxxiii.
  PORTA PINTI. *Rom.* vii.
  PORTA SAN FREDIANO. *Rom.* xxi, lxvii.
  PORTA SAN GALLO. *Rom.* xxi, xxxvii, lxvii, lxx.
  PORTA SAN PIERO. *Rom.* xxxii, xlii.
  PORTA SANTA CROCE. *Rom.* viii, l, lvi.

GIOTTO'S CAMPANILE. *Rom.* mentioned Proem, iii.

HOSPITALS.
  HOSPITAL FOR POOR TRAVELLERS (outside Porta Santa Croce). *Rom.* xxv, xxix–xxx.
  HOSPITAL OF SAN MATTEO. *Rom.* xlii, xlvi.
  SPEDALE DEGL' INNOCENTI (Foundling Hospital). *Rom.* xiv.

LOGGIA DE' CERCHI. *Rom.* i.

LOGGIA, ORCAGNA'S. *Rom.* Proem, viii, xlix, lxv.

MERCATO VECCHIO, *or,* OLD MARKET. *Rom.* i–iii, viii, x, xvi.

OLTRARNO. *Rom.* Proem, v, xxx, lxvii.

G

ORCAGNA'S LOGGIA. *See above*, LOGGIA, ORCAGNA'S.

PALACES (including public buildings).

BARGELLO. *Rom.* viii, lx.

MEDICI (*referred to as* "PALACE OF THE VIA LARGA"). *Rom.* xii, xix, xxi, xxvi.

PITTI. *Rom.* mentioned Proem.

SCALA (CASA GHERARDESCA). *Rom.* vii, xiii.

SPINI. *Rom.* xlv.

VECCHIO. *Rom.* Proem, viii, xlv, liv–lv, lx, lxiii, lxv–lxvi, lxxii.

PIAZZA. *See below under* SQUARES.

PRATO, THE. *Rom.* x.

RUCELLAI GARDENS. *Rom.* xxxviii–xxxix.

SAN GIORGIO, HILL OF. *Rom.* xxxiii, l.

SAN MARTINO. *Rom.* i.

SAN MINIATO, HILL OF. *Rom.* Proem, liii.

SQUARES.

PIAZZA D' OGNISSANTI. *Rom.* x.

PIAZZA DE' MOZZI. *Rom.* v, xliv, lxvii.

PIAZZA DEL DUOMO. *Rom.* ii, viii, xxii, xxv, xxix–xxxi, xlv, xlvii.

PIAZZA DELL' ANNUNZIATA. *Rom.* xiii–xiv.

PIAZZA DELLA SIGNORIA. *Rom.* viii, xvi, xxi, xxxv, xlix, l, lx, lxv–lxvii, lxx, lxxii.

PIAZZA DI SAN GIOVANNI. *Rom.* iii, viii, xvi, xlv.

PIAZZA DI SAN MARCO. *Rom.* xli, lxii.

PIAZZA DI SANTA CROCE. *Rom.* xxvi, xxxvii, lxiii.

STINCHE. Prison. *Rom.* xxxix, xlii.

STREETS.

BORGO DE' GRECI. *Rom.* xx.

BORGO DEGLI ALBIZZI. *Rom.* xlix, lxxi.

BORGO DI SAN LORENZO. *Rom.* xx.

BORGO LA CROCE. *Rom.* lvi.

BORGO PINTI. *Rom.* xiii, xxxvii, Epilogue.

BORGO SANTA CROCE. *Rom.* xxvi.

CALIMARA. *Rom.* Proem, iii.

CORSO DEGLI ADIMARI. *Rom.* ix.

FERRAVECCHI. *Rom.* i–ii, xvi.

LUNG ARNO. *Rom.* xx.

OGNISSANTI. *Rom.* i, x, xxii.

POR' SANTA MARIA. *Rom.* xlii–xliii.

PORTA ROSSA. *Rom.* x.

VIA DE' BARDI. *Rom.* v, x–xi, xviii, xx, xxx, lxiv, lxvi–lxvii.

VIA DE' BENCI. *Rom.* xx, xxvi.

VIA DE' CERRETANI. *Rom.* xxii.

VIA DE' FEBBRAI. *Rom.* xiv.

VIA DE' LIBRAJ. *Rom.* l.

VIA DE' MARTELLI. *Rom.* xxix.

VIA DEL COCOMERO. *Rom.* xi, lxiii.

VIA DEL FOSSO. *Rom.* xliv.

VIA DEL GARBO. *Rom.* i, xxx.

VIA DEL MAGLIO. *Rom.* xiii.

VIA DEL PALAGIO. *Rom.* li.

VIA DELL' ORIUOLO. *Rom.* xxv.

VIA DELLA SCALA. *Rom.* xxxviii.

VIA GUALFONDA. *Rom.* xviii, xxviii.

VIA GUICCIARDINI. *Rom.* x.

VIA LARGA. *Rom.* xii, xix, xxi, xxix.

VIA SAN GALLO. *Rom.* lxx.

VIA SAN SEBASTIANO. *Rom.* xiii.

TETTO DE' PISANI. *Rom.* lxv, lxxii.

FLORENTINE CITIZEN, SPIRIT OF. See SPIRIT OF A FLORENTINE CITIZEN.

FLOSS. River at St. Ogg's near which Mr. Tulliver's mill is situated. *M. F.* Bk. 1, i, v–vi; Bk. 3, v; Bk. 5, i; Bk. 6, i–ii, xiii; Bk. 7, v.

"A wide plain, where the broadening Floss hurries on between its green banks to the sea, and the loving tide, rushing to meet it, checks its passage with an impetuous embrace. On this mighty tide the black ships—laden with the fresh-scented fir-planks, with rounded sacks of oil-bearing seed, or with the dark glitter of coal—are borne along to the town of St. Ogg's, which shows its aged, fluted red roofs and the broad gables of its wharves between the low wooded hill and the river brink, tinging the water with a soft purple hue under the transient glance of this February sun. . . . Just by the red-roofed town the tributary Ripple flows with a lively current into the Floss." Bk. 1, i.

As children Tom and Maggie Tulliver play along the Ripple and Floss, and later Maggie, Lucy Deane, and Stephen Guest go boating on it. The trading ships that carry Tom's venture in Laceham goods sail down the Floss, and when Stephen Guest and Maggie go away together they are rowing on the river. When the great flood in September endangers the mill, Maggie rescues Tom in her rowboat, and it is in the swollen Floss that the two are drowned.

Note.—The original of the Floss is the River Trent, on which the town of Gainsborough (the original of " St. Ogg's ") is situated. The Trent is particularly liable to flooding in that region, and various destructive floods of the kind described in the catastrophe of " Mill on the Floss " have occurred in the neighbourhood of Gainsborough. The worst of these was the flood of 1770, referred to in the story as having taken place 60 years before that in which Tom and Maggie perish.

" FLOW ON, THOU SHINING RIVER " (*Real*). A song which Rosamond Vincy sings to Mr. Featherstone. *Mid.* xii.[1]

FLUFF. Maltese dog belonging to Grandcourt. *D. D.* xii.

FLY. Black-and-tan terrier. *Mid.* lii.

FODGE, MASTER. Poll's small son, " most inveterate in ill-behaviour during service time." *Amos B.* ii.

FODGE, POLL. An insubordinate inmate of Shepperton workhouse. *Amos B.* ii.

---

[1] The words are by Thomas Moore, the music by Sir John Stevenson.

"Poll Fodge—known to the magistracy of her county as Mary Higgins—a one-eyed woman, with a scarred and seamy face, the most notorious rebel in the workhouse, said to have once thrown her broth over the master's coat-tails." Ch. ii.

FORD, OLD "MESTER". "A true Staffordshire patriarch." *Mr. G.'s L. S.* xxi.

FORD, HIRAM. A wagoner. *Mid.* lvi.

FORTINBRAS, LORD. Mr. Calibut's son-in-law. *F. H.* xx.

"FORWARD, YOUNG WRESTLER FOR THE TRUTH!" First line of "Six Stanzas" addressed by Miss Pratt to the Rev. Mr. Tryan. *J. R.* iii.

FOSSO, VIA DEL (*Real*). Street in Florence along which Baldassarre Calvo goes to purchase a knife at Niccolò Caparra's shop. *Rom.* xliv.

Note.—This was the Via del Fosso (now a part of the Via de' Benci) which extended from the Ponte alle Grazie to the Borgo S. Croce. A part of the present Via Giuseppe Verdi which continues the Via de' Benci to the north was also called the Via del Fosso.

FOTHERGILL, MISS. Mrs. Prettyman's maiden name. *B. J.* ii.

FOUNDLING HOSPITAL. *See* SPEDALE DEGL' INNOCENTI.

FOWLER. A tenant on one of Squire Cass's farms. *S. M.* iii, viii–ix. When he pays his rent to the squire's son Godfrey, Dunsey gets the money from Godfrey as the price of his silence regarding the latter's marriage.

"FOX AND HOUNDS." Hotel in Duffield, Transome's headquarters. *F. H.* xxx.

FOXHOLM CHURCH. Mr. Heron's church, where Mr. Gilfil and Tina are married. *Mr. G.'s L. S.* xxi.

FOXHOLM PARSONAGE. The peaceful home of the Herons. *Mr. G.'s L. S.* xx.

FRANCES, AUNT. The Dodsons' aunt. *M. F.* Bk. 1, vii.

FRANCESCO. Workman engaged in decorating the ceiling of the saloon at Cheverel Manor. *Mr. G.'s L. S.* ii, v.

FRANCESO, FRA. *See* PUGLIA, FRA FRANCESO DI.

FRANCISCANS, *or*, FRATI MINORI (*Hist.*). The monastic order which opposes Savonarola and the Dominicans. *Rom.* Proem, xliii, lxiii, lxv.

"Frati Minori, or Franciscans, in that age all clad in grey, with the knotted cord round their waists, and some of them with the *zoccoli*, or wooden sandals, below their bare feet;—perhaps the most numerous order in Florence, owning many zealous members who loved mankind and hated the Dominicans." Ch. xliii.

Note.—The Franciscans (also called the Minorites or Lesser Brethren), a religious order founded 1209 by St. Francis of Assisi. The principal Franciscan Convent and Church in Florence was Santa Croce.

FRANCO, MATTEO (*Hist.*). An "untainted sceptic", one of Lorenzo de' Medici's circle at Careggi. *Rom.* xxxix.

Note.—Matteo Franco (1447–1494), poet, a friend of Luigi Pulci. The two exchanged a long series of abusive sonnets, full of slang and the language of the market place.

FRANKFORT (*Real*). The German city where Daniel Deronda attends services in the old synagogue of the Orthodox Jews and is seen by his grandfather's friend Joseph Kalonymos. *D. D.* xxxii, li; mentioned *Mid.* xvi.

Note.—Frankfort-am-Main, a German city with an important Jewish population, including a group of ultra-Orthodox Jews.

FRASER, MR. Daniel Deronda's tutor, "an able young Scotchman who acted as Sir Hugo Mallinger's secretary." *D. D.* xvi.

FRATE, THE. Common way of referring to Fra Girolamo. *See* SAVONAROLA, FRA GIROLAMO.

FRATI MINORI. *See* FRANCISCANS.

FRATI NERI (BLACK BRETHREN). *See* AUGUSTINIANS.

FRATI PREDICATORI. *See* DOMINICANS.

FRATI SERVITI. *See* SERVITES.

FRATI UMILIATI. *See* HUMBLED BRETHREN.

FREDIANO, SAN (PORTA). *See* PORTA SAN FREDIANO.

FREELY, ADMIRAL, K.C.B. A fictitious great-uncle of Edward Freely, whose portrait the latter hangs over the parlour mantelpiece in order to impress the Palfreys. *B. J.* ii, iii.

FREELY, MR. EDWARD. The name which David Faux assumes when he returns from the West Indies, opens a confectioner's shop in Grimworth, and courts Penny Palfrey. *B. J.* ii–iii.

FREEMAN'S END. A picturesque but sadly neglected farmhouse belonging to Mr. Brooke, and inhabited by the Dagleys. *Mid.* xxxix.

FREIBERG (*Real*). A town where Dorothea Brooke enjoyed hearing the famous organ, on her way home from Lausanne. *Mid.* vii.

Note.—Freiburg, or Fribourg, in Switzerland; the organ in the cathedral is one of the largest and finest in Europe.

FREKE. Clergyman. *Mid.* viii.

FRENCH, MRS. Sir Hugo Mallinger's housekeeper. *D. D.* xvi.

FRESHITT. Parish near Middlemarch, where Sir James Chettam lives. *Mid.* iv, vi, xxxiv, xl.

FRESHITT HALL. Home of Sir James Chettam. *Mid.* vi, ix, xxxii, xlix–l, liv–lvi, lxii, lxiv, lxxvii, lxxxiv.

"FREUDVOLL, LEIDVOLL, GEDANKENVOLL." One of Klesmer's own compositions, which he plays at the Arrowpoints'. *D. D.* v.

FRIAR'S GATE.[1] The "Focus of aristocracy" in Milby. *J. R.* ii.

FRICK. Hamlet in Lowick, where public opinion is against railways. *Mid.* lvi.

---

[1] *Note.*—This was Bond Gate, Nuneaton.

FRIPP, DAME. A dirty old woman to whom Mr. Gilfil was kind. *Mr. G.'s L. S.* i.

FUGLEMAN, MR. A critic whose recent remarks about the Iliad Mr. Hintze cites. *T. S.* v.

FULKE. A colonial governor. *Mid.* xlix.

FULLILOVE. Timber-merchant at Grimworth. *B. J.* ii.

FULLILOVE, MISS. The timber-merchant's daughter. *B. J.* ii.

FURLEY, MR. The man who holds the mortgage on Mr. Tulliver's land. *M. F.* Bk. 3, i, viii.

FURNESS, MR. Curate; "a tall young man, with blond hair and whiskers." *Amos B.* vi.
Note.—His prototype was the Rev. W. S. Bucknill, vicar of Burton-Hastings, near Nuneaton, 1844–73. (Manuscript notes.)

G

GABBADEO, MAESTRO. "As wise a doctor as sits at any door," to whom Bratti claims to have sold a ring to ward off pestilence. *Rom.* xiv.

GABRIEL. Angel, "the messenger of mildest death that draws the parting life." *P.—D.M.*

GADDI, FRANCESCO (*Hist.*). A Florentine who can speak French. *Rom.* xxvi–xxvii.

He is one of those present at the entry of the French king, Charles VIII, into Florence. When the rain interrupts Luca Corsini's Latin oration, Gaddi is asked to speak in French, but hangs back, and Tito Melema makes a speech in French in his place.
Note.—In reality Francesco Gaddi, an officer of the palace, made the speech in French, which, in the novel, is made by the fictitious character, Tito Melema.

GADSBY. One of Mr. Riley's acquaintances. *M. F.* Bk. 1, iii.

GADSBY, MRS. A yeomanry captain's wife, a former kitchen-maid, fond of hunting. *D. D.* vii.

GADSMERE. Grandcourt's place in a coal mining district where Mrs. Glasher and her children live for several years. In his will he leaves it to Gwendolen as her place of residence. *D. D.* xxv, xxviii–xxx, xxxvi, xliv, xlviii, lix, lxiv–lxv.

" Imagine a rambling, patchy house, the best part built of grey stone, and red-tiled, a round tower jutting at one of the corners, the mellow darkness of its conical roof surmounted by a weather-cock making an agreeable object either amidst the gleams and greenth of summer or the low-hanging clouds and snowy branches of winter; the ground shady with spreading trees: a great cedar flourishing on one side, backward some Scotch firs on a broken bank where the roots hung naked, and beyond, a rookery: on the other side a pool overhung with bushes, where the water-fowl fluttered and screamed: all around, a vast meadow which might be called a park, bordered by an old plantation and guarded by stone lodges which looked like little prisons. Outside the gate the country, once entirely rural and lovely, now black with coal-mines." Ch. xxx.

GAGGIO, SAN (CHURCH). *See* SAN GAGGIO, CHURCH OF.

GALLO, SAN (GATE OF). *See* PORTA SAN GALLO.

GAMBIT, DOCTOR. Medical man of a Benefit club in Middlemarch. *Mid.* xlv, lxxi.

GANYMEDE. An old-young writer, "once a girlishly handsome and precocious youth" who had produced a "Comparative estimate of European nations" before he was well out of his teens and continues to regard himself as wonderfully young when he is fat and middle-aged. *T. S.* xii.

GARBO (*Real*). A cloth-producing quarter of Florence. *Rom.* i, xxx. In chapter xxx this is mentioned as the Via del Garbo where Baldassarre Calvo buys a book.

Note.—Guido Biagi, in his edition of *Romola* points out that the Garbo was not properly a quarter, but merely a certain length of street, corresponding to that portion of the present Via della Condotta between the Via Calzaiuoli and the Piazzetta delle Farine. The woollen cloth manufactured in the Via del Garbo was a finer quality than that from San Martino, the other cloth-producing section. (*See Romola*, Biagi ed. vol. 1, p. 11.)

GARDNER, MARIA. A Milby girl who "had a lovely 'crop' of dark brown ringlets". *J. R.* v.

GARNETT. An acquaintance of Mr. Tulliver's. *M. F.* Bk. 1, vii.

GARRATT. Servant at Freshitt Hall. *Mid.* l.

GARSTIN, PETER. Mine owner; Whig candidate for North Loamshire. *F. H.* ii, vii, xi, xvi–xvii, xx, xxix–xxxi.

"Garstin was a harsh and wiry fellow; he seemed to suggest that sour whey, which some say was the original meaning of Whig in the Scottish." Ch. xvi.

GARTH, ALFRED. Mr. and Mrs. Garth's son who is destined to be an engineer. *Mid.* xxiv–xxv, xl.

GARTH, BEN. Mary's youngest brother; "an energetic young male with a heavy brow," who hates grammar. *Mid.* xxiv, xl, lvii, lxxxvi, Finale.

GARTH, CALEB. Land agent and builder; a man with a strong sense of honour and an enthusiastic interest in his work. *Mid.* xvii, xxiii–xxv, xxxv, xxxviii–xl, xlv, lii–lvii, lxii, lxvi, lxviii–lxix, lxxi, lxxxv–lxxxvi, Finale.

"A large amount of painful experience had not sufficed to make Cable Garth cautious about his own affairs, or distrustful of his fellow-men when they had not proved themselves untrustworthy. . . . He was one of those rare men who are rigid to themselves and indulgent to others. He had a certain shame about his neighbour's errors, and never spoke of them willingly." Ch. xxiii.

"His virtual divinities were good, practical schemes, accurate work, and the faithful completion of undertakings : his prince of darkness was a slack workman. . . . In fact, he had a reverential soul with a strong, practical intelligence. But he could not manage finance : he knew values well, but he had no keenness of imagination for monetary results in the shape of profit and loss : and having ascertained this to his cost, he determined to give up all forms of his beloved 'business' which required that talent. He . . . was one of those precious men within his own district whom everybody would choose to work for them, because he did his work well, charged very little, and often declined to charge at all. It is no wonder, then, that the Garths were poor, and 'lived in a small way'. However, they did not mind it." Ch. xxiv.

"With regard to a large number of matters about which other men are decided or obstinate, he was the most easily manageable man in the world. He never knew what meat he would choose ; and if Susan had said that they ought to live in a four-roomed cottage, in order to save, he would have said, ' Let us go,' without inquiring into details. But where Caleb's feeling and judgment strongly pronounced, he was a ruler ; and in spite of his mildness and timidity in reproving, every one about him knew that on the exceptional occasion, when he chose, he was absolute." Ch. lvi.

He had failed in the building business but had eventually paid his creditors in full. He has faith in Fred Vincy, and when Fred disappoints his own family by deciding not to enter the Church, he takes him into his office as his assistant, at the cost of additional work for himself, and gives him help that enables him to marry his daughter Mary. He accepts a good position from Mr. Bulstrode, but when he learns of Mr. Bulstrode's dishonest career, his uncompromising honesty forces him to give this up.

Note.—It is generally agreed that many of Caleb Garth's marked characteristics—his occupation as builder and land agent, his uncompromising uprightness, delight in his work, love of the soil, perhaps even his domestic submissiveness — were drawn from Robert Evans, George Eliot's father, although the character is not an exact portrait of the original. (*See* Cooke, *George Eliot*, pp. 4–5 ; Cross, *George Eliot's Life*, vol. 1, p. 2 ; Dictionary of National Biography, article *Cross, Mary Ann*.)

GARTH, CHRISTY. Eldest son of Mr. and Mrs. Garth, who has taken to books instead of business. *Mid.* xl, lvii.

"Christy, who held it the most desirable thing in the world to be a tutor, to study all literatures and be a regenerate Porson . . . a square-browed, broad-shouldered masculine edition of his mother . . . was always as simple as possible." Ch. lvii.

GARTH, JIM. Young son of Mr. and Mrs. Garth. *Mid.* xl, lvii.

GARTH, LETTY. Mary's little sister. *Mid.* xxiv, xl, lvii, lxxxvi–Finale.

GARTH, MARY. Elder daughter of Mr. and Mrs. Garth; an attractive girl with plain features, a clever tongue, a sense of humour, and a warm heart. *Mid.* xi–xii, xiv, xvii, xxii–xxv, xxxi–xxxiii, xxxv–xxxvi, xl, lii, lvi–lvii, lix, lxiii, lxvi, lxxxvi–Finale.

"Mary Garth . . . had the aspect of an ordinary sinner: she was brown; her curly dark hair was rough and stubborn; her stature was low: and it would not be true to declare in satisfactory antithesis, that she had all the virtues . . . Advancing womanhood had tempered her plainness, which was of a good human sort, such as the mothers of our race have very commonly worn in all latitudes under a more or less becoming headgear. Rembrandt would have painted her with pleasure, and would have made her broad features look out of the canvas with intelligent honesty. For honesty, truth-telling fairness, was Mary's reigning virtue: she neither tried to create illusions, nor indulged in them for her own behoof, and when she was in a good mood she had humour enough in her to laugh at herself." Ch. xii.

"She has a broad face and square brow, well-marked eyebrows and curly dark hair, a certain expression of amusement in her glance which her mouth keeps the secret of, and for the rest, features entirely insignificant. . . . If you made her smile, she would show you perfect little teeth; if you made her angry, she would not raise her voice, but would probably say one of the bitterest things you have ever tested the flavour of; if you did her a kindness, she would never forget it." Ch. xl.

As children, she and Fred Vincy had been sweethearts, and no one else ever replaces him in her affections, although she shows much scorn for his imperfections, and steadily opposes his plan of taking orders, for which she thinks he is not suited. While she has great admiration for Mr. Farebrother, who is in love with her, she remains faithful to Fred and marries him after saying, "I should never like scolding any one else so well, and that is a point to be thought of in a husband."

GARTH, MRS. SUSAN. Caleb's wife; a good, unworldly woman with much force and some oddities of character. *Mid.* xvii, xxiii–xxv, xl, lii, lvi–lvii, lxviii, lxxxvi–Finale.

"Mrs. Garth never committed herself by over-hasty speech; having, as she said, borne the yoke in her youth, and learned self-control. She had that rare sense which discerns what is unalterable, and submits to it without murmuring. Adoring her husband's virtues, she had very early made up her mind to his incapacity of minding his own interests, and had met the consequences cheerfully. She had been magnanimous enough to renounce all pride in tea-pots or children's frilling. . . . She had sometimes taken pupils in a peripatetic fashion, making them follow her about in the kitchen with their book or slate." Ch. xxiv.

Devoted entirely to her family, she is anxious to have her husband's good qualities and solid work appreciated at their full value and to give the children as good an education as possible, training them herself while they are small, and scheming and planning for their further education. Although she has always regarded Fred Vincy with a motherly feeling, she is disappointed when her daughter Mary accepts him as a husband when she might have married Mr. Farebrother.

GARUM. The rich parish in which Mr. and Mrs. Pullet reside. *M. F.* Bk. 1, xi.

GARUM FIRS. The farm belonging to Mr. and Mrs. Pullet, where Tom and Maggie Tulliver and Lucy Deane visit, and where Maggie pushes Lucy into the pond. *M. F.* Bk. 1, viii–x ; Bk. 6, xii.

"All the farmyard life was wonderful there — bantams, speckled and top-knotted ; Friesland hens, with their feathers all turned the wrong way ; guineafowls that flew and screamed and dropped their pretty-spotted feathers ; pouter-pigeons and a tame magpie ; nay, a goat, and a wonderful brindled dog, half mastiff, half bull-dog, as large as a lion. Then there were white railings and white gates all about, and glittering weathercocks of various design, and garden-walks paved with pebbles in beautiful patterns—nothing was quite common at Garum Firs : and Tom thought that the unusual size of the toads there was simply due to the general unusualness which characterized uncle Pullet's possessions as a gentleman farmer. Toads who paid rent were naturally leaner. As for the house, it was not less remarkable : it had a receding centre, and two wings with battlemented turrets, and was covered with glittering white stucco." Bk. 1, ix.

GASCOIGNE, ANNA. The rector's elder daughter, " whose shy face was a tiny copy of his own." *D. D.* iii, v–viii, x–xi, xiv, xxiv, xxviii, xxxi, xliv, xlviii, lii, lviii, lxix.

She is devoted to her brother Rex, becomes attached to her beautiful cousin Gwendolen Harleth, and is very unhappy when Rex falls in love with Gwendolen and is refused.

GASCOIGNE, EDWY. A younger son of the rector's. *D. D.* iii, xxiv.

GASCOIGNE, MR. HENRY. Rector of Pennicote ; Mrs. Davilow's brother-in-law, a kindly, cheerful, and somewhat worldly man, who had once been in the army. *D. D.* ii–xi, xiii–xv, xxi, xxiv, xxvi, xxviii, xxxi, xliv, xlviii, lv, lviii–lix, lxiv, lxix.

" He had some agreeable virtues, some striking advantages, and the failings that were imputed to him all leaned toward the side of success.

"One of his advantages was a fine person, which perhaps was even more impressive at fifty-seven than it had been earlier in life. There were no distinctively clerical lines in the face, no official reserve or ostentatious benignity of expression, no tricks of starchiness or of affected ease. . . . He had a native gift for administration, being tolerant both of opinions and conduct, because he felt himself able to overrule them, and was free from the irritations of conscious feebleness . . . No clerical magistrate had greater weight at sessions, or less of mischievous impracticableness in relation to worldly affairs. Indeed, the worst imputation thrown out against him was worldliness: it could not be proved that he forsook the less fortunate, but it was not to be denied that the friendships he cultivated were of a kind likely to be useful to the father of six sons and two daughters." Ch. iii.

Proud of her beauty and charm, he is greatly interested in having his wife's niece, Gwendolen Harleth, make a suitable marriage. Notwithstanding his worldliness he meets financial losses with his usual cheerfulness and proceeds to make the necessary adjustments with great spirit.

GASCOIGNE, LOTTA. The rector's little daughter. *D. D.* iii, lii.

GASCOIGNE, MRS. NANCY. The rector's devoted wife; Mrs. Davilow's sister. *D. D.* ii–iv, vi–xi, xiv, xxi, xxiv, xxviii, xliv, lviii.

" Mrs. Gascoigne bore a family likeness to her sister. But she was darker and slighter, her face was unworn by grief, her movements were less languid, her expression more alert and critical as that of a rector's wife bound to exert a beneficent authority. Their closest resemblance lay in a non-resistant disposition, inclined to imitation and obedience . . . [she] believed herself the most enviable of wives, and her pliancy had ended in her sometimes taking shapes of surprising definiteness." Ch. iii.

GASCOIGNE, REX. Eldest son of Mr. and Mrs. Gascoigne; the pride of the family. *D. D.* iii, vi–viii, xxiv, xxxvii, xliv, xlviii, lii, lviii, lxix.

" He was a fine open-hearted youth, with a handsome face strongly resembling his father's and Anna's, but softer in expression than the one, and larger in scale than the other: a bright, healthy, loving nature, enjoying ordinary, innocent things so much that vice had no temptation for him, and what he knew of it lay too entirely in the outer courts and little-visited chambers of his mind for him to think of it with great repulsion. Vicious habits were with him 'what some fellows did'—'stupid stuff' which he liked to keep aloof from." Ch. vi.

While still a young student at Oxford he falls deeply in love with his cousin, Gwendolen Harleth, who rejects him, and he is long in recovering from the effects of his unsuccessful love affair. When financial reverses overtake his family he meets misfortune manfully, and makes every effort to help them. As he has never lost his fondness for Gwendolen, he is profoundly moved by the news of her husband's death.

GASCOIGNE, WARHAM. The rector's son, who goes to India. *D. D.* iii, vi, lviii.

GASKIN, CAPTAIN. Mr. Gascoigne's name before he took orders and changed it to Gascoigne. *D. D.* iii.

GATE, MRS. An aristocratic matron of Grimworth, who has high connexions frequently visiting her. *B. J.* ii.

GAWAINE. Arthur Donnithorne's friend at Norburne. *Adam B.* xii, xvi, xxv-xxvi.

GAWCOME. One of the lessees of the collieries near Gadsmere. *D. D.* xxx.

GEDGE, MR. Landlord of the "Royal Oak", at Shepperton. *Adam B.* xvii.

GELL. A young man who is taken into the firm of Guest & Co. *M. F.* Bk. 6, v.

GENEVA (*Real*). The city where Latimer completes his education, where he knows Charles Meunier and where he has the severe illness which gives him the power of clairvoyance. *L. V.* i.

Note.—The Swiss city of Geneva, on Lake Geneva, is a noted educational centre containing many private schools patronized by foreigners.

GENOA (*Real*). City in Italy, where Daniel Deronda meets his mother, and where Mr. and Mrs. Grandcourt are staying when Grandcourt is drowned. *D. D.* l-li, liii-lvii, lix, lxiv. In *Romola*, Baldassarre Calvo is taken to Genoa, when a Genoese merchant rescues him from slavery at Corinth, and in Genoa he sees the man who has bought Tito Melema's onyx ring. *Rom.* xxx.

"GENTLEMAN'S MAGAZINE" (*Real*). *Mid.* xii; *Mr. G.'s L. S.* ii.

Note.—The *Gentleman's Magazine*, London, founded 1731.

GERMAN COZEN, MR. See COZEN, MR. GERMAN.

GHERARDESCA, CASA. See SCALA PALACE.

GHIRLANDAJO, DOMENICO (*Hist.*). A great painter who "was making the walls of the churches reflect the life of Florence." *Rom.* i, xxv.

Note.—Domenico Curradi Ghirlandajo (1449-1494), a Florentine artist who was trained as a goldsmith but later became a painter. He painted principally frescoes in Florence.

GHITA, MONNA. Tessa's mother, a peasant woman who sells

vegetables in the Mercato Vecchio. *Rom.* ii, x, xiv, xvi.

"She was a stout but brawny woman, with a man's jerkin slipped over her green serge gamurra or gown, and the peaked hood of some departed mantle fastened round her sun-burnt face, which, under all its coarseness and premature wrinkles, showed a half-sad, half-ludicrous maternal resemblance to the tender baby-face of the little maiden." Ch. ii.

GIANNETTA. Little mule belonging to Tessa. *Rom.* xxxiii.

GIANNI. Former owner of the little boat in which Romola puts to sea. *Rom.* lxi.

GIBBS. Servant. *D. D.* liv.

GIBBS, MISS JANET. Mrs. Patten's niece, "a single lady of fifty, who has refused the most ineligible offers out of devotion to her aged aunt." *Amos. B.* i, vi. *Note.*—Nuneaton lists give her prototype variously as Miss Ibbetson, or Mrs. George Morris. (Manuscript notes.)

GIBBS, JOHN. Wagoner. *M. F.* Bk. 1, v.

GIBSON. A schoolmate of Tom Tulliver's. *M. F.* Bk. i, v.

GIDEON. Optical instrument-maker, member of the Philosophers' Club, and Mordecai's opponent in argument; a Jew who is neither ashamed nor proud of his race. *D. D.* xlii.

GILES. An unsuccessful candidate for Parliament, who "spent ten thousand pounds and failed because he did not bribe enough." *Mid.* xxxviii.

GILFIL, REV. MAYNARD. Sir Christopher Cheverel's ward and chaplain, later vicar of Shepperton and Knebley; a man greatly beloved by his parishioners. *Mr. G.'s L. S.* i–ii, iv–xxi, Epilogue; mentioned *Amos B.* i.

"The Vicar did not shine in the more spiritual functions of his office; and indeed, the utmost I can say for him in this respect is, that he performed those functions with undeviating attention to brevity and despatch. He had a large heap of short sermons, rather yellow and worn at the edges, from which he took two every Sunday, securing perfect impartiality in the selection by taking them as they came without reference to topics; and having preached one of these sermons at Shepperton in the morning, he mounted his horse and rode hastily with the other in his pocket to Knebley, where he officiated in a wonderful little church. . . . Here, in an absence of mind to which he was prone, Mr. Gilfil would sometimes forget to take off his spurs before putting on his surplice, and only become aware of the omission by feeling something mysteriously tugging at the skirts of that garment as he stepped into the reading-desk." Ch. i.

"The dear old Vicar, though he had something of the knotted whimsical character of the poor lopped oak, had yet been sketched out by nature as a noble tree. The heart of him was sound, the grain was of the finest, and in the grey-haired man who filled his pocket with sugar-plums for the little children, whose most biting words were directed against the evil-doing of the rich man, and who, with all his social pipes and slipshod talk, never sank below the highest level of his parishioners' respect, there was the main trunk of the same brave, faithful, tender nature that had poured out the finest, freshest forces of its life-current in a first and only love—the love of Tina." Epilogue.

All through his youth he loves the little Italian, Caterina, and tries to watch over her during her unhappy love affair with the worthless Captain Wybrow. After she partially recovers from the shock of Captain Wybrow's death he marries her, and has a few months of great happiness as her husband. When she dies, that side of his life is closed for ever, and he lives a solitary life among his parishioners, all of whom admire and respect him greatly.

Note.—The Reverend Bernard Gilpin Ebdell, who married Sally Shilton ("Caterina"), was the original of Maynard Gilfil. It has been suggested that some touches in his character are taken from the Reverend Henry Hake, vicar of Chilvers Coton from 1844–1859. (*See* Andrews, *Bygone Warwickshire*, p. 271; Olcott, *George Eliot*, pp. 15, 33; also article by George Morley in *Gentleman's Magazine*, n.s., vol. 45, p. 583.)

Bernard Gilpin Ebdell, vicar of Chilvers Coton, was the clergyman who, in 1819, baptized Mary Ann Evans. He was vicar 1786–1828.

GILFIL, MRS. MAYNARD. *See* SARTI, CATERINA.

GILLS. Stone-cutter in Sproxton, "a wide-mouthed, wiry man." *F. H.* xi.

GILSBROOK. Place where David Faux's family live. *B. J.* ii–iii.

GIORGIO, SAN (HILL). *See* SAN GIORGIO, HILL OF.

GIOVANNI, SAN (PIAZZA). *See* SAN GIOVANNI, PIAZZA DI.

GIRDLE, MRS. Wife of the miller at Pennicote. *D. D.* xxxi.

GIROLAMO, FRA. *See* SAVONAROLA, FRA GIROLAMO.

GIULIANO, FRA (*Hist.*). A Franciscan monk who was to pair with Fra Domenico in the Trial by Fire. *Rom.* lxv.
Note.—Fra Giuliano Rondinelli.

GIUSEPPE. A maker of violins, held by some people to be as good as Stradivarius. *P.*—*Strad.*

GLASGOW (*Real*). Place where Felix Holt had studied and where, for a while, he lived a wild life. *F. H.* iv–v, xiii.
Note.—Glasgow is the seat of the important University of Glasgow, founded 1451.

GLASHER, COLONEL. Lydia's husband whom she forsook for Mr. Grandcourt. *D. D.* xiv.

GLASHER, ANTONIA, AND JOSEPHINE. Two of the pretty little daughters of Mrs. Glasher and Grandcourt. *D. D.* xxx.

"The three little girls ... dark-eyed, delicate-featured brunettes with a rich bloom on their cheeks, their little nostrils and eyebrows singularly finished as if they were tiny women."

GLASHER, HENLEIGH. The handsome little son of Mrs. Glasher and Grandcourt, who becomes his father's heir, and is to take his name, when Grandcourt dies. *D. D.* xiii–xiv, xxx, xlviii, lix.

GLASHER, LYDIA. The beautiful woman, who, nine years before the opening of the story, left her husband and child for Grandcourt. *D. D.* xiii–xiv, xxv, xxvii–xxviii, xxx–xxxi, xxxvi, xlviii, lix.

"An impressive woman, whom many would turn to look at again in passing; her figure was slim and sufficiently tall, her face rather emaciated, so that its sculpturesque beauty was the more pronounced, her crisp hair perfectly black, and her large, anxious eyes also what we call black. Her dress was soberly correct, her age perhaps physically more advanced than the number of years would imply, but hardly less than seven-and-thirty. An uneasy-looking woman." Ch. xiii.

For years after their elopement, Grandcourt remained much attached to her, though his passion eventually burned itself out. Embittered by Grandcourt's failure to marry her, she centres all her feeling on an anxious love for her four children and an intense desire that Grandcourt shall marry her for their sake.

When she learns from Mr. Lusk that Grandcourt is courting Gwendolen Harleth, she arranges a meeting with Gwendolen, tells her story, and obtains Gwendolen's promise not to marry Grandcourt. When she learns that in spite of this promise Gwendolen has accepted Grandcourt, she determines to do as much as she can, without harming her children's prospects, to spoil any satisfaction that Gwendolen may feel in the marriage, and on the wedding day sends to her Grandcourt's family diamonds with a bitter note which throws the bride into hysterics.

GLEGG, MR. A retired wool-stapler, a kind, stingy, white-haired old gentleman. *M. F.* Bk. 1, vii, xii; Bk. 2, ii; Bk. 3, ii–viii; Bk. 5, ii, vi; Bk. 6, xii; Bk. 7, iii.

"Mr. Glegg, having retired from active business as a wool-stapler, for the purpose of enjoying himself through the rest of his life, had found this last occupation so much more severe than his business, that he had been driven into amateur hard labour as a dissipation, and habitually relaxed by doing the work of two ordinary gardeners ... Now good Mr. Glegg himself was stingy in the most amiable manner : his neighbours called him "near", which always means that the person in question is a lovable skinflint. If you expressed a preference for cheese-parings, Mr. Glegg would remember to save them for you, with a good-natured delight in gratifying your palate, and he was given to pet all animals which required no appreciable keep. There was no humbug or hypocrisy about Mr. Glegg." Bk. 1, xii.

In his good-humoured way he feels a sincere pity for the Tulliver family, and eventually he lends Tom Tulliver a little money to trade with.

GLEGG, MRS. JANE. Mrs. Tulliver's oldest sister; a handsome, thrifty, ill-tempered woman, the embodiment of the Dodson spirit. *M. F.* Bk. 1, ii, iv, vi–vii, ix, xii–xiii; Bk. 3, iii, vii–viii; Bk. 5, ii, v; Bk. 6, iv, xii–xiii; Bk. 7, ii–iv.

"The Dodsons were certainly a handsome family, and Mrs. Glegg was not the least handsome of the sisters. . . . no impartial observer could have denied that for a woman of fifty she had a very comely face and figure, though Tom and Maggie considered their aunt Glegg as the type of ugliness. It is true she despised the advantages of costume, for though, as she often observed, no woman had better clothes, it was not her way to wear her new things out before her old ones. Other women, if they liked, might have their best thread-lace in every wash, but when Mrs. Glegg died it would be found that she had better lace laid by in the right-hand drawer of her wardrobe, in the Spotted Chamber, than ever Mrs. Wooll of St. Ogg's had bought in her life, although Mrs. Wooll wore her lace before it was paid for. So of her curled fronts: Mrs. Glegg had doubtless the glossiest and crispest brown curls in her drawers, as well as curls in various degrees of fuzzy laxness; but to look out on the week-day world from under a crisp and glossy front would be to introduce a most dreamlike and unpleasant confusion between the sacred and the secular. Occasionally, indeed, Mrs. Glegg wore one of her third-best fronts on a week-day visit, but not at a sister's house." Bk. 1, vii.

She and her brother-in-law, Mr. Tulliver, frequently disagree, and she is disliked by the Tulliver children because of her disagreeable temper and domineering ways. Her sense of family loyalty, however, as well as her desire for gain, leads her to help Tom Tulliver when he is trying to make money in trade to pay his father's debts, and she surprises everyone by offering Maggie Tulliver a home after Maggie returns from her flight with Stephen Guest.

Note.—Mrs. Everard, George Eliot's aunt (her mother's sister), one of the Pearson sisters, was the original of Aunt Glegg. Her portrait, corresponding fairly closely to the quoted description, is in the possession of the Reverend Frederic Rawlins Evans, George Eliot's nephew, and a reproduction of this is given in Olcott, *George Eliot*, p. 94. *See also* note and references under Dodsons.

GOBY, MR. The "whittaw", or saddler, from Treddleston. *Adam B.* vi.

GOBY, MRS. A patient that Dr. Lydgate "had wanted to cut up". *Mid.* xlv.

"GOD REST YOU, MERRY GENTLEMEN" (*Real*). A "Christmas carril" which little Aaron Winthrop sings. *S. M.* x.
Note.—The most popular of Christmas carols, author unknown.

GODWIN. The doctor who looks after Arthur Donnithorne's broken arm. *Adam B.* v.

GOFFE, MR. An unsuccessful farmer, tenant at Rabbit's End, who held that one thing was as mauling as another, and that an election was no worse than the sheeprot. *F. H.* viii, xxxi.

GOGOFF, MR. AND MRS. Guests of Grandcourt. *D. D.* xii.

"GOLDEN KEYS." Hotel in Wanchester. *D. D.* xxii.

"GOLDEN LION." Inn at St. Ogg's, where Mr. Tulliver meets and pays his creditors. *M. F.* Bk. 3, iii, vi–vii; Bk. 5, vi.

GOLLO. Husband of Tessa's cousin, Nannina. *Rom.* xiv.

"GONDOLIER'S SONG." See "OTELLO, GONDOLIER'S SONG FROM."

GONFALONIERE. See SIGNORIA.

GOOD MEN OF ST. MARTIN (BUONOMINI DI SAN MARTINO) (*Hist.*). A society which aided poor people of good family in Florence. *Rom.* v, xii.

Note.—Founded in the first half of the 15th century by Saint Antonine, Prior of San Marco.

GOODRICH, MR. Drawing-master at Mr. Stelling's. *M. F.* Bk. 2, iv.

GOODWIN. Member of the Philosophers' Club; a wood-inlayer, "well-built, open-faced, pleasant-voiced." *D. D.* xlii.

"GOODWIN SANDS OPINION." A journal which published a review of Vorticella's "Channel Islands". *T. S.* xv.

GORE, MR. Mr. Tulliver's attorney, who, as Mr. Tulliver fears, is no match for Lawyer Wakem. *M. F.* Bk. 2, ii; Bk. 3, i, iii, vii–viii.
"Lawyer Gore . . . was a bald, round-featured man, with bland manners and fat hands; a gamecock that you would be rash to bet upon against Wakem. Gore was a sly fellow; his weakness did not lie on the side of scrupulosity: but the largest amount of winking, however significant, is not equivalent to seeing through a stone wall." Bk. 2, ii.

GORO. A large man with a fat cheek and glassy eye who joins in the popular talk in the market and streets whenever there is any excitement. *Rom.* i, xxii, lxiii.

GÖTTINGEN (*Real*). One of the places where Mordecai Cohen had studied. *D. D.* xl.
Note.—A university town in Hanover, Germany.

GOTTLIB, MR. A banker who had a run on his bank in 1816. *F. H.* xx.

GOWER STREET (*Real*). The street in London where Mr. Tryan found Lucy lying dead. *J. R.* xviii.

Note.—A street in the Bloomsbury section of London running north from Bedford Square.

"GRACEFUL CONSORT" (*Real*). A song from "The Creation" which Lucy Deane and Stephen Guest sing. *M. F.* Bk. 6, i.

Note.—"Graceful consort at thy side," a duet from "The Creation" by Haydn (1732–1809).

GRAHN, DOCTOR. Armgart's physician, who cures the singer of her sharp illness, but does not save her voice. *P.*—*Armg.* iii–iv.

GRAINGER. A sick man whom treatment reduced to a skeleton. *Mid.* x.

"GRAMPIAN HEIGHTS AND THEIR CLIMBERS, *or*, THE NEW EXCELSIOR." One of many articles written against Proteus Merman by supporters of Grampus. *T. S.* iii.

GRAMPUS. A colonial governor. *Mid.* xlix.

GRAMPUS, GREENLAND. A great authority, author of an epoch-making book, whose theory about the Magicodumbras and the Zuzumotzis Proteus Merman discovers to be wrong. *T. S.* iii.

GRANBY, MR. *Amos B.* vi.

GRANDCOURT, MISS. Maiden name of Grandcourt's mother; an heiress whose husband took her name. *D. D.* xvi.

GRANDCOURT, GWENDOLEN. See HARLETH, GWENDOLEN.

GRANDCOURT, HENLEIGH MALLINGER. Sir Hugo Mallinger's younger brother who married Miss Grandcourt and took her name along with her estates. *D. D.* xvi.

GRANDCOURT, MR. HENLEIGH MALLINGER. Sir Hugo Mallinger's nephew and presumptive heir; a cold, selfish, immovable man, who has worn out all gratifications except that of bending others to his will. *D. D.* ix–xv, xxv–xxxii, xxxv–xxxvi, xliv–xlv, xlviii, lii, liv–lvi, lix.

"Grandcourt could hardly have been more unlike all her imaginary portraits of him. He was slightly taller than herself, and their eyes seemed to be on a level; there was not the faintest smile on his face as he looked at her, not a trace of self-consciousness or anxiety in his bearing; when he raised his hat he showed an extensive baldness surrounded with a mere fringe of reddish-blond hair, but he also showed a perfect hand; the line of feature from brow to chin undisguised by beard was decidedly handsome, with only moderate departures from the perpendicular, and the slight whisker, too, was perpendicular. It was not possible for a human aspect to be freer from grimace or solicitous wrigglings; also it was perhaps not possible for a breathing man wide awake to look less animated. . . . His complexion had a faded fairness resembling that of an actress when bare of the artificial white and red; his long narrow grey eyes expressed nothing but indifference." Ch. xi.

Although possessed of large estates, he has spent so freely on his pleasures that he feels some need of ready money. Some years before, he had run away with the beautiful and dashing Mrs. Glasher and his passion for her had been the strongest of which he was capable, although it had not induced him to marry her when her husband's death finally left her free. He comes to Diplow with some idea of courting the rich Miss Arrowpoint, but is attracted by Gwendolen Harleth's beauty and independence, and, led on by the fact that she holds him off and even goes away to escape his attentions, makes up his mind to marry her. For a while he feels as much liking for her as his worn-out nature permits, but her attitude toward Deronda, innocent though it is, arouses his jealousy and he determines to break her spirit and bend her to his idea of what his wife should be, heedless of the hatred which this arouses in her. He is drowned in the Mediterranean, on a boating trip which he had forced her into taking, and leaves a will which gives his estates to his illegitimate son by Mrs. Glasher and a mere pittance to Gwendolen.

GRANGE. *See* TIPTON GRANGE.

GRANT, BERTHA. A slim, fair-haired sylph, beautiful, cold, and entirely selfish, who becomes Latimer's wife. *L. V.* i–iii.

"She was keen, sarcastic, unimaginative, prematurely cynical, remaining critical and unmoved in the most impressive scenes." Ch. i.

She becomes engaged to Latimer's elder brother, the popular, worldly Alfred. When Latimer becomes the heir, after Alfred's sudden death, she marries him for his wealth without feeling any affection for him. Because he does not give her the kind of social success she craves, her indifference turns to hate and she plans to poison him, but her dying maid reveals her plans.

GRAPNELL & Co. The firm whose failure swallows up all of Mrs. Davilow's money. *D. D.* ii, xv.

GRATTAN. A lad who shot his mother by accident, and who is befriended by Dr. Kenn. *M. F.* Bk. 6, ii.

GRAVES, MISS. Teacher. *D. D.* xxi.

GRAY, MRS. Mrs. Pullet's milliner. *M. F.* Bk. 1, ix.

GREAT COUNCIL (*Hist.*). The "Council after the Venetian mode" favoured by Savonarola, which was adopted as the new form of government in Florence at the end of 1494. *Rom.* xxxii, xxxv–xxxvi, xxxix, xlv, lii, lviii–lix.

Note.—The Great Council (Consiglio Maggiore) had power to create all the chief magistrates and approve all laws. All citizens were eligible who had attained the age of 29, had paid their taxes, and were *beneficiati*. Whenever this number of *beneficiati* exceeded 1,500 the number was divided into thirds, each third serving six months. As the total number at the first Great Council was 3,200, about 1,000 sat at a time.

GRECI, BORGO DE'. *See* BORGO DE' GRECI.

GRECO, MESSER. Name by which Tito Melema is frequently addressed. *See* MELEMA, TITO.

GREEN, THE. *See* HAYSLOPE GREEN.

GREEN ARBOUR. The spot in Cardell Chase where the Archery Club meets for a roving archery match. *D. D.* xiv.

"GREEN DRAGON." Public-house in Middlemarch where there was a billiard room, "which some anxious mothers and wives regarded as the chief temptation in Middlemarch." *Mid.* xviii, xxiii, li, lviii, lxvi, lxx–lxxi.

"GREEN MAN." Inn at Windsor where Hetty Sorrel stops on her journey to find Arthur Donnithorne. *Adam B.* xxxvi–xxxvii.

It is from the landlord and landlady of the "Green Man" that Hetty Sorrel learns that Arthur Donnithorne is no longer at Windsor.

"GREEN MAN." Public-house at Brassing. *Mid.* xxxii.

"GREEN MAN." Public-house in Milby. *J. R.* iv.

"GREENLAND GRAMPUS AND PROTEUS MERMAN." One of the articles written on the Merman-Grampus controversy. *T. S.* iii.

GREGARINA. A lady "whose distinction was that she had had cholera and who did not feel herself in her true position with strangers until they knew it." *T. S.* xv.

GRETCHEN. Armgart's maid. *P.— Armg.*

GRETCHEN'S SONGS IN FAUST (*Real*). Songs, with Prince Radzivill's music, which Mirah Cohen sings to Klesmer when he is trying her voice. *D. D.* xxxix.

Note.—Anton Heinrich, Prince of Radziwill (1775–1833), a player, singer, and composer whose best known work was his *Compositions to Goethe's Dramatic Poem of Faust.*

GRIFFIN. The Asshers' maid. *Mr. G.'s L. S.* v, vii, xvi.

GRIFFIN, AND WIFE. Parishioners of Mr. Tyke's. *Mid.* xvii.

GRIMWORTH. The town where David Faux settles as Edward Freely and opens his confectioner's shop. *B. J.* ii–iii.

GRINSELL, LORD. An acquaintance of the Dowager Lady Chettam. *Mid.* lv.

GRIPP & Co. Publishers in Middlemarch who print the book which Mary Garth writes for her children. *Mid.* Finale.

GROSVENOR PLACE (*Real*). Street in London where the Klesmers live. *D. D.* xlviii.

Note.—Grosvenor Place, a fine residence street just west of Buckingham Palace Gardens.

GROSVENOR SQUARE (*Real*). The square in London where the

Grandcourts live. *D. D.* xliv–xlv, xlviii, lviii, lxiv.
  Note.—One of the most fashionable and aristocratic squares in London, a little east of Hyde Park.

GROVE. *See* FIR-TREE GROVE.

GROWLER. The Poyser's bull-dog. *Adam B.* vi, viii, xviii, xx, xxii, xxxii, xlix.

GRUBY, MR. Grocer in Milby. *J. R.* i–ii.[1]

GUALFONDA, VIA (*Real*). Street in Florence where the artist Piero di Cosimo lives. *Rom.* xviii, xxviii.
  Note.—The Via Gualfonda (now spelled Valfonda) extends from the Piazza della Stazione to the Viale Filippo Strozzi. George Eliot follows the authority of Bottari's footnote to Vasari in locating Piero di Cosimo's dwelling there, but Guido Biagi points out that that is an error, as Piero di Cosimo lived, according to his own declaration in the Rent Rolls of 1498, in the Via della Scala. (*See* Biagi ed. of *Romola*, vol. i, p. 237.)

"GUARDIAN" (*Real*). A paper read by Mr. Gascoigne's family. *D. D.* vii.
  Note.—The *Guardian*, London, first published 1846.

GUARINO (*Hist.*). An Italian scholar who brought back manuscripts from Greece. *Rom.* iv, vi.
  Note.—Guarino da Verona (1370–1460), Italian philologist and teacher, at one time professor of rhetoric in Florence. He brought back many manuscripts from Greece, and grief over the loss of some of these at sea is said to have turned his hair white before he landed.

GUCCIO. One of the populace in the Mercato Vecchio when the news of the death of Lorenzo de' Medici is discussed. *Rom.* i, xxii.

GUEST, MISS, AND MISS LAURA. Stephen Guest's sisters, who "associated chiefly on terms of condescension with the families of St. Ogg's, and were the glass of fashion there". *M. F.* Bk. 6, i–ii, vi, ix–x; Bk. 7, iv.

GUEST, MR. Stephen's father; senior member of the firm of Guest and Co. *M. F.* Bk. 6, i–ii, v.

GUEST, STEPHEN. Lucy Deane's handsome, idle lover. *M. F.* Bk. 3, v; Bk. 6, i–iii, vi–vii, ix–xi, xiii–xiv; Bk. 7, ii, v.

"The fine young man who is leaning down from his chair to snap the scissors in the extremely abbreviated face of the King Charles lying on the young lady's feet is no other than Mr. Stephen Guest, whose diamond ring, attar of roses, and air of nonchalant leisure, at twelve o'clock in the day, are the graceful and odoriferous result of the largest oil-mill and the most extensive wharf in St. Ogg's . . . a rather striking young man of five-and-twenty, with a square forehead, short dark-brown hair standing erect, with a slight wave at the end, like a thick crop of corn, and a half-ardent, half sarcastic

---

[1] His prototype was a Mr. Barnacle. (Manuscript information.)

glance from under his well-marked horizontal eyebrows." Bk. 6, i.
Although he and Lucy Deane are tacitly engaged, he falls passionately in love with Maggie Tulliver, and, after a brief struggle, yields to this passion. He prevails on Maggie to leave St. Ogg's with him and is keenly disappointed when she decides not to marry him but to return to her family. Years later he and Lucy come together again and are married.

GUEST & Co. A prosperous firm in St. Ogg's, owning ships and mills, with a banking concern attached. *M. F.* Bk. 1, vii ; Bk. 3, v, vii–viii ; Bk. 6, v.

Lucy Deane's father is a member of the firm, and Tom Tulliver is employed there after his father's failure.

GUICCIARDINI, PIERO (*Hist.*). A keen Florentine, a member of the Signoria, who is strongly opposed to the sentence of death passed on Bernardo del Nero and the other Mediceans. *Rom.* lviii, lxxi.

Note.—Piero Guicciardini (1454–1513), who was a member of the Signoria in 1484, 1489, 1497, and 1513.

GUICCIARDINI, VIA (*Real*). Street in the Oltrarno quarter of Florence, near one corner of which Tito Melema is first seen by Fra Luca. *Rom.* x.

Note.—This street, which leads south from the Ponte Vecchio, is named from the houses of the Guicciardini families there. At an earlier date it was called the Borgo di Piazza.

GUILDENSTERN. *P.—C. B. P.*

" GUN STREET CHAPEL." An Independent chapel. *Amos B.* ii.

Note.—This may be a reference to some real chapel in Gun Street, Manchester, though no such building is there now. In the original manuscript of the story the chapel is called " Bullock Lane Chapel ".

GUNNS, THE MISS. Wine-merchant's daughters ; fashionable young ladies, " rather hard-featured than otherwise." *S. M.* xi, xiii.

GYP. Adam Bede's sheep-dog. *Adam B.* i–ii, iv, x–xi, xxvii, xxx, xxxv, xxxviii, li.

GYPSIES. A band of Gypsies, encamped on Dunlow Common ; Maggie Tulliver, unhappy and jealous of her cousin, Lucy Deane, runs away to join them and impress them with her superior knowledge. *M. F.* Bk. 1, xi.

Note.—Maggie's adventure with the Gypsies is one of the incidents in *Mill on the Floss*, which are partly autobiographic. George Eliot, in her childhood, had an experience with a band of Gypsies, though the details of her adventure may not have agreed with Maggie's. (*See* Deakin, *Early Life of George Eliot*, p. 18.) The Gypsies are mentioned also in the autobiographic poem, *Brother and Sister*.

GYPSIES, SPANISH. *See* ZINCALI.

" GYPSY." Mr. Dempster's pet name for Janet. *See* Dempster, Janet.

H

HACKBUTT, MR. A rich tanner of fluent speech, a leading citizen of Middlemarch. *Mid.* xviii, xxxvii, xlv, lx, lxiv, lxxi.

HACKBUTT, MRS. The tanner's wife, who thinks that Mrs. Bulstrode should part from her husband. *Mid.* lxxiv.

HACKBUTT, FANNY. One of Mrs. Garth's pupils. *Mid.* xxiv.

HACKIT, MR. Churchwarden at Shepperton; a farmer, "a shrewd substantial man, whose advice about crops is always worth listening to, and who is too well-off to want to borrow money." *Amos B.* i–ii, v–vi, viii–x; *mentioned Mr. G.'s L. S.* i.

Note.—Some suggestions for the character of Mr. Hackit were taken from the personality of George Eliot's father, Robert Evans. (*See* Blind, *George Eliot*, p. 13; Deakin, *Early Life of George Eliot*, p. 126.)

HACKIT, MRS. A sharp-tongued, very kind-hearted and benevolent woman with the courage of her opinions. *Amos B.* i–ii, v–x, Conclusion; mentioned *Mr. G.'s L. S.* i.

"Mrs. Hackit declines cream; she has so long abstained from it with an eye to the weekly butter-money, that abstinence, wedded to habit, has begotten aversion. She is a thin woman with a chronic liver-complaint, which would have secured her Mr. Pilgrim's entire regard and unreserved good word, even if he had not been in awe of her tongue, which was as sharp as his own lancet. She has brought her knitting—no frivolous fancy knitting, but a substantial woollen stocking; the click-click of her knitting-needles is the running accompaniment to all her conversation, and in her utmost enjoyment of spoiling a friend's self-satisfaction, she was never known to spoil a stocking." Ch. i.

Although, in her blunt way, she tells Mr. Barton of her disapproval when he allows the Countess to quarter herself on him, she is a true friend to him and his family and a great help to him and Milly in their time of trouble. She is present at Milly's death.

Note.—The original of Mrs. Hackit was Mrs. Robert Evans, George Eliot's mother. Mrs. Evans was an intimate friend of Mrs. Emma Gwyther ("Milly Barton") and the picture of Mrs. Hackit's relation to Milly Barton is true except in the detail of her being with Milly during Milly's last illness, as Mrs. Evans ("Mrs. Hackit") died a few months before Mrs. Gwyther ("Milly"). (*See* Blind, *George Eliot*, p. 14; Cooke, *George Eliot*, p. 5, 281; Deakin, *Early Life of George Eliot*, p. 126.)

HAFIZ. The Meyricks' Persian cat. *D. D.* xviii, xx, lii.

HALL FARM. The Poysers' farm at Hayslope. *Adam B.* ii–iii, v–ix, xiv–xv, xviii–xx, xxxviii, xlviii–xlix, lii–liii.

"Evidently that gate is never opened: for the long grass and the great hemlocks grow close against it; and, if it were opened, it is so rusty that the force necessary to turn it on its hinges would be likely to pull down the square stone-built pillars, to the detriment of the two stone lionesses which grin with a doubtful carnivorous affability above a coat of arms, surmounting each of the pillars. . . It is a very fine old place, of red brick, softened by a pale powdery lichen, which has dispersed itself with happy irregularity, so as to bring the red brick into terms of friendly companionship with the limestone ornaments surrounding the three gables, the windows, and the door-place. But the windows are patched with wooden panes, and the door, I think, is like the gate—it is never opened: how it would groan and grate against the stone floor if it were! For it is a solid, heavy, handsome door, and must once have been in the habit of shutting with a sonorous bang behind a liveried lackey, who had just seen his master and mistress off the grounds in a carriage and pair. . . But at present one might fancy the house in the early stage of a chancery suit, and that the fruit from that grand double row of walnut-trees on the right hand of the enclosure would fall and rot among the grass." Ch. vi.

The Hall Farm furnishes the setting for several of the important scenes in *Adam Bede*. Hetty Sorrel lives there with her aunt and Uncle Poyser, and Dinah Morris stays there when she is at Hayslope. It is in the farm dairy that Arthur Donnithorne sees Hetty, and in the garden, much later, Adam Bede and Hetty become engaged. In the Hall Farm kitchen Mrs. Poyser " has her say out " with her landlord, Squire Donnithorne, and in the kitchen, also, the Harvest Home supper is celebrated.

Note.—While several originals of the Hall Farm have been suggested, the balance of opinion is in favour of Corley Hall, an old Jacobean house about four miles from Coventry and not far from George Eliot's childhood home at Nuneaton. The description of Corley Hall agrees in the main with that of the Hall Farm, except that the lionesses on the gatepost are griffins. Some remains of the " fine double row of walnut-trees " may still be seen, though many have fallen. The description of the Hall Farm garden may possibly have been taken from George Eliot's own garden at Griff House.

HALLIWELL. Lawyer, of the firm of Dymock and Halliwell. *F. H.* xxxv.

HALM - EBERSTEIN, LEONORA, PRINCESS. Daniel Deronda's unknown mother, a famous prima donna known as Alcharisi, who bitterly resented being a Jewess. *D. D.* xxxvi, l–li, liii.

" She was covered, except as to her face and part of her arms, with black lace hanging loosely from the summit of her whitening hair to the long train stretching from her tall figure. Her arms, naked from the elbow, except for some rich bracelets, were folded before her, and the fine poise of her head made it look handsomer than it really was . . . her eyes were piercing and her face so mobile that the next moment she might look like a different person . . . there was a play of the brow and nostril which made a tacit language . . . She was a remarkable-looking being . . . Her worn beauty had a strangeness in it as if she were not quite a human mother, but a Melusina, who had ties with some world which is independent of ours. . ."

"This woman's nature was one in which all feeling—and all the more when it was tragic as well as real—immediately became matter of conscious representation; experience immediately passed into drama, and she acted her own emotions. In a minor degree this is nothing uncommon, but in the Princess the acting had a rare perfection of physiognomy, voice, and gesture." Ch. li.

Brought up by a stern and orthodox father who believed intensely in his race and in the inferiority of women, she had come to hate both his authority and the thought of being a Jewess. At her father's wish she had married her cousin Charisi, but had bent his gentle nature to her will and had gone on the stage, where her wonderful voice and acting made her the leading prima donna of her time. With all her ambition centred on a great career she had no love for her baby (Daniel), and after her husband's early death she persuaded Sir Hugo Mallinger, one of her admirers, to take Daniel to England and bring him up in ignorance of his birth. Some time after, thinking that her voice was failing, she married the Prince Halm-Eberstein and retired from the stage. Believing that she had done the best thing for Daniel in having him brought up as a Christian Englishman, she had never intended to reveal herself to him, but when suffering from an incurable disease she becomes conscience stricken at the thought that she has thwarted her father's desire to have a grandson, and summons Deronda to meet her at Genoa, where she makes herself and his race known to him without responding in any way to the affection which he offers her.

Note.—In his *Life and Writings of Isaac Disraeli, by his Son,* Benjamin Disraeli, Lord Beaconsfield, gives an account of Isaac Disraeli's mother, which in some respects, particularly her intense resentment of her race and its social disadvantages and her lack of affection for her son, so resembles the Princess Halm-Eberstein, that it seems probable that George Eliot must have taken some touches in the portrait of Deronda's mother, and in the scene between mother and son, from this original. (*See* Disraeli's

Life and Writings of Mr. Disraeli; also article in Temple Bar, vol. 49, p. 542.)

HALSELL COMMON. Open ground between Donnithorne Chase and Norburne over which Arthur Donnithorne gallops. *Adam B.* xii.

HALSELL COMMON. A piece of ground crossed by Will Ladislaw on his way to and from Lowick. *Mid.* xxxvii, xlvi.

HALSELL WOOD. A wood near Middlemarch. *Mid.* xlvi, lviii.

HAMBURG (*Real*). City where Mirah Cohen had once lived and where her brother Mordecai had studied. *D. D.* xx, xl.
Note.—The free city of Hamburg, on the Elbe, in Germany.

"HAND AND BANNER." The tavern in Holborn, the meeting-place of the Philosophers' Club, to which Mordecai Cohen takes Daniel Deronda. *D. D.* xl, xlii, xlvi.
Note.—The original of the "Hand and Banner" was a tavern in Red Lion Square, Holborn, where a philosophical club, to which G. H. Lewes belonged in his youth, used to meet. For description and note of the club itself *see* "Philosophers".

HANMER, MR. Engineer to whom Alfred Garth is to be apprenticed. *Mid.* xxiv–xxv.

HARDY, JIM. Coal-carrier. *J. R.* xxvi.

HARDY, JUSTICE. *Adam B.* xliii.

HARFAGER, CLARA. A girl with some money, "whose friends don't know what to do for her." *Mid.* lxii.

"HARK THE EROL ANGILS SING" (*Real*). A Christmas hymn which Dolly Winthrop likes. *S. M.* x.
Note.—"Hark! the herald angels sing," a well-known Christmas hymn by Charles Wesley, written 1739.

HARLETH, GWENDOLEN. The autocrat of the Davilow family; a beautiful, selfish, undisciplined girl who marries Grandcourt to escape poverty. *D. D.* i–vii, ix–xv, xxi, xxiii–xxix, xxxi–xxxii, xxxv–xxxvi, xliv–xlv, xlviii, l, lii, liv–lvii, lix, lxi, lxiv, lxix–lxx.

"Was she beautiful or not beautiful? and what was the secret of form or expression which gave the dynamic quality to her glance? Was the good or the evil genius dominant in those beams? Probably the evil; else why was the effect that of unrest rather than of undisturbed charm? ... The Nereid in sea-green robes and silver ornaments, with a pale sea-green feather fastened in silver falling backward over her green hat and light-brown hair, was Gwendolen Harleth." Ch. i.

"Having always been the pet and pride of the household, waited on by mother, sisters, governess, and maids, as if she had been a princess in exile, she naturally found it difficult to think her own pleasure less important than others made it, and when it was positively thwarted, felt an astonished resentment, apt, in her cruder days, to vent itself in one of those passionate acts which look like a contradiction of habitual tendencies ... Gwendolen's nature was not remorseless, but she liked to make her penances easy." Ch. iii.

"She meant to do what was pleasant to herself in a striking manner; or, rather, whatever she could do so as to strike others with admiration and get in that reflected way a more ardent sense of living, seemed pleasant to her fancy. . ."

"In her beauty, a certain unusualness about her, a decision of will which made itself felt in her graceful movements and clear unhesitating tones . . . However, she had the charm, and those who feared her were also fond of her; the fear and the fondness being perhaps both heightened by what may be called the irridescence of her character—the play of various, nay, contrary tendencies." Ch. iv.

Her beauty and aloofness attract the rich Mallinger Grandcourt, and she is about ready to accept him when she learns that he ought to marry Mrs. Glasher. Promising Mrs. Glasher not to marry Grandcourt, she goes away to escape his attentions, gambles at Leubronn, where she is influenced by seeing Daniel Deronda as she is losing, and is called home by the news that all her mother's property has been lost. As the only way of earning money herself which she can find is a hated position as governess, she marries Grandcourt in spite of her promise to Mrs. Glasher, attempting to quiet her conscience by the plea that she is doing it for her mother, to whom she is really attached. The false position in which she finds herself soon makes her unhappy, and she turns to Daniel Deronda, whose effect on her at Leubronn she has not forgotten, for spiritual aid, thereby arousing her husband's resentment and jealousy. Grandcourt's cruel and contemptuous attitude so arouses her hatred that she trifles with the idea that she could kill him, and when he is drowned before her eyes, she feels that her momentary delay in throwing him a rope makes her a murderess. In her remorse and despair she turns to Deronda as her only help, and from him gradually attains the beginning of a new spiritual attitude and unselfishness.

Note.—When George Eliot was at Homburg in 1872 she was much impressed by a young lady whom she saw gambling there. This incident furnished the model for Gwendolen Harleth's gambling at Leubronn. (See Cross, *George Eliot's Life*, vol. 3, p. 172; also article in *Nineteenth Century*, vol. 17, p. 483.)

HARRY. A boy employed at Dorlcote Mill. *M. F.* Bk. 1, iv–v.

HART, DR. The doctor who is called in when Captain Wybrow is found dead. *Mr. G.'s L. S.* xiv–xv, xix.

HARTOPP, MRS. BESSIE. Widow of one of Sir Christopher Cheverel's tenants. *Mr. G.'s L. S.* ii.

"HARVEST HOME" (*Real*). Song. *Adam B.* liii.

"As Adam was going homewards, on Wednesday evening, in the six o'clock sunlight, he saw in the distance the last load of barley winding its way towards the yard-gate of the Hall Farm, and heard the chant of " Harvest Home ! " rising and sinking like a wave."

Note.—A " Harvest Home " song formed part of the ceremonial of bringing home the last load of grain. There were various versions, one beginning :
" Harvest home, harvest home
We have ploughed, we have sowed,
We have reaped, we have mowed,
We have brought home every load,
Hip, hip, hip, Harvest Home."

" HARVEST-SONG " (*Real*). Song sung at the Harvest Supper at the Hall Farm. *Adam B.* liii.
" Now the great ceremony of the evening was to begin—the harvest-song, in which every man must join ; he might be in tune, if he liked to be singular, but he must not sit with closed lips."
Note.—The Harvest Song, "Here's a health unto our master," was common in the Midland counties. There are several versions with slight differences in the words.

HASSAN. A Gypsy, Zarca's lieutenant. *Sp. G.* iii–v.

HATHERCOTE. Village near Treby. *F. H.* xxxi, xxxiii.

HAUTBOY. Quoted by Hinze, the too deferential man, as regarding Chaucer as a poet of the first order. *T. S.* v.

HAWKINS. *F. H.* xvii.

HAWKINS, BROTHER. A member of Mr. Lyon's congregation. *F. H.* xxiv.

HAWLEY, ARABELLA. A young lady who had gone into a consumption. *Mid.* xxxvi.

HAWLEY, MR. FRANK. Lawyer and town clerk in Middlemarch, notorious for his bad language. He is one of Mr. Bulstrode's chief opponents. *Mid.* xviii, xxxvii–xxxviii, xlv–xlvi, li, lxxi–lxxii, lxxvi.

HAWLEY, YOUNG. A law student who is an accomplished billiard player. *Mid.* lxvi.

HAXEY, JOB. Weaver who wove Mrs. Tulliver's linen. *M. F.* Bk. 3, ii.

HAYDN'S CANZONETS (*Real*). *Mid.* xvi.
Note.—Songs by Franz Joseph Haydn (1732–1809).

HAYNES, MR. A man who wanted to take Offendene, the place where Mrs. Davilow lives. *D. D.* ii, xxi, lxiv.

HAYSLOPE. The village in Loamshire where Adam Bede lives ; the scene of many of the incidents in *Adam Bede*. *Adam B.* i, and following chapters.
" That rich undulating district of Loamshire to which Hayslope belonged, lies close to a grim outskirt of Stonyshire, overlooked by its barren hills as a pretty blooming sister may sometimes be seen linked in the arm of a rugged, tall, swarthy brother. . . . High up against the horizon were the huge conical masses of hill, like giant mounds intended

to fortify this region of corn and grass against the keen and hungry winds of the north; not distant enough to be clothed in purple mystery, but with sombre greenish sides visibly specked with sheep . . . And directly below them the eye rested on a more advanced line of hanging woods, divided by bright patches of pasture or furrowed crops . . . Then came the valley, where the woods grew thicker, as if they had rolled down and hurried together from the patches left smooth on the slope, that they might take the better care of the tall mansion which lifted its parapets and sent its faint blue summer smoke among them." Ch. ii.

Note.—The original of Hayslope, Loamshire, is the little village of Ellastone, Staffordshire, where Robert Evans, George Eliot's father ("Adam Bede") lived in his youth. (*See* Masefield, *Staffordshire*, p. 132; Mottram, *True Story of George Eliot*, p. 56; Parkinson, *Scenes from the George Eliot Country*, p. 87.) Roston, where Robert Evans was born, has occasionally been mistakenly suggested as an original.

HAYSLOPE CHURCH. The ancient church where Mr. Irwine preaches and where Adam Bede sings in the village choir. *Adam B.* ii, ix, xviii.

"I cannot say that the interior of Hayslope Church was remarkable for anything except for the grey age of its oaken pews— great square pews mostly, ranged on each side of a narrow aisle. It was free, indeed, from the modern blemish of galleries. The choir had two narrow pews to themselves in the middle of the right-hand row . . . The pulpit and desk, grey and old as the pews, stood on one side of the arch leading into the chancel, which also had its grey square pews for Mr. Donnithorne's family and servants. Yet I assure you these grey pews, with the buff-washed walls, gave a very pleasing tone to this shabby interior, and agreed extremely well with the ruddy faces and bright waistcoats." Ch. xviii.

Note.—Ellastone Church is the original of Hayslope Church.

HAYSLOPE GREEN. "A piece of unenclosed ground, with a maple in the middle of it," where Dinah Morris preaches in Hayslope. *Adam B.* i–ii, v.

"The Green lay at the extremity of the village, and from it the road branched off in two directions, one leading farther up the hill by the church, and the other winding gently down towards the valley. On the side of the Green that led towards the church, the broken line of thatched cottages was continued nearly to the churchyard gate; but on the opposite, north-western side, there was nothing to obstruct the view of gently-swelling meadow, and wooded valley, and dark masses of distant hill." Ch. ii.

Note.—Ellastone Green was the original of Hayslope Green.

It is, however, no longer an open green, but is now occupied by several small houses.

HAZELOW, TOM. Cousin of Bill the stone-sawyer, who can read anything "right off". *Adam B.* xxi.

"HEARTS AND DIAMONDS." A work for which Kate Meyrick designed the frontispiece. *D. D.* lii.

HEIDELBERG (*Real*). The German university where Will Ladislaw had studied. *Mid.* ix.

Note.—A university town in Baden, the seat of the oldest university in Germany.

HELOISA. A lady who disapproves of Laura's attempts to disguise her age. *T. S.* xiii.

HEPHZIBAH. See EPPIE.

"HERE AND THERE, OR A TRIP FROM TRURO TO TRANSYLVANIA." Title of Monas' one book. *T. S.* xv.

HERMIONE. Character from the "Winter's Tale" which Gwendolen Harleth represents in private theatricals at Offendene. *D. D.* vi.

HERMITAGE. Arthur Donnithorne's retreat in Fir Tree Grove, where he and Hetty Sorrel meet and where he has two momentous interviews with Adam Bede. *Adam B.* xii–xiii, xxvii–xxviii, xlviii.

HERNANDO. A member of Duke Silva's retinue. *Sp. G.* ii.

HERON, REV. ARTHUR. Mr. Gilfil's brother-in-law. *Mr. G.'s L. S.* xx.

HERON, MRS. LUCY. Mr. Gilfil's gentle sister, who cares for Caterina in her time of sorrow. *Mr. G.'s L. S.* xix–xxi.

HERON, OSWALD, *alias* OZZY. Mrs. Heron's little son, "a broadchested, tawny-haired boy of five." *Mr. G.'s L. S.* xx–xxi.

HERONS, OF FENSHORE. *F. H.* xl.

"HERZ, MEIN HERZ" (*Real*). A song which Mirah Cohen is singing just as her father returns. *D. D.* lxvi.

Note.—"Herz, mein Herz, warum so traurig," a popular German song written by J. R. Wÿss (1812), with music by J. L. F. Glück.

"HESTHER." Mr. Bates' old humpbacked housekeeper. *Mr. G.'s L. S.* vii.

HETTON COPPICE. The little woods in which Hetty Sorrel left her baby to perish. *Adam B.* xliii, xlv.

HETTON-DEEPS. Village in lead mines region, the scene of Dinah Morris's first preaching. *Adam B.* viii.

HETTON PARISH. *Adam B.* xliii.

HETTY. See SORREL, HESTER.

HIBBERT, MISS. *Mr. G.'s L. S.* v.

HICKES. The old butler at Transome Court. *F. H.* i–ii.

HICKES, MRS. The butler's wife. See DENNER.

HICKS. A rural doctor. *Mid.* x, xxvi.

HIERIA. The hamadryad who never knew that she grew old. *E. E.* —*L. F.*

HIGGINS, MR. Mrs. Higgin's deceased husband. *Mr. G.'s L. S.* i.

HIGGINS, MRS. An elderly widow of Shepperton. *Mr. G.'s L. S.* i.

HIGGINS, MARY. Poll Fodge's real name. *See* FODGE, POLL.

HIGH ASH. Part of Sir Christopher Cheverel's estate. *Mr. G.'s L. S.* xiv.

HIGH CROSS. A well-known point in Cardell Chase. *D. D.* xiv.

HIGH STREET, Milby. *J. R.* ii, iv, vi.

HIGHBURY (*Real*). Location of the dissenting church in which Mr. Bulstrode had been a power when he lived in London. *Mid.* liii.

Note.—The district of Highbury, north of Islington, which forms a suburb of London.

HILLBURY. *F. H.* xl.

HINCKLEY (*Real*). One of the places through which Hetty Sorrel passes on her journey in search of Arthur Donnithorne. *Adam B.* xxxvi.

Note.—Hinckley in Leicestershire, about 14 miles south-west of Leicester.

HINDA. Prettiest and boldest of the three Gypsy girls that tease Juan, the minstrel. *Sp. G.* iii.

HINZE. "The too deferential man." *T. S.* v.

"He is the superlatively deferential man, and walks about with murmured wonder at the wisdom and discernment of everybody who talks to him. He cultivates the low-toned tête-à-tête, keeping his hat carefully in his hand and often stroking it, while he smiles with downcast eyes as if to relieve his feelings under the pressure of the remarkable conversation which it is his honour to enjoy."

HITA. A Gypsy girl, one of the three that tease Juan the minstrel. *Sp. G.* iii.

"HO PERDUTO IL BEL SEMBIANTE" (*Real*). One of the songs which Caterina sings to Sir Christopher Cheverel. *Mr. G.'s L. S.* ii.

Note.—In the first edition of *Mr. Gilfil* George Eliot describes this song as being from Gluck's *Orfeo*, but in the revised edition she changed the text to read: "Sir Christopher's favorite airs, by Gluck and Paisiello." It is by Giovanni Paisiello (1741-1816), and, when Caterina sang it, was one of the new songs of the day, as it had been sung two years before, in 1786, at Naples, by the popular prima donna, Anna Morichelli. It is from Paisiello's cantata *Amor vendicato*, first presented at Naples, 30th June, 1786. That cantata seems to have been called sometimes *Dafne ed Alceo*, from its principal characters.

HOBB'S LANE. By-road in Treby, down which Felix Holt vainly tries to lead the election mob. *F. H.* xxxiii.

HOLBORN (*Real*). A street in London near which the Cohens' pawnshop is located. *D. D.* xxxiii.

HOLDSWORTH, MICHAEL. A careless farmer, whose fallows are foul. *Adam B.* xviii, xxiii.

HOLDSWORTH, YOUNG MIKE. *Adam B.* xxi.

HOLLIS, MR. A guest of Grandcourt's at Diplow Hall. *D. D.* xii.

HOLLIS, LADY FLORA. Wife of the above; "a lively middle-aged woman well endowed with curiosity." *D. D.* xii–xiii, xv.

HOLLOW PASTURES. The land which Squire Donnithorne proposes to let the Poysers have instead of the Lower and Upper Ridges. *Adam B.* xxxii.

"HOLLOWS." Farm belonging to Sir Christopher Cheverel. *Mr. G.'s L. S.* ii.

"HOLLY BUSH." Public-house by the Stone Pits, at Hayslope. *Adam B.* i–ii.

"HOLLY MOUNT." The house in which Janet Dempster settles Mrs. Pettifer so that Mr. Tryan may have a comfortable home. *J. R.* xxv–xxviii.

HOLT, MR. Felix Holt's father, a quack doctor; an ignorant man who at his death left his widow the receipts for certain worthless medicines as a means of support. *F. H.* iv–v.

HOLT, FELIX. A Radical; a young watch-maker of superior education and strong opinions, who devotes his life to the service of the poor and unfortunate. *F. H.* iii–v, x, xiii, xv–xviii, xxii, xxiv, xxvii, xxx, xxxii–xxxiv, xxxvii–xxxviii, xli, xliii–xlvii, xlix–Epilogue.

"The minister, accustomed to the respectable air of provincial townsmen, and especially to the sleek well-clipped gravity of his own male congregation, felt a slight shock as his glasses made perfectly clear to him the shaggy-headed, large-eyed, strong-limbed person of this questionable young man, without waistcoat or cravat. . . . he was a peculiar-looking person, but not insignificant, which was the quality that most hopelessly consigned a man to perdition. He was massively built. The striking points in his face were large clear grey eyes and full lips." Ch. v.

"His strong health, his renunciation of selfish claims, his habitual preoccupation with large thoughts and with purposes independent of everyday casualties, secured him a fine and even temper, free from moodiness or irritability. He was full of long-suffering towards his unwise mother . . . he had chosen to fill his days in a way that required the utmost exertion of patience, that required those little rill-like out-flowings of goodness which in minds of great energy must be fed from deep sources of thought and passionate devotedness. In this way his energies served to make him gentle; and now, in this twenty-sixth year of his life, they had ceased to make him angry, except in the presence of something that roused his deep indignation." Ch. xxx.

He has been well educated and could live in comfortable and "respectable" circumstances, but prefers to give up outside refinements to live in poverty among the people whom he wishes to serve. His father had invented some quack medicines upon the sale of which his widowed mother lived comfortably, but Felix, who knows that the medicines are worthless, forces her to give up selling them, and provides for her himself. Mrs. Holt, who objects strongly to giving up the medicines, asks the Reverend Mr. Lyon to reason with Felix, and through the minister Felix meets Esther, with whom he soon falls in love, although at first he sees only surface qualities and faults about which he lectures her. He is interested in the parliamentary campaign in which Harold Transome is the Radical candidate, and fears that some of the practices which he has seen will result in trouble. When a serious election riot does occur, Felix tries to turn the mob and unintentionally kills a constable. He is tried for manslaughter and sentenced to four years' imprisonment in spite of the testimony of his friends, including Esther Lyon, who is now known to be the rightful possessor of the Transome estates. Eventually he is pardoned and learns that Esther has given up wealth and position because she returns his love. The two are married and move away from Treby.

Note.—Some features of Felix Holt were drawn from Gerald Massey, the socialist-poet. (*See* Collins, *Studies*, p. 148 ; Dict. nat. biog.) Another original has been suggested in John Farn, of the vicinity of Nuneaton, a ribbon weaver and labour agitator with a gift for oratory. *See* article in *Great Thoughts from Master Minds*, March, 1901, pp. 369–70. The description of the election riot was suggested by a riot in Nuneaton which George Eliot herself saw when she was thirteen years old. (*See* Cross, *George Eliot's Life*, vol. l, pp. 27–9.)

HOLT, MRS. MARY. Mother of Felix ; a foolish, ignorant, and loquacious woman. *F. H.* iii–v, xxii, xxxii, xxxvii–xxxviii, xli, xliii, xlvi, l–Epilogue.

" She was a tall elderly woman, dresssed in black, with a light-brown front and a black band over her forehead . . . Mrs. Holt was not given to tears ; she was much sustained by conscious unimpeachableness, and by an argumentative tendency which usually checks the too great activity of the lachrymal gland." Ch. iv.

When Felix makes her give up the sale of the worthless medicines by which she has supported herself, she feels deeply injured and never loses an opportunity to talk of this and of her son's obstinacy in giving up what she considers a more genteel position to become a watchmaker.

HOLT'S CARTHARTIC LOZENGES. One of the quack medicines to which Felix is heir. *F. H.* iii–v.

HOLT'S RESTORATIVE ELIXER. A quack medicine to which Felix is heir. *F. H.* iii–v.

HOME FARM. One of the farms on the Transome estate. *F. H.* i, xliii.

HOME, SWEET HOME (*Real*). A song which Rosamond Vincy sings to Peter Featherstone, although she detests it. *Mid.* xii.
Note.—This well-known song by John Howard Payne, from his opera "Clari, or the Maid of Milan" which was first produced in 1823, was a comparatively new song when Rosamond Vincy sang it. The music is by Sir Henry Bishop.

HOOD, JEM. The bassoon-man. *Amos B.* i.

HOOPOE, OF JOHN'S. A critic who thinks that Toucan of Magdalen is the author of a certain work. *T. S.* xi.

HOPKINS, MR. Draper in Middlemarch. *Mid.* xxxvi, lxxi.

HORATIO. *P.—C. B. P.*

HORNER, REVEREND MR. An Independent minister at Milby who, "elected with brilliant hopes, was discovered to be given to tippling and quarreling with his wife." *J. R.* ii.

HORROCK, MR. "The vet," a non-committal man of neutral expression in whose company Fred Vincy goes to Houndsley horse-fair. *Mid.* xxiii, lx, lxvi.
"Costume, at a glance, gave him a thrilling association with horses (enough to specify the hat-brim which took the slightest upward angle just to escape the suspicion of bending downward), and nature had given him a face which by dint of Mongolian eyes, and a nose, mouth, and chin seeming to follow his hat-brim in a moderate inclination upward, gave the effect of a subdued unchangeable skeptical smile." Ch. xxiii.

HOSPITAL FOR POOR TRAVELLERS (*Real*). A convent hospital outside the Porta Santa Croce, Florence, to which Piero di Cosimo directs Baldassarre Calvo after the latter escapes from the French soldiers. *Rom.* xxv, xxix–xxx.
Note.—In the fifteenth century Florence had many hospitals of both types, those for the care of the sick and those for the entertainment of poor travellers. At least one of the second type was to be found near each gate of the city.

HOSPITAL OF SAN MATTEO (*Real*). Hospital in Florence which Romola visits during the famine. *Rom.* xlii–xliii, xlvi.
Note.—The Ospedale di San Matteo, in the Piazza di San Marco, founded in the fourteenth century. It is now the Academia delle Belle Arti.

"HOUND OF THE LORD." A Dominican; a play (Domini Canes) upon the name of the order. Name applied to Fra Girolamo. *Rom.* viii.

HOUNDSLEY. A town near Middlemarch where a horse-fair is held, and where Fred Vincy makes an ill-judged purchase of a horse. *Mid.* xxiii–xxiv, xxvi.

HUDSON. Mrs. Grandcourt's maid. *D. D.* xxxi.

HUMBLED BRETHREN (*Hist.*). "Frati Umiliati, or Humbled Brethren, from Ognissanti, with a glorious tradition of being the earliest workers in the wool-trade," one of the monastic orders that take part in the procession of the Madonna de l'Impruneta. *Rom.* xliii.

Note.—The Humiliati (or Umiliati) an Italian order founded in the twelfth century, and suppressed by Pius V in 1570. Their principal centre in Florence was the Church and Convent of Ognissanti, and the wool trade industries of Ognissanti were developed by them.

HURTADO. A young gentleman of Duke Silva's household. *Sp. G.* ii.

"HUSH, YE PRETTY WARBLING CHOIR" (*Real*). One of the tunes played by Uncle Pullet's musical snuff-box. *M. F.* Bk. 1, ix.

Note.—An air from Handel's masque or pastoral opera, "Acis and Galatea", composed about 1720. The words of the greater part, including this song, are by John Gay.

HUSKISSON (*Hist.*). A statesman who is killed by the new railroad. *Mid.* xxxvii, xli; mentioned *F. H.* Introduction.

Note.—William Huskisson (1770–1830), who was killed at the opening of the Liverpool and Manchester Railroad, 15th September, 1830.

HUTCHINS. A servant of Grandcourt. *D. D.* xxv.

HYNDMARSH, MR. Grocer in St. Ogg's. *M. F.* Bk. 3, vii.

I

"I LOVE THEE STILL." *See* "AH, PERCHÈ NON POSSO ODIARTI."

"ICH HAB' DICH GELIEBET UND LIEBE DICH NOCH" (*Real*). A song by Heine to which Klesmer has set music of his own. *D. D.* xxii.

IDIONE. The hamadryad who was sad because she grew old. *E. E.* —*L. F.*

ILSELY. A town near Middlemarch. *Mid.* lxviii.

IMPRUNETA (L'), CHURCH OF (*Real*). A church six miles from Florence which contained the shrine of the sacred image of the unseen Madonna dell' Impruneta. *Rom.* xlii–xliii.

Note.—The Church of Santa Maria dell' Impruneta, founded by the Buondelmonte family, consecrated in 1054, and rebuilt about 1470. One of the chapels contains the miracle-working statue of the Virgin. This church, in the village of Impruneta, is famous for its Della Robbias.

IMPRUNETA, MADONNA DELL' (*Real*). An image of the Virgin of extreme sanctity which is brought from the Church of l'Impruneta outside Florence and carried in solemn procession through the city to break the famine of 1496. *Rom.* viii, xlii–xliii.

"For a century and a half there were records how the Florentines, suffering from drought, or flood, or famine, or pestilence, or the threat of wars, had fetched the potent image within their walls, and had found deliverance. And grateful honour had been done to her and her ancient church of L'Impruneta. . . . The Florentines were deeply convinced of her graciousness to them, so that the sight of her tabernacle within their walls was like the parting of the cloud, and the proverb ran, that the Florentines had a Madonna who would do what they pleased." Ch. xlii.

Note.—A famous wonder-worker image which was found buried at Impruneta and was said to have uttered a cry when the workman's spade struck it. It was probably made by a Luca, of the eleventh century, though legend attributed it to St. Luke.

"INDEPENDENT MONITOR." One of the journals in which Vorticella's one book is noticed. T. S. xv.

IÑEZ. Fedalma's old trusted nurse. Sp. G. i–ii.

INFIRMARY. The old hospital in Middlemarch; Mr. Tyke and Mr. Farebrother are both candidates for its chaplaincy, and Mr. Tyke is elected because Dr. Lydgate votes for him as Bulstrode's candidate. Mid. xiii, xvi, xviii, xlv, lxvii, lxxvi.

INNKEEPER, AT SNOWFIELD. The man who takes Adam Bede from Snowfield back to Oakburne in his "taxed cart", when Adam is searching for Hetty Sorrel. Adam B. xxxviii.

INNOCENT VIII, POPE (Hist.). Rom. mentioned Proem, viii.

Note.—Giovanni Battista Cibo (1432 – 92), pope, as Innocent VIII, 1484 – 92. He was the pope who made Giovanni de' Medici a cardinal at the age of fourteen, and his son, Franceschetto, married a daughter of Lorenzo de' Medici.

IRWINE, MRS. The rector's handsome mother and Arthur Donnithorne's godmother; a lively, exacting old lady, who is one of the reasons why the rector cannot afford to marry. Adam B. v, viii, xvi, xxv, xxvi, xxxiii, xl, lv.

"That stately old lady, his mother, a beautiful aged brunette, whose rich-toned complexion is well set off by the complex wrappings of pure white cambric and lace about her head and neck. She is as erect in her comely embonpoint as a statue of Ceres; and her dark face, with its delicate acquiline nose, firm proud mouth, and small intense black eye, is so keen and sarcastic in its expression that you instinctively substitute a pack of cards for the chessmen and imagine her telling your fortune. The small brown hand with which she is lifting her queen is laden with pearls, diamonds, and turquoises; and a large black veil is very carefully adjusted over the crown of her cap, and falls in sharp contrast on the white folds about her neck . . . she is clearly one of those children of royalty who have never doubted their right divine and never met with any one so absurd as to question it." Ch. v.

IRWINE, THE REVEREND ADOLPHUS. "Rector of Broxton, Vicar of Hayslope, and Vicar of Blythe, a pluralist at whom the severest Church-reformer would have found it difficult to look sour." *Adam B.* i–ii, v–ix, xvi–xviii, xxii–xxv, xxxiii, xxxix–xliii, xlvi, lv, Epilogue.

"His was one of those large-hearted, sweet-blooded natures that never know a narrow or a grudging thought; epicurean, if you will, with no enthusiasm, no self-scourging sense of duty; but yet, as you have seen, of a sufficiently subtle moral fibre to have an unwearying tenderness for obscure and monotonous suffering . . . He really had no very lofty aims, no theological enthusiasm . . . He had that charity which has sometimes been lacking to very illustrious virtue —he was tender to other men's failings, and unwilling to impute evil. He was one of those men, and they are not the commonest, of whom we can know the best only by following them away from the market-place, the platform, and the pulpit, entering with them into their own homes, hearing the voice with which they speak to the young and aged about their own hearth-stone, and witnessing their thoughtful care for the every-day wants of every-day companions, who take all their kindness as a matter of course, and not as a subject for panegyric." Ch. v.

" ' Mrs. Poyser used to say . . . Mr. Irwine was like a good meal o' victual, you were the better for him without thinking on it, and Mr. Ryde was like a dose o' physic, he gripped you and worreted you, and after all he left you much the same.' " Ch. xvii.

He is very fond of Arthur Donnithorne, who has been his pupil, and he is a friend of Adam Bede also. He cautions Arthur not to turn Hetty Sorrel's pretty head, but from a too great delicacy of feeling does not encourage the confession which Arthur later tries to make to him. When Hetty Sorrel is arrested for child-murder, he is notified and has to break the news to Adam Bede and the Poysers. During the time of Hetty's trial he stands by Adam Bede, trying to help him in any possible way, and he is one of the witnesses in Hetty's behalf.

IRWINE, MISS ANNE. The Rector's half-invalid sister, to whom he is devoted. *Adam B.* v, viii, xvii, xxv–xxvi, lv.

"And Mr. Irwine's sisters, as any person of family within ten miles of Broxton could have testified, were such stupid uninteresting women! It was quite a pity handsome, clever Mrs. Irwine should have had such commonplace daughters . . . But no one ever thought of mentioning the Miss Irwines, except the poor people in Broxton village, who regarded them as deep in the science of medicine, and spoke of them vaguely as 'the gentle-folks'." Ch. v.

IRWINE, MISS KATE. The Rector's plain, self-sacrificing sister, a thin, middle-aged woman. *Adam B.* v, viii, xxv–xxvi, lv.

ISIDOR, FATHER. Duke Silva's uncle, a Prior of San Domingo and an Inquisitor; "a holy, high-born, stern Dominican." *Sp. G.* i–ii, iv. He is bitterly opposed to Duke Silva's proposed marriage to Fedalma, on the ground that she is of alien race and a heretic. Finding it impossible to dissuade the Duke, he is on the point of having her seized by the Inquisition, but she escapes him by going off with her father, Zarca. When Zarca and the Moors take Bedmár, the Prior is captured; Zarca saves him from immediate death by burning at the hands of the mob, and has him hanged instead. Before his death he sees Duke Silva in Gypsy dress and curses him as a traitor.

ISMAËL. Gypsy boy, in love with Hinda. *Sp. G.* iii.

"IT WAS IN THE PRIME." One of Pablo's songs, in the *Spanish Gypsy. Sp. G.* i.

"ITALIA, THE." *See* ALBERGO D'ITALIA.

"I'VE BEEN ROAMING" (*Real*). One of the songs sung by Rosamond Vincy. *Mid.* xvi.

Note.—The words of this song were written by George Darley (1795–1846), poet, critic, and mathematician, and were published in 1826 under his pseudonym of Guy Penseval in his *Labours of Idleness*. The music is by C. E. Horn.

J

JABAL. Lamech's eldest son who "bore upon his face The look of that calm river-god, the Nile, Mildly secure in power that needs not guile." *P.—L. J.*

JABEZ. Footman at Transome Court. *F. H.* i.

JACKSON, MISS. Mrs. Barton's maiden aunt, who had withdrawn herself and her income from the Barton home after a slight "tiff" with Amos. *Amos B.* v, ix.[1]

JACOB, BROTHER. *See* FAUX, JACOB.

JACOBS, MR. Schoolmaster, whose academy Tom Tulliver attends when a small boy. *M. F.* Bk. 1, iii, vii; Bk. 2, i.

JACOPO. The youthful acolyte who, when he first sees Romola in the plague-stricken village, thinks that she is the Madonna come to aid the sufferers. *Rom.* lxviii–lxix.

JAKIN, MRS. Bob's mother, "a dreadfully large, fat woman." *M. F.* Bk. 1, vi; Bk. 3, vi; Bk. 5, iii; Bk. 6, iv; Bk. 7, i, v.

JAKIN, BOB. Tom Tulliver's ragged holiday companion and staunch friend, gifted with volubility, much native wit, and cunning. *M. F.* Bk. 1, vi; Bk. 3, vi; Bk. 4, iii; Bk. 5, ii, v–vii; Bk. 6, iv, xiv; Bk. 7, i, iii, v.

"Bob knew, directly he saw a bird's egg, whether it was a swallow's, or a tomtit's, or a yellow-hammer's; he found out all the wasps' nests, and could set all sorts of traps; he could climb the trees like a squirrel, and had

---

[1] A Nuneaton list gives a Miss Wicken as her prototype. (Manuscript notes.)

quite a magical power of detecting hedgehogs and stoats ; and he had courage to do things that were rather naughty, such as . . . killing a cat that was wandering *incognito* . . . For a person suspected of preternatural wickedness, Bob was really not so very villainous-looking ; there was even something agreeable in his snub-nosed face, with its close-curled border of red hair." Bk. 1, vi.

When he grows up he becomes a prosperous packman, with a ready tongue and unfailing good nature which, together with his broad thumb, worst even Aunt Glegg in a bargain. His friendship for Tom Tulliver and his admiration for Maggie prompt him to help Tom make some money by trading. For awhile Tom Tulliver lodges in Bob's house by the river, and it is from Bob's house that Maggie, who is lodging there when the flood comes, goes in her row-boat to rescue Tom at the mill.

Note.—The original of Bob Jakin was William Jaques, a schoolmate of George Eliot's at Griff. (*See* Blind, *George Eliot*, p. 21 ; Cooke, *George Eliot*, p. 7.)

JAKIN, MRS. PRISSY. Bob's wife, " a tiny woman, with the general physiognomy of a Dutch doll." *M. F.* Bk. 6, iv ; Bk. 7, i.

JAMAICA (*Real*). The colony to which David Faux had gone to seek his fortune and from which, as Edward Freely, he returns to settle in Grimworth. *B. J.* ii–iii.

Note.—The principal island of the British West Indies.

JAMES, MR. The Doctor's assistant who married the Doctor's niece secretly. *Adam B.* xv.

JANE. The Cass's maid. *S. M.* xvii–xviii.

JANET. *See* DEMPSTER, JANET.

JARRETT. Village carpenter. *D. D.* vi.

JAY, BETTY. A poor inhabitant of Raveloe. *S. M.* iii.

JEFFRIES. Servant of Mrs. Davilow's. *D. D.* xxi.

JENNINGS. A man who wrote a poem on croquet. *D. D.* v.

JENNINGS, MRS. A newcomer in Shepperton, who excites unfavourable comment when she does not put on black at Mr. Gilfil's death. *Mr. G.'s L. S.* i.[1]

JERMYN, MISS. The lawyer's daughter. " She considers herself a judge of what is ladylike, and she is vulgarity personified." *F. H.* v, ix, xix, xlii.

JERMYN, MRS. The lawyer's wife. *F. H.* ii, xlii.

JERMYN, LOUISA. The lawyer's second daughter, one of Esther Lyon's pupils. *F. H.* v, xix, xlii.

JERMYN, MATTHEW. Lawyer ; Mrs. Transome's former lover, a selfish and unscrupulous man. *F. H.* Introd., i–iii, v, vii–ix, xv–xxi, xxv, xxviii–xxx, xxxiii–xxxvii, xli–xlii, xlvi–xlvii, Epilogue.

" He was grey, but still remarkably handsome ; fat, but tall enough to bear that trial to man's dignity. There was as strong a

---

[1] A Nuneaton list gives a Mrs. Wilkinson as her prototype. (Manuscript notes.)

suggestion of toilette about him as if he had been five-and-twenty instead of nearly sixty. He chose always to dress in black and was especially addicted to black satin waistcoats, which carried out the general sleekness of his appearance; and this, together with his white, fat, but beautifully-shaped hands, which he was in the habit of rubbing gently on his entrance into a room, gave him very much the air of a lady's physician." Ch. ii.

"Jermyn was able and politic enough to have commanded a great deal of success in his life, but he could not help being handsome, arrogant, fond of being heard, indisposed to any kind of comradeship, amorous and bland towards women, cold and self-contained towards men." Ch. xxix.

When a handsome and sentimental young man he had been Mrs. Transome's lover and had compromised her. He had used his hold over her to secure his own material advancement, and in managing the Transome estate had grown rich and had married and maintained an expensive family. When Harold Transome returns as heir to the Transome estate and discovers Mr. Jermyn's mismanagement and crookedness, he quarrels with him, and in a public quarrel Mr. Jermyn informs Harold that he is his father.

JEROME, MRS. SUSAN. Thomas Jerome's handsome wife, who is not always in sympathy with her husband's benevolent plans. *J. R.* viii, xi, xxv–xxvi.

"Mrs. Jerome was like her china, handsome and old-fashioned. She was a buxom lady of sixty, in an elaborate lace cap fastened by a frill under her chin, a dark, well-curled front concealing her forehead, a snowy-neckerchief exhibiting its ample folds as far as her waist, and a stiff grey silk gown." Ch. viii.

JEROME, MR. THOMAS. A retired corn-factor of Milby, a benevolent Dissenter, and one of Mr. Tryan's firm supporters. *J. R.* ii, viii–xiii, xxii, xxv–xxvi, xxviii.

"If you had heard the tone of mingled good-will, veneration, and condolence in which this greeting was uttered, even without seeing the face that completely harmonized with it, you would have no difficulty in inferring the ground-notes of Mr. Jerome's character. To a fine ear that tone said as plainly as possible— 'Whatever recommends itself to me, Thomas Jerome, as piety and goodness, shall have my love and honour. Ah, friends, this pleasant world is a sad one, too, isn't it? Let us help one another, let us help one another.' And it was entirely owing to this basis of character, not at all from any clear and precise doctrinal discrimination, that Mr. Jerome had very early in life become a Dissenter. In his boyish days he had been thrown where Dissent seemed to have the balance of piety, purity, and good works on its side, and to become a Dissenter seemed to him identical with choosing God instead of mammon." Ch. viii.

Note.—In the lists of originals prepared in Nuneaton after the publication of *Scenes of Clerical Life*, the original of Mr. Jerome was given as a Mr. Everard. (*See* Olcott, *George Eliot*, p. 16.)

JESSON'S BOY. *J. R.* xvi.

JET. The Countess Czerlaski's spaniel. *Amos. B.* iii, v, vii.

JETSOME. A young and worthless protegé of Lawyer Wakem's, who is put in charge of Dorlcote Mill after Mr. Tulliver's death. *M. F.* Bk. 6, v, xii.

JOB. *See* TUDGE, JOB.

JOB. Kitty's "follyer". *J. R.* xxi.

JOB, OLD. A man who speaks in dialect. *Mid.* xxiv.

JOCOSA. Gwendolen Harleth's name for Miss Merry, the governess. *See* MERRY, MISS.

JODSON, MR. Former occupant of the house where Mrs. Davilow lives after leaving Offendene. *D. D.* xliv, lviii.

JOHN. Mr. Jermyn's footman. *F. H.* xxi.

JOHN. Servant at Camp Villa, who empties the gravy tureen on Mrs. Barton's newly turned black silk dress. *Amos B.* iii.

JOHN. Sir James Chettam's groom. *Mid.* iii.

JOHN, OLD. The Donnithorne's head groom. *Adam B.* xii, xxix, xxxii.

JOHNS, MR. A Baptist minister with a solemn twang. *T. S.* ix.

JOHNS, REV. MR. Of Gun Street Chapel. *Amos B.* ii.

Note. — Possibly William Johns (1771–1845), a Unitarian minister, author and teacher. He taught in Manchester for thirty years.

JOHNSON. *Mid.* xxxix.

JOHNSON, MR. JOHN. Electioneering agent; a vulgar, not over-scrupulous man, who grows prosperous in the service of Lawyer Jermyn and later turns against him. *F. H.* xi, xvii, xxi, xxviii–xxxi, xxxiii–xxxiv, xxxvii, xlvi–xlvii, Epilogue.

"A smartly-dressed personage on horseback, with a conspicuous expansive shirt-front and figured satin stock. He was a stout man, and gave a strong sense of broadcloth." Ch. xi.

"THE JOLLY COLLIERS." Inn at Shepperton. *Amos B.* vii.

JONAS, MR. Dyer. *Mid.* lxxi.

JONAS. Servant. *Mid.* v.

JORTIN. *S. M.* iv.

JOSÉ. A young gentleman of Duke Silva's household. *Sp. G.* ii.

JOSEPH. Mr. Trumbull's assistant. *Mid.* lx.

JOYCE. A young farmer. *F. H.* xx.

JUAN. Poet and minstrel; a friend both to Duke Silva and to the Spanish Gypsy, Fedalma, with whom he is unselfishly in love. *Sp. G.* i–v.

"So Juan was a troubadour revived
Freshening life's dusty road with babbling rills
Of wit and song, living mid harnessed men
With limbs ungalled by armour."
Bk. 1.

Juan forms a connecting link in several parts of the plot. His light talk with the Gypsy prisoner, Zarca, enables the Gypsy to recognize Fedalma as his lost daughter. When Fedalma throws in her lot with her father and the Gypsies escape from Bedmár, Juan goes with them to the Gypsy camp at Guadix, and is there when Duke Silva, for love of Fedalma, joins the Gypsies. When Fedalma after her father's death is embarking for Africa it is Juan who sees the pilgrim Silva on the strand, and urges Fedalma to a last interview with the lover from whom she is separated for ever.

JUBAL. Youngest son of Lamech who invents the lyre and discovers music. *P.—L. J.*

He wanders through the world for long years, seeking higher music and greater songs. After many years he returns, an old man, to find a newer generation celebrating him and his discovery of music in great festival. They believe, however, that he is dead, and when he proclaims himself the Jubal whom they are honouring he is jeered at and thrust out alone, to die. Dying, he is consoled by a vision of the greatness of his gift to man in the discovery of song.

JUDENGASSE (*Real*). A street in Frankfort which Daniel Deronda explores. *D. D.* xxxii.

JUDITH, AUNT. Mrs. Poyser's favourite sister; Dinah Morris's Methodist aunt who had brought her up when she was left an orphan. *Adam B.* vi, viii, x.

JULIA, AUNT. Mr. Casaubon's aunt, who had made a runaway match and been disinherited; Will Ladislaw's grandmother. *Mid.* ix, xxviii, xxxvii, liv.

JUNO. Mr. Irwine's brown setter. *Adam B.* v, xvi.

K

KALONYMOS, JOSEPH. A faithful friend of Daniel Deronda's grandfather, from whom Daniel eventually obtains his grandfather's papers. *D. D.* xxxii, li, lx.

As a substantial merchant with business in distant parts of the earth he is a type of the "wandering Jew". At Frankfort he sees Daniel Deronda in the Synagogue, ascertains his name, and suspects that he is the grandson of his old friend, Charisi. He then goes to Daniel's mother, who had told him that her son had died years before, accuses her of falsehood to her father, and is the means of her sending for Daniel and revealing his parentage and race to him.

KATE. One of Agatha's old cousins. *P.—Agatha.*

KEATING. A gentleman fond of hunting. *S. M.* iii–iv.

KECK, MR. Editor of the "Middlemarch Trumpet". *Mid.* xxxviii, xlvi.

KELL, MRS. Housekeeper at Tipton Grange. *Mid.* lxii.

KEMP, BROTHER. A musical member of Mr. Lyon's congregation, with a heavy bass. *F. H.* xiii, xxiv, xxxvii.

KENCH, MASTER. Constable at Raveloe. *S. M.* vii.

KENCH YARD, BATHERLEY. The place where Molly Farren had lodged with her baby. *S. M.* xiv.

KENN, DR. Vicar of St. Ogg's, a kind friend to Maggie Tulliver. *M. F.* Bk. 5, v; Bk. 6, i–ii, vi, ix; Bk. 7, i–v.

"That plain, middle-aged face, with a grave, penetrating kindness in it, seeming to tell of a human being who had reached a firm, safe strand, but was looking with helpful pity towards the strugglers still tossed by the waves." Bk. 6, ix.

When Maggie Tulliver returns to St. Ogg's after leaving it with Stephen Guest, he takes her into his family as governess for his young children and treats her with great kindness. He eventually advises her to leave St. Ogg's for a time, being led to this step by the prevalent feeling in the parish, which he is unable to overcome.

KENN, MRS. The vicar's invalid wife, who dies. *M. F.* Bk. 6, vi, ix; Bk. 7, i.

KENNEL YARD, ST. OGG'S. The place where one of Bob Jakin's friends who owns ferrets lives. *M. F.* Bk. 1, vi.

KEW BRIDGE. (*Real*). The bridge over the Thames, under which Daniel Deronda rows just before he first sees Mirah Cohen. *D. D.* xvii.

KEW GARDENS (*Real*). The place near which Daniel Deronda rescues Mirah Cohen when she is attempting to drown herself in the Thames. *D. D.* xvii.

Note.—Kew Gardens, the Royal Botanic Gardens, on the Thames, about sixteen miles from London.

"KEY TO ALL MYTHOLOGIES." The *magnum opus* which is the ambition of Mr. Casaubon's life and which he is unable to complete. *Mid.* vii, x, xxix, xxxvii, xlii, xlviii, l.

"The difficulty of making his Key to all Mythologies unimpeachable weighed like lead upon his mind . . . even his religious faith wavered with his wavering trust in his own authorship." Ch. xxix.

KEZIA. Mrs. Tulliver's good-hearted, bad-tempered housemaid, who is faithful to her mistress in time of trouble. *M. F.* Bk. 1, ii, v, vii; Bk. 3, vi, viii.

"Having declared her intention of staying till the master could get about again, 'wage or no wage,' she had found a certain recompense in keeping a strong hand over her mistress, scolding her for 'moithering' herself, and going about all day without changing her cap, and looking as if she was 'mushed'. Altogether, this time of trouble was rather a Saturnalian time to Kezia: she could scold her betters with unreproved freedom." Bk. 3, viii.

KIBBLE. Silversmith in Brassing. *Mid.* xxxvi.

KIMBLE, DOCTOR. The lively Raveloe doctor, who becomes

intense and bitter over cards and brandy. *S. M.* ii–iii, ix–xi, xiii, xvi.

"But Doctor Kimble (country apothecaries in old days enjoyed that title without authority of diploma), being a thin and agile man, was flitting about the room with his hands in his pockets, making himself agreeable to his feminine patients, with medical impartiality, and being welcomed everywhere as a doctor by hereditary right—not one of those miserable apothecaries who canvas for practice in strange neighbourhoods, and spend all their income in starving their one horse, but a man of substance, able to keep an extravagant table like the best of his patients. Time out of mind the Raveloe doctor had been a Kimble." Ch. xi.

KIMBLE, MRS. The doctor's wife and Squire Cass's sister ; a stout, good-natured lady. *S. M.* x–xi, xiii.

KING STREET. The street in Treby Magna where the election riot starts. *F. H.* xxxi, xxxiii, xlvi.

KING'S LORTON. The rural parish where Mr. Stelling is in charge when Tom Tulliver is sent to school to him. *M. F.* Bk. 1, vii ; Bk. 2, i, iv, vii.

KING'S TOPPING. An estate of the Mallingers which had been in the family for centuries. *D. D.* xvi, xxxvi.

KINGSTOWN (*Real*). The town in Jamaica, where David Faux had been forced to "devise cakes and patties in a kitchen". *B. J.* iii.

Note.—Kingston, the capital and principal commercial city of Jamaica, in the British West Indies.

KIRKE, MISS. An invalid in St. Ogg's who refuses to have Maggie Tulliver as a reader and companion. *M. F.* Bk. 7, iv.

KITTY. The Dempster's housemaid. *J. R.* xvii, xxi, xxv.

KITTY. Mr. Gilfil's black mare. *Mr. G.'s L. S.* xix.

KITTY. One of Mrs. Poyser's maids, "a rare girl to spin, for all she squinted." *Adam B.* vi.

KITTY. Servant at Transome Court. *F. H.* i.

KLESMER, HERR JULIUS. A great musician who marries Miss Arrowpoint, the heiress. *D. D.* v–vi, x–xii, xxi–xxiii, xxxv, xxxvii, xxxix, xlv, xlviii, lii, lxx.

"Herr Klesmer being a felicitous combination of the German, the Sclave, and the Semite, with grand features, brown hair floating in artistic fashion, and brown eyes in spectacles. His English had little foreignness except its fluency ; and his alarming cleverness was made less formidable just then by a certain softening air of silliness which will sometimes befall even Genius in the desire of being agreeable to Beauty." Ch. v.

While he discourages Gwendolen Harleth, when after the loss of her mother's fortune she consults him about going on the stage, he appreciates Mirah Cohen's talent and helps her in her musical career.

Note.—The original of Klesmer was said to have been Liszt, whom George Eliot met at Weimar. (*See* article by Lord Acton in *Nineteenth Century*, vol. 17, p. 483.)

KLESMER, MRS. JULIUS. *See* ARROWPOINT, MISS CATHERINE.

KNEBLEY. Parish near Shepperton. *Mr. G.'s L. S.* i.
Note.—The original of Knebley is Astley, in Warwickshire.

KNEBLEY ABBEY. Home of the Oldinport family. *Mr. G.'s L. S.* i.
Note.—Astley Castle, near Arbury, was the original of Knebley Abbey.

KNEBLEY CHURCH. Church where Mr. Gilfil officiates on Sunday afternoons. *Mr. G.'s L. S.* i; mentioned *Amos B.* vi.
"A wonderful little church . . . with a checkered pavement which had once rung to the iron tread of military monks, with coats of arms in clusters on the lofty roof, marble warriors and their wives without noses occupying a large proportion of the area, and the twelve apostles, with their heads very much on one side, holding didactic ribbons, painted in fresco on the walls." Ch. i.
Note.—The original of Knebley Church was Astley Church, a mile west of Arbury Park. (*See* Andrews, *Bygone Warwickshire*, p. 271; Parkinson, *Scenes*, pp. 12, 52.)

KNIGHTSBRIDGE (*Real*). A street in London out of which Mirah Cohen has just turned when she sees her father following her. *D. D.* lxii.

KNOTT, BESSIE. Dorcas's curly-headed little girl of three. *Mr. G.'s L. S.* xix.

KNOTT, DANIEL. Former coachman at Cheverel Manor; husband of Dorcas. *Mr. G.'s L. S.* xix.

KNOTT, DANIEL (YOUNG). Dorcas's son, "a flaxen-haired lad of nine." *Mr. G.'s L. S.* xix.

KNOTT, DORCAS. A former maid at Cheverel Manor; a great favourite of Caterina's, with whom Caterina seeks refuge on leaving Cheverel Manor. *Mr. G.'s L. S.* iv, xvi, xix.

KNOWLES. *Adam B.* xxxii.

L

LABRON, MR. Lawyer in Treby, agent for the Debarrys. *F. H.* ii, vii, xix-xx, xxiv, xxviii.

LACEHAM. Town on the Floss, where Maggie Tulliver and her cousin Lucy are sent to boarding school, and where, later, Bob Jakin and Tom Tulliver get the lace goods with which they trade. *M. F.* Bk. 2, vii; Bk. 5, ii.
Note.—The original of Laceham was Nottingham, noted for its lace manufacture.

"LACEHAM COURIER." Newspaper. *M. F.* Bk. 6, xiii.

LADBROOK, MISS. Guest at the New Year's Eve dance at the Red House. *S. M.* xi.

LADBROOK, MRS. *S. M.* xi.

LADIES' CHARITY, WANCHESTER. *D. D.* xxi.

LADISLAW. Will Ladislaw's deceased father, whom he resembles; a musician in poor health who had married the daughter of Mr. Bulstrode's first wife. *Mid.* xxxvii, lx.

LADISLAW. Will Ladislaw's grandfather, a Polish refugee and musician; Mr. Casaubon's Aunt Julia had been disinherited for marrying him. *Mid.* xxxvii.

LADISLAW, DOROTHEA. *See* BROOKE, DOROTHEA.

LADISLAW, WILL. Mr. Casaubon's second cousin; a generous, gay, and rather irresponsible young man with Bohemian tendencies. *Mid.* ix–x, xix–xxii, xxix–xxx, xxxiv, xxxvii–xxxix, xlii–xliii, xlvi–li, liv, lviii–lxii, lxiv, lxxi, lxv, lxxvii–lxxxiv, Finale.

"Will Ladislaw's smile was delightful, unless you were angry with him beforehand; it was a gush of inward light illuminating the transparent skin as well as the eyes, and playing about every curve and line as if some Ariel were touching them with a new charm, and banishing forever the traces of moodiness . . . The first impression on seeing Will was one of sunny brightness, which added to the uncertainty of his changing expression. Surely, his very features changed their form; his jaw looked sometimes large and sometimes small; and the little ripple in his nose was a preparation for metamorphosis. When he turned his head quickly his hair seemed to shake out light, and some persons thought they saw decided genius in this coruscation." Ch. xxi.

His grandmother, Mr. Casaubon's aunt, had been disinherited because she made a *mésalliance*, by marrying a poor Pole, and Mr. Casaubon, who feels an inherited responsibility for this, had educated Will. With artistic tastes, some ability as a writer, and a disregard for worldly considerations he has some difficulty in choosing a profession. When he meets Dorothea as Mr. Casaubon's wife he first becomes interested in her, and then grows to love her with constancy and devotion, and for the sake of being near her settles in Middlemarch as editor of Mr. Brooke's paper. His sense of honour causes him to refuse Mr. Bulstrode's offer of money, dishonestly gained, which should have been his mother's. When Dorothea, after a short widowhood, gives up position and fortune to marry him, he enters public life, without promise of marked success.

Note.—It has been suggested that some traits in the character of Will Ladislaw were drawn, perhaps unconsciously, from George Henry Lewes, who, also, was a man of versatile talent and lively manner. Some critics, however, do not recognize Lewes as the original. Those who consider Lewes as the prototype find one of their arguments in the author's very evident fondness for the character of Ladislaw. (*See* Bonnell, *Charlotte Brontë, George Eliot, Jane Austen*, p. 240; Deakin, *Early Life of George Eliot,*

p. 89; Parkinson, *Scenes from the George Eliot Country*, p. 140.)

LAENNEC, DR. (*Hist.*). A physician under whom Lydgate studied in Paris. *Mid.* lxxvi.

Note.—René Théophile Hyacinthe Laennec (1781 – 1826), a famous French physician, discoverer of auscultation of the heart, who taught in Paris from 1822.

LAERTES. A guest at the college breakfast party. *P.—C. B. P.*

LAKINS. Poor family in Milby. *J. R.* xxiii.

LAMB, JONATHAN. The old parish clerk in Milby. *J. R.* v.

Note.—In the lists of originals prepared in Nuneaton after the publication of the *Scenes of Clerical Life*, a Mr. Wheway was given as the original of Jonathan Lamb. (*See* Olcott, *George Eliot*, p. 16.)

LAMB, LEONARD, B.A. An acquaintance of Mr. Raffles, called Ba-Lamb. *Mid.* xli.

LAMBERT, FRIEND. A member of Mr. Lyon's church. *F. H.* xviii.

LAMBETH (*Real*). The part of London where Mirah Cohen had lived with her mother. *D. D.* xx.

Note.—A metropolitan borough of London, on the south bank of the Thames.

LAMBRA. Fedalma's dead mother. *Sp. G.* i.

LAMECH. Jubal's father. *P.—L. J.*

LAMMETER, MR. Nancy's father; a grave and dignified man. *S. M.* v-vi, ix, xi, xiii, xvi-xvii, xx, Conclusion.

"That grave and orderly senior was not going to bate a jot of his dignity by seeming elated at the notion of a match between his family and the Squire's ... His spare but healthy person, and high-featured, firm face, that looked as if it had never been flushed by excess, was in strong contrast not only with the Squire's, but with the appearance of the Raveloe farmers generally—in accordance with a favourite saying of his own, that 'breed was stronger than pasture'." Ch. xi.

LAMMETER, OLD MR. Mr. Lammeter's deceased father, "a fine old gentleman" who "came from a bit north'ard". *S. M.* vi.

LAMMETER, NANCY. The gentle, modest, but firm young beauty of Raveloe; later Godfrey Cass's wife. *S. M.* iii, viii–xi, xiii, xvi–xx, Conclusion.

"Everything belonging to Miss Nancy was of delicate purity and nattiness ... and as for her own person, it gave the same idea of perfect unvarying neatness as the body of a little bird ... when at last she stood complete in her silvery twilled silk, her lace tucker, her coral necklace, and coral eardrops, the Miss Gunns could see nothing to criticise except her hands, which bore the traces of butter-making, cheese-crushing, and even still coarser work ... There is hardly a servant-maid in these days who is not better informed than Miss Nancy; yet she had the essential attributes of a lady—

high veracity, delicate honour in her dealings, deference to others, and refined personal habits . . . she was slightly proud and exacting, and as constant in her affection towards a baseless opinion as towards an erring lover." Ch. xi.

She marries Godfrey Cass, to whom she is much attached, and rules him firmly but kindly, believing strictly in her own convictions. In spite of the fact that she grieves deeply over the death of her own baby, she will not consent to take another in its place, and steadily refuses Godfrey's suggestion that they adopt Eppie. When Eppie is nearly grown up, Godfrey confesses that she is his own child, and then Nancy agrees to take her, and is much disappointed, for her husband's sake, when Eppie chooses to stay with old Silas Marner, her adoptive father.

LAMMETER, PRISCILLA. Nancy's plain sister; a cheerful, unselfish, blunt old maid, devoted to her father. *S. M.* v, xi, xvi–xvii, xx, Conclusion.

"LANCET" (*Real*). A medical periodical, the attitude of which on the coronership is discussed by the medical men in Middlemarch. *Mid.* xvi.

Note.—The *Lancet*, London, founded 1823 by Thomas Wakley.

LANDINO, CRISTOFORO (*Hist.*). A scholar who criticized Bardo de' Bardi. *Rom.* vi–vii, xiii.

Note.—Cristoforo Landino (1424–1504), Italian philologist, who held the chair of rhetoric and poetry at Florence, 1457–1504. His name is best known for his edition of Dante, with commentaries, and for his *Disputationes Camaldulenses*.

LANDOR, MISS. The belle of Milby. *J. R.* ii–iii.

LANDOR, MR. Banker in Milby; one of Mr. Tryan's supporters. *J. R.* i–ii, vii, ix, xxii, xxviii.

Note.—The original of Mr. Landor was a Mr. Craddock. (Manuscript information; also Olcott, *George Eliot*, p. 16.)

LANDOR, MRS. Wife of the Milby attorney. *Amos B.* iv.

LANDOR, MR. BENJAMIN. Lawyer, the banker's son. *J. R.* i–iii, viii, xx; mentioned as "the Milby attorney". *Amos B.* iv.

LANDOR, MR. EUSTACE. A young dandy in Milby, the banker's son. *J. R.* ii.[1]

"LANDS END TIMES." A journal that reviews Vorticella's one book. *T. S.* xv.

LANGEN, BARON VON. A visitor at Leubronn; "a gentleman with a white mustache and clipped hair; solid-browed, stiff, and German." *D. D.* i–ii, xiv–xv.

LANGEN, BARONESS VON. The English wife of the above, in whose care Gwendolen Harleth visits Leubronn. *D. D.* i, xiv–xv.

LANIGER. A man with "a temper but no talent for repartee", who is persuaded that his harsh critic Mordax is a wolf at heart. *T. S.* viii.

---

[1] *Note.*—A Nuneaton list gives Mr. T. J. Craddock as his original. (MS. notes.)

LANTERN YARD. The street in a great manufacturing town, where the chapel of Silas Marner's youth was situated. *S. M.* i–ii, x, xii, xxi.
Note.—An article by F. W. Humberstone, in the *Coventry Herald*, 14–15th November, 1919, suggests that the original of Lantern Yard may have been Vicar's Lane, in Coventry, which had several of the features of Lantern Yard.

LAPIDOTH, *otherwise* COHEN. Mirah and Mordecai's unscrupulous father; an actor who called his family Lapidoth, a name of his Polish forefathers. *D. D.* xx, lii, lxii, lxvi–lxviii.

"Once a handsome face, with bright colour, it was now sallow and deep-lined, and had that peculiar impress of impudent suavity which comes from courting favour while accepting disrespect. He was lightly made and active, with something of youth about him which made the signs of age seem a disguise; and in reality he was hardly fifty-seven." Ch. lxii.

He had deserted his wife and son, and taken Mirah to America with him when she was a small child. Later they returned to Europe, and he urged his daughter to accept the dishonourable attentions of the Count, causing her to flee from him in fear. After Mirah is settled in London with her brother, he finds them there, and while staying with them steals Daniel Deronda's diamond ring and disappears.

LAPIDOTH, MIRAH. *See* COHEN, MIRAH.

LAPP. River at Treby. *F. H.* Introd., i, xxxii.

LARCHER, MRS. The carrier's wife. *Mid.* xxvi, xlv, lx.

LARCHER, MR. CAIUS. A young dandy of Middlemarch whom Rosamond Vincy looks down on. *Mid.* xxvii.

LARCHER, EDWIN, ESQ. A prosperous carrier, who has a sale when he moves. It is at this sale that Will Ladislaw is recognized by Raffles. *Mid.* xviii, lx.

LARGA, VIA (*Real*). Street in Florence where the Palace of the Medici is located. *Rom.* xii–xiii, xix, xxi, xxvi, xxix.
Note.—The old Via Larga (now part of the Via Cavour) took its name both from its size and from the many rich palaces which it contained.

"LASCIA CH'IO PIANGA" (*Real*). Song which Mab Meyrick practises. *D. D.* lxi.
Note.—An aria by Handel.

LASSMANN, MR. The man whose speculations cause the failure of the firm of Grapnell & Co. and result in the loss of Mrs. Davilow's fortune. *D. D.* ii, xxi.

"LAST ROSE OF SUMMER" (*Real*). Song. *Mid.* vii.
Note.—A well-known song, with words by Thomas Moore, first published 1813, in his *Irish Melodies*; the air is altered from an older one called the "Groves of Blarney".

K

"LATCHGATE ARGUS." A journal that reviews Vorticella's one book. *T. S.* xv.

LATIMER. A shy, poetic, sensitive young man who develops the gift of insight into the minds of others and has his life ruined by this double consciousness. *L. V.* i–ii.

He falls in love with Bertha Grant, his brother Alfred's fiancée, and his clairvoyance shows him both her cold cruel nature and the fact that he is destined to marry her. After his brother's sudden death, Latimer marries Bertha, but the union is unhappy. Latimer discovers that Bertha has planned to kill him, and they separate, Latimer awaiting in solitude the death from heart disease, of which his clairvoyance tells him the exact date.

LATIMER'S FATHER. A successful banker and land holder, whose affection and pride centre in his elder son, Alfred. *L. V.* i–ii.

LAURA. A lady disapproved of by Heloisa because she disguises her age. *T. S.* xiii.

LAURE, MADAME. Lydgate's first love, a beautiful French actress. Having tired of her husband, whom she was supposed to stab in a play, she turned the play into reality and killed him, and later told Lydgate that she did not like husbands. *Mid.* xv.

LAUSANNE (Real). Town where Dorothea and Celia Brooke had finished their education, in a Swiss family. *Mid.* i, vii, xxi, xlviii, lxxxi.

Note.—Lausanne, near Lake Geneva, the capital of the Canton of Vaud, in Switzerland.

LAWE, LADY. *D. D.* v.

LAWE, MISS. The handsome daughter of Lady Lawe, whose beauty is eclipsed by that of Gwendolen Harleth. *D. D.* v.

LAXETER. Town where Mr. Tryan had formerly held a curacy. *J. R.* iii, xi.

LEDRU, ANNETTE. A beautiful French woman, Esther Lyon's mother, who died before the opening of the story. *F. H.* vi, xxi, xxv.

Having married a young Englishman, Maurice Christian Bycliffe, against the will of her family, she had followed him to England, where her baby was born and where she learned of her husband's death. After great kindness and devotion from Mr. Lyon she married him, but lived for only a few years.

LEEDS (Real). Town to which Dinah Morris goes on a visit to Methodist friends, at the time of Hetty Sorrel's journey and crime. *Adam B.* xxx, xxxviii, xl, xlv.

Note.—Leeds, the largest town in Yorkshire; a manufacturing city, with a large Methodist element.

LEEK. Farmer. *D. D.* xxi.

LEEK MALTON. Town. *F. H.* xx, xxxi.

LEGHORN (Real). The Italian port to which the French aid for Florence at the time of the famine is sent. *Rom.* xlii–xliii.

Note.—Leghorn, on the Mediterranean, about fifty miles south-west of Florence.

LEICESTER (*Real*). One of the places to which Hetty Sorrel goes on her journey to Windsor to find Arthur Donnithorne. *Adam B.* xxxv-xxxvi.

Note.—Leicester, the county town of Leicestershire, about twenty-six miles from Derby (the "Stoniton" of *Adam Bede*).

LEMON, MRS. Mistress of the school where Rosamond Vincy was educated. *Mid.* xi, xvi, xxvii, xliii, xlv.

"The chief school in the county, where the teaching included all that was demanded in the accomplished female—even to extras, such as the getting in and out of a carriage." Ch. xi.

LENONI, MR. Name by which Mr. Christian greets Dominic. *F. H.* xix.

LENTULUS. A conceited man, "surprised at his own originality," who is reserved in praising his contemporaries because he sees how superior his own work on the same lines would have been if he had ever taken it up. *T. S.* iv.

LEO. Armgart's devoted old music master, who, when his own music is forgotten, trains her voice to perfection. After she loses her voice, his story and example encourage her to "bury her dead joy" and live for others. *P.—Armg.* i, iv-v.

LEO, JOSEPH. Mirah Cohen's music master at Vienna. *D. D.* xx, xxxix.

LEONARDI, CAMILLO (*Hist.*). A learned man who prescribes for Bardo de' Bardi the wearing of certain rings as a cure for numbness. *Rom.* vi.

Note.—Camillo Leonardo (or Camillus Leonardus), of Pesaro, an astronomer and physician of the latter part of the fifteenth century. He wrote several books, especially one entitled *Speculum lapidum* (first ed. 1502), a work on precious stones, their history, properties, virtues against disease, etc.

LEONORA, AUNT. The Princess Halm-Eberstein's aunt, who gave her niece the ambition to be a singer, as she had been. *D. D.* li.

"LET US TAKE THE ROAD" (*Real*). A song from the "Beggar's Opera" sung by Lucy Deane, Philip Wakem, and Stephen Guest. *M. F.* Bk. 6, vii.

LETHERALL, MR. The man who advises Latimer's father to give him a scientific education. *L. V.* i.

"LETTERS TO A YOUNG MAN ON HIS ENTRANCE INTO LIFE." Title of a book written by Miss Pratt. *J. R.* iii.

LETTY. Servant at Transome Court. *F. H.* xxxix.

LEUBRONN. The continental resort where Gwendolen Harleth gambles and attracts the attention of Daniel Deronda. *D. D.* i–iii, xv, xxv, xxix.

Note.—In her picture of Leubronn, George Eliot may have had in mind Homburg, where the sight of a young woman gambling once suggested to her that incident in Gwendolen Harleth's career.

LEYBURN, MISS. The daughter of the county member. *M. F.* Bk. 6, i.

LEYBURN, MR. An M.P. from St. Ogg's. *M. F.* Bk. 6, ii.

LIBRAJ, VIA DE' (*Real*). Street in Florence where Tessa meets the young Piagnoni who demand her necklace for the Bonfire of Vanities. *Rom.* l.

Note.—The street formerly called Via de' Libraj is that part of the present Via del Proconsolo between the Borgo degli Albizi and the Piazza San Firenze.

LICHTENBERG PALACE. A picture gallery in Vienna frequently visited by Latimer and his family. *L. V.* i.

Note.—Possibly meant for the Liechtenstein Picture Gallery in Vienna.

LILLO. Small son of the contadina Tessa and Tito Melema. *Rom.* xxxiii–xxxiv, lvi, lxx, Epilogue.

When as a child of three years old he runs away from home, he is found and taken home by Romola, who thus finds her husband's "other wife" and his children.

LILLY. Copying clerk; member of the Philosophers' club. *D. D.* xlii.

"Lilly, the pale, neat-faced copying clerk, whose light-brown hair was set up in a small parallelogram above his well-filled forehead, and whose shirt, taken with an otherwise seedy costume, had a freshness that might be called insular, and perhaps even something narrower." Ch. xlii.

LIMP, MR. "A meditative shoemaker, with weak eyes and a piping voice." *Mid.* lxxi.

LINDA, COUNTESS. The fair, gentle young court lady to whom the saintly peasant Agatha talks of her simple faith. *P.—Agatha.*

LINDUM. Town near St. Ogg's. *M. F.* Bk. 3, i; Bk. 6, xiii.

Note.—The original of Lindum was Lincoln.

LINGON, MISS. Mrs. Transome's maiden name. *See* TRANSOME, MRS. ARABELLA.

LINGON, REVEREND JOHN. Mrs. Transome's brother; rector of Little Treby. *F. H.* i–ii, xix, xxxi, xxxiii, xliii, xlvi–xlvii, Epilogue.

"The rector of Little Treby had been a favourite in the neighbourhood since the beginning of the century . . . He had always been called Jack Lingon, or Parson Jack—sometimes, in older and less serious days, even 'Cockfighting Jack'. He swore a little when the point of a joke seemed to demand it, and was fond of wearing a coloured bandana tied loosely over his cravat, together with large brown leather leggings; he spoke in a pithy familiar way that people could understand, and had none of that frigid mincingness called dignity, which some have thought a peculiar clerical disease." Ch. xix.

Although he had always been a Tory, family feeling makes him support his nephew, Harold Transome, when the latter comes out as a Radical candidate.

LINNET, MRS. A matter-of-fact, rather vulgar widow; a member of Mr. Tryan's congregation. *J. R.* iii, vi, x, xiii, xxi, xxv–xxvi.

LINNET, MISS MARY. Mrs. Linnet's elder daughter, an amiable, colourless woman past her first youth, who is in love with Mr. Tryan. *J. R.* iii, v–vi, xi, xxi, xxv–xxvi.

"She had always combined a love of serious and poetical reading with her skill in fancywork, and the neatly-bound copies of Dryden's *Virgil*, Hannah More's *Sacred Dramas*, Falconer's *Shipwreck*, Mason *On Self-Knowledge*, *Rasselas*, and Burke *On the Sublime and Beautiful*, which were the chief ornaments of the book-case . . . had been bought with her pocket-money when she was in her teens . . . Miss Linnet had dark ringlets, a sallow complexion, and an amiable disposition. As to her features, there was not much to criticize in them, for she had little nose, less lip, and no eyebrow; and as to her intellect, her friend Mrs. Pettifer often said: 'She didn't know a more sensible person to talk to than Mary Linnet' . . . While most people thought it a pity that a sensible woman like Mary had not found a good husband." Ch. iii.

Note.—In the lists of originals prepared in Nuneaton after the publication of *Scenes of Clerical Life*, the originals of the Misses Linnet were the Misses Hill. Mrs. Linnet was Mrs. Hill. (Manuscript notes.)

LINNET, MISS REBECCA. Mrs. Linnet's younger daughter, a headstrong, unpopular woman. Like her sister, she is in love with Mr. Tryan, for whose sake she gives up finery. *J. R.* iii, v, x–xi, xxv–xxvi.

"Rebecca was always spoken of sarcastically, and it was a customary kind of banter with young ladies to recommend her as a wife to any gentleman they happened to be flirting with— her fat, her finery, and her thick ankles sufficing to give piquancy to the joke, notwithstanding the absence of novelty." Ch. iii.

LINTER, LADY SARA. Mr. G.'s *L. S.* v.

LIPPUS. A blunderer, who ruins his chance by a too elaborate personal canvas. *T. S.* i.

LIRET, MONSIEUR. Vaudois clergyman in Lausanne, who gave conferences on the history of the Waldenses. *Mid.* ii, v.

LISA. A fair young girl of Palermo who falls deeply and innocently in love with King Pedro, when she sees him at a tournament. Wasting away with her hopeless love, and grieving over the thought of dying

while the king is still ignorant of her feeling for him, she confides her story to Minuccio, the sweet singer, and bids him sing it to the king. Touched by Minuccio's song, the king visits Lisa and bids her live, and he and his Queen take Lisa and Perdicone, whom she marries happily, under their protection. Thereafter the King always calls himself Lisa's faithful knight. *P.—Lisa.*
Note.—The poem "How Lisa loved the King" is a poetical version of one of Boccaccio's tales. The original story is given in the *Decamerone*, tenth day, novel seven.

LISA, MONNA. The deaf old woman who looks after Tessa and her children. *Rom.* xxxiii–xxxiv, l, lvi, lxx.

"LITTLE CORDUROYS." *See* BOND, TOMMY.

LITTLE TREBY. Village near Treby Magna. *F. H.* Introd., i–ii, xix, xxvii, Epilogue.

LITTLESHAW. Village in Stonyshire, where Tommy Trounsem was discovered. *F. H.* xxviii–xxix, xxxv.

LIVERPOOL (*Real*). *Adam B.* xl, xliv; *B. J.* i; mentioned *J. R.* ii; *Mid.* lxx.

In *Adam Bede* Arthur Donnithorne lands at Liverpool on his return from Ireland; in *Brother Jacob* David Faux sails from Liverpool to seek his fortune in America.

LIZZIE. Mr. Jerome's little granddaughter. *J. R.* viii, xxvi.

LOAMFORD. Town where Felix Holt is imprisoned and tried. In *Middlemarch* Loamford is a town in the vicinity of Middlemarch. *F. H.* xxxiii, xxxvii, xli–xlii, xlv–xlvii; mentioned *Adam B.* xi; *Mid.* lviii.

LOAMSHIRE. The county in which Hayslope, the main scene of *Adam Bede*, is situated. *Adam B.* i, and following chapters.

"That rich undulating district of Loamshire to which Hayslope belonged lies close to a grim outskirt of Stonyshire, overlooked by its barren hills as a pretty blooming sister may sometimes be seen linked in the arm of a rugged, tall, swarthy brother; and in two or three hours' ride the traveller might exchange a bleak, treeless region, intersected by lines of cold grey stone, for one where his road wound under the shelter of woods, or up swelling hills, muffled with hedgerows and long meadow-grass and thick corn; and where at every turn he came upon some fine old country seat nestled in the valley or crowning the slope, some homestead with its long length of barn and its cluster of golden ricks, some grey steeple looking out from a pretty confusion of trees and thatch and dark-red tiles." Ch. ii.

Note.—The original of Loamshire in *Adam Bede* is Staffordshire, the county in which George Eliot's father, Robert Evans ("Adam Bede") lived before moving to Warwickshire.

LOAMSHIRE. The county in which Middlemarch is situated. *Mid.* i.

LOAMSHIRE, NORTH. The section in England in which the Transome estates are situated; the scene of the novel *Felix Holt*. *F. H.* Introduction, and following chapters.

LOAMSHIRE MILITIA. Captain Arthur Donnithorne's regiment. *Adam B.* v, xxxvi.

LOGGIA, ORCAGNA'S. *See* ORCAGNA'S LOGGIA.

LOGGIA DE' CERCHI (*Real*). Arcade in Florence under which Bratti finds Tito Melema sleeping. *Rom.* i–ii.

Note.—The Loggia dei Cerchi, which in the fifteenth century was an arcade near the houses of the famous Cerchi family, is now enclosed, forming the lower story of a house at the corner of the Via dei Cerchi and the Via de' Cimatori. Parts of the columns of the Loggia showing the Arms of the Cerchi can still be seen.

LOLA. A fat Spanish girl at the Inn. *Sp. G.* i.

LOLIGO. A fluent writer, in the great Merman-Grampus controversy. *T. S.* iii.

LOLLO. The conjurer's impish lad, who assists the conjurer at the Fierucola and later, as a prank, cuts the bonds of the old prisoner, thus releasing Baldassarre Calvo. *Rom.* xiv, xxii.

LOLO. Dog. *M. F.* Bk. 6, i.

LONDON (*Real*). London is a main scene in *Daniel Deronda*, through the residence there of the Cohens and the Meyricks, etc., and it is mentioned, as a very minor scene, in several of the stories of provincial life. *Adam B.* mentioned xxxvii; *Amos B.* vii; *D. D.* vi, xvi–xx, xxxii–xxxiv, xxxvii–xliii, xlv–l, lii, lxi–lxiii, lxv–lxviii, lxx; *F. H.* ii, vi, xvii, xxx; *J. R.* ii, xviii; *M. F.* Bk. 6, i; *Mid.* xv–xvi, liii, lviii, lxi, lxxv–lxxvii, lxxix, lxxxiv, Finale.

Various localities and buildings in London and its vicinity are mentioned in the different novels. All of these which have any part, however small, in the plots of the stories, are entered separately in their alphabetical places in the Dictionary, and the fuller information, including the historical notes, is given under these separate entries. The following list will show at a glance what localities in London and its immediate vicinity are mentioned.

BEDFORD ROW. *F. H.* xvii, xxx, Epilogue.

BLACKFRIARS BRIDGE. *D. D.* xx, xxviii, xl.

BLACKHEATH. *F. H.* xxi.

BROMPTON. *D. D.* xlvi, lxii, lxvi–lxvii.

CHELSEA. *D. D.* xvii, and later.

CRYSTAL PALACE. *D. D.* xxxiv.

FINSBURY. *Mid.* xli.

GOWER STREET. *J. R.* xviii.

GROSVENOR PLACE. *D. D.* xlviii.

GROSVENOR SQUARE. *D. D.* xliv–xlv, xlviii, lviii, lxiv.

HIGHBURY. *Mid.* liii.

HOLBORN. *D. D.* xxxiii.

KEW BRIDGE. *D. D.* xvii.

KEW GARDENS. *D. D.* xvii.

KNIGHTSBRIDGE. *D. D.* lxii.

LAMBETH. *D. D.* xx.
MARBLE ARCH. *D. D.* lii.
NATIONAL GALLERY. *D. D.* xxxviii.
PARK LANE. *D. D.* xvii, xxviii, xxxvii, xlv, lxiv.
PUTNEY. *D. D.* xvii.
REGENT STREET. *D. D.* xxxix.
RICHMOND BRIDGE. *D. D.* xvii.
ROTTEN ROW. *D. D.* xxxiii, xlviii.
THAMES (River). *D. D.* xvii, xx, xl.
LONDON ROAD. "That pleasant issue from Middlemarch called London Road, which was also the road to the New Hospital." *Mid.* lx, lxvi.
LONG, MR. ST. JOHN (*Hist.*). A medical charlatan, who claimed to have extracted mercury from the temples of a patient. *Mid.* xlv.
Note.—John St. John Long (1798-1834), an ex-artist who established a medical practice in London in 1827, and claimed to have an entirely original method of treating consumption, etc. He was twice tried for manslaughter, and eventually died of a consumption which he refused to treat by his own method.
LONG MEADOWS. The residence of the Palfreys. *B. J.* ii.
LOPEZ, CAPTAIN. A Spanish captain, in charge of the guard of the Gypsy prisoners. *Sp. G.* i.
LORENZO, *formerly called* Ephraim. Innkeeper at Bedmár; the son of a converted Jew. *Sp. G.* i–ii.
LORENZO, SAN (BORGO). *See* BORGO SAN LORENZO.

LORENZO, SAN (CHURCH). *See* SAN LORENZO.
LORTON. *See* KING'S LORTON.
LOUIS (*Hist.*). A French physician, a fever specialist, under whom Lydgate had studied in Paris. *Mid.* xvi, lxxvi.
Note.—Pierre Charles Louis (1787–1872), whose well-known work on typhoid fever was published in 1829.
"LOVE IN HER EYES SITS PLAYING" (*Real*). A song which Philip Wakem sings for Maggie Tulliver. *M. F.* Bk. 5, iii.
Note.—A song from Handel's *Acis and Galatea*; the words are by John Gay.
LOVEGOOD. Sir James Chettam's manager. *Mid.* iii–iv, xxxiv, xxxviii.
LOWER AND UPPER RIDGES. The land which Squire Donnithorne wishes Mr. Poyser to give up to Thurle. *Adam B.* xxxii.
LOWICK. Parish near Middlemarch. *Mid.* iii–iv, vii, ix, xii, xxxiv–xxxv, xl, xlvii, lii, lvi–lvii, lxx–lxxi, lxxxiv.
Note.—The parish of Lowick in Middlemarch is imaginary, though its name is real. When George Eliot chose the name she did not remember that there was any place of the name in England, but there are actually three parishes named Lowick, one of them in a Midland county. (*See* Cross, *George Eliot's Life*, vol. 3, p. 212.)
LOWICK CHURCH. The church of which first Mr. Casaubon, and

later Mr. Farebrother, is rector. *Mid.* ix, xlvii.

LOWICK GATE. Street in Middlemarch where the Vincys live. *Mid.* xxvi–xxvii, xxxi, xxxvi, xliii, lx, lxix–lxx, lxxviii.

LOWICK MANOR. The residence of Mr. Casaubon and Dorothea. *Mid.* ix, xxvii–xxix, xxxiv, xxxvii, xlii, xlix–l, liv, lvi, lxiv, lxxii, lxxvi.

" It had a small park, with a fine old oak here and there, and an avenue of limes toward the south-west front, with a sunk fence between park and pleasure ground, so that from the drawing-room windows the glance swept uninterruptedly along a slope of greensward till the limes ended in a level of corn and pastures, which often seemed to melt into a lake under the setting sun . . . The building, of greenish stone, was in the old English style, not ugly, but small-windowed and melancholy-looking ; the sort of house that must have children, many flowers, open windows, and little vistas of bright things, to make it seem a joyous home." Ch. ix.

LOWICK PARSONAGE. The home of the Farebrother family after Mrs. Casaubon gives the Lowick living to Mr. Farebrother. *Mid.* ix, liv, lvii, lix, lxvi, lxxi, lxxx, lxxxii.

LOWME, MR. An elderly man in Milby who prides himself on his aristocracy. *J. R.* ii, iv, xiv, xxv.

" Mr. Lowme, one of the most aristocratic men in Milby, said to have been ' brought up a gentleman ', and to have had the gay habits accordant with that station, keeping his harriers and other expensive animals. He was now quite an elderly Lothario, reduced to the most economical sins ; the prominent form of his gaiety being this of lounging at Mr. Gruby's door, embarrassing the servant-maids who came for grocery, and talking scandal with the rare passers-by." Ch. ii.

Note.—In the lists of originals prepared in Nuneaton after the publication of *Scenes of Clerical Life,* the original of Mr. Lowme is said to have been a Mr. Towle. (See Olcott, *George Eliot,* p. 16.)

LOWME, MRS. Mr. Lowme's wife, a firm believer in Mr. Pilgrim's skill. *J. R.* ii, vii, x, xxv.

LOWME, THE MISSES. *J. R.* vii.

LOWME, MR. BOB. The possessor of beautiful whiskers which meet under his chin. *J. R.* ii.

LUCA, FRA. The religious name of Romola's brother Bernardino de' Bardi, who has left his family to become a Dominican monk. *Rom.* v, viii, x–xiii, xv, xvii.

He had been brought up to share in his father's studies, but, in spite of the fact that he was the blind man's one hope, had turned from scholarship to mysticism, deserting his father to join the Dominicans, and had become a wanderer and hermit in Eastern lands. On his way home, broken in health, he meets a man who has seen Baldassarre Calvo, Tito Melema's deserted father, and from him receives a letter to Tito begging him to save his father from slavery. He delivers the note, and is thus the one person who knows that Tito is aware that his father is alive. Although he has this knowledge, which might have saved his sister Romola from her disastrous marriage to Tito Melema, he does not warn her of it, but instead, when dying, gives her a visionary, mystical warning which merely distresses her. It is at Fra Luca's death bed that Romola first sees Savonarola, who is later to influence her so greatly.

LUCIA, SANTA (CHURCH). *See* SANTA LUCIA, CHURCH OF.

LUCKRETH. A village on the River Floss, which Maggie and Stephen pass when they leave St. Ogg's together. *M. F.* Bk. 6, xiii.

Note.—It has been suggested that the original of Luckreth was Stockwith, a village on the Trent ("Floss"), about three and one-half miles north of Gainsborough ("St. Oggs"). (*See* article by John F. Fraser in the *Bookman* (London), vol. 9, p. 55.)

LUCY. The girl whose life Mr. Tryan ruined in his college days. *J. R.* xviii.

LUFF, MR. Draper at Grimworth. *B. J.* ii.

LUKE. *See* MOGGS, LUKE.

LUKIN, DR. *F. H.* iv.

LUKYN. An inhabitant of Treby. *F. H.* xxi, xxiv.

LUKYN, OLD MRS. *F. H.* xxii.

LUNDY, BOB. Butcher at Raveloe; "a jolly, smiling, red-haired man, who was not disposed to answer rashly," a frequenter of the Rainbow Inn. *S. M.* vi.

LUNG ARNO (*Real*). Quai along the Arno in Florence, where on the day of his betrothal Tito Melema first sees that Tessa is following him. *Rom.* xx, xliii.

"LUNGI DAL CARO BENE" (*Real*). Music which Will Ladislaw and Mrs. Lydgate are playing when Dorothea interrupts them. *Mid.* xliii.

Note.—A cavatina, by Giuseppe Sarti (1729–1802).

LUNIGIANA (*Real*). The region where the prisoners brought to Florence by the French had been captured. *Rom.* xxii–xxiii.

Note.—A picturesque region of Central Italy, including the lower valley of the Magra and the mountains to the west.

LUNN, MR. Sally's father. *B. J.* i.

LUNN, SALLY. An early flame of David Faux's. *B. J.* i.

LUPO. A crazy man at Peretola, of whom Baldassarre Calvo reminds Tessa. *Rom.* xxxiv.

LUSH, MR. THOMAS CRANMER. Mr. Grandcourt's general factotum and toady, a man educated for the Church, who preferred the lazy luxury of the life of a rich man's companion to the activity of a clerical career. *D. D.* xi–xv, xxv, xxvii–xxviii, xxx, xxxvi, xlv, xlviii, liv.

"A middle-aged man, with dark, full face and fat hands ... prominent eyes, fat though not clumsy figure, and strong black grey-besprinkled hair of frizzy thickness." Ch. xi.

"Mr. Lush had passed for a scholar once, and had still a sense of scholarship when he was not trying to remember much of it; but the bachelor's and other arts which softened manners are a time-honoured preparation for sinecures, and Lush's present comfortable provision was as good as a sinecure in not requiring more than the odour of departed learning... Lush's love of ease was well satisfied at present, and if his puddings were rolled towards him in the dust, he took the inside bits and found them relishing." Ch. xii.

He schemes to have Grandcourt marry the rich Miss Arrowpoint, and disapproves of his attentions to Gwendolen Harleth. Failing to influence Grandcourt, he arranges to have Mrs. Glasher see Gwendolen, hoping that the story of Mrs. Glasher's relations with Grandcourt may drive Gwendolen to refuse him. From the beginning Gwendolen feels a marked antipathy for Mr. Lush, and when she marries Grandcourt her influence banishes him for awhile, but he is eventually recalled, and is the one deputed to tell Gwendolen of the disagreeable provisions in her husband's will.

LYDDY. Mr. Lyon's old servant, much given to despondency and groans. *F. H.* iv–vi, xiii–xvi, xviii, xxii, xxvi–xxvii, xxxii, xxxviii, xl, li.

LYDGATE, CAPTAIN. Sir Godwin's third son; a fop and a critic of feminine charms, whose admiration greatly pleases Rosamund and leads her to disobey her husband and so lose her baby. *Mid.* lviii, lxiv.

LYDGATE, CHARLES. Tertius Lydgate's uncle. *Mid.* lxv.

LYDGATE, SIR GODWIN. Uncle of Tertius Lydgate, who refuses to help his nephew when he is in need of money. *Mid.* xxxvi, xliii, lviii, lxiv–lxv.

LYDGATE, ROSAMOND. *See* VINCY, ROSAMOND.

LYDGATE, TERTIUS. A talented young doctor with a great enthusiasm for the best in his profession. *Mid.* x–xiii, xv–xviii, xxvi–xxvii, xxix–xxxi, xxxiv, xxxvi, xl, xlii–xlvi, xlvii, l–lii, lvi, lviii–lix, lxiii–lxxix, lxxxi–lxxxii, Finale.

"One of Lydgate's gifts was a voice habitually deep and sonorous, yet capable of becoming very low and gentle at the right moment. About his ordinary bearing there was a certain fling, a fearless expectation of success, a confidence in his own powers and integrity, much fortified by contempt for petty obstacles or seductions of which he had had no experience. But this proud openness was made lovable by an expression of unaffected goodwill." Ch. xiii.

"His scientific interest soon took the form of a professional enthusiasm; he had a youthful belief in his bread-winning work ... and he carried to his studies ... the conviction that the medical profession as it might be was the finest in the world ... But he did not simply aim at a more genuine kind of practice than was common. He was ambitious of a wider effect: he was fired with the possibility that he might work out the proof of an anatomical conception and make a link in the chain of discovery . . . Lydgate was ambitious above all to contribute towards enlarging the scientific, rational basis of his profession." Ch. xv.

He settles in Middlemarch, intending not only to be a good doctor, but also to carry on scientific investigation, for which he is well fitted. Captivated by Rosamond Vincy's beauty and grace, he marries her and soon discovers that she is absolutely selfish and unresponsive to his tender love, with no sympathy for his high aims. His opposition to accepted medical usages makes him unpopular with the other physicians of Middlemarch, and his connexion with Mr. Bulstrode leads him into trouble. His wife has only blame for him, and all his endeavours to economize are stubbornly opposed by her. The struggle between him and Rosamond, who demands position and luxury at any price, ends in the subjection of his higher self, and his noblest aims are sacrificed to worldly success. To meet the demands of her ambition he is forced to move to London, and become a fashionable physician, and dies there at a comparatively early age.

Note.—The high-minded, medical side of Lydgate is said to have been drawn from the Rt. Hon. Sir T. Clifford Allbutt, Regius Professor of Physic, Cambridge, who, when *Middlemarch* was written, was head of the Leeds Fever Hospital which George Eliot visited. The portraiture is but partial and the circumstances different. (Manuscript notes.) George Eliot's friend and biographer, Mr. Oscar Browning, has also been suggested as the prototype, in part. (Browning, *Memories of Sixty Years*, p. 193.)

"LYDIA" (*Real*). A tune which Mr. Barton sets in church, thereby scandalizing Mr. Farquhar. *Amos B.* ii.

Note. — Composed by Thomas Phillips (1774–1841), and used in Nonconformist hymnbooks before it was adopted in the Church of England.

LYON, ESTHER. A beautiful and charming girl who gives up the wealth and social position that she might claim in order to marry Felix Holt. *F. H.* iv–vi, x, xiv–xvi, xviii–xix, xxii, xxiv–xxvii, xxx, xxxii, xxxvi–Epilogue.

"A very delicate scent, the faint suggestion of a garden, was wafted as she went. He would not observe her, but he had a sense of an elastic walk, the tread of small feet, a long neck, and a high crown of shining brown plaits with curls that floated backward—things, in short, that suggested a fine lady . . . Esther had that excellent thing in woman, a soft voice with a clear fluent utterance. Her sauciness was always charming, because it was without emphasis, and was accompanied with graceful little turns of the head." Ch. v.

"She had one of those exceptional organizations which are quick and sensitive without being in the least morbid; she was alive to the finest shades of manner, to the nicest distinctions of tone and accent . . . Her own pretty instep, clad in a silk stocking, her little heel, just rising from a kid slipper, her irreproachable nails and delicate wrist, were the objects of delighted consciousness to her; and she felt that it was her superiority which made her unable to use without disgust any but the finest cambric handkerchiefs and freshest gloves. Her money all went in the gratification of these nice tastes, and she saved nothing from her earnings . . . she hated all meanness, would empty her purse impulsively on some sudden appeal to her pity, and if she found out that her father had a want she would supply it with some pretty device of a surprise." Ch. vi.

She had been brought up as the daughter of Rufus Lyon, the Independent minister, and while fond of her father has little sympathy with his simple tastes and life. Through her father she meets Felix Holt, and while at first repelled by his surface roughness, soon becomes interested in him and in the lectures that he gives her. Fearing that she may hear the story from someone else, Rufus Lyon tells her that he is not her real father, and that she is the daughter of Maurice Christian Bycliffe. She is much touched by his story of his devotion and marriage to her mother, and gains a different appreciation of his life and character. Later, after she learns that she is the rightful owner of the Transome estates, she goes to Transome Court to visit Mrs. Transome, and there is courted by Harold Transome. What she sees at Transome Court shows her that wealth does not necessarily bring happiness, and as Felix Holt's trial for manslaughter has opened her eyes to the strength of her real feeling for him, she gives up her claim to the estate to marry Felix.

Note.—While George Eliot's portrait of Esther Lyon is not autobiographic to anything like the same extent as that of the character of Maggie Tulliver (in *Mill on the Floss*), there are some things in it— the fastidiousness, niceness about dress, etc.—for which the author's own tastes and habits supplied the original. (*See* Parkinson, *Scenes from the George Eliot Country*, p. 85; Timmins, *History of Warwickshire*, p. 151.)

LYON, REV. RUFUS. The ardent minister of the Independent Chapel in Treby Magna, and Esther Lyon's reputed father, a man of many lovable oddities and much nobility of character. *F. H.* iii–vi, x, xiii–xvi, xviii–xix, xxii–xxvii, xxx, xxxii, xxxvi– xxxviii, xl–xli, xliv–xlvi, l, Epilogue.

"He was walking about now, with his hands clasped behind him, an attitude in which his body seemed to bear about the same proportion to his head as the lower part of a stone Hermes bears to the carven image that crowns it. His face looked old and worn, yet the curtain of hair that fell from his bald crown and hung about his neck retained much of its original auburn tint, and his large, brown, short-sighted eyes were still clear and bright. At the first glance, every one thought him a very odd-looking rusty old man; the free-school boys often hooted after him and called him "Revelations"; and to many respectable church people old Lyon's little legs and large head seemed to make Dissent additionally preposterous. But he was too shortsighted to notice those who tittered at him—too absent from the world of small facts and petty impulses in which titterers live." Ch. iv.

"Once in his life he had been blinded, deafened, hurried along by rebellious impulse; he had gone astray after his own desires, and had let the fire die out on the altar; and as the true penitent, hating his self-besotted error, asks from all coming life duty instead of joy, and service instead of ease, so Rufus was perpetually on the watch lest he should ever again postpone to some private affection a great public opportunity which to him was equivalent to a command." Ch. xv.

Twenty-two years before the opening of the story Rufus Lyon was an eloquent and successful minister of a large Independent Chapel, when Annette Ledru came suddenly into his life. The death of her husband, Maurice Christian Bycliffe, had left her penniless in a strange land, and Mr. Lyon took her and her baby into his home, in spite of the criticism of his congregation, fell deeply in love with her, and gave up his high calling to watch over her and her child. After a time the grateful Annette married him and when she died, three years later, he returned to the ministry, and brought up the baby, Esther, as his own daughter. At the opening of the story he is leading, in humble surroundings, a life of wrapt absorption in his work and loving devotion to Esther, who still believes herself his daughter. When events make him believe that she should no longer be kept in ignorance of her parentage he tells her the full story and leaves her free to decide whether or not she will claim the inheritance and rank to which she is apparently entitled.

Note.—The original of Rufus Lyon was the Reverend Francis Franklin, a Baptist minister, who for fifty-four years, from 1799 until his death in 1852, was pastor of the Cow Lane Chapel, in Coventry. Mr. Franklin was the father of the Misses Franklin, whose school in Coventry George Eliot attended, and the character of Rufus Lyon is said by those who remembered him, to be a faithful portrait. (*See* Cross, *George Eliot's Life*, vol. 1, pp. 24-5; Negri, *George Eliot*, vol. 2, p. 62; also article in *Our Times*, June, 1881.)

LYON, MRS. RUFUS. *See* LEDRU, ANNETTE.

LYTHERLY. A town in the neighbourhood of Raveloe. *S. M.* xi, Conclusion (Lytherley).

M

MACARTHY. A recluse who dies young leaving behind him many manuscripts. *E. E.* 1.

MACCHIAVELLI, NICCOLÒ (*Hist.*). A young friend of Tito Melema, who is to succeed Tito as Secretary to the Ten if the latter has to leave Florence suddenly. *Rom.* iii, xii, xvi, xxv, xxxix, xlv, lii, lx, lxiii, lxv.

"He was a young man about Tito's own age, with keen features, small close-clipped head, and close-shaven lip and chin, giving the idea of a mind as little encumbered as possible with material that was not nervous. The keen eyes were bright with hope and friendliness, as so many other young eyes have been that have afterwards closed on the world in bitterness and disappointment; for at that time there were none but pleasant predictions about Niccolò Macchiavelli, as a young man of promise, who was expected to mend the broken fortunes of his ancient family." Ch. xvi.

Note.—Niccolò di Bernardo dei Macchiavelli (1469-1527), Florentine statesman and author, Secretary to the Ten, 1498-1512.

MACEY, MR. Parish clerk and tailor at Raveloe; a discursive and argumentative old gentleman who delights in relating the events which have taken place in the parish in the past; generally admired for his "'cuteness". *S. M.* i, vi-viii, x-xi, xiv, xvi, xix, Conclusion.

MACEY, SOLOMON. Fiddler, brother of the parish clerk at Raveloe; "a small hale old man, with an abundant crop of long white hair reaching nearly to his shoulders." *S. M.* vi, xi.

MACKWORTH. A visitor at Leubronn. *D. D.* i.

MADDALENA, SUORA (*Hist.*). A seer of visions. *Rom.* xxxvi.

Note.—Suora Maddalena Panatiere da Trina (1443-1503), a member of the third order of St. Dominic.

MADELEY, DR. Physician from Rotherby, called in to attend Milly Barton. *Amos B.* viii; mentioned *J. R.* xxvii.[1]

MADONNA DELL' IMPRUNETA. *See* IMPRUNETA, MADONNA DELL'.

MAGICODUMBRAS. A subject about which Proteus Merman discovers the great Grampus to be all wrong. *T. S.* iii.

MAGLIO, VIA DEL (*Real*). Street in Florence through which Romola and Monna Brigida have to take a round-about way to San Marco because of the crowd of the Fierucola. *Rom.* xiii.

---

[1] Nuneaton lists give his prototype as either Dr. Miller or Dr. Bourne. (MS. notes.)

Note.—The street formerly called Via del Maglio from the popular game Del Maglio played there by the young Florentines, is now the Via Lamarmora extending northward from San Marco.

MAGNIFICENT, THE. *See* MEDICI, LORENZO DE'.

MAGNIFICENT EIGHT. *See* EIGHT.

MAGNIFICO, IL. *See* MEDICI, LORENZO DE'.

"MAID OF ARTOIS" (*Real*). Music which Stephen Guest brings to Lucy Dean. *M. F.* Bk. 6, vi. *Note.*—An opera by W. M. Balfe.

"MAIDEN, CROWNED WITH GLOSSY BLACKNESS." Juan's song about Fedalma. *Sp. G.* i.

MAINWARING. One of Fred Vincy's acquaintances. *Mid.* xii.

MAINZ (*Real*). The city in Germany where Joseph Kalonymos' banking establishment is located; Daniel Deronda goes there to get his grandfather's papers from Kalonymos. *D. D.* li, lix–lx, lxiii. *Note.*—Mainz (or Mayence), on the Rhine just below the confluence of the Main and the Rhine.

MAKEPIECE. Electioneering agent. *F. H.* xvii, xxxv.

MALAM, JUSTICE. The Justice of the Peace whom it is proposed to invoke when Silas Marner's gold is stolen. *S. M.* vii–x.

"Justice Malam was naturally regarded in Tarley and Raveloe as a man of capacious mind, seeing that he could draw much wider conclusions without evidence than could be expected of his neighbours who were not on the Commission of the Peace." Ch. x.

MALINGRE, HUGUES LE. The ancestor of the Mallingers "who came in with the Conqueror". *D. D.* xvi.

MALLINGER, AMABEL. One of Sir Hugo Mallinger's three daughters. *D. D.* lii, lxix.

MALLINGER, SIR FRANCIS. Sir Hugo's father, whose will gave Sir Hugo only a life interest in the lands, for want of a son. *D. D.* xv.

MALLINGER, HENLEIGH. *See* GRANDCOURT, Henleigh Mallinger.

MALLINGER, SIR HUGO. A genial baronet and M.P., who is on poor terms with his own nephew and heir, Henleigh Mallinger Grandcourt, and is much attached to his ward and reputed nephew, Daniel Deronda. *D. D.* i, iii, ix–x, xv–xvii, xx, xxv, xxviii, xxxii–xxxiii, xxxv–xxxvii, xli, xlv, xlviii, xlix–lii, lv, lix, lxiv–lxv, lxix–lxx.

"Sir Hugo was an easy-tempered man, tolerant both of differences and defects; but a point of view different from his own concerning the settlement of the family estates fretted him rather more than if it had concerned Church discipline, or the ballot, and faults were the less venial for belonging to a person whose existence was inconvenient to him. In no case could Grandcourt have been a nephew after his own heart; but as the presumptive heir to the Mallinger estates he was the sign and embodiment of a chief grievance in the baronet's life—the want of a son to inherit the lands." Ch. xv.

"Hardly any man could be more good-natured than Sir Hugo; indeed, in his kindliness, especially to women, he did actions which others would have called romantic; but he never took a romantic view of them, and in general smiled at the introduction of motives on a grand scale, or of reasons that lay very far off." Ch. xxxii.

In his youth he had been deeply in love with a beautiful prima donna, the Italian Jewess, Alcharisi, and at her request, after her husband's death, had taken charge of her young son, Daniel Deronda, to bring him up in England, as an Englishman and in ignorance of his race. When he marries, he has only daughters, and so gradually gives to his ward the affection that he would have given a son, ignorant of the fact that the secrecy maintained about his parentage has made Daniel believe that he is Sir Hugo's illegitimate son. He wishes Daniel to enter English public life, and when the latter, after his parentage and race are revealed to him, by his unknown mother, elects to call himself a Jew and work for his race, Sir Hugo is disappointed but is too genuinely attached to Daniel to oppose him.

MALLINGER, LOUISA, LADY. Sir Hugo's gentle wife, who "felt apologetically about herself as a woman who had produced nothing but daughters in a case where sons were required". *D. D.* xv–xvii, xx, xxv, xxviii, xxxii–xxxiii, xxxv–xxxvii, xlv, lxix–lxx.

"She had reddish blond hair (the hair of the period), a small Roman nose, rather prominent blue eyes and delicate eyelids, with a figure which her thinner friends called fat, her hands showing curves and dimples like a magnified baby's." Ch. xxviii.

MALLINGER, THERESA. One of Sir Hugo Mallinger's three daughters. *D. D.* xxviii, lii.

MALTHOUSE YARD. The location of the Independent Chapel and of Mr. Lyon's house in Treby Magna. *F. H.* iii–vi, xiii–xv, xviii, xxii, xxv, xxxii, xxxviii, xli–xlii, xlvi, Epilogue.

Note.—The original of Rufus Lyon's chapel in Malthouse Yard was Cow Lane Chapel, Coventry, where the Reverend Francis Franklin ("Rufus Lyon") preached for fifty-four years. George Eliot went to this chapel when she was a student in the Misses Franklin's school.

"MAMSEY." Name by which Mr. Dempster sometimes addressed his mother. See DEMPSTER, OLD MRS.

MANETTI, SIBILLA. The old woman with whom Tessa and her children are stranded after Tito's death. *Rom.* lxx.

MANTRAP, SIR GAVIAL. A swindler who is excused and pitied by some, because he has such good morals. *T. S.* xvi.

MARBLE ARCH (*Real*). Spot near which Mirah Cohen first sees her father when he returns to London. *D. D.* lii.

Note.—The Marble Arch, a triumphal arch, erected in 1828 in front of Buckingham Palace and removed about 1850 to its present site at the north-east corner of Hyde Park.

MARCO, SAN (CONVENT AND CHURCH). *See* SAN MARCO, CONVENT AND CHURCH.

MARCO, SAN (PIAZZA). *See* SAN MARCO, PIAZZA.

MARCOS, FATHER. A priest who says Fedalma is an infidel. *Sp. G.* i.

MARIA, POR' SANTA. *See* POR' SANTA MARIA.

MARIA NOVELLA, SANTA. *See* SANTA MARIA NOVELLA.

MARIANO, FRA (*Hist.*). A Dominican who was ready to enter the Fire. *Rom.* lxiv.

Note.—Fra Mariano degli Ughi.

MARIANO, FRA (*Hist.*). A monk who preaches against Savonarola. *Rom.* xii.

Note.—Fra Mariano da Genazzano, an Augustinian who preached against Savonarola at the instigation of Lorenzo de' Medici.

MARIOTTO. A merry-eyed youth of seventeen, who joins in the sport of the mock marriages at the Peasants' Fair. *Rom.* xiv.

MARKET, OLD. *See* MERCATO VECCHIO.

MARKET BEWLEY. *M. F.* Bk. 1, vii.

MARKET-WOMAN. The messenger who delivers to Lorenzo, concealed in an apple, a letter from the Gypsy chief, Zarca, to the Moor, El Zagal. *Sp. G.* ii.

MARKHAM, MR. *Mr. G.'s L. S.* ii, xiv.

"MARKIS O' GRANBY." The former name of "Dickison's", Basset. *M. F.* Bk. 1, viii.

MARLOWE, BROTHER. An aged Wesleyan preacher. *Adam B.* viii.

MARNER, SILAS. Linen weaver at Raveloe. *S. M.* i–ii, iv–viii, x, xii–xxi, Conclusion.

"Strangely Marner's face and figure shrank and bent themselves into a constant mechanical relation to the objects of his life, so that he produced the same sort of impression as a handle or a crooked tube, which has no meaning standing apart. The prominent eyes that used to look trusting and dreamy, now looked as if they had been made to see only one kind of thing that was very small, like tiny grain, for which they hunted everywhere; and he was so withered and yellow, that, though he was not yet forty, the children always called him 'Old Master Marner'." Ch. ii.

"Yet few men could be more harmless than poor Marner. In his truthful simple soul, not even the growing greed and worship of gold could beget any vice directly injurious to others. The light of his faith quite put out, and his affections made desolate, he had clung with all the force of his nature to his work and his money; and like all objects to which a man devotes himself, they had fashioned him into correspondence with themselves. His loom, as he wrought in it without ceasing, had in its turn wrought on him, and confirmed more and more the monotonous craving for its monotonous response. His gold, as he hung over it and saw it grow, gathered his power of loving together into a hard isolation like its own." Ch. v.

In his youth he had been an artisan in a large manufacturing town where, in spite of the fact that he was subject to occasional cataleptic attacks, he led a contented life, his strong interests being his membership in a dissenting church, his friendship for William Dane, and his approaching marriage. Falsely accused of a robbery through his friend's treachery, and driven from church and home, he had wandered to Raveloe where he settled. With all faith in both men and religion lost through his cruel experience, he leads there a lonely life as a recluse and miser, his one pleasure the contemplation of the growing hoard of gold which he saves slowly by hard and constant toil. When his money is stolen, and the little golden-haired Eppie, an unclaimed child, comes, as he thinks, in place of the gold, he brings her up as his daughter, and through her needs and affection regains his joy in life.

Note.—The plot of Silas Marner shows some marked resemblance to a Polish story by Kraszewski called *Jermola the Potter*. The similarity is most striking in the case of the central figure, Jermola, a deserted lonely old man left in poverty by the well-to-do family to which he had given a lifetime of service. Like Silas Marner, old Jermola finds a deserted infant near his hut, adopts it, and through love for it and the efforts which he has to make to support it, is restored to a happy and useful life. Unlike Silas, however, his life ends in tragedy, as the child is taken from him. (*See also* note under *Silas Marner* in *Synopses*.)

"MARQUIS OF GRANBY." Inn at Treby Magna, the stronghold of the Tories. *F. H.* iii, xv, xix–xx, xxxi, xxxiii.

MARRABLES. A florid laboratory assistant; member of the Philosophers' Club. *D. D.* xlii.

MARRIOTT, ELLEN. A pretty Milby girl. *J. R.* v.

MARSEILLES (*Real*). French Mediterranean port from which the Grandcourts start on their yachting trip. *D. D.* xlviii, liv; mentioned *Rom.* xlii.

MARSHALL. Jeweller at Wanchester. *D. D.* xxi.

MARTELLI, VIA DE' (*Real*). Street in Florence by which the syndics return from their interview with Charles VIII in the Via Larga. *Rom.* xxix.

Note.—Via de' Martelli is a short street leading from the Piazza del Duomo to the Via Cavour (formerly Via Larga). Its earlier name of *Via degli Spadai* was changed to Martelli, from the houses of the Martelli family.

MARTHA. Maid at Cheverel Manor. *Mr. G.'s L. S.* vi, xvi, xviii.

MARTHA. Mr. Gilfil's old housekeeper; David's wife. *Mr. G.'s L. S.* i.

MARTHA. Rosamond Lydgate's servant. *Mid.* lxxvii – lxxviii, lxxxi.

MARTHA. Servant of the Tullivers. *M. F.* Bk. 1, vii, ix.

MARTIN, MRS. Sally's mother. *J. R.* xii.

MARTIN, SALLY. A deformed girl in Milby, befriended by Janet Dempster. *J. R.* iii, vi, xii.

MARUFFI, FRA SALVESTRO (*Hist.*). A Dominican brother of San Marco, designated by Savoranola as Romola's confessor. *Rom.* xli, xliv, lviii–lix, lxvi, lxxi–lxxii.

"It was not that there was anything manifestly repulsive in Fra Salvestro's face and manner, any air of hypocrisy, any tinge of coarseness; his face was handsomer than Fra Girolamo's, his person a little taller . . . But his face had the vacillating expression of a mind unable to concentrate itself strongly in the channel of one great emotion or belief . . . Such an expression is not the stamp of insincerity; it is the stamp simply of a shallow soul, which will often be found sincerely striving to fill a high vocation . . . Fra Salvestro had a peculiar liability to visions." Ch. xli.

Note.—Fra Silvestro Maruffi, one of the two Dominicans arrested with Savonarola and executed with him. He was, according to Villari, a weak and frivolous man.

The spelling used by Villari, and by most other authorities, is Silvestro, but some, including Nerli, whose work was used by George Eliot, give the form Salvestro.

MARULLO, MICHELE (*Hist.*). Greek soldier - poet, husband of Alessandra Scala. *Rom.* iii, vii, xii.

Note. — Michael Tarchaniota Marullus, humanist, died 1500.

MARZOCCO (*Real*). The stone lion, emblem of the Florentine Republic. *Rom.* i, vii, xxxv, lxv, lxxii.

Note.—The Marzocco, or stone lion, was set up in various parts of Florence. The one which was in the Piazza della Signoria at the time of *Romola* was by Donatello, and represented a lion seated on his haunches with the right forepaw resting on a shield on which the Florentine lily was carved. This has been replaced by a bronze cast and the original moved to the Museo Nazionale.

"MASANIELLO, DUET IN" (*Real*). Duet which Stephen Guest and Philip Wakem sing. *M. F.* Bk. 6, vii.

Note.—"Masaniello" is the name given in England to D. F. E. Auber's opera "La muette de Portici".

MASKERY, MRS. A Methodist, the wheelwright's plain-looking wife. *Adam B.* v, x.

MASKERY, WILL. A wheelwright who used to be a wild drunken fellow before he became a Methodist. *Adam B.* i–ii, v, xviii.

   Note.—The name Maskery is one of the real names which George Eliot took from the neighbourhood of Ellastone, where her father, Robert Evans ("Adam Bede") lived as a young man. (*See* Mottram, *True Story of George Eliot*, p. 15; Parkinson, *Scenes from the George Eliot Country*, p. 96.)

MASO. The Bardi's old serving man, who serves Romola as long as she lives in the Via de' Bardi and accompanies her on her attempted flight from Florence, when she is turned back by Savonarola. *Rom.* v–vi, xii–xiii, xvi, xx, xxvii–xxviii, xxxi, xxxvi–xxxvii, xli, xlvi, liv, lvi, lxvii.

MASSEY, BARTLE. The caustic, keen-witted old schoolmaster of Hayslope, who is patient with backward pupils, but bitter towards all women. *Adam B.* v, xi, xvi, xviii, xxi, xxiii–xxiv, xxxii, xl–xlii, xlvi, liii, lv.

"The face wore its mildest expression: the grizzled bushy eyebrows had taken their more acute angle of compassionate kindness, and the mouth, habitually compressed with a pout of the lower lip, was relaxed so as to be ready to speak a helpful word or syllable in a moment. This gentle expression was the more interesting because the schoolmaster's nose, an irregular aquiline twisted a little on one side, had rather a formidable character; and his brow, moreover, had that peculiar tension which always impresses one as a sign of a keen impatient temperament: the blue veins stood out like cords under the transparent yellow skin, and this intimidating brow was softened by no tendency to baldness, for the grey bristly hair, cut down to about an inch in length, stood round it in as close ranks as ever." Ch. xxi.

He is a man of ability and education who has been made a crabbed woman-hater by some experience of his youth. He is at odds with Joshua Rann on the subject of church music, and often comments sharply on Hayslope doings and sayings. To Adam Bede, who had been a pupil in his night-school, Bartle Massey is a loyal friend, giving up all of his own interests to go to Stoniton to stay with Adam during Hetty Sorrel's trial.

   Note.—Bartle Massey is one of the real names used by George Eliot in *Adam Bede*. The master of the school which her father, Robert Evans ("Adam Bede") attended near Roston, was named Bartle Massey, and, according to the account of him given by Mottram, had some of the characteristics of the Bartle Massey of the story. (*See* Mottram, *True Story of George*

Eliot, pp. 15, 24; Parkinson, *Scenes from the George Eliot Country*, p. 96.)

MATTEO. Servant to Bernardo Rucellai. *Rom.* xxxiv.

MAWMSEY, MR. Grocer, the chief representative of the retail trader in Middlemarch. *Mid.* xlv, li, lx. " Mr. Mawmsey was not only an overseer . . . he was also asthmatic and had an increasing family . . . he was an important man ; indeed, an exceptional grocer, whose hair was arranged in a flame-like pyramid, and whose retail deference was of the cordial, encouraging kind—jocosely complimentary, and with a certain considerate abstinence from letting out the full force of his mind." Ch. xlv.

MAWMSEY, MRS. The grocer's wife, the mother of a large family who has a great esteem for medicine. *Mid.* xlv, li, lx.

MAXIMILIAN, EMPEROR (*Hist.*). *Rom.* xlii, xlv, xlix

Note.—Maximilian I (1459–1519), Holy Roman emperor, 1493–1519.

MAXUM, OLD. *See* OLD MAXUM.

MAZZINGHI, DOMENICO (*Hist.*). One of the Ten, an ardent disciple of Savonarola. *Rom.* lxiv.

Savonarola employs Mazzinghi to write a letter to the Florentine ambassador in France to prepare the way for a later letter from Savonarola himself to the French king. By guile Tito Melema secures from Savonarola the letter to the French king which Savonarola had meant to entrust to Mazzinghi and after this letter has been sent by a courier it is captured by agents of the Duke of Milan, through information supplied by Tito.

Note.—There is some dispute as to the actual historical facts in the matter of the letters. According to Villari, none of Savonarola's own letters to the princes were ever sent, and the letter which fell into the hands of the Duke of Milan was the one which Mazzinghi had written to the Florentine ambassador. Mazzinghi died 1520.

MEDICEAN LIBRARY (*Real*). The library of Lorenzo de' Medici, which Savonarola acquired for the Convent of San Marco. *Rom.* xxvii, lxiv.

Note.—The most important part of the Medicean Library of the Dominicans of San Marco is now preserved in the great Biblioteca Medicea-Laurenziana, of Florence.

MEDICEANS (*Hist.*). The political party in Florence to which Romola's god-father and his friends belong. *Rom.* xxii, xxv, xxxix, xliv–xlvii, lii, lvi-lviii, lxvi.

MEDICI, GIOVANNI DE', CARDINAL (*Hist.*). Piero's " keener younger brother ", a friend of Tito Melema. *Rom.* xiii, xix–xxi, liv.

Note.—Giovanni de' Medici (1475–1521), created Cardinal at the age of thirteen, and in 1513 made Pope as Leo X.

MEDICI, LORENZO DE', *called* IL MAGNIFICO, OR, THE MAGNIFICENT

(*Hist.*). *Rom.* Proem, i–iii, v, viii–ix, xiv, xx–xxi, xxxix.

He does not figure as a character in *Romola*, but the news of his death is discussed in the Mercato Vecchio in the opening chapters, and he is frequently mentioned.

Note.—Lorenzo de' Medici (1448-92), virtual ruler of Florence, patron of arts and letters and himself a writer.

MEDICI, PIERO DE' (*Hist.*). The son and successor of Lorenzo the Magnificent, who is driven from Florence by the exasperated citizens and makes an unsuccessful attempt to return. *Rom.* Proem, iii, vi, viii, xiii, xvi, xix, xxi–xxii, xxviii, xxxix, xlv, lii, liv, lvii, lix.

Note.—Piero de' Medici (1471-1503).

MEDICI, PALACE OF THE. See PALACE OF THE VIA LARGA.

MEDITERRANEAN (*Real*). *D. D.* xlviii, liv–lvi. *Rom.* lxi, lxviii.

The Mediterranean is a definite part of the scene in two of the novels. In *Daniel Deronda* Gwendolen Harleth and her husband, Grandcourt, go yachting on the Mediteranean, and Grandcourt is drowned in it while sailing a small boat near Genoa, and Gwendolen is rescued from drowning when she leaps overboard after him. In *Romola*, Romola de' Bardi, sick at heart after her god-father's execution, sets herself adrift in a small fishing boat, hoping that she may never return; instead she is carried to the plague-stricken village, where, in helping the sufferers, she wins back some peace and strength for herself.

" MEDLEY PIE." A lively and judicious publication that reviews Vorticella's one book. *T. S.* xv.

MEDLICOTE, LORD. A patron of Mr. Bulstrode's hospital, who has given the land and the timber. *Mid.* xiii, xxiii–xxiv, xlv, lvi.

MEDWIN. A London lawyer. *F. H.* xxi, xxix.

" MEET ME BY MOONLIGHT " (*Real*). One of the songs which Rosamond Vincy sings. *Mid.* xvi.

Note.—" Meet me by moonlight alone," by J. A. Wade, composed and published 1826, had an extraordinary vogue, and was therefore one of the popular songs in Rosamond Vincy's day.

MEG. Captain Donnithorne's mare. *Adam B.* xii, xxix.

MEGALOSAURUS. " Greatest of fossils." *T. S.* iii.

MEGATHERIUM, LORD. A gouty old nobleman. *Mid.* vi.

MELEMA, TITO. A handsome young Greek scholar; a bright, gentle, likeable and entirely selfish egoist, who, by always taking the easy course, ends by being a traitor to everyone to whom he should have been loyal. *Rom.* i–xiv, xvi–xxiii, xxvi–xxvii, xxix–xxxvi, xxxviii–xxxix, xliii, xlv–xlviii, l, liii, lv–lviii, lx, lxii–lxv, lxvi–lxvii.

" And he had been docile, pliable, quick of apprehension, ready to acquire; a very bright lovely boy, a youth of even splendid grace, who seemed quite without vices, as if that beautiful form represented a vitality so exquisitely poised and balanced that it could know no uneasy desires, no unrest—a radiant presence for a lonely man to have won for himself. If he were silent when his father expected some response, still he did not look moody; if he declined some labour—why he flung himself down with such a charming, half-smiling, half-pleading air, that the pleasure of looking at him made amends ... the curves of Tito's mouth had ineffable good humour in them. And then, the quick talent to which everything came readily, from philosophical systems to the rhymes of a street ballad caught up at a hearing!" Ch. ix.

"[He] made almost every one fond of him, for he was young, and clever, and beautiful, and his manners to all were gentle and kind. I believe, when I first knew him, he never thought of anything cruel or base. But because he tried to slip away from everything that was unpleasant, and cared for nothing else so much as his own safety, he came at last to commit some of the basest deeds—such as make men infamous. He denied his father, and left him to misery; he betrayed every trust that was reposed in him, that he might keep himself safe and get rich and prosperous." Epilogue.

He owes everything to his foster-father, Baldassarre Calvo, who had brought him up as his own son. On a trip to Delos their boat was attacked by pirates and Baldassarre was captured, while Tito, who was carrying all their fortune in gems, escaped by swimming. In Florence, to which he makes his way after this misfortune, his brightness and charm at once win him friends—Tessa, the contadina, shares her breakfast with him, and Nello, the barber, takes him under his protection and introduces him to the blind scholar, Bardo de' Bardi, through whose aid he succeeds in selling his gems and obtaining a post as professor of Greek. He acts as secretary to Bardo, winning both the confidence of the old scholar and the love of Bardo's beautiful daughter, Romola. Tito has allowed himself to keep up an acquaintance with Tessa, and eventually as a jest goes through a mock marriage with her. After selling his gems for a large sum he had made no attempt to use the money to find his father, persuading himself, instead, that the old man must be dead, and he even rejects a direct appeal for aid which the monk, Fra Luca, brings him from his father. His marriage to Romola is at first happy, but many things, especially his bad faith in selling her father's library, soon make her see that he is faithless and conscienceless, and they drift apart. When Baldassarre Calvo, as an escaped prisoner, comes upon Tito in Florence, Tito denies him and later even carries his treachery so far as to have Baldassarre imprisoned for two years. His tact and versatility have made him useful to many people, and he serves all three political parties at the same time, without any real loyalty to any, considering nothing but his own interest, working against Savonarola while pretending to be of his party, and even consenting to the death of Romola's godfather. He over-reaches himself, however, by arousing the resentment of Dolfo Spini whom he serves for his own ends, is attacked by Spini's followers, the Compagnacci, and, just as he succeeds in escaping from them, is found and killed by his deserted old father, the most sinned against of the many whom his selfishness has injured.

MELIBOEUS. *T. S.* xiii.

MELISSA. A sentimental lady who pities the swindler, Sir Gavial Mantrap, because he "is an excellent family man". *T. S.* xvi.

MELSPRING. Town. *Mid.* lxxxiv.

"MEMORY, TELL TO ME." One of the songs of Juan, the minstrel, in the *Spanish Gypsy*. *Sp. G.* i.

MENGAN, MRS. Captain Lydgate's sister, who stays two nights with Rosamond on her way from town. *Mid.* lviii, lxiv.

MENICO, FRA (*Hist.*). A monk who preaches against Savonarola. *Rom.* i, xii.

Note.—Fra Domenico da' Ponza, a friend of the Duke of Milan and a noted enemy of Savonarola, preached against Savonarola in Santa Croce in 1495.

MERCATO VECCHIO, OR OLD MARKET (*Real*). The important centre of Florentine popular life, where Tito Melema on his first day in Florence hears the populace discuss the news of Lorenzo de' Medici's death, and first sees Tessa. *Rom.* i–iii, viii, x, xvi.

"A broad piazza, known to the elder Florentine writers as the Mercato Vecchio, or the Old Market. This piazza, though it had been the scene of a provision market from time immemorial, and may, perhaps, says fond imagination, be the very spot to which the Fesulean ancestors of the Florentines descended from their high fastness to traffic with the rustic population of the valley, had not been shunned as a place of residence by Florentine wealth. In the early decades of the fifteenth century, which was now near its end, the Medici and other powerful families of the *popolani grassi*, or commercial nobility, had their houses there, not perhaps finding their ears much offended by the loud roar of mingled dialects, or their eyes much shocked by the butchers' stalls, which the old poet Antonio Pucci accounts a chief glory, or *dignità*, of a market that, in his esteem, eclipsed the markets of all the earth beside." Ch. i.

Note.—The Mercato Vecchio, which in the time of Romola was the "heart of Florence" and the centre of Florentine commerce, was the oldest part of Florence. It no longer exists, having been swept away 1885–9 to make way for the modern Piazza Vittorio Emanuele. Its life and manners are described by many of the older Florentine writers, notably Antonio Pucci and Franco Sacchetti, the latter of whom has been called the " Echo of the Old Market ".

MERCER, JOSEPH. An old man in Milby. *J. R.* iii.

MERMAN, JULIA. Proteus Merman's devoted wife, who is involved in his misfortunes. *T. S.* iii.

MERMAN, PROTEUS. A young man of promise who discovers an error in the epoch-making work of Grampus; he is ruined by the resulting controversy, while Grampus annexes his idea and takes all the credit for himself. *T. S.* iii.

MERRY, MISS. Governess in the Davilow family; a plain, elderly woman devoted to the family. *D. D.* iii–iv, vi–vii, xxi, xxiii–xxiv, xxvii–xxviii, xxxv, xliv, lviii.

MERULA (*Hist.*). A scholar who sought patronage. *Rom.* v.

Note.—Giorgio Merula (1424–94), a scholar and emendator of manuscripts. He was attached to the Court of Milan and flattered that Court in his history of Milan.

MERULA. *T. S.* xi.

" MESSENGER." Newspaper. *M. F.* Bk. 5, vi.

" MESSIAH." An oratorio of which Caleb Garth is fond. *Mid.* lvi.

Note.—The *Messiah*, by Handel.

METHURST. *F. H.* xxi.

METHURST, LADY ALICIA. An acquaintance of Lady Debarry's. *F. H.* vii.

MEUNIER, CHARLES. Latimer's school friend who becomes, in later life, a famous physician. *L. V.* i–ii.

He performs the experiment which revives Bertha's maid, who has apparently died, long enough for her to accuse Bertha of planning to poison Latimer.

MEUNIER'S, MADAME. A school. *D. D.* xxi.

MEYRICK, MRS. A cheerful little woman who has made a brave struggle against poverty and who takes charge of Mirah Cohen when Daniel Deronda rescues her from drowning. *D. D.* xvii–xviii, xx, xxxii, xxxvii, xxxix, xlvi–xlvii, lii, lxi, lxvii–lxviii, lxx.

" She was a lively little woman, half French, half Scotch, with a pretty articulateness of speech that seemed to make daylight in her hearer's understanding. Though she was not yet fifty, her rippling hair, covered by a quakerish net cap, was chiefly gray, but her eyebrows were brown as the bright eyes below them; her black dress, almost like a priest's cassock with its row of buttons, suited a neat figure hardly five feet high." Ch. xviii.

MEYRICK, AMY. Mrs. Meyrick's daughter; a teacher. *D. D.* xvii–xviii, xx, xxxii, xxxvii, xxxix, xlvii, lii, lxx.

" The daughters were to match the mother . . . Everything about them was compact, from the firm coils of their hair, fastened back *à la Chinoise*, to their grey skirts in puritan non-conformity with the fashion ... All four, if they had been waxwork, might have been packed easily in a fashionable lady's travelling trunk. Their faces seemed full of speech, as if their minds had been shelled, after the manner of horse-chestnuts, and become brightly visible." Ch. xviii.

Note.—It has been suggested that George Eliot's Coventry friends, the Hennell sisters (Miss Sara Hennell and Mrs. Bray) may have been to a slight extent the originals of the Meyrick sisters. (*See* Blind, *George Eliot*, p. 36; Olcott, *George Eliot*, p. 184.)

MEYRICK, HANS. Daniel Deronda's eccentric young artist friend, who "was made for mishaps". *D. D.* xvi–xviii, xxxii, xxxvii, xxxix, xlv, xlvii, lii, lxi, lxvii.

"Only to look at his pinched features and blond hair hanging over his collar reminded one of pale quaint heads by early German painters; and when this faint coloring was lit up by a joke, there came sudden creases about the mouth and eyes which might have been moulded by the soul of an aged humorist ... There was no want of ability or of honest, well-meaning affection. ... The only danger was that the incalculable tendencies in him might be fatally timed, and that his good intentions might be frustrated by some act which was not due to habit but to capricious, scattered impulses. He could not be said to have any one bad habit; yet at longer or shorter intervals he had fits of impish recklessness, and did things that would have made the worst habits." Ch. xvi.

A lasting friendship had been formed between Hans and Daniel at the University, where Daniel befriended the less fortunate Hans, and gave up the opportunity of getting a scholarship himself in order to help Hans obtain a much-needed one. When he meets Mirah at his mother's house he falls in love with her and does not lose hope of winning her until she marries Daniel.

MEYRICK, KATE. Mrs. Meyrick's daughter, who earns her living by drawing. *D. D.* xvii–xviii, xx, xxxii, xxxix, xlvii, lii, lxx.

MEYRICK, MAB. Mrs. Meyrick's musical daughter; an impulsive, warm-hearted girl resembling her brother in appearance. *D. D.* xvii–xviii, xx, xxxii, xxxvii, xxxix, xlvii, lii, lxi, lxx.

MICHAEL. Angel "of pensive brow, snow-vest, and flaming sword". *P.—D. M.*

MICHAEL, MASTER. Innkeeper. *P.—Agatha.*

MICHELE, FRA. A Carthusian lay brother, in the service of the Mediceans, who carries a ring from Tito Melema to Giannozzo Pucci. *Rom.* xlv.

MICO. Minuccio's poet friend. *P.—Lisa.*

MICROPS. A "Cetacean of unanswerable authority". *T. S.* iii.

MIDDLEMARCH. A provincial town, the principal scene of the novel,

Middlemarch. *Mid.* vi, and following chapters.

For outline of the story *see* section of Synopses.

Note.—George Eliot's impressions of her residence in Coventry provide the original for the picture of "Middlemarch", although the picture is not developed with the detail shown in the portrait of Nuneaton as "Milby". (*See* Stephen, *George Eliot*, p. 34, 174; also his article on George Eliot in the *Dictionary of National Biography*.)

One of the recognitions of George Eliot's connexion with Coventry is the decision to name all new streets opened in the Radford Garden suburbs (a region which was once one of her favourite walks) from her novels, and of the two streets, opened by 1922, one is "Middlemarch Road" and the other "Lydgate Road". Coventry has also a "George Eliot Road".

"MIDDLEMARCH PIONEER." The paper which Mr. Brooke buys when he wishes to enter Parliament and which Will Ladislaw edits for him. *Mid.* xxx, xxxvii–xxxviii, xlvi, xlix, li, lx–lxii, lxiv.

"MIDDLEMARCH TRUMPET." The paper which opposes Mr. Brooke. *Mid.* xxxvii–xxxviii, xlvi, li, lxiv.

MIDDLETON, Mr. Mr. Gascoigne's curate, an "unexceptional young clergyman with pale whiskers and square-cut collar" who falls in love with Gwendolen Harleth. *D. D.* iii, vi, ix.

MIDSUMMER DAY FESTIVAL. *See* SAN GIOVANNI, FESTA OF.

MILAN (*Real*). The Italian city where Lady Cheverel aids the poor musician Signor Sarti, and later rescues his orphan daughter, the little Caterina. *Mr. G.'s L. S.* iii; mentioned *Rom.* Proem, i, viii–ix, xxi–xxii, lvii, lxiii.

MILAN, DUKE OF. *See* SFORZA, LUDOVICO.

MILBY. Market-town; scene of the story of *Janet's Repentance*, and of some of the action in the other *Scenes of Clerical Life*. *J. R.* i–xxviii; *Amos B.* ii–iv, vi; *Mr. G.'s L. S.* i.

"It was a dingy-looking town, with a strong smell of tanning up one street and a great shaking of hand-looms up another ... To a superficial glance, Milby was nothing but dreary prose: a dingy town, surrounded by flat fields, lopped elms, and sprawling manufacturing villages, which crept on and on with their weaving-shops, till they threatened to graft themselves on the town." Ch. ii.

Note.—The easily recognized original of Milby is the market and manufacturing town of Nuneaton, Warwickshire. The name was taken from an old corn-mill in Nuneaton, on the Anker, called Milby Mill. (*See* Dryden, *Memorials of Old Warwickshire*, p. 124; Parkinson, *Scenes*, pp. 12, 55–8.)

MILBY CHURCH. *J. R.* ii, iv, vi, ix, xxviii.

Note.—The original of Milby Church is the parish church of St. Nicholas, at Nuneaton.

MILBY VICARAGE. Scene of the Clerical Meeting, where Amos Barton's shortcomings are discussed. *Amos B.* iii, vi; spoken of as the "Parsonage", *J. R.* v–vi. *Note.*—This is the Vicarage in Nuneaton, near the Church.

MILL ON THE FLOSS. For the mill itself, *see* DORLCOTE MILL.

MILLER. Second-hand book-seller, member of the Philosophers' Club, who liked his joke. *D. D.* xlii.
"Miller, the broad man, an exceptional second-hand bookseller who knew the insides of books, had at least grandparents who called themselves German, and possibly far-away ancestors who denied themselves to be Jews . . . was implicitly accepted as a sort of moderator." Ch. xlii.

MILLS, MR. Squire Donnithorne's butler. *Adam B.* xxiii, xxvi, xliv, lv.

MINCHIN, DR. One of the two leading physicians of Middlemarch, who opposes Lydgate and his innovations. *Mid.* xv–xvi, xviii, xxvi, xlv, lxiii.
"He objected to the rather free style of anecdote in which Dr. Sprague indulged, preferring well-sanctioned quotations, and liking refinement of all kinds; it was generally known that he had some kinship to a bishop, and sometimes spent his holidays at 'the palace'.
"Dr. Minchin was soft-handed, pale-complexioned, and of rounded outline, not to be distinguished from a mild clergyman in appearance." Ch. xviii.

MINIATO, SAN (CONVENT). *See* SAN MINIATO, CONVENT OF.

MINIATO, SAN (HILL). *See* SAN MINIATO, HILL OF.

MINNY. Lucy Deane's King Charles spaniel, a gift from Tom Tulliver. *M. F.* Bk. 6, i–ii, iv, vi.

MINT. *See* ZECCA.

MINUCCIO. The great singer, who reveals to King Pedro, by means of his song, the touching story of gentle Lisa's love.
". . . a singer of most gentle fame,
A noble, kindly spirit, not elate
That he was famous, but that song was great." *P.—Lisa.*

MIRAH. *See* COHEN, MIRAH.

MIRANDOLA, PICO DELLA. *See* PICO DELLA MIRANDOLA, GIOVANNI.

MISCHIEF. Dolfo Spini's fine staghound. *Rom.* lxiii.

"MR. MERMAN AND THE MAGICO-DUMBRAS." One of the works called forth by the great Merman-Grampus controversy. *T. S.* iii.

MITCHELL. Coachman. *F. H.* vii.

MIXTUS. A "half-breed"; a successful business man who has gained great wealth but finds the spiritual and intellectual interests and ideals of his youth submerged in the society which his lively and worldly wife collects around her. *T. S.* ix.

MOFFAT, MR. Auctioneer and broker. *B. J.* ii.

MOGGS, MRS. Luke's wife. *M. F.* Bk. 1, iv; Bk. 5, vii.

MOGGS, LUKE. The head miller at Dorlcote Mill, with whom Maggie Tulliver is fond of conversing, "wishing him to think well of her understanding." *M. F.* Bk. 1, iv–v; Bk. 2, i, vi; Bk. 3, ii, iv, vi, viii–ix; Bk. 5, vii; Bk. 6, v.
"A tall, broad-shouldered man of forty, black-eyed and black-haired, subdued by a general mealiness, like an auricula." Bk. 1, iv.

MOLE, MRS. Mrs. Steene's friend. *B. J.* ii.

MOLLY. Mrs. Poyser's housemaid. *Adam B.* vi, viii, xviii, xx, xxvi, xxxii, xxxv, xlix, lii.

MOLLY, LADY. A titled relative of Gwendolen Harleth. *D. D.* iii.

MOLTON. A village where Bertha Grant's maid Fletcher lives after she marries. *L. V.* ii.

"MOMENTS WITH MR. MERMAN." One of the works called forth by the great Merman-Grampus controversy. *T. S.* iii.

MOMPERT, DR. A Bishop. *D. D.* xxi, xxiv.

MOMPERT, MRS. The bishop's wife, with whom Gwendolen Harleth is about to take a position as governess when she accepts Grandcourt's offer. *D. D.* xxiv, xxvi, xxviii.

MOMPERTS, THE THREE MISS. The bishop's daughters. *D. D.* xxi, xxiv, xxvi.

MONAS. The author of a single book, entitled *Here and There*, or *A trip from Truro to Transylvania*. *T. S.* xv.

MONK. St. Bernard dog which takes care of Dorothea Brooke and her sister in their walks. *Mid.* ii, xxxix.

MONK'S TOPPING. An estate of the Mallingers, which came from a grant under Henry the Eighth. *D. D.* xvi.

"MOOR, THE" (*Real*). A druggist's shop which pretends to rival Nello's barber shop as a resort for the *eruditi*. *Rom.* iii.
Note.—The Pharmacia del Moro, or del Saracino (both names were used), which had a Moor's head for a sign, was one of the oldest and best known in Florence, and by the beginning of the sixteenth century was already established at the Canto alla Paglia, at the corner of the Borgo San Lorenzo and the Piazza San Giovanni. It belonged to the Grazzini family, and among the members of that family who practised there was the poet Anton Francesco Grazzini, called Il Lasco (1503–84).

MORDAX. "The watch-dog of knowledge," an intellectual worker who is admirable and kindly in his personal relations, but a biting critic and fierce antagonist if he is corrected or his opinions challenged. *T. S.* viii.

MORDECAI. *See* COHEN, EZRA MORDECAI.

MORELLO, MOUNT. (*Real*). A hill near Florence. *Rom.* Proem, iv.
Note.—A mountain north of Florence.

MORGAN, MISS. Governess in the Vincy family. *Mid.* xi–xii, xvi, xxvii, xxxvi.

"Miss Morgan, who was brown, dull, and resigned, and altogether, as Miss Vincy often said, just the sort of person for a governess." Ch. xvi.

MORO. Black spaniel belonging to Harry Transome. *F. H.* xix, xl, xlii–xliii.

MORRIS, DINAH. Mrs. Poyser's niece, a beautiful and saintly young Methodist preacher whose one thought is to obey an imperative call to preach the gospel and to spend herself in the service of those who need her. *Adam B.* i–iii, v–vi, viii, x–xi, xiv–xv, xxv, xxx, xxxv, xxxvii–xxxviii, xlv–xlvii, xlix–lii, liv–lv, Epilogue.

"She stood and turned her grey eyes on the people. There was no keenness in the eyes; they seemed rather to be shedding love than making observations; they had the liquid look which tells that the mind is full of what it has to give out, rather than impressed by external objects. She stood with her left hand towards the descending sun, and leafy boughs screened her from its rays; but in this sober light the delicate colouring of her face seemed to gather a calm vividness, like flowers at evening. It was a small oval face, of a uniform transparent whiteness, with an egg-like line of cheek and chin, a full but firm mouth, a delicate nostril, and a low perpendicular brow, surmounted by a rising arch of parting between smooth locks of pale reddish hair. The hair was drawn straight back behind the ears, and covered, except for an inch or two, above the brow, by a net Quaker cap. The eyebrows, of the same colour as the hair, were perfectly horizontal and firmly pencilled; the eyelashes, though no darker, were long and abundant; nothing was left blurred or unfinished. It was one of those faces that make one think of white flowers with light touches of colour on their pure petals. The eyes had no peculiar beauty, beyond that of expression; they looked so simple, so candid, so gravely loving, that no accusing scowl, no light sneer could help melting away before their glance." Ch. ii.

She lives at Snowfield, where she works in a mill, but at the opening of the story she is visiting her aunt at Hayslope, where she preaches movingly on the village Green. Seth Bede has long been in love with her, but Adam Bede has never seen her until, at the time of his father's death, she comes to his cottage to help his grief-stricken mother. Her sense of religious duty causes her to try to lead vain little Hetty Sorrel to a higher life, and while she produces no religious impression on Hetty, she leaves with her a sense of love which makes the girl turn to her later in her despair.. Dinah is away from home when Hetty is tried for murder and sentenced to death, but she hurries to Hetty's prison as soon as the news reaches her, and there prays and talks with the stricken girl until she touches her heart and induces her to make the confession which she had obstinately refused to make. She goes with Hetty to the place of execution, and is with her when the reprieve arrives at the last minute. When his grief about Hetty has been somewhat softened, Adam Bede discovers that he is in love with Dinah, and eventually she marries him.

Note.—The original of Dinah Morris was Elizabeth Evans, the wife of George Eliot's uncle, Samuel Evans, although, as George Eliot herself says, the character is not an exact portrait. Mrs. Evans, whom George Eliot speaks of as "my Methodist Aunt Samuel", was an eloquent and well-known Wesleyan preacher, and some of her characteristics and experiences appear in Dinah Morris. One of Elizabeth Evans's striking experiences, when she induced an ignorant girl who had been convicted of child-murder to make a confession, and afterwards rode in the cart with her to the place of execution, gave George Eliot the idea for the climax of *Adam Bede*. Her connexion with Dinah Morris has been commemorated in the table erected to her memory in the Ebenezer Wesleyan Chapel in Wirksworth ("Snowfield") which reads "Elizabeth Evans, known to the world as Dinah Bede". (*See* Cross, *George Eliot's Life*, vol. 2, pp. 65–7; for a detailed account of the life of Elizabeth Evans, *see* Mottram, *True story of George Eliot in relation to Adam Bede*.)

MORTEIRA. Family name of Princess Halm-Eberstein's mother. *D. D.* liii.

MORTON, MR. *M. F.* Bk. 1, xii.

MOSES. *P.—D. M.*

MOSS, MR. Mr. Tulliver's brother-in-law, an unsuccessful farmer who borrowed three hundred pounds from Mr. Tulliver and has much ado to pay his rent. *M. F.* Bk. 1, vi, viii; Bk. 2, ii; Bk. 3, iii, viii; Bk. 4, ii.

"A man without capital, who, if murrain and blight were abroad, was sure to have his share of them, and who, the more you tried to help him out of the mud, would sink the farther in. . . . Mr. Moss, who, when he married Miss Tulliver, had been regarded as the buck of Basset, now wore a beard nearly a week old, and had the depressed, unexpectant air of a machine-horse." Bk. 1, viii.

MOSS, BABY. *M. F.* Bk. 2, ii.

MOSS, GEORGY. Son of Mr. and Mrs. Moss. *M. F.* Bk. 1, viii.

MOSS, MRS. GRITTY. Mr. Tulliver's sister, who has made a poor marriage and received much help from her brother. *M. F.* Bk. 1, vi–viii; Bk. 2, ii; Bk. 3, iii–iv; Bk. 4, ii; Bk. 6, ix, xi.

"Besides being poorly off, and inclined to 'hang on' her brother, [she] had the good-natured submissiveness of a large, easy-tempered, untidy, prolific woman, with affection enough in her not only for her own husband and abundant children, but for any number of collateral relations." Bk. 2, ii.

Moss, LIZZY. Little daughter of Mr. and Mrs. Moss, "a black-eyed child of seven who resembles her cousin Maggie Tulliver." *M. F.* Bk. 1, viii.

Moss, WILLY. The twelve-year old son of Mr. and Mrs. Moss. *M. F.* Bk. 6, xi.

"MOSSLANDS." A remote part of the grounds of Cheverel Park; a little island where Mr. Bates lives. *Mr. G.'s L. S.* vii, xv, xvii.

MOST CHRISTIAN KING. *See* CHARLES VIII.

MOTT, MR. *S. M.* xvi.

MOZZI, PIAZZA DE' (*Real*). Piazza in Florence at the end of the Via de' Bardi. *Rom.* v, xliv, lxvii.

Note.—The Piazza de' Mozzi, named after the Mozzi family, bankers to the popes, extends from the Via de' Bardi to the Ponte alle Grazie.

MUDPORT. Town where Maggie Tulliver and Stephen Guest part after their flight. *M. F.* Bk. 1, ii–iii; Bk. 2, iv; Bk. 6, xiii–xiv; Bk. 7, i, v.

MUDPORT FREE SCHOOL. *M. F.* Bk. 1, iii.

MUGELLO (*Real*). A region from which the contadini come to Florence for the San Giovanni festa.

Note.—The Mugello, a district north-east of Florence.

MUMPS. Bob Jakin's "bull-terrier of brindled coat and defiant aspect". *M. F.* Bk. 4, iii; Bk. 5, iii; Bk. 6, iv; Bk. 7, i.

MUSCAT, MR. An influential member of Mr. Lyon's congregation. *F. H.* iv–v, xxiv, xxxi, xxxvii.

MUSCAT, MRS. Wife of the above, "who had once been a beauty and was as nice in her millinery as any Trebian lady belonging to the Establishment." *F. H.* vi, xvi, xviii, xxiv.

MUSCAT, YOUNG. Son of Mr. and Mrs. Muscat; an unsuccessful admirer of Esther Lyon's. *F. H.* xxii.

MUSIC MASTER AT MRS. LEMON'S SCHOOL. Rosamond Vincy's music teacher, the organist at St. Peter's. *Mid.* xvi.

"Her master ... was one of those excellent musicians here and there to be found in our provinces ... Rosamond, with the executant's instinct, had seized his manner of playing, and gave forth his large rendering of noble music with the precision of an echo ... A hidden soul seemed to be flowing forth from Rosamond's fingers; and so indeed it was, since souls live on in perpetual echoes, and to all fine expression there goes somewhere an originating activity, if it be only that of an interpreter." Ch. xvi.

Note.—His original was Edward Simms, junior, organist at St. Michael's, Coventry, 1828-86, who taught George Eliot. His compositions are in the Cathedral Library, Coventry.

N

NADAR. A Gypsy captain. *Sp. G.* iv–v.

NALDO. A "painter of eclectic school", without power of application. He furnishes the contrast to Stradivarius in the poetic dialogue between the two. *P.—Strad.*

NALDO, MESSER. Name which Tito Melema assumes in his relations with Tessa. *Rom.* xxxiii–xxxiv, lvi. *See also* MELEMA, TITO.

NANCY. One of Mrs. Poyser's maids. *Adam B.* vi–vii, xx, xxii, xxxii, xlix, lii.

NANNI. Tailor; one of the crowd in the Mercato Vecchio that discuss the news of the death of Lorenzo de' Medici. *Rom.* i.

NANNINA. Tessa's cousin, who married Gollo. *Rom.* xiv.

NANNY. The Barton's devoted maid-of-all-work, "who had a warm heart and a still warmer temper." *Amos B.* ii, v, vii–x.

NAPLES (*Real*). *D. D.* li; *Rom.* Proem, i, xxi, xxx, xlii; mentioned *F. H.* xxi.

Note.—The Naples which figures in *Daniel Deronda* and *Felix Holt* is the city of Naples; that in *Romola* is the Kingdom of Naples, which in the fifteenth century was one of the five great powers of Italy. At the beginning of *Romola* its ruler was the "Spanish-born old King Ferdinand", who was succeeded 1494 by his son Alfonso.

NAPLES, CARDINAL OF (*Hist.*). A friend of Savonarola, whose name is forged to a letter intended to lure Savonarola from Florence. *Rom.* xlvi.

Note.—Olivier Caraffa, created cardinal 1464, who was archbishop of Naples 1458-84. He died at Rome in 1511.

NARDI, JACOPO (*Hist.*). A young Florentine of two-and-twenty, an adherent of Savonarola, who stands by Romola at Savonarola's execution. *Rom.* lxxii.

Note.—Jacopo Nardi (1476-1556), author and historian, best known for his *Istorie della Città di Firenze*.

NARWHAL, LORD. Grampus's friend. *T. S.* iii.

NASH. A bone-setter. *D. D.* vii.

NASH, NANCY. A charwoman, who is cured by Dr. Lydgate after her illness had been incorrectly diagnosed by Dr. Minchin. *Mid.* xlv.

NATIONAL GALLERY, LONDON (*Real*). One of the places in which Mordecai Cohen frequently lingers, hoping to find in the portraits a type of a great Jewish leader. *D. D.* xxxviii.

NAUMANN, ADOLF. A good-natured German painter in Rome who admires the beauty of Mrs. Casaubon so much that he asks

Mr. Casaubon to sit for Thomas Aquinas, in order to have an opportunity of painting Dorothea also. *Mid.* xix–xx, xxii, xxx.

Note.—The character of Naumann was probably suggested by Johann Friedrich Overbeck (1789–1869), a German artist who worked at Rome 1810–1869. (*See* Jacobs, *George Eliot*, p. 72.)

NAUPLIA (*Real*). The port from which Tito Melema and Baldassarre Calvo had sailed on their last voyage. *Rom.* vi.

Note.—A Greek port, at the head of the Gulf of Nauplia.

NELL. One of Agatha's old cousins. *P.*—*Agatha.*

NELLO. A lively and talkative barber who is proud of the fact that his shop, the "Apollo and Razor", is the resort of the *eruditi* of Florence. *Rom.* i–vi, viii, xiii, xvi, xxii, xxix, xlv, xlvii.

"A man of slim figure, whose eye twinkled rather roguishly. He wore a close jerkin, a skull-cap lodged carelessly over his left ear as if it had fallen there by chance, a delicate linen apron tucked up on one side, and a razor stuck in his belt." Ch. i.

His shop on the Piazza di San Giovanni is an informal meeting place for all Florentines prominent in art, literature, or politics, and Nello's lively comment on news and personalities forms a gay chorus to the story. When Tito Melema comes to Florence, Nello at once takes him under his protection, introduces him to the two Cennini and to other patrons of his shop, and takes him to see the blind Bardo de' Bardi. Completely won by Tito's charm and beauty, he champions him against all criticism and believes in him to the last.

Note.—The character of Nello is drawn from that of Domenico di Giovanni, *called* Il Burchiello (1404 – 48), the barber poet of Florence. Burchiello's portrait in the Uffizi has below it a painting of his shop, from which the description of Nello's shop is taken.

NERI (*Hist.*). The owners of a considerable range of houses on the Via de' Bardi, in one of which Romola de' Bardi and her blind father live. *Rom.* v.

NERLI (*Hist.*). Member of the Arrabbiati. *Rom.* xxxix.

Note.—Tanai de' Nerli and his son Jacopo di Tanai de' Nerli were both prominent in Florentine politics at this date. Jacopo was a chief of the Arrabbiati and an opponent of Savonarola.

NERO, BERNARDO DEL (*Hist.*). A stern, upright, old Florentine, who is faithful to his political party, loyally devoted to his personal friends, such as blind Bardo de' Bardi, and affectionately watchful of his god-daughter, Romola. *Rom.* v–vi, viii, xii–xiii, xvii, xix–xx, xxvii, xxxi–xxxii, xxxv–xxxvii, xxxix, xlv, xlviii–xlix, lii, liv, lvi–lvii, lix–lx.

He sympathizes with blind Bardo's ambition to have his library preserved intact, and endeavours both through his interest with the Medici and by means of personal financial aid to have this carried out. His own pride, and his affection for Romola make him suspicious of Tito Melema in the beginning, and he never overcomes his dislike for him. For many years a friend of Lorenzo de' Medici, he remains faithful to Lorenzo's sons, though he takes no part himself in the Medicean conspiracy. Partly through Tito Melema's treachery he is arrested as a conspirator, tried hastily, and executed in spite of Romola's efforts to intercede for him with Savonarola. His death, and her suspicion of Tito's part in it, finally drive Romola away from Tito.

Note.—Bernardo del Nero, executed 1497 at the age of 75, was a prominent citizen who had been Gonfaloniere in 1497. Though he had been a Medicean all his life he had no active part in the conspiracy which cost him his life, his only connexion with it being a knowledge of the conspiracy which he had failed to reveal.

NEW FEVER HOSPITAL. The new hospital in Middlemarch which Mr. Bulstrode establishes and largely maintains, putting Dr. Lydgate in charge of the work. *Mid.* xiii, xliii–xlv, lx, lxiii, xlvii, lxix, lxx, lxxvi, lxxxi.

NEW PITS. Name given to the more modern part of Sproxton. *F. H.* xi.

NEW YORK (*Real*). The American city where, in *Daniel Deronda*, Mirah Cohen and her father, Lapidoth, live for some time, and where, in *Middlemarch*, Raffles goes with the money which Bulstrode has paid him to leave England. *D. D.* xx; *Mid.* liii.

NEWCASTLE (*Real*). *M. F.* Bk. 6, v, xii.

Note.—Newcastle-upon-Tyne, the county town of Northumberland, situated about nine miles from the mouth of the Tyne.

NICCOLI, NICCOLÒ (*Hist.*). *Rom.* v.

Note.—Niccolò de' Niccoli (1363–1437), humanist and bibliophile, an enthusiastic collector of manuscripts who spent his whole fortune in their purchase.

NICCOLÒ, FRA (*Hist.*). Savonarola's secretary. *Rom.* lxiv.

Note.—Niccolò da Milano, who acted as Savonarola's secretary 1495-8.

NICHOLAS V, POPE (*Hist.*). The Pope who, while he was still Thomas of Sarzana, honoured Bardo de' Bardi with his personal notice. *Rom.* v, xii.

Note.—Tomaso Parentucelli or Tomaso da Sarzana (1398–1455); pope, as Nicholas V, 1447-55. A patron of learning as well as a man of great erudition, he collected many manuscripts and employed hundreds of scholars and copyists.

NIMROD. Mr. Transome's old black retriever. *F. H.* i, vii–viii, xl, xliii.

NINNA. Daughter of the contadina Tessa and Tito Melema. *Rom.* l, lvi, lxx, Epilogue.

NISBETT. *Amos. B.* vi.

NOBLE, MISS HENRIETTA. Mrs. Fairbrother's sister, a tiny, meek old lady with a benevolent disposition, who is very fond of Will Ladislaw. *Mid.* xvii, xlvi, l, lii, lvii, lxiii, lxxx, lxxxiii.

NOFRI. Tessa's cross-grained stepfather who used to beat her. *Rom.* x, xiv, xx, xxxiii, l, lvi.

NOLA, JACOPO DI. Name by which Tito pretends to identify his father, Baldassarre Calvo, as a former servant. *Rom.* xxxix, xlviii.

NOLAN, MRS. Wife of the retired merchant; formerly Miss Pendrell. *F. H.* xx, xxxi.

NOLAN, BARUCH. A retired London hosier believed to understand politics; a wealthy and esteemed inhabitant of Treby, whose Hebrew extraction is ignored *F. H.* xx, xxiv, xxxi.

"A wiry old gentleman past seventy, whose square tight forehead, with its rigid hedge of grey hair, whose bushy eyebrows, sharp dark eyes, and remarkable hooked nose, gave a handsome distinction to his face in the midst of rural physiognomies." Ch. xx.

NORBURNE. A place not far from Hayslope where Arthur Donnithorne goes to see Mr. Gawaine. *Adam B.* xii.

Note.—The original of Norburne, was Norbury, near Ellastone ("Hayslope").

NORTH LOAMSHIRE. *See* LOAMSHIRE, NORTH.

"NORTH LOAMSHIRE HERALD." Tory newspaper. *F. H.* i, iv, viii, xlvii.

NORTH QUAY. Place where Joshua Rigg plans to set up his moneychanger's shop. *Mid.* liii.

NORTON. A village through which Hetty Sorrel passes on her journey back from Windsor. *Adam B.* xxxvii.

NOUNA. A Gypsy. *Sp. G.* iii.

NUNZIATA, CHURCH OF THE. *See* ANNUNZIATA, CHURCH OF THE.

NUNZIATA, PIAZZA DELL'. *See* ANNUNZIATA, PIAZZA DELL'.

NUTTINGWOOD. Place where old Mrs. Vulcany lives. *D. D.* iii.

NUTTWOOD, MR. Dissenter and deacon; a grocer in Treby Magna. *F. H.* iii–iv, xiii, xxxvii.

NUTTWOOD, MRS. The grocer's wife. *F. H.* vi.

O

"O BIRD THAT USED TO PRESS." One of the songs which Pablo sings. *Sp. G.* ii.

"O ME, O ME, WHAT FRUGAL CHEER." The first line of a song written by Will Ladislaw. *Mid.* xlvii.

"O PATRIA MIA." *See* ODE TO ITALY.

"O WHISTLE AND I WILL COME TO THEE, MY LAD" (*Real*). The tune which the hand of the

Liberal candidate plays at the election in Treby. *F. H.* xxxi.

Note.—" O whistle and I'll come to thee, my lad," a song with words by Robert Burns set to an older air, the origin of which is in doubt.

OAKBOURNE. A "pretty town within sight of the blue hills" about ten miles from Hayslope. *Adam B.* xi, xxxvi, xxxviii.

Note.—The original of Oakbourne is the town of Ashbourne, about five miles from Ellastone (" Hayslope ").

OATES, JINNY. The cobbler's daughter at Raveloe. *S. M.* viii.

OATES, SALLY. The cobbler's wife. *S. M.* i–ii.

She suffers from heart disease and dropsy, as had Silas Marner's mother, and Silas, moved by pity, takes her a preparation of foxglove, which helps her greatly.

OBERE STRASSE. Street in Leubronn in which is located Mr. Wiener's shop where Gwendolen Harleth pawns her necklace. *D. D.* ii.

ODDO. A dyer who helped erect barricades against the French in 1494. *Rom.* xxii.

" ODE TO ITALY (O PATRIA MIA) " (*Real*). Leopardi's " Ode to Italy " which Mirah sings, set to the music of her old teacher, Joseph Leo. *D. D.* xxxix, xlv.

Note.—The ode by Count Giacomo Leopardi (1798–1837), written 1818 and entitled *All' Italia.* The first line begins " O patria mia ".

" ŒDIPUS AND ANTIGONE AT COLONOS." Subject of a picture which Piero di Cosimo paints for Giovanni Vespucci, using Romola and her father as models. *Rom.* xviii, xxviii.

OFFENDENE. House near Wanchester where Gwendolen Harleth lives with her mother, and where she returns after her husband's death. *D. D.* ii–vii, ix, xiii–xv, xxi, xxv, xxvii–xxix, xxxv, xliv, lxiv–lxv, lxix.

" The house was but just large enough to be called a mansion, and was moderately rented, having no manor attached to it, and being rather difficult to let with its sombre furniture and faded upholstery. But inside and outside it was what no beholder could suppose to be inhabited by retired tradespeople." Ch. iii.

OGG, ST. The patron saint of St. Ogg's, a legendary boatman on the river Floss. *M. F.* Bk. 1, xii.

OGG'S, ST. (Town). *See* ST. OGG'S.

OGNISSANTI (*Real*). Monastery of the Frati Umiliati in Florence. *Rom.* xliii.

Note.—The suppressed Minorite monastery of Ognissanti, on the east side of the Piazza Manin, now a barracks. It was occupied from 1256 by the Frati Umiliati or Humbled Brethren, workers in the wool trade. In 1554 it was ceded to the Franciscans.

OGNISSANTI (*Real*). The street in Florence where the dyers carried on their trade. *Rom.* i, x, xxii.

Note.—This was the Borgo Ognissanti, near the monastery of Ognissanti, where for several centuries the Frati Umiliati had carried on an extensive industry in woollen manufacture and such allied trades as dyeing, etc.

OGNISSANTI, PIAZZA D' (*Real*). Place in Florence where Tito Melema and Tessa rest on their way to the Prato. *Rom.* x.

Note.—This is the square now called the Piazza Manin.

"OH, NO, WE NEVER MENTION HER" (*Real*). One of the songs sung by Miss Rebecca Linnet. *J. R.* iii.

Note.—Written by Thomas Haynes Bayly (1797–1839).

OLD BROWN. A horse. *Adam B.* xxii.

"OLD GOGGLES." Name given to Mr. Jacobs by the boys in his school. *M. F.* Bk. 2, i.

OLD HALL, ST. OGG'S. The scene of the bazaar which is the culmination of Maggie Tulliver's social career. *M. F.* Bk. 1, xii ; Bk. 4, iii ; Bk. 6, ix.

"It was the Normans who began to build that fine old hall, which is like the town telling of the thoughts and hands of widely-sundered generations; but it is all so old that we look with loving pardon at its inconsistencies, and are well content that they who built the stone oriel, and they who built the Gothic façade and towers of finest small brickwork with the trefoil ornament, and the windows and battlements defined with stone, did not sacrilegiously pull down the ancient half-timbered body, with its oak - roofed banqueting-hall." Bk. 1, xii.

"The fine old hall, with its open roof and carved oaken rafters, and great oaken folding-doors, and light shed down from a height on the many-coloured show beneath : a very quaint place, with broad faded stripes painted on the walls, and here and there a show of heraldic animals of a bristly, long-snouted character, the cherished emblems of a noble family once the seigniors of this now civic hall. A grand arch, cut in the upper wall at one end, surmounted an oaken orchestra, with an open room behind it . . . Near the great arch over the orchestra was the stone oriel with painted glass, which was one of the venerable inconsistencies of the old hall." Bk. 6, ix.

Note. — The original of the Old Hall, St. Ogg's, is the Old Hall, Gainsborough, the ancient residence of the lords of the manor of Gainsburgh, an interesting specimen of an old baronial hall. (For a history and description of this building, which is still standing, *see* Stark, *History and Antiquities of Gainsburgh*.)

OLD MARKET. *See* MERCATO VECCHIO.

"OLD MAXUM." A pauper patriarch of ninety-five, stone deaf. *Amos B.* ii.[1]

---

[1] A Nuneaton list gives a Mr. Taylor as his prototype. (Manuscript notes.)

OLD PALACE. *See* PALAZZO VECCHIO.

"OLD PASTURES." *S. M.* xi.

OLD PITS. Name given to the older part of Sproxton. *F. H.* xi.

OLD TOPPING. Borough. *M. F.* Bk. 3, vii.

OLD WOMAN, SNOWFIELD. The woman with whom Dinah Morris lodged. *Adam B.* xxxviii.

OLDING, JOHN. A labourer at Tadd's Hole, near Stoniton, who finds the dead body of Hetty Sorrel's baby and gives evidence against Hetty at the trial. *Adam B.* xliii.

OLDINPORT, MR. The squire of Shepperton parish who helps Amos Barton when he is in need of money. *Amos B.* ii, v, ix; mentioned *Mr. G.'s L. S.* i.

Note.—The original of Mr. Oldinport was the Right Honourable Charles Newdigate Newdegate, Member of Parliament for Warwickshire 1843–84. (*See* Olcott, *George Eliot*, pp. 14, 24.)

OLDINPORT, MR. The squire of Knebley parish in Mr. Gilfil's time; an exacting landlord, cousin and predecessor of the Mr. Oldinport of Amos Barton. *Mr. G.'s L. S.* i.

Note.—The original of this Mr. Oldinport was Francis Parker Newdigate, who succeeded to the Arbury Hall estates in 1806 on the death of Sir Roger Newdigate, the last baronet. (*See* Olcott, *George Eliot*, pp. 15, 24.)

OLDINPORT, FELICIA, LADY. *Mr. G.'s L. S.* i.

"OLDINPORT ARMS." Inn. *Mr. G.'s L. S.* i.

Note.—The original of the "Oldinport Arms" is the "Newdegate Arms", Nuneaton.

OLDINPORT FAMILY. *Amos B.* i; *Mr. G.'s L. S.* xxi.

OLIVER. A Middlemarch M.P., who is to be turned out because he is a Peelite. *Mid.* xxxviii.

OLTRARNO (*Real*). The section of Florence in which Romola lived. *Rom.* Proem, v, x, xxx, lxvii.

Note.—Oltrarno, that is, the part of the city beyond, or on the south side of, the Arno, one of the four quarters into which Florence was divided in 1342.

OMNIBUS COLLEGE. Fred Vincy's college. *Mid.* lii.

ORCAGNA'S (OR ORGAGNA'S) LOGGIA (*Real*). The spacious loggia on the Piazza della Signoria, Florence, in which the Franciscans and Dominicans were placed at the time of the Trial by Fire. *Rom.* Proem, viii, xlix, lxv.

Note.—Orgagna's Loggia is the beautiful arcade near the Palazzo Vecchio which is usually called the Loggia de' Lanzi (from the Swiss lancers posted there under Cosimo I), although the name Loggia dell' Orgagna is also used. Its earlier names were Loggia dei Signori or Loggia dei Priori; at the time of the Trial by Fire, it was called Loggia dei Signori. It was ordered by the General Council of Florence in 1356, and though perhaps designed by Orgagna, was not built until 1376–82, several years after Orgagna's death.

ORCHARD STREET. The Milby street in which the Dempsters' house is situated, and the scene of the Sunday evening demonstration against Mr. Tryan. *J. R.* iv–v, ix, xiii–xv, xxi, xxiii, xxv, xxviii.

"Orchard Street, which opened on the prettiest outskirt of the town—the church, the parsonage, and a long stretch of green fields." Ch. iv.

Note.—Church Street, Nuneaton, is the original of Orchard Street, Milby.

ORCHARDS, THE. Home of the Osgoods at Raveloe. *S. M.* iii.

ORGANIST, Shepperton. *Amos B.* i.
Note.—Original: Richard Stratton.

ORIUOLA, VIA DELL' (*Real*). Street in Florence. *Rom.* xxv.

Note—The Via dell' Orivola (Oriuola) leads from the Duomo in the direction of Porta alla Croce. It was so named in the fourteenth century because the first Florentine clock (oriulo or orologico) was made there, 1353.

"ORPHEUS" (*Real*). An opera by Gluck, in the title role of which Armgart scores her great success. *P.*—*Armg.* i ; mentioned *Mr. G.'s L. S.* xx; in the first edition of *Mr. G.'s L. S.* mentioned also in ch. ii, but this reference is omitted in the revised edition.

Note.—" Orpheus and Euridice," or " Orfeo ed Euridice ", by Christoph Wilibald Gluck, first performed 1762. The song " Che farò senza Euridice ", which Caterina Sarti sings, in *Mr. Gilfil's Love Story*, is from this opera, and in the first edition of *Mr. Gilfil* both " Che farò " and Caterina's other song, " Ho perduto il bel sembiante " were mentioned as being in the " Orpheus ". In the revised edition, however, George Eliot omitted in chapter ii, the name of the opera and changed the text to read " Sir Christopher's favourite airs, by Gluck and Paisiello ".

ORTO DE' RUCELLAI. *See* RUCELLAI GARDENS.

OSGOOD, MISS. Mr. Osgood's sister who married Mr. Lammeter and died before the opening of the story. *S. M.* vi.

OSGOOD, MR. One of the landed gentry of Raveloe, Mr. Lammeter's brother-in-law. *S. M.* iii, x, xvi–xvii, Conclusion.

OSGOOD, MRS. A fine-looking, grey-haired lady much attached to her niece, Nancy Lammeter. *S. M.* ii–iii, v, x–xi.

"An elderly lady . . . whose full white muslin kerchief, and mob-cap round her curls of smooth grey hair, were in daring contrast with the puffed yellow satins and top-knotted caps of her neighbours." Ch. xi.

OSGOOD, GILBERT. Nancy Lammeter's cousin, whom she refused. *S. M.* xi.

"OTELLO, GONDOLIER'S SONG FROM" (*Real*). The song which Daniel Deronda is singing on the Thames, just before he rescues Mirah Cohen from drowning. *D. D.* xvii.

Note.—"Otello," an opera by Rossini, with libretto based on Shakespeare's play, Othello.

OTTLEY, MR. Farmer in whose house Molly has been at service before going to Mrs. Poyser. *Adam B.* vi.

"OVER THE HILLS AND FAR AWAY" (*Real*). A tune which Solomon Macey plays at the New Year's dance at the Red House. *S. M.* xi.

Note.—This song is found in George Farquhar's play *The Recruiting Officer*, first produced 1706. There is also a song to the same air and with the same refrain "Over the Hills", etc., in Gay's *Beggar's Opera*.

OXFORD (*Real*). *Adam B.* xvi; *D. D.* vii–viii, xii; *F. H.* vii–viii; *L. V.* i; *M. F.* Bk. 1, iii.

The English university where Arthur Donnithorne in *Adam Bede*, Rex Gascoigne and Mr. Lush in *Daniel Deronda*, Philip Debarry in *Felix Holt*, Latimer's brother, Alfred, in the *Lifted Veil*, and Mr. Stelling in *Mill on the Floss* have been educated.

OYSTER CLUB, GRIMWORTH. *B. J.* ii–iii.

P

PABLO. The lame son of Roldan, the juggler; a mournful twelve-year-old boy, with a beautiful voice. *Sp. G.* i–ii.

"He sings God-taught such marrow-thrilling strains
As seem the very voice of dying Spring,
A flute-like wail that mourns the blossoms gone."

PACK. Collier at Sproxton. *F. H.* xi, xxxi.

PADDIFORD CHURCH. The little Chapel-of-ease on Paddiford Common, of which Mr. Tryan is curate. *J. R.* ii, viii, xxi.

PADDIFORD COMMON. A poor district in Milby, the scene of the Reverend Mr. Tryan's labour. *J. R.* i–iii, viii, xi, xxv–xxvi.

"Paddiford Common . . . was hardly recognizable as a common at all, but was a dismal district where you heard the rattle of the handloom, and breathed the smoke of the coal-pits." Ch. ii.

Note.—The original of Paddiford Common is Stockingford, between Nuneaton and Arbury.

PADDIFORD LENDING LIBRARY. *J. R.* iii.

PADRONCELLO. Tina's name for Sir Christopher Cheverel. *See* CHEVEREL, SIR CHRISTOPHER.

PADUA (*Real*). *Rom.* xvi.

Note.—Padua, a city of northern Italy, which at the time of *Romola* was under Venetian rule.

PAGLIA, CANTO DI. *See* CANTO DI PAGLIA.

PAINE, MAT. Lawyer Dempster's clerk. *J. R.* iv, vii.

PALACE OF THE PEOPLE. *See* PALAZZO VECCHIO.

PALACE OF THE VIA LARGA (*Real*). The home of the Medici before their expulsion from Florence, where Charles VIII is lodged after his entry into Florence. *Rom.* xii, xix, xxi, xxvi, xxix.

Note.—This is the Palazzo Medici (sometimes called Palazzo Riccardi after its later owners) in the Via Cavour (formerly Via Larga). It was erected about 1444–52 by Michelozzo for Cosimo Pater Patriæ. It is now a government building occupied by the prefecture.

PALAGIO, VIA DEL (*Real*). Street in Florence by which Romola and Monna Brigida return after the latter has given up her "vanities" to the Piagnoni. *Rom.* li.

Note.—The old Via del Palagio del Podestà now forms the first part of the Via Ghibellina as far as the Via Giuseppe Verdi.

PALAZZO VECCHIO (*Real*). The home of the Gonfaloniere and Signoria, the seat of the government of Florence. Savonarola is imprisoned here. *Rom.* Proem, vii–viii, xxiii, xxviii–xxix, xxxv, xxxviii, xliii, xlv, xlvii–xlviii, liv–lv, lx, lxii–lxiii, lxv–lxvi, lxxii.

Note.—The Palazzo Vecchio, on the Piazza della Signoria, was begun in 1298 from Arnolfo di Cambio's designs and completed and extended at later dates. Until 1532 it was the seat of the government of Florence, and then for awhile the palace of Cosimo I. Since 1871 it has been a civic building. Its earlier name was Palazzo del Popolo, dei Signori, or della Signoria, and Guido Biagi points out that it could not have been called Palazzo Vecchio in the time of Romola, as that name was not used until 1550.

PALERMO (*Real*). Scene of the poem "How Lisa loved the King." *P.—Lisa.*

Note.—Palermo, the capital and largest city of Sicily, on the north coast of the island. At the time of *Lisa* Sicily was ruled by King Pedro III, of Aragon, and his queen, Constance (daughter of Manfred of Beneventum), through whom Pedro had acquired his Sicilian rights.

PALFREY, MR. A farmer who farmed his own land; Penelope's father. *B. J.* ii–iii.

PALFREY, MRS. Penelope's mother. *B. J.* ii–iii.

PALFREY, SQUIRE. Mr. Palfrey's deceased father "respected by the last Grimworth generation as a man who could afford to drink too much in his own house". *B. J.* ii.

PALFREY, LETITIA. Penny's elder sister, who has a prouder style of beauty and a more worldly ambition and is engaged to a woolfactor. *B. J.* ii–iii.

PALFREY, MISS PENELOPE. The pretty blue-eyed girl who is on the point of marrying Edward Freely when it is discovered that he is the disgraced David Faux. *B. J.* ii–iii.

"Her yellowish flaxen hair did not curl naturally, I admit, but its bright, crisp ringlets were such smooth, perfect miniature tubes. . . . She wore them in a crop, for in those days . . . young ladies wore crops long after they were twenty, and Penelope was not yet nineteen. Like the waxen ideal, she had round blue eyes, and round nostrils in her little nose, and teeth such as the ideal would be seen to have if it ever showed them. Altogether she was a small round thing, as neat as a pink and white double daisy, and as guileless." Ch. ii.

PARERGA. Mr. Casaubon's published pamphlets, preliminary to his great unpublished "Key to all Mythologies", "by which he tested his public and deposited small monumental records of his march." *Mid.* xxix.

PARIS (*Real*). *D. D.* xii, xxiii, xxv; *Mid.* x, xv–xviii, xlv, lxvi; mentioned *Amos B.* iv. In *Middlemarch* Paris is one of the places where Dr. Lydgate had studied medicine.

PARK HOUSE. The home of the Guest family in St. Ogg's. *M. F.* Bk. 6, ii, vi, ix–x.

PARK LANE (*Real*). The street in London where Sir Hugo Mallinger lives. *D. D.* xvii, xxviii, xxxvii, xlv, lxiv.

PARK STREET. Street in Treby Magna, part of the route taken by the election rioters. *F. H.* xxxiii.

PARLEY STREET. A street in Middlemarch. *Mid.* xlv.

PARLIAMENTARY CANDIDATE SOCIETY (*Real*). *Mid.* li.

Note.—A society "instituted to support reform by promoting the return of fit and proper members to Parliament", active at the time of the Reform Bill.

PARROT, MR. One of Mr. Gilfil's parishioners; a farmer. *Mr. G.'s L. S.* i.

PARROT, MRS. The farmer's wife. *Mr. G.'s L. S.* i.

PARROT, BESSIE. A flaxen-headed little girl. *Mr. G.'s L. S.* i.

PARROT, MISS SELINA. *Mr. G.'s L. S.* i.

PARRY, MR. Amos Barton's predecessor at Shepperton; a popular preacher. *Amos B.* i–ii; *J. R.* xi, xxvi.[1]

PARTRIDGE. *M. F.* Bk. 1, iii.

PASH. Watchmaker; a member of the Philosophers' Club. "A small dark, vivacious, triple-baked Jew," ready in debate. *D. D.* xlii.

PASTON, MR. Minister of the church in Lantern Yard in Silas Marner's youth. *S. M.* i, xxi.

PATCH, NED. Pedlar. *F. H.* xxviii.

PATCH, OLD. Parish clerk, one of the Christmas Eve singers who sing under the windows of Dorlcote Mill at midnight. *M. F.* Bk. 2, ii.

"PATRIOT." Newspaper. *F. H.* xxiv.

PATTEN, MRS. A rich old lady of Shepperton, tenant of Cross Farm. *Amos B.* i, v–vi; *Mr. G.'s L. S.* i.

"Mrs. Patten, a childless old lady, who had got rich chiefly by the negative process of spending nothing . . . She is a pretty little old woman of eighty, with a close

---

[1] A Nuneaton list gives Mr. Docker as his prototype. (Manuscript notes.)

cap and tiny flat white curls round her face, as natty and unsoiled and invariable as the waxen image of a little old lady under a glass-case ; once a lady's-maid, and married for her beauty. She used to adore her husband, and now she adores her money, cherishing a quiet blood-relation's hatred for her niece, Janet Gibbs, who, she knows, expects a large legacy, and whom she is determined to disappoint." *Amos B.* Ch. i.

Note.—The original of Mrs. Patten is said to have been a Mrs. Hutchings or Hutchins. (Manuscript information ; also Olcott, *George Eliot,* p. 14.)

PAZZI (*Hist.*). Member of the party of the Arrabbiati. *Rom.* xxxix.

Note.—A well-known Florentine family several members of which were politically prominent at the date of *Romola.*

PAZZINI (LA). Fruit woman in Milan, with whom the Sartis lodged. *Mr. G.'s L. S.* iii.

PEACOCK, MR. Lydgate's predecessor in Middlemarch. *Mid.* xi, xvii–xviii, xxvi–xxvii, xlv, lxiv.

PEASANTS' FAIR. *See* FIERUCOLA.

PEDRO. Servant at Lorenzo's Inn. *Sp. G.* i.

PEDRO, KING OF ARAGON (*Hist.*). The gallant ruler of Sicily with whom young Lisa falls in love when she sees him at a tournament. When he learns from the minstrel Minuccio that the maiden is dying for love of him, he visits her and bids her live and he and his queen, Constance, take Lisa and her suitor, Perdicone, under their protection and advance their fortunes. Thereafter King Pedro wears Lisa's favour, and calls himself her faithful knight. *P.—Lisa.*

Note.—George Eliot's poem tells the story of Lisa and King Pedro, without change of plot, from the tale in Boccaccio's *Decamerone,* tenth day, novel seven. The king in the story is Pedro III, King of Aragon, who acquired his claims in Sicily through his queen, Constance, daughter of Manfred of Beneventum, King of Sicily. Pedro became King of Aragon in 1276, King of Sicily in 1282, and died 1285.

PEGWELL. Corn-factor. *Mid.* xxiii.

PELLEY'S BANK. *M. F.* Bk. 6, v.

PELTON, SQUIRE. A man who flogged his dogs to frighten his wife. *D. D.* xxxi.

PENDRELL, MISS. *See* NOLAN, MRS.

PENDRELL, MR. Banker in Treby Magna. *F. H.* v, xxiv.

PENDRELL, MRS. The banker's wife. *F. H.* xxiv.

"PENLLWY UNIVERSE." A journal which notices Vorticella's one book. *T. S.* xv.

PENNICOTE. Parish of which Mr. Gascoigne is rector. *D. D.* iv, vi–vii, xxxi, lxix.

PENNICOTE CHURCH. *D. D.* xxi, xxxi.

PENNICOTE RECTORY. Home of the Gascoigne family. *D. D.* ii–iii, vi–viii, xxi, xxiv, xliv, lviii, lxix.

PENTREATH, LADY. Lord Pentreath's handsome wife. *D. D.* xxxv–xxxvi, xlv.

"She was one of those women who are never handsome till they are old, and she had had the wisdom to embrace the beauty of age as early as possible. What might have seemed harshness in her features when she was young, had turned now into a satisfactory strength of form and expression which defied wrinkles, and was set off by a crown of white hair." Ch. xxxvi.

PENTREATH, LORD. A representative of the old aristocracy; a neighbour of the Mallingers. *D. D.* xxxv–xxxvi, xlv.

PEPE. The small son of Lorenzo, the innkeeper. *Sp. G.* i.

PEPIN. The too ready writer; a busy "general writer" who feels a "certain surprise that there have not been more persons equal to himself". *T. S.* xiv.

PEPÍTA. A Spanish girl who watches the juggling in the Plaça Santiago; she is in love with Juan the Minstrel. *Sp. G.* i.

PEPPER, MRS., OF FIBB'S END. One of Bob Jakin's customers. *M. F.* Bk. 5, iii.

"PER PIETÀ NON DIRMI ADDIO" (*Real*). A song by Beethoven, which Mirah Cohen sings. *D. D.* xxxii, xlv.

PERDICONE. Lisa's suitor, whom she marries later. *P.—Lisa.*

PERETOLA (*Real*). A village near Florence. *Rom.* x, xvi, xxxiv, lvi.

Note.—A village about three miles from Florence, beyond the Porta al Prato.

PERRY. One of Latimer's servants. *L. V.* i.

PESTH (*Real*). One of the cities where Mirah Cohen and her father, Lapidoth, had been. *D. D.* xx.

Note.—Pesth, now part of Budapest, the capital of Hungary (formed by the union of Buda and Pesth in 1873), was at the time of *Daniel Deronda* a separate city.

PETTIFER, MRS. Janet Dempster's kind friend who shelters her when her husband turns her out at midnight. *J. R.* iii, xi–xii, xv–xvi, xviii–xxiii, xxv–xxvii.

"The small, elderly lady in dowdy clothing, who is also working diligently, is Mrs. Pettifer, a superior-minded widow, much valued in Milby, being such a very respectable person to have in the house in case of illness, and of quite too good a family to receive any money-payment — you could always send her garden-stuff that would make her ample amends." Ch. iii.

Note.—The original of Mrs. Pettifer was a Mrs. Robinson. (Manuscript information; also Olcott, *George Eliot*, p. 16; Coventry, *Centenary*, p. 5.)[1]

PHILEMON. *T. S.* xiii.

PHILLIPS, SAM. A stone-sawyer who had learned to read at the age of twenty. *Adam B.* xxi.

"PHILOSOPHERS', THE." A club at the "Hand and Banner" frequented by Mordecai. *D. D.* xlii.

---

[1] Some Nuneaton lists give Mrs. Craddock as the prototype.

"Half a dozen men of various ages, from between twenty and thirty to fifty, all shabbily dressed, most of them with clay pipes in their mouths . . . This was the soberest of clubs . . . Certainly a company select of the select among poor men, being drawn together by a taste not prevalent even among the privileged heirs of learning and its institutions; and not likely to amuse any gentleman in search of crime or low comedy." Ch. xlii.

Note.—The original of the "Philosophers'" was a philosophical club, meeting in Red Lion Square, to which G. H. Lewes once belonged. (*See* Blind, *George Eliot*, pp. 105, 268; also article by G. H. Lewes in *Fortnightly Review*, vol. iv, p. 384.)

PHIPPS, MISS. The unattractive daughter of the Milby banker. *Amos B.* iv.

Note.—Perhaps the same as the Miss Phipps in *Janet's Repentance*.

PHIPPS, MISS. A young lady fond of fine clothes. *J. R.* ii, v, x.[1]

PHIPPS, MR. Mrs. Phipps's amiable husband. *J. R.* xiii, xxv.

Note.—In the lists of originals prepared in Nuneaton after the publication of *Scenes of Clerical Life* the original of Mr. Phipps is given as a Mr. Bull. (*See* Olcott, *George Eliot*, p. 16.)

PHIPPS, MRS. One of Mr. Pratt's chief patients in Milby; "a woman of decided opinions, though of wheezy utterance." *J. R.* ii, x, xxiii, xxi, xxv–xxvi.

Note.—The original of Mrs. Phipps was Mrs. Bull. (Manuscript information.)

PHIPPS, MRS. The wife of the Milby banker. *Amos B.* iv.

PHIPPS, MR. ALFRED. A young Milby dandy. *J. R.* ii.

PHIPPS, NED. *J. R.* vi.

PHŒBE. The Meyricks' servant. *D. D.* xviii.

PHŒBE. Mrs. Pettifer's servant. *J. R.* xvi.

PIAGNONI (*Hist.*). The name given to the adherents or party of Savonarola; the democratic party. *Rom.* xii, xxv, xliii, xlv, xlix–li, lvii, lxiv–lxvi.

Note.—The name Piagnoni, which means snivellers or funeral mourners (i.e. paid mourners), was given to the followers of Savonarola because they constantly denounced the sins of the city and advocated a sober, restrained life. In the politics of the period, the Piagnoni, or party of the people, were opposed both to the Mediceans and to the Arrabbiati, or aristocratic party.

PIAZZA. For names of squares beginning with the word Piazza *see* the significant part of the name, e.g. Mozzi, Piazza de'.

PICCOLA, VIA. A little street in Florence, beyond San Ambrogio, where Tessa and her children live after they move from San Giorgio. *Rom.* l.

---

[1] A Nuneaton list gives a Miss Bull as her prototype. (Manuscript notes.)

PICKARD, REV. MR.[1] *Mr. G.'s L.S.* i.

PICO DELLA MIRANDOLA, GIOVANNI (*Hist.*). Scholar and friend of Savonarola. *Rom.* iii–iv, xvi, xxv, xxix, xxxix.

"Pico della Mirandola, once a Quixotic young genius with long curls, astonished at his own powers and astonishing Rome with heterodox theses; afterwards a more humble student with a consuming passion for inward perfection, having come to find the universe more astonishing than his own cleverness." Ch. xxxix.

Note.—Giovanni Pico della Mirandola (1463–94), an Italian philosopher and theologian; precocious and gifted, he was called the "Phœnix of the Age".

PIERO, SAN (Porta). *See* PORTA SAN PIERO.

PIERRE. Latimer's servant at Geneva. *L. V.* i.

PIETRA (*Real*). The village near which Romola's flight from Florence is arrested by her encounter with Savonarola. *Rom.* xxxvii.

Note.—A village on the road to Bologna about two miles north of Florence.

PIEVANO, THE. The parish priest whom Romola persuades to return to the care of his plague-stricken village. *Rom.* lxviii–lxix.

PILGRIM, MR. A prosperous doctor in Milby. *Amos B.* i, v–vi; *J. R.* i–ii, vi, xiii, xxii–xxv; mentioned *Mr. G.'s L. S.* i.

"Mr. Pilgrim, the doctor from the nearest market-town, who, though occasionally affecting aristocratic airs, and giving late dinners with enigmatic side-dishes and poisonous port, is never so comfortable as when he is relaxing his professional legs in one of those excellent farm-houses where the mice are sleek and the mistress sickly." *Amos B.* Ch. i.

"Pilgrim was tall, heavy, rough-mannered, and spluttering . . . The doctor's estimate, even of a confiding patient, was apt to rise and fall with the entries in the day-book; and I have known Mr. Pilgrim discover the most unexpected virtues in a patient seized with a promising illness. . . . Doubtless this *crescendo* of benevolence was partly due to feelings not at all represented by the entries in the day-book; for in Mr. Pilgrim's heart, too, there was a latent store of tenderness and pity which flowed forth at the sight of suffering." *J. R.* Ch. ii.

Note.—The original of Mr. Pilgrim was a well-known doctor, Mr. Bucknill. (Manuscript information; also Olcott, *George Eliot*, p. 14; Parkinson, *Scenes*, p. 57.)

PILULUS. *T. S.* xiii.

PINK, MR. Saddler, whose shop is the centre of gossip in Treby Magna. *F. H.* xxviii, xxxi.

"Mr. Pink professed a deep-dyed Toryism; but he regarded all fault-finding as Radical and somewhat impious, as disturbing to trade, and likely to offend the gentry or the servants through whom their harness was ordered. . . . It was only the 'Papists' who lived far enough off to be spoken of uncivilly." Ch. xxviii.

---

[1] A Nuneaton list gives Mr. Hartnill as his prototype. (Manuscript notes.)

PINKERTON. The old Tory member of Parliament from Middlemarch. *Mid.* vi, li.

PINTI, BORGO. *See* BORGO PINTI.

PINTI, PORTA. *See* PORTA PINTI.

PIPPO'S SHOP. Shop where Tessa buys sweetmeats for her children. *Rom.* l.

PISA (*Real*). A city conquered by Florence, which had rebelled. *Rom.* viii–ix, xxi, xxvii, xxix, xxxii, xxxv, xlii–xliii, xlv–xlvi.

Note.—Pisa, a city forty-nine miles west of Florence. Captured by Florence in 1406, it re-asserted its independence in 1494 at the time of the visit of Charles VIII of France, and was in a state of rebellion during most of the time of *Romola.*

PISTOJA (*Real*). Town where Romola breaks her journey when returning to Florence. *Rom.* xiv, lxiii, lxix–lxx.

Note.—Pistoja, or Pistoia, is an ancient town in Tuscany, on the Ombrone, twenty-one miles north-west of Florence.

PITT, MR. (*Hist.*). A great statesman with whom Mr. Nolan boasts of having had an interview. *F. H.* iii, xx.

Note.—William Pitt, the younger (1759–1806).

PITTI, LUCA (*Hist.*). Builder of the great Pitti Palace. *Rom.*, mentioned Proem.

Note.—Luca Pitti, Gonfaloniere of justice, who built the Pitti Palace about 1440.

PITTI, PIERO (*Hist.*). "One of the Magnificent Eight," a guest at the supper in the Rucellai Gardens. *Rom.* xxxix.

Note.—Piero Pitti, a Medicean, son of Luca Pitti.

PITTMAN, THE MISSES. Lawyer Pittman's four tall daughters, "with cannon curls surmounted by large hats, and long drooping ostrich feathers of parrot green." *J. R.* ii.

PITTMAN, MR. An old lawyer in Milby, Mr. Dempster's partner. *J. R.* ii, xxv.

"No one in Milby considered old Pittman a virtuous man, and the elder townspeople were not at all backward in narrating the least advantageous portions of his biography in a very round unvarnished manner. Yet I could never observe that they trusted him any the less, or liked him any the worse." Ch. ii.

Note.—In the lists of originals prepared in Nuneaton after the publication of *Scenes of Clerical Life* a Mr. Greenway was given as the original of Mr. Pittman. (*See* Olcott, *George Eliot*, p. 16.)

PIVART, MR. Owner of a farm on the Ripple. *M. F.* Bk. 2, ii, vii; Bk. 3, i. He takes measures for irrigation which Mr. Tulliver regards as an infringement of his water power and the lawsuit which results ruins Mr. Tulliver.

PLAÇA SANTIAGO. *See* SANTIAGO, PLAÇA.

PLESSY, LORD. A nobleman who lies in bed all day and plays at dominoes. *Mid.* xxxviii.

PLYMDALE, MR. A wealthy manufacturer and prominent citizen of Middlemarch. *Mid.* xi, xiii, xviii, li, lxiv, lxxiv.

PLYMDALE, NED. Son of Mr. and Mrs. Plymdale, and a rejected lover of Rosamond Vincy; "one of the good matches in Middlemarch, though not one of its leading minds." *Mid.* xxvii, xxxi, lviii, lxiv.

PLYMDALE, MRS. SELINA. The manufacturer's well-meaning wife; Mrs. Bulstrode's intimate friend. *Mid.* xvi, xxxi, lxiv, lxxi, lxxiv.

POD'S END. *F. H.* xx.

POGGIO (*Hist.*). An admirable scholar whom Bardo de' Bardi does not consider entirely free from faults. *Rom.* vi.

Note.—Giovanni Francesco Poggio Bracciolini (1380–1459), chancellor and historiographer of Florence, an author and scholar best known for his researches in monasteries and his recovery of many manuscripts.

POINÇON, MADAME. A strict acquaintance of the Brooke sisters. *Mid.* i.

POLITIAN. *See* POLIZIANO, ANGELO.

POLIZIANO, ANGELO (*Hist.*). A Florentine scholar, the rejected suitor of Alessandra Scala, who indulges in a literary quarrel with Bartolommeo Scala. *Rom.* ii–iii, v, vii, ix, xiii, xvi, xxix, xxxix.

"Angelo Poliziano, chief literary genius of that age, a born poet, and a scholar without dulness, whose phrases had blood in them and are alive still." Ch. xxxix.

Note.—Angelo Ambrosini, *called* Poliziano, or Politian (1454–94), Italian scholar and poet, professor of Greek and Latin at Florence. His *Miscellanea*, a collection of critical observations on the ancient authors, was published 1489.

POLLAJUOLO, ANTONIO (*Hist.*). Goldsmith "whom patronizing Popes had seduced from his native Florence to more gorgeous Rome ". *Rom.* xxxix.

Note.—Antonio Pollaiuolo (1429–98), Florentine goldsmith, medallist, metal-caster, and painter.

POLLARD'S END. Section of Treby Magna. *F. H.* xxviii, xxxiii.

POMFRET, MRS. Lady's maid at Donnithorne Chase. *Adam B.* vii, xii–xiii, xxxi.

PONTANUS (*Hist.*). A scholar who sought patronage. *Rom.* v, lvii.

Note.—Giovanni Pontano (1426–1503), a scholar, head of the Neapolitan Academy, who made an elaborate address of welcome to Charles VIII when that king entered Naples.

PONTE ALLA CARRAJA (*Real*). Bridge across the Arno, in Florence, the last one passed by Tito when he tries to escape the mob by swimming. *Rom.* x, lxvii.

Note.—The Ponte alla Carraia, then called Ponte Nuovo, was built 1218–20 at the expense of the Frati Umiliati. It was destroyed by an inundation in 1333, restored in 1337, partially rebuilt in 1559, and widened in 1867.

PONTE RUBACONTE, OR PONTE ALLE GRAZIE (*Real*). Bridge across the Arno, in Florence, near Romola's house. *Rom.* v, xx, xxvi–xxvii, xxxvi–xxxvii, xliv, lxvii.
Note.—The Ponte alle Grazie was built in 1237 for Rubaconte da Mandella. It was formerly called the Ponte Rubaconte, its other name, alle Grazie, coming from the chapel of Santa Maria delle Grazie, on the right bank. It was modernized in 1874, when the old houses on the bridge were demolished.

PONTE SANTA TRINITÀ (*Real*). Bridge across the Arno, in Florence, the first one passed by Tito Melema when he tries to escape the mob by swimming. *Rom.* xliii, xlv, lxvii.
Note.—The Ponte Santa Trinità, one of the most beautiful bridges in Italy, was built in 1252, and rebuilt in 1567–70 by Ammanati. It takes its name from the Church of Santa Trinità near by.

PONTE VECCHIO (*Real*). The bridge across the Arno in Florence, from which Tito Melema leaps when pursued by the mob. *Rom.* Proem, v, x, xxi, xlii–xliii, xlvii, lxvii.
Note.—The oldest bridge in Florence, said to date originally from Roman times; several times demolished, it was finally rebuilt by Taddeo Gaddi in 1345.

PONTO. Mr. Gilfil's old brown setter. *Mr. G.'s L. S.* i.

POOLE. *J. R.* xxv.

POR' DEL PRATO (*Real*). Gate in Florence beyond which Tessa's mother and step-father live. *Rom.* viii (Porta al Prato), x, xxxiii.
Note.—This is the Porta al Prato, formerly a part of the walls, at the end of the Via del Prato. Guido Biagi points out that the form of the name used by George Eliot, Por del Prato, is incorrect. It was called *al Prato* because just within it was a large field.

POR' SANTA MARIA (*Real*). Street in Florence, near which Romola comes upon the starving Baldassarre Calvo. *Rom.* xx, xlii–xliii.
Note.—The Por' Santa Maria, so named from a gate in the first circuit of the old walls, leads northward from the Ponte Vecchio.

PORPESSE, M. A French savant who takes notice of the great Merman - Grampus controversy. *T. S.* iii.

PORTA PINTI (*Real*). Gate in Florence near which Bartolommeo Scala lived. *Rom.* vii.
Note.—The gate at the end of the Borgo Pinti (Via de' Pinti), erected about the end of the thirteenth century. It was pulled down in the nineteenth century.

PORTA ROSSA (*Real*). Street in Florence by which Tito Melema and Tessa go to Ognissanti, during the San Giovanni festa. *Rom.* x.

Note.—Via Porta Rossa, so named from a gate in the second circuit of walls built of brick, is a street which leads westward from Via Calzaiuoli.

PORTA SAN FREDIANO (*Real*). The gate by which Charles VIII enters Florence. *Rom.* xxi, xlv, lxvii.

Note.—The Porta San Frediano was erected 1332. It was the gate looking toward Pisa, and through it Charles VIII entered 17th November, 1494.

PORTA SAN GALLO (*Real*). Gate by which Tito Melema plans to make his final departure from Florence. *Rom.* xxi, xxxvii, lxvii, lxx.

Note.—The Porta San Gallo, at the end of the Via di San Gallo, was begun in 1284.

PORTA SAN PIERO (*Real*). The gate of Florence "that looks toward Siena and Rome". *Rom.* xxxii, xxxvi, xlii.

Note.—The Porta San Piero Gattolino, now called the Porta Romana.

PORTA SANTA CROCE (*Real*). Gate in Florence near which Tessa and her children live. *Rom.* viii, xxv, l, lvi.

Note.—The Porta alla Croce was built about 1287 under the direction of Arnolfo. The space in which it stands is now called the Piazza Beccaria.

PORTE SAINT MARTIN (*Real*). The theatre in Paris where Madame Laure was acting when Lydgate was in love with her. *Mid.* xv.

Note.—An old well-known theatre in Paris.

PORTER. LADY, The lady in whose family the Countess Czerlaski had been a governess. *Amos B.* iii–iv.

PORTER, SIR WILLIAM. *Amos B.* iii.

POULTER, MR. The village schoolmaster at King's Lorton, an old Peninsular soldier, who is employed to drill Tom Tulliver. *M. F.* Bk. 2, iv.

POWDERELL, MR. A retired ironmonger of Middlemarch, a man of some standing. *Mid.* xviii, xlv, lx.

POWDERELL, MRS. The ironmonger's wife, who privately takes Widgeon's Purifying Pills when she is under Lydgate's care. *Mid.* xlv.

POWDERELLS. A Lowick family, which had sat in the same pew with the Waules for generations. *Mid.* xii.

POWERS, BILL. Leader of the beer drinkers at the "Bear and Ragged Staff". *J. R.* iv.

POYSER, MARTIN. Mrs. Poyser's husband and Hetty Sorrel's uncle; a substantial, jovial farmer, the tenant of the Hall Farm, and the "broadest man in the parish". *Adam B.* ii, v–vi, ix, xiv, xviii, xx, xxii–xxvi, xxx–xxxvi, xxxviii, xl, xlii–xlviii, xlix, lii–liii, lv.

"A portly figure, with a ruddy black-eyed face, which bore in it the possibility of looking extremely acute, and occasionally contemptuous, on market-days, but had now a predominant after-supper expression of hearty good-nature . . . he was of so excellent a disposition that he had been kinder and more respectful than ever to his old father since he had made a deed of gift of all his property, and no man judged his neighbours more charitably on all personal matters; but for a farmer, like Luke Britton, for example, whose fallows were not well cleaned, who didn't know the rudiments of hedging and ditching, and showed but a small share of judgment in the purchase of winter stock, Martin Poyser was as hard and implacable as the north-east wind." Ch. xiv.

" Mr. Poyser was in his Sunday suit of drab, with a red-and-green waistcoat, and a green watch-ribbon having a large cornelian seal attached, pendant like a plumb-line from that promontory where his watch-pocket was situated; a silk handkerchief of a yellow tone round his neck; and excellent grey-ribbed stockings, knitted by Mrs. Poyser's own hand, setting off the proportions of his leg. Mr. Poyser had no reason to be ashamed of his leg, and suspected that the growing abuse of top-boots and other fashions tending to disguise the nether limbs, had their origin in a pitiable degeneracy of the human calf. Still less had he reason to be ashamed of his round, jolly face, which was good-humour itself." Ch. xviii.

He is proud of his wife's superior acuteness and cleverness, and of the unblemished record of his family which has " held up its head and paid its way as far back as its name was in the parish register ". His easy good nature is a marked contrast to his wife's keen tongue and critical habit, but when his niece, Hetty Sorrel, brings disgrace on the family he is harder towards her than is his faultfinding wife.

POYSER, MARTY. Mr. and Mrs. Poyser's elder son, aged nine. *Adam B.* xiv, xviii, xx, xxii, xxvi, xxx, xxxiv, xlix.

" The ' little uns ' addressed were Marty and Tommy, boys of nine and seven, in little fustian tailed coats and knee-breeches, relieved by rosy cheeks and black eyes; looking as much like their father as a very small elephant is like a very large one." Ch. xviii.

POYSER, OLD MARTIN. Martin Poyser's aged father who has retired from active life to a comfortable chair in the chimney-nook. *Adam B.* xiv, xviii, xx, xxii–xxiii, xxxi, xxxiv, xl.

" Old Martin Poyser, a hale but shrunken and bleached image of his portly black-haired son—his head hanging forward a little, and his elbows pushed backwards so as to allow the whole of his forearm to rest on the arm of the chair. His blue handkerchief was spread over his knees, as was usual indoors, when it was not hanging over his head; and he sat watching what went forward with the quiet *outward* glance of healthy old age." Ch. xiv.

" Like all old men whose life has been spent in labour, he liked to feel that he was still useful—that there was a better crop of onions in the garden because he was by at the sowing—and that the cows would be milked the better if he stayed at home on a Sunday afternoon to look on. He always went to church on Sacrament Sundays, but not very regularly at other times; on wet Sundays, or whenever he had a touch of rheumatism, he used to read the three first chapters of Genesis instead." Ch. xviii.

POYSER, MRS. RACHEL. The sharp-tongued mistress of the Hall Farm; a shrewd, capable woman, with a gift for epigram and a flow of conversation which has many unexpected turns but no end. *Adam B.* ii, vi–ix, xiv, xviii, xx, xxii–xxvii, xxx–xxxv, xxxviii, xl, xlix, lii -liii, lv.

"Do not suppose, however, that Mrs. Poyser was elderly or shrewish in her appearance; she was a good-looking woman, not more than eight-and-thirty, of fair complexion and sandy hair, well-shapen, light-footed: the most conspicuous article in her attire was an ample checkered linen apron, which almost covered her skirt; and nothing could be plainer or less noticeable than her cap and gown, for there was no weakness of which she was less tolerant than feminine vanity, and the preference of ornament to utility. The family likeness between her and her niece Dinah Morris, with the contrast between her keenness and Dinah's seraphic gentleness of expression, might have served a painter as an excellent suggestion for a Martha and Mary. Their eyes were just of the same colour, but a striking test of the difference in their operation was seen in the demeanour of Trip, the black-and-tan terrier, whenever that much-suspected dog unwarily exposed himself to the freezing arctic ray of Mrs. Poyser's glance. Her tongue was not less keen than her eye, and, whenever a damsel came within earshot, seemed to take up an unfinished lecture, as a barrel-organ takes up a tune, precisely at the point where it had left off." Ch. vi.

"She has the spirit of three men, with that pale face of hers; and she says such sharp things, too."

"Sharp! yes, her tongue is like a new-set razor. She's quite original in her talk, too; one of those untaught wits that help to stock a country with proverbs. I told you that capital thing I heard her say about Craig—that he was like a cock who thought the sun had risen to hear him crow. Now that's an Æsop's fable in a sentence." Ch. xxxiii.

She is a pattern dairywoman and housekeeper, with standards of excellence which none of her much-berated maids, even under the spur of her sharp tongue, ever succeeds in living up to. She keeps her eyes open for her neighbours' foibles and weaknesses, summing them up in keen, though homely, epigrams, and is strict with her husband's niece, Hetty Sorrel, whom she rightly suspects of selfishness and vanity. When the parsimonious Squire Donnithorne tries to impose upon her good-natured husband, Mrs. Poyser " speaks her mind " to the Squire, routing him in a battle of words which delights the whole neighbourhood. In spite of her sharp tongue she is a kindly woman, much attached to her family and fond of her niece Dinah Morris, whose saintliness she appreciates though she does not approve of her Methodism and self-denial.

Note.—For several of Mrs. Poyser's traits—her kindliness, shrewd common sense, and witty tongue—George Eliot's own mother, Mrs. Robert Evans (Christiana Pearson) was the original. Mr. John W. Cross, in *George Eliot's Life*, describes Mrs. Robert Evans as a "woman with an unusual amount of force—a shrewd practical person, with a considerable dash of the Mrs. Poyser vein in her." Cross, vol. 1, p. 13.

The name Poyser was a real name in the neighbourhood of Ellastone (the "Hayslope" of *Adam Bede*), and an actual Mrs. Poyser, a farmer's wife, is said to have lived there at the time when George Eliot's father, Robert Evans, was still in Ellastone. A writer in *Notes and Queries*, whose father had been clerk to William Evans, George Eliot's uncle, states that a Mrs. Poyser was Mr. William Evans' housekeeper, which might explain the use of the name. (*See Notes and Queries*, Ser. vi, vol. 8, p. 351.)

POYSER, TOMMY. Mr. and Mrs. Poyser's second son, a lad of seven years. *Adam B.* xiv, xviii, xx, xxii, xxvi, xxx, xxxiv, xlix, lii.

POYSER, TOTTY (CHARLOTTE). Mr. and Mrs. Poyser's three-year-old daughter, the spoiled darling of the Hall Farm. *Adam B.* vi–vii, xiv, xviii, xx, xxii–xxiv, xxvi, xxx, xxxii, xlix, lv.

"A little sunny-haired girl between three and four, who, seated on a high chair at the end of the ironing - table, was arduously clutching the handle of a miniature iron with her tiny fat fist and ironing rags with an assiduity that required her to put her little red tongue out as far as anatomy would allow." Ch. vi.

PRAGUE (*Real*). The European city, where, in *Daniel Deronda*, Mirah Cohen escapes from her father, Lapidoth. In the *Lifted Veil*, Latimer has a vision of this city in his first experience of clairvoyance; when he visits the city later he realizes the exactness of his vision. *D. D.* xviii, xx; *L. V.* i–ii.

Note.—The ancient city of Prague, now the capital of Czechoslovakia, which at the time of *Daniel Deronda* belonged to Austria.

PRATO (*Real*). A town near Florence where the doctor Maestro Tacco once lived. *Rom.* x, xiv, xvi, lxiii, lxx.

Note.—Prato, ten miles northwest of Florence, on the Bisenzio, an affluent of the Arno.

PRATO, THE (*Real*). "A large, open space within the walls, where the

Florentine youth played at their favourite Calcio." *Rom.* x, xxvi, xxix, xxxiv.

> *Note.*—A large triangular field formerly just within the Porta al Prato, where the Florentines used to play games and where the tiltings took place.

PRATO, POR' DEL. *See* POR' DEL PRATO.

PRATT. Mr. Casaubon's butler, "a red-cheeked man given to lively converse with Tantripp," Dorothea's maid. *Mid.* xxvii, xlviii, liv.

PRATT, MISS. The doctor's sister and housekeeper. *J. R.* iii, ix, xxv.

> "Miss Pratt was an old maid with a cap, a braided 'front', a backbone and appendages. Miss Pratt was the one bluestocking of Milby, possessing, she said, no less than five hundred volumes, competent, as her brother the doctor often observed, to conduct a conversation on any topic whatever, and occasionally dabbling a little in authorship, though it was understood that she had never put forth the full powers of her mind in print." Ch. iii.

PRATT, MISS ELIZA. The doctor's daughter; a handsome girl, somewhat in love with Mr. Tryan. *J. R.* iii, x–xi.

PRATT, MR. RICHARD. Doctor; Mr. Pilgrim's rival in Milby, and an adherent of Mr. Tryan. *J. R.* i–ii, ix–xi, xiii, xxvii.

> "Pratt was middle sized, in sinuating, and silvery-voiced.

. . . Pratt elegantly referred all diseases to debility, and, with a proper contempt for symptomatic treatment, went to the root of the matter with port wine and bark. . . . There was the most perfect unanimity between Pratt and Pilgrim in the determination to drive away the obnoxious and too probably unqualified intruder as soon as possible . . . But by their respective patients these two distinguished men were pitted against each other with great virulence." Ch. ii.

> *Note.*—The original of Mr. Pratt was a Mr. Bond. (*See* Olcott, *George Eliot,* p. 16.)

PRENDERGAST, THE HON. AND REV. MR. Non-resident rector of Milby. *J. R.* i–iii, v–vi, xxvi.

> "Mr. Prendergast looked much more dignified with his plain white surplice and black hair. He was a tall commanding man, and read the Liturgy in a strikingly sonorous and uniform voice." Ch. vi.

> *Note.*—The original of the Hon. and Rev. Mr. Prendergast was the Hon. and Rev. R. B. Stopford, vicar of Nuneaton. (*See* Olcott, *George Eliot,* pp. 16, 39.)

PRETTYMAN, MR. Grocer at Grimworth. *B. J.* ii–iii.

PRETTYMAN, MRS. The grocer's wife. *B. J.* ii.

PRIEST. *P.*—*C. B. P.*

PRIMROSE. Mr. Gascoigne's grey nag. *D. D.* vii.

PRIOR. A deceased clergyman with whom Amos Barton had been friendly. *Amos B.* vi.

PRIOR, THE. *See* ISIDOR, FATHER.

PRISON STREET. A street in the town where Silas Marner lived in his youth. *S. M.* xxi.

PRISONERS, THREE. Three prisoners captured by the French at Lunigiano and Fivizzano, who are led by French soldiers through the streets of Florence and released by the exasperated populace. As they escape in different directions, the oldest, Baldassarre Calvo, accidentally comes upon his ungrateful son, Tito Melema, who refuses to recognize him. *Rom.* xxii–xxiii.

" In the van of the crowd were three men in scanty clothing; each had his hands bound together by a cord, and a rope was fastened round his neck and body, in such a way that he who held the extremity of the rope might easily check any rebellious movement by the threat of throttling. The men who held the ropes were French soldiers, and by broken Italian phrases and strokes from the knotted end of the rope, they from time to time stimulated their prisoners to beg." Ch. xxii.

Note.—The three prisoners were real, and an account of their release by the populace and their escape through the city is given in Villari's *Savonarola*. The only fictitious things in George Eliot's account are her making Baldassarre Calvo one of the prisoners and his subsequent encounter with Tito Melema.

PRITCHARD. Servant in the Vincy family. *Mid.* xi, xxvi.

PRITCHLEY. District near Treby. *F. H.* xvii.

PROCTER, MR. Printer and stationer, who keeps a circulating library. *J. R.* iii, vii (Proctor).

PROTHEROE. Doctor from Brassing. *Mid.* xlv.

PROWD, MR. Watchmaker in Treby Magna. *F. H.* iv, xxii.

PRYME, MR. A client of Lawyer Dempster's with whom he quarrels. *J. R.* xiii–xiv.

PUCCI, GIANNOZZO (*Hist.*). An accomplished young member of the Medicean party, a guest at the supper in the Rucellai Gardens. *Rom.* xxxix, xlv, lvi–lvii, lx.

He receives messages from Piero de' Medici of which Tito Melema is the bearer, and is one of the Mediceans arrested and executed at the same time as Romola's godfather, Bernardo del Nero.

Note.—Giannozzo Pucci (1460–97).

PUFF. Mrs. Transome's Blenheim spaniel. *F. H.* vii.

PUG. One of Mr. Irwine's dogs. *Adam B.* v, xvi.

PUGH, MR. The young curate of Whittlecombe who has "neat, black whiskers, and a pale complexion". *Amos B.* vi.

PUGLIA, FRA FRANCESCO DI (*Hist.*). A Franciscan who, when preaching the Quaresimal sermons at Santa Croce in 1498, challenges Savonarola to prove his doctrines by walking through fire. *Rom.* lxiii, lxv.

Note.—Fra Francesco di Puglia attacked Savonarola with

great violence in the sermons which he preached against him. The historical facts are substantially as stated by George Eliot.

PULCI, LUIGI (*Hist.*). Poet, whose verses and opinions are constantly quoted by Nello the Barber. *Rom.* Proem, iii, vi, viii, xvi, xxxix, xlix, lvii.

Note.—Luigi Pulci (1432–84), Italian poet, author of *Il Morgante Maggiore.*

PULINARI, SAN. *See* SAN PULINARI.

PULLER. A Cambridge student. *D. D.* xvi.

PULLET, MR. A gentleman-farmer with a decided fondness for lozenges, who is pronounced to be a nincompoop by Tom Tulliver, and whose musical snuff-box delights Maggie Tulliver. *M. F.* Bk. 1, vii, ix–x, xiii; Bk. 3, iii; Bk. 5, ii, v; Bk. 6, ii, xii.

" Mr. Pullet was a small man with a high nose, small twinkling eyes, and thin lips, in a fresh-looking suit of black, and a white cravat, that seemed to have been tied very tight on some higher principle than that of mere personal ease. He bore about the same relation to his tall, good-looking wife, with her balloon sleeves, abundant mantle, and large be-feathered and be-ribboned bonnet, as a small fishing-smack bears to a brig with all its sails spread." Bk. 1, vii.

PULLET, MRS. SOPHY. Mrs. Tulliver's favourite sister; a tall, good-looking, well-dressed lady, much given to tears, who is thought tolerable by the Tulliver children " chiefly because she was not their Aunt Glegg ". *M. F.* Bk. 1, ii–iv, vi–x, xiii; Bk. 3, ii–iii; Bk. 5, ii, v; Bk. 6, ii–iii, xii; Bk. 7, iii.

" It was not everybody who could afford to cry so much about their neighbours who had left them nothing; but Mrs. Pullet had married a gentleman farmer, and had leisure and money to carry her crying and everything else to the highest pitch of respectability." Bk. 1, vii.

She pities Mrs. Tulliver's bad luck with her children, so unlike the Dodsons, and helps to send Maggie to a boarding school " which would not prevent her being so brown, but might tend to subdue some other vices in her."

Note.—For the original of Mrs. Pullet as one of the Dodson sisters, *see* note under Dodsons.

" PULPIT " (*Real*). A religious paper in which one of Amos Barton's sermons is printed. *Amos B.* iii.

Note.—The " Pulpit ", a magazine of sermons published in London, 1824–71.

PUMMEL. Theophrastus Such's valet and factotum, " an excellent respectable servant whose spelling is unvitiated by non-phonetic superfluities " and who is never surprised. *T. S.* viii.

PUMPITER. " The considerable provincial town " where Vorticella, the authoress of one book, lives. *T. S.* xv.

" PUMPITER GAZETTE AND LITERARY WATCHMAN." A journal which

reviews Vorticella's one book. *T. S.* xv.

"PUMPSHIRE POST." A journal which reviews Vorticella's one book. *T. S.* xv.

PURCELL'S SONGS (*Real*). Lucy Deane's favourites among the songs sung by Stephen Guest. *M. F.* Bk. 6, ii.
Note.—Henry Purcell (1658–95), a well-known English musician, composer of many songs both secular and religious.

"PURIFYING PILLS." *See* WIDGEON'S PURIFYING PILLS.

PURWELL, THE HON. AUGUSTUS. *Mr. G.'s L. S.* i.

"PUSH OFF THE BOAT." One of the songs of Juan the minstrel in the *Spanish Gypsy. Sp. G.* iii.

PUTNEY (*Real*). Place on the Thames where Daniel Deronda had a boat. *D. D.* xvii.
Note.—A village on the Thames six miles from London.

PUTTY, JAMES. A successful electioneering agent, admired by Mr. Johnson. *F. H.* xvii, xxiv, xxx–xxxi.

PYE'S CROFT. The place out of which Mrs. Linnet thinks Lawyer Dempster cheated her. *J. R.* iii, xiii, xxv.

PYM. Arthur Donnithorne's valet. *Adam B.* xii, xxviii–xxix.

PYRAMID OF VANITIES (*Real*). The great pile of gauds and vanities brought together for the bonfire of Vanities in the Piazza della Signoria, Florence. *Rom.* xlix.

"There were tapestries and brocades of immodest design, pictures and sculptures held too likely to incite to vice; there were boards and tables for all sorts of games, playing-cards along with the blocks for printing them, dice, and other apparatus for gambling; there were worldly music-books, and musical instruments in all the pretty varieties of lute, drum, cymbal, and trumpet; there were masks and masquerading-dresses used in the old carnival shows; there were handsome copies of Ovid, Boccaccio, Petrarca, Pulci, and other books of a vain or impure sort; there were all the implements of feminine vanity." Ch. xlix.

Q

QUALLON, MR. The banker at Wanchester, one of the Gascoignes' and Davilows' social circle. *D. D.* iii, v, vii.

QUETCHAM HALL. The Arrowpoints' magnificent place. *D. D.* iii, v, ix, xii, xv, xxi–xxii, xxxv, lxix.

QUICKSETT. A Cambridge student. *D. D.* xvi.

QUILLINGHAM. Home of Sir Godwin Lydgate, where Lydgate and Rosamond go on their honeymoon. *Mid.* xxxvi, xlv, lviii, lxiv–lxv, lxxv.

QUINQUAGESIMA, STRADA. The dirty narrow street in Milan, where Caterina's father, Signor Sarti, lived. *Mr. G.'s L. S.* iii.

QUINTIN. *Sp. G.* i.

QUORLEN. Tory printer in Treby Magna. *F. H.* xxiv, xxviii.

R

RABBINISCHE SCHULE (*Real*). The synagogue of the orthodox Jews in Frankfort where Daniel Deronda attends a service and is seen by his grandfather's old friend, Joseph Kalonymos. *D. D.* xxxii.

Note. — The Synagogue Beth Tefillah Jeschurun, in the Schutzenstrasse, built by the Israelitische Religionsgesellschaft in 1853, was, at the time of *Daniel Deronda* (1866), the only large synagogue of the orthodox Jews in Frankfort.

RABBITT'S END. Farm on the Transome estate. *F. H.* viii, xxxi.

RACHEL. Mrs. Hackit's housemaid. *Amos B.* viii.

RADBOROUGH, DEAN OF. An acquaintance of the Countess Czerlaski's. *Amos B.* iii.

RADLEY. *J. R.* xi.

RAFFLES, JOHN. Rigg Featherstone's step-father; a dissipated bully who had been associated with Mr. Bulstrode in his dishonourable transactions. *Mid.* xli, liii, lx–lxi, lxviii–lxxi, lxxiv. "He was a man obviously on the way towards sixty, very florid and hairy, with much grey in his bushy whiskers and thick curly hair, a stoutish body which showed to disadvantage the somewhat worn joinings of his clothes, and the air of a swaggerer." Ch. xli.

Discovering Mr. Bulstrode's whereabouts, he threatens to disclose the dishonesty of Bulstrode's early life, and is bribed to keep silence. At last he comes to Mr. Bulstrode at Stone Court ill and worn out from dissipation. Mr. Bulstrode, desiring his death, allows the doctor's orders to be disobeyed, and Raffles dies, but his death does not save Mr. Bulstrode, for Raffles had previously told the story of Mr. Bulstrode's dishonesty.

"**RAINBOW.**" Inn at Raveloe, the social centre of the villagers. *S. M.* i–viii, x, xiii, xviii, Conclusion.

"It was a place where he was likely to find the powers and dignities of Raveloe . . . the bright bar or kitchen on the right hand, where the less lofty customers of the house were in the habit of assembling, the parlour on the left being reserved for the more select society in which Squire Cass frequently enjoyed the double pleasure of conviviality and condescension." Ch. v.

"The conversation . . . had, as usual, been slow and intermittent when the company first assembled. The pipes began to be puffed in a silence which had an air of severity; the more important customers, who drank spirits and sat nearest the fire, staring at each other as if a bet were depending on the first man who winked; while the beer-drinkers, chiefly men in fustian jackets and smock-frocks, kept their eyelids down and rubbed their hands across their mouths, as if their draughts of beer were a funereal duty attended with embarrassing sadness." Ch. vi.

RALPH. The messenger sent to Liverpool to meet Arthur Donnithorne and tell him of the Old Squire's death. *Adam B.* xl.

RAM, MR. Second-hand bookdealer, in whose shop Daniel Deronda first meets Mordecai. *D. D.* xxxiii, xl.

"He was an elderly son of Abraham, whose childhood had fallen on the evil times at the beginning of this century, and who remained amid this smart and instructed generation as a preserved specimen, soaked through and through with the effect of the poverty and contempt which were the common heritage of most English Jews seventy years ago. He had none of the oily cheerfulness observable in Mr. Cohen's aspect ... Mr. Ram dealt ably in books in the same way that he would have dealt in tins of meat and other commodities—without knowledge or responsibility as to the proportion of rottenness or nourishment they might contain." Ch. xl.

"RAM INN." Headquarters in Treby Magna for the Transome interests during the election. *F. H.* vii, xix-xx, xxxi, xxxiii.

RAMBLE, SQUIRE. *Mr. G.'s L. S.* xix.

RAMON. An old trumpeter in Duke Silva's train, who "takes his trumpeting as solemnly as angel charged to wake the dead". *Sp. G.* i.

RANN, JOSHUA. Shoemaker and parish clerk in Hayslope—"a man in rusty spectacles, with stubby hair, a large occiput, and a prominent crown." *Adam B.* ii, v, xviii, xxv, lv.

"Where that good shoemaker got his notion of reading from, remained a mystery even to his most intimate acquaintances. I believe, after all, he got it chiefly from Nature, who had poured some of her music into this honest conceited soul, as she had been known to do into other narrow souls before his. She had given him, at least, a fine bass voice and a musical ear; but I cannot positively say whether these alone had sufficed to inspire him with the rich chant in which he delivered the responses. The way he rolled from a rich deep forte into a melancholy cadence, subsiding, at the end of the last word, into a sort of faint resonance, like the lingering vibrations of a fine violoncello, I can compare to nothing for its strong calm melancholy but the rush and cadence of the wind among the autumn boughs." Ch. xviii.

He is opposed to the "Methodisses" who will, he fears, get the upper hand in the parish if the Squire and rector are not more active against them, and is frequently at odds about the church service with Bartle Massey, the schoolmaster, who is his chief rival in the church choir.

RANN, SALLY. *Adam B.* ii.

RAPPIT, MR. The hairdresser from St. Ogg's, who is sent for after Maggie Tulliver cuts off her hair. *M. F.* Bk. 1, ix.

RATCLIFFE. *J. R.* vi.

RATTLER. Horse on which Arthur Donnithorne gallops to Norburne. *Adam B.* xii.

RAVELOE. Village in the Midlands; scene of the story of *Silas Marner. S. M.* i–Conclusion.

"Raveloe was a village where many of the old echoes lingered, undrowned by new voices . . . it lay in the rich central plain of what we are pleased to call Merry England, and held farms which, speaking from a spiritual point of view, paid highly desirable tithes. But it was nestled in a snug well-wooded hollow, quite an hour's journey on horseback from any turnpike, where it was never reached by the vibrations of the coach-horn, or of public opinion. It was an important-looking village with a fine old church and large churchyard in the heart of it, and two or three large brick-and-stone homesteads, with well-walled orchards and ornamental weather-cocks, standing close upon the road, and lifting more imposing fronts than the rectory, which peeped from among the trees on the other side of the churchyard." Ch. i.

Note.—No village has been definitely identified as the original of Raveloe, though Bulkington, in Warwickshire, about three miles south-east of Nuneaton, has been suggested as a possible original. (See Coventry Libraries Committee, *Catalogue of the George Eliot Centenary Exhibition,* p. 12.)

RAYMOND, MISS. Lady Mallinger's maiden name. *D. D.* xvi.

RAYMOND, MR. Lady Mallinger's brother. *D. D.* xxxv, xlviii.

RAYMOND, MRS. Lady Mallinger's sister-in-law; an independent lady. *D. D.* xxxv–xxxvi, xlviii.

RAYMOND, EDGAR. The Raymond's four-year-old son. *D. D.* xxxv.

RAYNOR, MRS. Janet Dempster's mother. *J. R.* iii–v, vii, xiii–xvi, xix–xxviii.

"Mrs. Raynor had supported herself in her widowhood by keeping a millinery establishment, and in this way had earned money enough to give her daughter what was then thought a first-rate education, as well as to save a sum which, eked out by her son-in-law, sufficed to support her in her solitary old age. Always the same clean, neat old lady, dressed in black silk, was Mrs. Raynor: a patient, brave woman, who bowed with resignation under the burden of remembered sorrow, and bore with meek fortitude the new load that the new days brought with them." Ch. v.

Note.—It has been suggested that Mrs. Nancy Wallington, the mother of Mrs. Buchanan ("Janet") was the original of Janet's mother, Mrs. Raynor.

RAYNOR, JANET. *See* DEMPSTER, JANET.

"RECORD" (*Real*). A periodical which Amos Barton would have taken in if he had been able to afford it. *Amos.* B. ii.

Note.—The *Record,* first published 1828, represented the views of the Evangelical element of the Church of England.

RECTORY, THE. *See* PENNICOTE RECTORY.

RED DEEPS. The place near Dorlcote Mill where Maggie Tulliver and Philip Wakem, her lover, meet. *M. F.* Bk. 5, i, iii–v; Bk. 6, vii–viii, x.

"Just where this line of bank sloped down again to the level, a by-road turned off and led to the other side of the rise, where it was broken into very capricious hollows and mounds by the working of an exhausted stone-quarry —so long exhausted that both mounds and hollows were now clothed with brambles and trees, and here and there by a stretch of grass which a few sheep kept close-nibbled." Bk. 5, i.

Note.—A little valley between Nuneaton and Griff House called Griff Bottoms or Griff Hollows was the original of the "Red Deeps".

RED HOUSE. Squire Cass's home at Raveloe. *S. M.* iii, viii–xi, xiii, xvi–xx, Conclusion.

"The Squire's wife had died long ago, and the Red House was without that presence of the wife and mother which is the fountain of wholesome love and fear in parlour and kitchen . . . The fading grey light fell dimly on the walls, decorated with guns, whips, and foxes' brushes, on coats and hats flung on the chairs, on tankards sending forth a scent of flat ale, and on a half-choked fire, with pipes propped up in the chimney-corners: signs

of a domestic life destitute of any hallowing charm." Ch. iii.

"RED LION." Inn at Batherley. *S. M.* viii.

"RED LION." Inn at Houndsley. *Mid.* xxiii.

"RED LION." Inn at Milby, frequented by Lawyer Dempster and his cronies. *J. R.* i–iv, vi–vii.

Note.—It is generally admitted that the original of the "Red Lion", Milby, was the quaint old "Bull Hotel", in Nuneaton.

"RED LION." Public-house. *F. H.* xxviii.

"RED ROVER." One of Mr. Macey's songs which had been a favourite with Squire Cass. *S. M.* vi.

Note.—This has been variously identified, but no one of the suggestions — songs entitled *Red Rover* by Neukomm (1833), Thomson (1835), and Linley (c. 1840), the old Rover ballad *Captain Ward*, and Dibdin's *Greenwich Pensioner*—meets the test of both date and title.

REDHILL ROAD, MILBY. *J. R.* xxv.

REGENT STREET, LONDON (*Real*). *D. D.* xxxix.

RENFREW, MRS. A colonel's widow; guest at a dinner party given by Mr. Brooke. *Mid.* x.

"REVELATIONS." Nickname given to Mr. Lyon by the schoolboys. *F. H.* iv.

REVISING BARRISTER, THE. An official who comes to Treby Magna before the Parliamentary election. *F. H.* xxviii.

RICHARDS, PATTY. *Mr. G.'s L. S.* xi.

RICHMOND BRIDGE (*Real*). Bridge over the Thames under which Daniel Deronda rows shortly before he rescues Mirah Cohen from drowning. *D. D.* xvii.

RICKETTS, DAME. An inhabitant of the Bridge Way, Milby. *J. R.* iv.

RIDOLFI (*Hist.*). Relatives of Niccolò Ridolfi, who avenge his execution by killing Francesco Valori. *Rom.* lxvi; family mentioned i.

RIDOLFI, GIOVAN BATTISTA (*Hist.*). A disciple of Savonarola; younger brother of Niccolò Ridolfi. *Rom.* lviii, lx.

Note.—Giovan Battista di Luigi Ridolfi, a member of Savonarola's party, was temporarily alienated by his brother's execution but later returned to his allegiance. He was very prominent at a later date, was ambassador to Venice, and to the Pope, and in 1512 Gonfaloniere of Justice.

RIDOLFI, NICCOLÒ (*Hist.*). Guest at the supper in the Rucellai Gardens. *Rom.* xxxix, lvi, lviii, lx.

He is a member of the Medicean party and is one of those arrested and executed at the same time as Bernardo del Nero, Romola's godfather.

Note.—Niccolò Ridolfi, head of the Ridolfi family; his son had married a sister of Piero de' Medici.

RIGG, MR. JOSHUA. *See* FEATHERSTONE, RIGG.

RILEY. "Auctioneer and vallyer"; Mr. Tulliver's friend through whose advice Tom is sent to school to Mr. Stelling. *M. F.* Bk. 1, ii–iii; Bk. 2, i, iv; Bk. 3, i, viii.

"Riley, you know—as can talk pretty nigh as well as if it was all wrote out for him, and knows a good lot o' words as don't mean much, so as you can't lay hold of 'em i' law; and a good solid knowledge o' business, too." Bk. 1, ii.

RINUCCINI, ALAMANNO (*Hist.*). A patron of learning in Florence. *Rom.* iii, xvii.

Note.—Alamanno Rinuccini (1426–1504), Florentine humanist and translator. He was Prior in 1495.

RIPPLE. The tributary of the Floss, on which Dorlcote Mill actually stood. *M. F.* Bk. 1, i, v; Bk. 2, ii; Bk. 5, i; Bk. 7, v.

"How lovely the little river is, with its dark, changing wavelets! It seems to me like a living companion while I wander along the bank and listen to its low placid voice, as to the voice of one who is deaf and loving." Bk. 1, i.

RIPSTONE. Market town. *Mr. G.'s L. S.* ii.

RIVER STREET. The street in St. Ogg's where the warehouse offices of Guest and Co. are located. *M. F.* Bk. 3, v.

RIVERSTON. Town near Middlemarch. *Mid.* lx, lxxiv, lxxxii.

ROBINS, CLARA. *J. R.* v.

ROBINSON. Attorney at Wanchester. *D. D.* lxix.

ROBISSON, MR. Mrs. Abel's former master. *Mid.* lxx.

RODD, MR. Baptist minister at Grimworth. *B. J.* ii.

RODHAM. Town where Mr. Strutt, the attorney, lives. *B. J.* ii.

RODNEY, JEM. Molecatcher and poacher, at first suspected by Silas Marner of being the thief who stole his money. *S. M.* i, v, vii.

ROE, MR. The "travelling preacher" stationed at Treddleston, who criticized Mr. Irwine. *Adam B.* v.

ROLDAN. The juggler, a disappointed middle-aged man, on whom life has been hard. He performs in the Plaça Santiago, and later is sent as a messenger by Duke Silva to obtain news of Fedalma in the Gypsy camp. *Sp. G.* i–ii.

ROMAGNA (*Real*). Section of Italy where Piero de' Medici was trying to gather forces in 1497. *Rom.* lvii–lix.

Note.—A region in the *compartimento* of Emilia including the modern provinces of Bologna, Ferrara, Ravenna and Forli. It formed the main part of the old exarchate of Ravenna which passed to the Pope in 1278.

ROME (*Real*). *D. D.* mentioned xxxvii, lii; *Mid.* x, xix–xxii, xxviii, xxx; *Rom.* iii, vii–viii, xvi, xix–xxi, xxxiv, xxxvi, xxxviii–xxxix, xlv–xlvi, lv, lvii, lxiii.

In *Middlemarch* Rome is the city to which Mr. and Mrs. Casaubon go on their wedding journey. In *Romola* Tito Melema twice goes there on political errands, and it is the centre of the agitation against Savonarola, under the Pope's leadership.

Note.—Under Alexander the Sixth (1492–1503), who was Pope during the period of *Romola*, the will of the Pope was absolute in Rome, and the Papal states of which he was the head were one of the five great powers of Italy.

ROMILLY (*Hist.*). A deceased acquaintance of Mr. Brooke's, who, if he were still living, could have helped to save Bruce, the sheep stealer, from hanging. *Mid.* iv, xlvi.

Note.—Sir Samuel Romilly (1757–1818), an English jurist and law reformer. He succeeded in having the death penalty abolished for a number of minor offences, including some kinds of stealing.

ROMOLA. *See* BARDI, ROMOLA DE'.

"ROOKERY." The appointed meeting-place of Tina and Capt. Wybrow, where Tina finds the captain dead " under the gloom of interlacing boughs ". *Mr. G.'s L. S.* xiii–xvii.

Note.—The original of the Rookery is a secluded part of the ground at Arbury Hall (" Cheverel Manor ").

"ROOKERY." A part of the grounds of Transome Court. *F. H.* ix.

ROSE, MRS. The farmer's wife. *F. H.* xxxi.

ROSE, REVEREND MR. Independent minister who failed at Salem chapel because his doctrine was a little too " high ". *J. R.* ii.

ROSE, MR. TIMOTHY. " A gentleman farmer from Leek Malton, against whose independent position nature

o

had provided the safeguard of a spontaneous servility." *F. H.* xx, xxxi.

ROSEMARY'S "BABES IN THE WOODS". "Something fresh and naïve in sculpture" of which Hinze asks Felicia's opinion. *T. S.* v.

ROSENKRANZ. *P.—C. B. P.*

ROSSETER. A town near Hayslope; the stranger on horseback, who stops to listen to Dinah Morris's preaching on the Green, is journeying to Rosseter. *Adam B.* ii, vi, xi, xx–xxii, xxv.

Note.—The original of Rosseter is the village of Rocester, in Staffordshire, near Ellastone.

ROTHERBY. Town near Shepperton and Milby. *Amos B.* viii; *Mr. G.'s L. S.* i; *J. R.* iii, xiv, xxvi–xxvii. *Note.*—Original: Coventry.

"ROTHERBY GUARDIAN." Newspaper. *J. R.* iv, xxv.

ROTTEN ROW (*Real*). Gwendolen, riding with Grandcourt in Rotten Row, sees Mrs. Glasher watching her. *D. D.* xxxiii, xlviii.

Note.—Rotten Row, the track for riders on the south side of Hyde Park, extending from Hyde Park corner to Kensington. Probably so called after the rotten soil of which it is composed, though other etymologies have been suggested.

ROUND POOL. The favourite fishing spot of Tom and Maggie Tulliver. *M. F.* Bk. 1, v–vi.

"That wonderful pool, which the floods had made a long while ago: no one knew how deep it was; and it was mysterious, too, that it should be almost a perfect round, framed in with willows and tall reeds, so that the water was only to be seen when you got close to the brink." Bk. 1, v.

Note.—A pool in the fields back of Griff House, the childhood home of George Eliot and her brother Isaac, was the original of the Round Pool where Tom and Maggie fished. (*See* Parkinson, *Scenes,* p. 14.)

ROVEZZANO (*Real*). *Rom.* i.

Note.—A village near Florence, on the road which leads from the Porta alla Croce.

"ROYAL GEORGE." Inn, at Treddleston, used by Mr. Poyser on market days. *Adam B.* xiv.

"ROYAL OAK." Inn at Oakbourne. *Adam B.* xxxviii.

"ROYAL OAK." Inn at Shepperton. *Adam B.* xvii.

"ROY'S WIFE OF ALDIVALLOCH" (*Real*). Song sung by Mr. Bates, the gardener. *Mr. G.'s L. S.* iv.

Note.—A favourite Scottish song, written near the end of the eighteenth century by Mrs. Elizabeth Grant, of Carron.

ROYSTON BATHS. *S. M.* xvii.

RUCELLAI, BERNARDO (*Hist.*). Purchaser of Tito Melema's most valuable gems; the host at the dinner in the Rucellai Gardens. *Rom.* ii–iii, ix, xvi, xxxvi, xxxviii–xxxix, xlv, lxvii.

Note.—Bernardo Rucellai (1448–1514), statesman, historian, and patron of learning, father of Giovanni Rucellai, the poet.

RUCELLAI, CAMILLA (*Hist.*). Prophetess, "chief among the feminine seers of Florence," who announces revelations hostile to Barnardo del Nero, Romola's godfather. *Rom.* xxix, xxxvi.

Note.—Camilla Bartolini Davanzi (1455-1520), who in 1484 married Ridolfo di Filippo Rucellai. She was divorced in 1496, and in 1500 entered the third order of St. Dominic, taking the name of Sister Lucia. In Savonarola's deposition at his trial, mention is made of a plot for the murder of Bernardo del Nero, which seemed to have originated in a revelation which Camilla Rucellai believed that she had received. Sister Lucia died in 1520, and was pronounced *beata* shortly after her death.

RUCELLAI GARDENS (*Real*). Scene of the political supper given by Bernardo Rucellai at which Baldassarre Calvo tries to reveal Tito Melema's deceit and ingratitude, but breaks down before he can prove his charge. *Rom.* xxxviii-xxxix.

Note.—The Rucellai Gardens, or, Orti Oricellari, a famous garden in the Via della Scala where in the time of Bernardo Rucellai, after the death of Lorenzo de' Medici, the meetings of the Platonic Academy in Florence were held.

RUGBY (*Real*). The school to which Mr. Casaubon had sent Will Ladislaw. *Mid.* ix.

Note.—Rugby School, a famous English public school at Rugby, founded in 1567 by Lawrence Sheriffe, citizen and grocer, of London.

RUPERT. Sir Christopher Cheverel's bloodhound. *Mr. G.'s L. S.* ii, v, vii, xiv.

"RUSSIE." Hotel in Leubronn. *D. D.* i.

RYDE, MR. Mr. Irwine's successor as rector of Broxton, a great contrast to Mr. Irwine. *Adam B.* xvii.

RYELANDS. Grandcourt's estate where he and Gwendolen spend their honeymoon. *D. D.* xxv, xxviii-xxxi, xxxv.

S

SAAD. Hita's dog. *Sp. G.* iii.

SACCHETTI, FRANCO (*Hist.*). A writer whose book is quoted by Niccolò Macchiavelli and Nello. *Rom.* xii, xxix.

Note.—Franco di Benci Sacchetti, *c.* 1330–*c.* 1400. The book mentioned is his *Novelle.*

SADLER. Draper in Middlemarch. *Mid.* xxvi.

ST. BOTOLPH'S. Mr. Farebrother's church, the oldest church in Middlemarch. *Mid.* xvi, l, lii, lxvi.

ST. JOHN'S DAY FESTIVAL. *See* SAN GIOVANNI, FESTA OF.

ST. OGG'S. Town on the Floss; the scene of much of the story of *The Mill on the Floss. M. F.* Bk. 1, ii, and later chapters.

"St Ogg's—that venerable town with the red-fluted roofs and the

broad warehouse gables, where the black ships unlade themselves of their burthens from the far north, and carry away, in exchange, the precious inland products, the well-crushed cheese and the soft fleeces ..."
"It is one of those old, old towns which impress one as a continuation and outgrowth of nature, as much as the nests of the bower-birds or the winding galleries of the white ants; a town, which carries the traces of its long growth and history like a millennial tree, and has sprung up and developed in the same spot between the river and the low hill from the time when the Roman legions turned their backs on it from the camp on the hillside, and the long-haired sea-kings came up the river and looked with fierce, eager eyes at the fatness of the land. It is a town 'familiar with forgotten years'." Bk. 1, xii.

Note.—The original of St. Ogg's is the town of Gainsborough, in Lincolnshire, on the River Trent (the "Floss").

ST. PETER'S. Mr. Thesiger's church in Middlemarch. *Mid.* xvi, xviii, lxiv.

ST. PETER'S, ROME (*Real*). One of the places which Dorothea and Mr. Casaubon visit on their honeymoon. *Mid.* xx.

Note.—St. Peter's (San Pietro in Vaticano), the great Cathedral in Rome.

ST. PETER'S PLACE. *Mid.* lxiv.

ST. URSULA. Parish. *M. F.* Bk. 1, iii.

SALEM CHAPEL. The Independent chapel in Milby. *J. R.* ii, viii, x.

SALKELD. An acquaintance of Arthur Donnithorne's. *Adam B.* xii.

SALLY. Mrs. Garth's servant. *Mid.* xxiv.

SALLY. Mrs. Glegg's maid. *M. F.* Bk. 1, xii.

SALLY. Mrs. Jerome's servant. *J. R.* viii.

SALLY. Mrs. Pullet's maid. *M. F.* Bk. 1, ix–x.

SALLY. Servant. *Mr. G.'s L. S.* i.

SALLY. A short-horned cow. *Adam B.* xviii.

SALT. Supercargo of the vessel which takes out Bob Jakin's and Tom Tulliver's ventures; "a briny chap." *M. F.* Bk. 5, ii.

SALT, MR. Wool-factor, "who only spoke when there was a good opportunity of contradicting." *F. H.* xx.

SALT, JIM, *called* "Sandy Jim". A carpenter in Jonathan Burge's workshop. *Adam B.* i–ii, xviii.

SALT, MRS. JIM. Sandy Jim's wife, always called "Timothy's Bess". *Adam B.* ii, xxv.

SALT, MARY. Mrs. Tiliot's maiden name. *See* TILIOT, MRS. MARY.

SALVESTRO, FRA. *See* MARUFFI, FRA SALVESTRO.

SALVIATI, THE (*Hist.*). A Florentine family, adherents of Savonarola. *Rom.* lxiii.

Note.—The Salviati were a distinguished family, opposed to the Medici, many of the members of which were prominent in Florentine history.

SALVIATI, MARCO (*Hist.*). A friend of Savonarola, who commands the body of three hundred armed citizens at the Trial by Fire. *Rom.* lxv.

Note.—His name is usually given as Marcuccio Salviati, but Nerli, in his *Commentarj*, one of the sources used by George Eliot, gives the name as Marco.

SAMPSON, MR. Driver of the North Loamshire coach. *F. H.* Introduction, vii.

SAMSON, OLD DOCTOR. Mr. G.'s *L. S.* xi.

SAN AMBROGIO (*Real*). Church in Florence near which Romola finds the run away Lillo. *Rom.* 1, lvi, lxx.

Note.—The Church of Sant' Ambrogio, on the Piazza Sant' Ambrogio, was built in the tenth century with a convent for Benedictines, the first convent for nuns in Florence.

SAN CASCIANO (*Real*). A town near Florence, falsely given as a proposed stopping-place of the Cardinal of Naples. *Rom.* xlvi.

Note.—San Casciano, in Tuscany, about ten miles south-east of Florence.

SAN FREDIANO, PORTA. See PORTA SAN FREDIANO.

SAN GAGGIO, CHURCH OF (*Real*). Church outside the gate of San Piero where the image of the Madonna dell' Impruneta was deposited before being brought into Florence. *Rom.* xxxvi, xlii.

Note.—The Monastery and Church of San Gaggio, outside the gate of San Piero Gattolino (later Porta Romana), founded 1345.

SAN GALLO (*Real*). A suburb just outside the San Gallo gate of Florence, where Tessa and her children are left stranded after Tito Melema's death. *Rom.* i, lxvii, lxx.

SAN GALLO, GATE OF. See PORTA SAN GALLO.

SAN GALLO, VIA (*Real*). One of the streets in Florence where Romola looks for Tessa. *Rom.* lxx.

Note.—The Via San Gallo continues Via dei Ginori northeast to the Piazza Cavour (Piazza della Porta a San Gallo).

SAN GIORGIO, HILL OF (*Real*). A hill behind the Via de' Bardi where Baldassarre Calvo finds a lodging in Tessa's house, and where he tries unsuccessfully to kill Tito Melema. *Rom.* xxxiii-xxxiv, l.

Note.—A hill south of Florence.

SAN GIOVANNI, CHURCH OF. See BAPTISTERY.

SAN GIOVANNI, FESTA OF (*Real*). The great summer festival of Florence, of which city San Giovanni was the patron saint; held on Midsummer Day (St. John's Day). *Rom.* viii, x.

"The day of San Giovanni . . . a day of peculiar rejoicing to Florence . . . ushered in by a vigil duly kept in strict old

Florentine fashion, with much dancing, with much street jesting, and perhaps with not a little stone-throwing and window-breaking, but emphatically with certain street sights such as could only be provided by a city which held in its service a clever Cecca, engineer and architect, valuable alike in sieges and shows." Ch. viii.

Tito Melema, after watching the San Giovanni procession, renews his acquaintance with the contadina Tessa, and after returning from an excursion with her sees Fra Luca, who gives him a letter from his lost foster-father Baldassarre Calvo.

SAN GIOVANNI, PIAZZA DI (*Real*). Square in Florence, where Nello's barber-shop is located. *Rom.* iii, viii, xvi, xlv.

Note. — The Piazza di San Giovanni, which took its name from the Battistero, or Church of San Giovanni Battista, adjoins the Piazza del Duomo. One of the oldest squares in Florence, it was the scene of the great religious festivals.

SAN JACOPO DEL POPOLO, BROTHERS OF. While searching for the unburied dead, during the famine of 1496 in Florence, members of this order find Baldassarre Calvo nearly dead of starvation. *Rom.* xlii.

SAN LORENZO (*Real*). The church in Florence where Savonarola preached during Lent, 1492. *Rom.* Proem, i, xii.

Note.—The ancient Church of San Lorenzo, consecrated by St. Ambrose in 393, was the first cathedral of Florence. Brunelleschi made the designs for its restoration in the first half of the fifteenth century. Some of Savonarola's most important sermons were preached in San Lorenzo.

SAN LORENZO, BORGO DI. *See* BORGO DI SAN LORENZO.

SAN MARCO, CONVENT AND CHURCH OF (*Real*). The Dominican monastery of which Savonarola is Prior. *Rom.* Proem, x–xi, xiii, xv–xvi, xxxix, xli, xliii, xlvi–xlvii, lvi, lviii–lix, lxii–lxiv, lxvi.

"San Marco ... the long corridors lined with cells—corridors where Fra Angelico's frescoes, delicate as the rainbow on the melting cloud, startled the unaccustomed eye here and there, as if they had been sudden reflections cast from an ethereal world, where the Madonna sat crowned in her radiant glory, and the Divine infant looked forth with perpetual promise." Ch. lxiv.

Romola's brother, the Dominican Fra Luca, dies at San Marco, and it is there, at his death bed, that Romola first sees Savonarola. When Bernardo del Nero is arrested Romola goes to San Marco to beg Savonarola for her godfather's life, and later Tito Melema goes to San Marco to obtain the letter by means of which he hopes to ruin Savonarola. After the proposed Trial by Fire, San Marco is attacked by the mob and Savonarola is arrested there.

Note.—The famous Monastery, with the adjoining Church of San Marco, on the Piazza

San Marco, was founded 1290 by the Silvestrini, and later, under Cosimo the Elder, was transferred to the Dominicans. In the fifteenth century the monastery was restored by Michelozzo and was decorated with frescoes by Fra Angelico da Fiesole. It was suppressed in 1867, and is now a museum. Several of the historical characters in *Romola*, including Pico della Mirandola and Angelo Poliziano, are buried in the church.

SAN MARCO, PIAZZA DI (*Real*). Square in Florence before the Church of San Marco ; the scene of Savonarola's open-air sermon to the crowd, 27th February, 1498. *Rom.* xli, lxii.

Note.—The Piazza di San Marco takes its name from the adjoining church and convent of San Marco. Its principal associations are with Savonarola and the Dominicans, but it was also a favourite playground for the popular game of *Palla e Maglio.*

SAN MARTINO (*Real*). A cloth-producing section of Florence. *Rom.* i, x.

Note.—Guido Biagi in his edition of *Romola* points out that San Martino was not properly a quarter but merely a certain length of street. The old Via San Martino now forms part of the Via Dante Alighieri.

SAN MATTEO, HOSPITAL OF. *See* HOSPITAL OF SAN MATTEO.

SAN MINIATO, CONVENT OF (*Real*). Convent, in the hospital of which Baldassarre Calvo is cared for when he is helpless. *Rom.* lxvii.

Note.—This was the ancient Benedictine monastery of San Miniato, connected with the Church of San Miniato on the hill of the same name, called after the martyr San Miniato who was buried there. During a later plague than the one mentioned in *Romola* the abbey was used as a lazaretto.

SAN MINIATO, HILL OF (*Real*). A famous hill overlooking Florence from the south, from which, in the Proem of *Romola*, the spirit of the ancient Florentine views the modern city and where, in the story, Baldassarre Calvo talks with Romola and tells her that Tito Melema has "another wife". *Rom.* Proem, liii.

Note.—San Miniato is a hill south of Florence from which a particularly fine view of the city is obtained. It is crowned by the Church of San Miniato.

SAN PIERO, PORTA. *See* PORTA SAN PIERO.

SAN PULINARI (*Real*). Church in Florence where Tessa became separated from her mother in the crowd. *Rom.* x.

Note.—The Church of San Pulinari was near the Loggia dell' Orcagna.

SAN SEBASTIANO, VIA (*Real*). Street in Florence along which Tito Melema goes to the Piazza dell'

Annunziata on the evening of the Fierucola. *Rom.* xiii.
Note.—This is the present Via Gino Capponi.

SAN SEVERINO, COUNT DI (*Hist.*). The "Milanese Count"; agent of the Duke of Milan, for whom he purchases Bardo de' Bardi's library from Tito Melema. *Rom.* xxxi–xxxii.
Note.—Giovan Francesco da San Severino, conte di Caiazzo (d. 1502), an officer in the army of Lodovico Sforza, duke of Milan. He and his brother Galeazzo were with Charles VIII in Florence.

SAN SPIRITO (*Real*). Convent and church of the Augustinians in Florence. *Rom.* xliii, lxx.
Note.—The Augustinian Church of Santo Spirito, on the Piazza Santo Spirito, which was attached to the monastery, was originally built in 1250 and twice rebuilt during the fifteenth century.

SAN STEFANO (*Real*). The church in Florence to the steps of which the starving Baldassarre Calvo is carried when Romola succours him. *Rom.* xlii–xliv.
Note.—The Church of Santo Stefano, supposed to have been founded in 790, is now known as the Church of SS. Stefano e Cecilia, the Cecilia having been added in 1783 when a church of that name was suppressed.

SANDEMAN, SQUIRE. *J. R.* viii.

SANDRO. Assistant to Nello the barber; a solemn dark-eyed youth. *Rom.* iii, xiii, xvi, xlv.

SANDY JIM. *See* SALT, JIM.

SANTA CROCE, BORGO. *See* BORGO SANTA CROCE.

SANTA CROCE, CHURCH OF (*Real*). The church in Florence in which Romola de' Bardi and Tito Melema are betrothed and in which later Bardo de' Bardi is buried. The Franciscan, Fra Francesco di Puglia, preaches his sermons against Savonarola in Santa Croce. *Rom.* Proem, xii, xv, xx, xxvii, xxxvi, l, lxiii, lxvi.

"The long dark mass of Santa Croce, where we buried our famous dead, laying the laurel on their cold brows, and fanning them with the breath of praise and of banners. But Santa Croce had no spire then." Proem.

Note.—The Church of Santa Croce, on the Piazza di Santa Croce, begun in 1294, completed in 1442, was built for the Franciscans in the form of a Latin cross. The façade is a nineteenth century addition. The number of famous dead buried there made it the Pantheon of Florence.

SANTA CROCE, PIAZZA DI (*Real*). The square in Florence where the public notice of the Trial by Fire, which Tito Melema reads and explains to the crowd, is posted. *Rom.* xxvi, xxxvii, lxiii.
Note.—The Piazza di Santa Croce, in front of the Franciscan church of Santa Croce from which it takes its name, was formerly the scene of tournaments and of the favourite Florentine game of Calcio.

SANTA CROCE, PORTA. *See* PORTA SANTA CROCE.

SANTA FELICITÀ, CHURCH OF (*Real*). A church in Florence close to the Via de' Bardi, near which Fra Luca gives Tito Melema the message from Baldassarre Calvo. *Rom.* xi.

Note.—Santa Felicità, a church south of the Ponte Vecchio, on the little Piazza Santà Felicità, is a church of very ancient origin, consecrated 1059, restored 1736.

SANTA LUCIA, CHURCH OF (*Real*). A small church near the Bardi house, in Florence. *Rom.* xx.

Note.—This is the small church of Santa Lucia dei Magnoli, in the Via de' Bardi, founded 1078.

SANTA MARIA, POR'. *See* POR' SANTA MARIA.

SANTA MARIA DEL FIORE, CATHEDRAL. *See* DUOMO.

SANTA MARIA NOVELLA, CHURCH OF (*Real*). Church in Florence, the façade of which had been completed at the expense of Bernardo Rucellai. *Rom.* i, xxxviii.

Note.—Santa Maria Novella was begun by the Dominicans about 1279. The façade, begun in 1350, was completed 1456-70. The richest patrons of the church were the Rucellai.

"SARACEN'S HEAD." A public-house in a market town near Shepperton. *Adam B.* xvii.

"SARACEN'S HEAD." Public-house in Bilkley. *Mid.* lxxi.

SARAH. The Cohens' servant. *D. D.* xlvi.

SARAH. The young servant-woman to whom Silas Marner was engaged and who forsook him for his friend William Dane. *S. M.* i.

SARGENT. Clergyman. *Amos B.* vi.

SARTI. Caterina's father, a broken-down musician of Milan who dies in great poverty, leaving his little daughter to the care of strangers. *Mr. G.'s L. S.* iii.

Note.—The original of Sarti was Dominic Motta, Lady Newdigate's Italian music master. He died at Arbury in 1791. (*See* Newdigate, *The Cheverels,* pp. 50, 105.)

SARTI, CATERINA *called* TINA. An affectionate and beautiful Italian girl with a fine voice, who is brought up by Sir Christopher and Lady Cheverel. *Mr. G.'s L. S.* i-xxi.

"You are at once arrested by her large dark eyes, which, in their inexpressive unconscious beauty, resemble the eyes of a fawn; and it is only by an effort of attention that you notice the absence of bloom on her young cheek, and the southern yellowish tint of her small neck and face, rising above the little black lace kerchief which prevents the too immediate comparison of her skin with her white muslin gown. Her large eyes seem all the more striking because the dark hair is gathered away from her face, under a little cap set at the top of her head, with a cherry colored bow on one side." Ch. ii.

"With one exception, her only talent lay in loving; and there, it is probable, the most astronomical of women could not have surpassed her. Orphan and protegée though she was, this supreme talent of hers found plenty of exercise at Cheverel Manor . . . the one other exceptional talent, you already guess, was music." Ch. iv.

"Said Mr. Bates, 'for she hasn't the cut of a gell as must work for her bread; she's as nesh an' dilicate as a paich-blossom—welly laike a linnet, wi' on'y joost body anoof to hold her voice.'" Ch. iv.

She falls in love with the handsome unscrupulous Captain Wybrow, and when he heartlessly forsakes her for Miss Assher, she is maddened by jealousy. She goes to meet him in the Rookery, thinking that she will kill him. When she reaches the Rookery she finds him dead. Many months later, when she has partially recovered from the shock, her affectionate heart leads her to marry Mr. Gilfil, her faithful lover, but she lives only a few months after their marriage.

Note.—The prototype of Caterina was Sally Shilton, a young girl with a beautiful voice who has brought up and educated by Lady Newdigate ("Lady Cheverel"). Sally Shilton married Bernard Gilpin Ebdell ("Maynard Gilfil") but did not die at an early age, as did Caterina. (*See* Newdigate, The Cheverels, pp. 75, 220, 228.)

SARZANA, THOMAS OF. *See* NICHOLAS V, POPE.

SASSO, MEO DI. The messenger who starts from Leghorn to bring to the starving Florentines the good news that the galleys from France, laden with corn and men, have reached Leghorn. *Rom.* xliii, xlv.

SATCHELL. Squire Donnithorne's incompetent old bailiff; when he has a paralytic stroke Adam Bede is given the management of the woods. *Adam B.* v, xviii, xxi.

SATCHELL, MRS. The bailiff's wife, whose cream and butter will not bear comparison with Mrs. Poyser's. *Adam B.* xxxii.

SAVONAROLA, FRA GIROLAMO (*Hist.*). A Dominican, Prior of the Convent of San Marco and head of the Piagnoni, or democratic party. *Rom.* Proem, i, viii, xii, xv–xvii, xxi, xxiii–xxvii, xxix, xxxi, xxxv, xxxix–xlvii, xlix–l, lii, lv, lviii–lix, lxii–lxvii, lxx–lxxii.

"The tone was not that of imperious command, but of quiet self-possession and assurance of the right, blended with benignity . . . His face was hardly discernible under the shadow of the cowl, and her eyes fell at once on his hands, which were folded across his breast and lay in relief on the edge of his black mantle. They had a marked physiognomy which enforced the influence of the voice: they were very beautiful and almost of transparent delicacy . . . the hands seemed to have an appeal in them against all hardness . . . In the act of bending, the cowl was pushed back, and the features of the monk had the full light of the tapers on them. They were very marked features, such as lend themselves to popular description. There was the high arched nose, the prominent under lip, the coronet of thick dark hair above the brow, all seeming to tell of energy and passion; there were the blue-grey eyes, shining mildly under auburn eyelashes, seeming, like the hands, to tell of acute sensitiveness." Ch. xv.

"There was nothing transcendent in Savonarola's face. It was not beautiful. It was strong-featured, and owed all its refinement to habits of mind and rigid discipline of the body." Ch. xl.

"Fra Girolamo's mind never stopped short of that sublimest end: the objects towards which he felt himself working had always the same moral magnificence. He had no private malice—he sought no petty gratification. Even in the last terrible days, when ignominy, torture, and the fear of torture, had laid bare every hidden weakness of his soul, he could say to his importunate judges: 'Do not wonder if it seems to you that I have told but few things; for my purposes were few and great.'" Ch. xxxv.

Savonarola, the great religious and political reformer of Florence, is the central figure in the historical part of *Romola*, and also, through the influence which he exerts over Romola herself, an important figure in the fictitious part of the plot. Romola first sees him at her brother's death-bed, but his principal connexion with her is when he meets her, on her attempted flight from her husband, and influences her by his exhortations to return to Tito and take up work for others though her personal happiness is gone. The main events in his career which figure in the novel are his preaching in the Duomo and elsewhere, his purification of the popular life of Florence, and his Bonfire of Vanities, the challenge which he receives from Fra Francesco and the attempted Trial by Fire, his last sermon and his arrest and execution.

Note.—Girolamo Savonarola, the great Florentine reformer, was born at Ferrara in 1452; he came to Florence in 1489, was excommunicated 1497, and arrested and executed 1498. George Eliot's picture of Savonarola's career and influence in Florence follows closely the account in the standard biography, that of Pasquale Villari, and is both historically accurate and sympathetic. The importance of her portrait is attested by the fact that *Romola* is mentioned seriously in the preface to the revised edition of Villari, and is cited frequently in the later biography by Lucas.

SAWYER'S COTTAGE. A poor little house where it is proposed that Mrs. Davilow and her family live when her money is lost. *D. D.* xxi, xxiii–xxiv.

SCADDON, HENRY. *See* CHRISTIAN, MAURICE.

SCALA, ALESSANDRA (*Hist.*). The beautiful and learned daughter of Bartolommeo Scala, who is one of the guests at the betrothal of Romola and Tito Melema. *Rom.* iii, vi–vii, xii, xx.

Note.—Alessandra Scala (1450–1506), a poetess and author of some Greek epigrams, who made an enemy of Poliziano by refusing to marry him.

SCALA, BARTOLOMMEO (*Hist.*). Secretary of the Florentine Republic and patron of Tito Melema; a self-made man, who carries on a literary quarrel with Angelo Poliziano. *Rom.* iii, vi–ix, xii, xx, xxiii, xlv.

Note.—Bartolommeo Scala (1430–95), a miller's son from Colle di Valdelsa, who came to Florence, studied there under the protection of Cosimo de' Medici and rose to wealth and power, becoming Gonfaloniere and Secretary of the Republic.

SCALA, VIA DELLA (*Real*). Street in Florence where the Rucellai Garden is located. *Rom.* xxxviii.

Note.—The Via della Scala, still so called, took its name from the foundling hospital which had been established there by Cione di Lapo Pollini and placed under the direction of the hospital of Santa Maria della Scala, in Siena.

SCALA PALACE (*Real*). The handsome palace close to the Porta Pinti where Bartolommeo Scala lived; "now known as the Casa Gherardesca." *Rom.* vii, xiii.

Note.—The Casa Gherardesca on the Via de' Pinti, originally built for Bartolommeo Scala, passed later to Alessandro de' Medici, Archbishop of Florence, afterwards Pope Leo XI, and eventually became the property of the Gherardesca family.

SCALES, MR. Sir Maximus Debarry's house steward and head butler, "a man most solicitous about his boots, wrist-bands, the roll of his whiskers, and other attributes of a gentleman." *F. H.* vii–viii, xii, xxviii.

SCANTLANDS. An outlying field on the Poyser Farm where there is a deep pool in which Hetty Sorrel thinks of drowning herself but lacks the necessary courage. *Adam B.* vi, xxxv.

SCARBOROUGH (*Real*). The place to which Lucy Deane goes with Stephen Guest's sisters. *M. F.* Bk. 7, iv.

Note.—Scarborough is a popular coast resort in Yorkshire.

SCHMIDT. Courier. *L. V.* i.

SCHUSTER STRASSE (*Real*). The street in Mainz, where Joseph Kalonymos' banking house is located. *D. D.* lx.

Note.—This is the Schuster Gasse.

SCINTILLA. Mixtus's worldly wife, a lively lady who knows nothing of Nonconformists except that they are unfashionable, and who cuts her husband off from his old friends and ideals. *T. S.* ix.

SEBASTIAN. *Sp. G.* i.

"SELTENERSCHEINENDE MONATSCHRIFT, OR HAYRICK FOR THE INSERTION OF SPLIT HAIRS." A learned journal of the Teutonic world. *T. S.* iii.

SELVA DE' RUCELLAI. *See* RUCELLAI GARDENS.

SEMPER. A poor speaker who makes many public speeches. *T. S.* xii.

SENECA. The Host's dog, a solemn mastiff. *Sp. G.* i.

SEPHARDO, SALOMO. A Jewish sage; the astrologer of Abderahmen's tower, whose aid and counsel Duke Silva seeks after Fedalma's departure. *Sp. G.* ii, iv.

SERVITES (*Hist.*). A monastic order; "that famous Florentine order founded by seven merchants who forsook their gains to adore the Divine Mother." *Rom.* i, xliii.

Note.—The Servites, or Frati Serviti (Servi Beatæ Mariæ Virginis) were an order founded in 1233 by Bonfiglio Monaldo and six other Florentines. The Church of the Serviti in Florence was the Annunziata.

SETH. *P.—L. J.*

"SEVEN STARS." Inn at Treby Magna from which Mr. Crow reads the Riot Act. *F. H.* xx, xxxi, xxxiii, xlvi.

SFORZA, LUDOVICO, DUKE OF MILAN (*Hist.*). Prospective patron of Tito Melema, to whom Tito sells Bardo de' Bardi's library. *Rom.* xxi, xxxi–xxxii, lvii, lxiv–lxv, lxxi.

"Ludovico Sforza—copious in gallantry, splendid patron of an incomparable Leonardo da Vinci—holding the ducal crown of Milan in his grasp, and wanting to put it on his own head rather than let it rest on that of a feeble nephew who would take very little to poison him, was much afraid of the Spanish-born old King Ferdinand and the Crown Prince Alfonso of Naples, who, not liking cruelty and treachery which were useless to themselves, objected to the poisoning of a near relative for the advantage of a Lombard usurper." Ch. xxi.

Note.—Ludovico Sforza, the Moor, who in 1481 assumed power in Milan. He was driven out in 1499 and was carried to France where he died in prison in 1508.

SHADE OF A FLORENTINE CITIZEN. *See* SPIRIT OF A FLORENTINE CITIZEN.

"SHALL I, WASTING IN DESPAIR." (*Real*). A song which Stephen Guest sings. *M. F.* Bk. 6, vii.

Note.—The words were written by George Wither, 1617. The original setting, by a seventeenth century composer is given in Chappell's *Popular Music of the Olden Time.*

SHARP, MRS. Lady Cheverel's maid, "of somewhat vinegar aspect and flaunting attire." *Mr. G.'s L. S.* ii–v, vii, xvii–xviii.

SHEPPERTON. Parish where the Bartons live, and where Mr. Gilfil was vicar, many years earlier. *Amos B.* i–iii, v–x, Conclusion; *Mr. G.'s L. S.* i, xxi, Epilogue; mentioned *J. R.* xi; mentioned *Adam B.* xvii.

"A flat ugly district this; depressing enough to look at even on the brightest days. The roads are black with coal dust, the brick houses dingy with smoke; and at that time—the time of handloom weavers—every other cottage had a loom at its window, where you might see a pale, sickly-looking man or woman pressing a narrow chest against a board, and doing a sort of tread-mill work with legs and arms. A troublesome district for a clergyman; at least to one . . . like Amos Barton." *Amos B.* Ch. ii.

Note.—The original of Shepperton is Chilvers Coton, a suburb of Nuneaton.

SHEPPERTON CHURCH. Amos Barton's church. *Amos B.* i, iii, vi.

"Shepperton Church was a very different-looking building five-and-twenty years ago. To be sure, its substantial stone tower looks at you through its intelligent eye, the clock, with the friendly expression of former days; but in everything else what changes! . . . I recall with a fond sadness Shepperton Church as it was in the old days, with its outer coat of rough stucco, its red-tiled roof, its heterogeneous windows patched with desultory bits of painted glass, and its little flight of steps with their wooden rail running up the outer wall, and leading to the schoolchildren's gallery." Ch. i.

Note.—The well-known original of Shepperton Church is the Church at Chilvers Coton, where George Eliot was baptised and which she attended as a child. (See Cross, *George Eliot's Life*, vol. 1, p. 2.)

SHERLOCK, REV. THEODORE, B.A. Curate in Treby Magna; a bashful young man of good birth. *F. H.* xxiii–xxiv.

The rector assigns to him the task of holding a public debate with Mr. Lyon, but on the day of the debate his timidity overcomes him and he leaves the town.

SHOE LANE. Street near Lantern Yard in Silas Marner's early home. *S. M.* xxi.

SHORT, MRS. The landlady of Camp Villa. *Amos B.* iii.

Note.—A Mrs. Fitchett is said to have been the original of Mrs. Short. (Manuscript information.)

"SHOULD I LONG THAT DARK WERE FAIR?" One of the songs of Juan, the minstrel, in the *Spanish Gypsy*. *Sp. G.* i.

SHRIKE. *T. S.* xi.

SHRUBS, THE. Mr. Bulstrode's residence in Middlemarch. *Mid.* liii, lx–lxi, lxvii–lxviii.

SHUTTLETON. *F. H.* xxiii.

SIENA (*Real*). Town to which Tito Melema is commissioned to go after offering to furnish evidence of another Medicean plot. *Rom.* xxxii, xlii, lvii.

Note.—Siena, a city in Tuscany thirty-one miles south-east of Florence.

SIGNA (*Real*). Location of the French camp. *Rom.* xxii–xxiii, xliii.

Note.—The little town of Signa about eight miles from Florence, founded by the

Florentines in 1377, to command the east end of the Gonfolino.

SIGNORA. An Italian singer who lived with Lapidoth and his daughter Mirah in New York. *D. D.* xx.

SIGNORIA (*Hist.*). The heads of the executive government of Florence, i.e. the Gonfaloniere and the eight Priori. *Rom.* Proem; i, iii, v, viii, xii, xxi, xxvi-xxvii, xxix, xxxi, xxxv, xlii-xliii, xlvi, xlviii, liv, lviii, lx, lxiii, lxv-lxvi, lxxi-lxxii.

Note.—The number of members of the Signoria had varied at different periods, but at the time of Romola (1492-98) it consisted of nine elected officers, the Gonfaloniere, who held office for two months, and eight Priori, also chosen for two months. During the period of office the members of the Signoria lived at the public expense in the Palazzo Vecchio.

SIGNORIA, PIAZZA DELLA (*Real*). The great square of Florence, scene of the San Giovanni festival, of the Bonfire of Vanities, of the proposed Trial by Fire, and finally of Savonarola's execution. *Rom.* viii, xvi, xxi, xxxv, xlvii, xlix-li, liv, lx, lxv-lxvii, lxx, lxxii.

"The Piazza della Signoria—that famous piazza, where stood then, and stand now, the massive turreted Palace of the People, called the Palazzo Vecchio, and the spacious Loggia, built by Orcagna—the scene of all grand State ceremonial." Ch. viii.

Note.—The picturesque Piazza della Signoria, the centre of Florentine life and ceremony, is of ancient construction and has preserved its present aspect since the fourteenth century. In the time of *Romola* it was called Piazza della Signoria. Later names were Piazza del Granduca and Piazza Nazionale, but it has now resumed its earlier name. A bronze tablet now marks the spot where the gallows upon which Savonarola was executed was erected.

"SILLY JIM." An inmate of the Shepperton workhouse, affected with hydrocephalus. *Amos B.* ii.

SILVA, DUKE. "Born de la Cerda, Calatravan Knight, Count of Segura, Fourth Duke of Bedmár." The Spanish Commander of Bedmár, who is betrothed to Fedalma, the Spanish Gypsy. *Sp. G.* i-v.

"On his surcoat white
Glitter the sword-belt and the jewelled hilt,
Red on the back and breast the holy cross,
And 'twixt the helmet and the soft-spun white
Thick tawny wavelets like the lion's mane
Turn backward from his brow pale, wide, erect,
Shadowing blue eyes—blue as the rain-washed sky
That braced the early stem of Gothic kings
He claims for ancestry. A goodly knight
A noble caballero, broad of chest
And long of limb." Book 1.

He is in command of the fortress of Bedmár, an outpost in Andalusia, but is not, so rumour goes, pressing his command against the Moors very vigorously because he is loath to leave his betrothed, Fedalma, a beautiful Gypsy girl who had been adopted by his mother, the Duchess Diana. Knowing that Fedalma is menaced by the Inquisition, he presses for an immediate marriage. When Fedalma, on learning that Zarca, the captured Gypsy chief, is her long-lost father casts in her lot with him and escapes with him from Bedmár, Duke Silva is broken-hearted. He follows Fedalma to the Gypsy camp, and when he cannot persuade her to return, elects to remain with her and become a Gypsy. Meanwhile the Moors and Gypsies attack Bedmár, and Silva brought back there finds his trust betrayed, his friends slain and his uncle, Father Isidor, the Inquisitor, about to be executed. Unable to prevail upon Zarca to spare the Prior's life, Silva kills Zarca, by that act separating himself for ever from Fedalma.

SIMEON, MR. (*Hist.*). *Amos. B.* ii.
Note. — Charles Simeon (1759-1836), an evangelical clergyman, holder of the living of Trinity Church, Cambridge.

SIMMONS. Mr. Featherstone's farm bailiff. *Mid.* xiv, xxxiii.

SIMS, MR. Auctioneer in Treby Magna. *F. H.* xxviii.

SINBAD. Lucy Deane's chestnut horse. *M. F.* Bk. 6, i, xii.

SINKER, MR. "The eminent counsel." *D. D.* xxxv.

"SIR ROGER DE COVERLY" (*Real*). A dance tune which Solomon Macey plays at the New Year's dance at the Red House. *S. M.* xi.
Note.—A popular dance tune, probably of North Country origin, from which Addison took the name of Sir Roger de Coverly in the *Spectator*.

SIRCOME, MR. An eminent miller. *F. H.* vii-viii, xx.

SISTER. The younger of the two children in the poem *Brother and Sister*. *P.—B. S.*
The little sister adores her brother, who is the hero and leader in their childish rambles near their country home, and finds her greatest happiness in being with him and pleasing him. Grown up and separated from him in later life, she can still exclaim :—
"But were another childhood-world my share,
I would be born a little sister there."
Note.—The poem *Brother and Sister* is autobiographic and describes the relation between George Eliot, the "Sister" of the poem, and her brother, Isaac Evans.

SISTINA, VIA (*Real*). The street in Rome where Mr. and Mrs. Casaubon stay on their wedding trip. *Mid.* xx.
Note.—A broad street beginning at the top of the Scala di Spagna and running southeast.

SITWELL, LADY. Sir Jasper's wife. *Mr. G.'s L. S.* i.

SITWELL, SIR JASPER. A country neighbour of Mr. Gilfil's. *Mr. G.'s L. S.* i.

SKIPPER'S LANE. The location of Mr. Lyon's first meeting. *F. H.* vi.

SKUNK. *T. S.* xi.

SLAUGHTER LANE. Street in Middlemarch where the "Tankard" is located. *Mid.* xlv, lxxi.

SLECK, OLD. Miner at Sproxton. *F. H.* xi.

SLOGAN, LORD. An Irish peer who was refused by Miss Arrowpoint. *D. D.* ix, xiv.

SLOMAN'S END. A hamlet three miles from Snowfield. *Adam B.* liv.

SLOPPETER. A noisy town. *Mr. G.'s L. S.* iv, xix.

SMITH, REVEREND MR. Independent minister of the Salem Chapel, Milby, with a talent for poetry, who exchanges verses with the ladies of his congregation. *J. R.* ii.

SMYRNA (*Real*). The Eastern city where Harold Transome had made his money. *F. H.* i, vii.
  Note.—The principal seaport of Asiatic Turkey, an important commercial city.

SNAP. Brown terrier belonging to Eppie. *S. M.* xvi.

SNELL, MRS. The landlord's wife. *S. M.* xiii.

SNELL, JOHN. Landlord of the "Rainbow", who always steers a middle course for the sake of business. *S. M.* vi–viii, Conclusion.
  "A man of a neutral disposition, accustomed to stand aloof from human differences as those of beings who were all alike in need of liquor." Ch. vi.

SNOWFIELD. The town in Stonyshire, "grim, stony, and unsheltered, up the side of a steep hill," where Dinah Morris lives. *Adam B.* iii, viii, xi, xiv–xv, xxxv, xxxviii.
  Note.—The original of Snowfield was Wirksworth, in Derbyshire ("Stonyshire"), where Elizabeth Evans ("Dinah Morris") lived.

SNUFF. The Cass's brown spaniel. *S. M.* iii.

SODERINI, PAGOLANTONIO (*Hist.*). "A keen Florentine." *Rom.* xvi, xxv–xxvi, xxxv, xxxix, lxvi, lxxi.
  Note.— Paolo Antonio Soderini, (1448–99), Gonfaloniere di Justizia in 1497.

SODERINI, TOMMASO (*Hist.*). His marriage to Fiammetta Strozzi is interfered with by Piero de' Medici. *Rom.* xvi.
  Note.—Tommaso Soderini (1470–1531), son of Pagolantonio Soderini. He married Fiammetta di Filippo di Matteo Strozzi, 1494.

"SOLDIER'S TEAR" (*Real*). One of the songs sung by Miss Rebecca Linnet. *J. R.* iii.
  Note.—Written by Thomas Haynes Bayly (1797–1839).

SORREL. Hetty's dead father, a good-for-naught. *Adam B.* xxxi.

SORREL, HESTER, *called* HETTY. Martin Poyser's niece, the village beauty of Hayslope; a shallow, selfish girl of seventeen years, whose dream of becoming the young squire's lady ends in

P

tragedy for herself and others. *Adam B.* iii–iv, vi–x, xii–xv, xviii–xxvii, xxix–xxxvii, xxxix, xlii–xliii, xlv–xlvii, Epilogue.

"There is one order of beauty which seems made to turn the heads not only of men, but of all intelligent mammals, even of women. It is a beauty like that of kittens, or very small downy ducks making gentle rippling noises with their soft bills, or babies just beginning to toddle and to engage in conscious mischief—a beauty with which you can never be angry, but that you feel ready to crush for inability to comprehend the state of mind into which it throws you. Hetty Sorrel's was that sort of beauty."

"It is of little use for me to tell you that Hetty's cheek was like a rose-petal, that dimples played about her pouting lips, that her large dark eyes hid a soft roguishness under their long lashes, and that her curly hair, though all pushed back under her round cap while she was at work, stole back in dark delicate rings on her forehead, and about her white shell-like ears; it is of little use for me to say how lovely was the contour of her pink-and-white neckerchief, tucked into her low plum-coloured stuff boddice, or how the linen butter-making apron, with its bib, seemed a thing to be imitated in silk by duchesses, since it fell in such charming lines, or how her brown stockings and thick-soled buckled shoes lost all that clumsiness which they must certainly have had when empty of her foot and ankle; of little use, unless you have seen a woman who affected you as Hetty affected her beholders, for otherwise, though you might conjure up the image of a lovely woman, she would not in the least resemble that distracting kittenlike maiden . . . Hetty's was a spring-tide beauty; it was the beauty of young frisking things, round-limbed, gambolling, circumventing you by a false air of innocence." Ch. vii.

Although she has been brought up by Mr. Poyser as if she had been his own daughter, she is incapable of feeling any gratitude and affection for him or his family. Her beauty attracts village suitors, including honest Adam Bede, whom her uncle favours, but she believes that her beauty destines her for a higher station. When she attracts the attention of the young squire, Arthur Donnithorne, she sees a rosy future for herself, ignorantly thinking that his passion, to which she has secretly yielded, must end in marriage. When Arthur Donnithorne breaks off his affair with her she is humiliated and sick at heart, but, later, seeing nothing better in the future, promises to marry Adam who is in ignorance of what her real relations with Arthur have been. As the time for their marriage approaches, Hetty realizes that the truth must soon come to light, and, under pretence of visiting Dinah Morris at Snowfield, journeys to Windsor to find Arthur Donnithorne and then not finding him, journeys back in despair, lacking the courage to kill herself, but determined to keep her disgrace from her family. On her way back her baby is born. She leaves it in a wood to die, and is arrested for child-murder, tried and sentenced to death. Through her trial and sentence she maintains a hard, obstinate silence, which breaks down only when Dinah Morris goes to her in prison and spends the last night in her cell, pleading with her to confess. Dinah accompanies her to the place of execution, and at the last minute Hetty's sentence is commuted to transportation, from which she never returns.

Note.—While Hetty herself is not a portrait, her tragedy, and, indeed, the germ of the plot of *Adam Bede*, were taken from a dramatic experience in the life of George Eliot's aunt, Elizabeth Evans ("Dinah Morris"). An ignorant girl, Mary Voce, had been tried at the Nottingham Assizes for child-murder, and had been sentenced to death. She had refused obstinately to confess her crime, and Mrs. Evans visited her in her cell, prayed over her all night, induced her to confess, and then rode with her to the place of execution and stayed with her until she was hanged. (*See* Cross, *George Eliot's Life*, vol. 2, pp. 65–6.)

SOUTHAMPTON (*Real*). *D. D.* vii-viii ; *F. H.* vi.

Note.—An English seaport on the Channel ; a principal port for transatlantic steamers.

SPANNING, DR. An acquaintance of Mr. Casaubon. *Mid.* xxxvii.

SPECKLE. Mr. Lammeter's grey horse. *S. M.* xvii.

SPEDALE DEGL' INNOCENTI (FOUNDLING HOSPITAL) (*Real*). *Rom.* xiv.

Note. — The Spedale degli Innocenti on the north-east side of the Piazza dell' Annunziata, was begun about 1419 by Brunelleschi, and completed 1451.

SPENCE, MR. Clerk at Guest & Co. *M. F.* Bk. 3, v.

SPEZIA (*Real*). *D. D.* 1, liv.

Note.—An important maritime town of Italy, on the Bay of Spezia, fifty miles south-east of Genoa.

SPICER, MR. Shoemaker and parish clerk at Lowick. *Mid.* lxx.

SPIKE. "A political molecule" who voted on the side of Progress though he was not inwardly attached to it under that name. *T. S.* vii.

SPILKINS. Landlord of the "Cross Keys", Treby Magna. *F. H.* xxviii.

SPILKINS, MR. A young man reckless with his pocket-money. *Mid.* lx.

SPINI, DOLFO (*Hist.*). Leader of the Compagnacci or Evil Companions. *Rom.* xxv, xxvii, xxxix, xlv-xlix, lix, lxiii, lxv–lxvi, lxxi–lxxii.

"Yet the tall, broad-shouldered personage greeted in that slight way looked like one who had considerable claims. He wore a richly embroidered tunic, with a great show of linen, after the newest French mode, and at his belt there hung a sword and poignard of fine workmanship. His hat, with a red plume in it, seemed a scornful protest against the gravity of Florentine costume, which had been exaggerated to the utmost under the influence of the Piagnoni. Certain undefinable indications of youth made the breadth of his face and the large diameter of his waist appear the more emphatically a stamp of coarseness, and his eyes had that rude desecrating stare at all men and things which to a refined mind is as intolerable as a bad odour or a flaring light." Ch. xlv.

An avowed enemy of Savonarola, he plots with Tito Melema against him, especially in the matter of the Trial by Fire, in which, guided by Tito's superior intelligence, he hopes to accomplish the Frate's overthrow. He becomes uneasy under Tito's somewhat condescending superiority, and after Savonarola's arrest, when his suspicions have been further aroused by the hints of Tito's enemy, the shifty notary Ser Ceccone, he orders his Compagnacci to make way with Tito.

Note.—Ridolpho Spini (d. 1519), usually called Doffo; the form Dolfo is used by Nerli in his *Commentarj*, one of the sources consulted by George Eliot. He was one of the seventeen commissioners appointed to conduct the examination of Savonarola.

SPINI PALACE (*Real*). "The great house with the loggia, over the bridge of the Santa Trinità." *Rom.* xlv.

Note.—The Palazzo Spini, now usually called the Palazzo Ferroni, dates from the beginning of the fourteenth century. It became the property of the Ferroni family in the eighteenth century.

SPIRIT OF A FLORENTINE CITIZEN. In the Proem to *Romola* the Spirit of a Florentine citizen who died during Lent of 1492 is imagined as revisiting modern Florence, and regarding the city from the hill of San Miniato. *Rom.* Proem.

"The Spirit is clothed in his habit as he lived; the folds of his well lined black silk garment or *lucco* hang in grave unbroken lines from neck to ankle; his plain cloth cap, with its *becchetto*, or long hanging strip of drapery, to serve as a scarf in case of need, surmounts a penetrating face, not, perhaps, very handsome, but with a firm, well cut mouth, kept distinctly human by a close-shaven lip and chin. It is a face charged with memories of a keen and various life passed below there on the banks of the gleaming river."

SPIRITO, SAN. *See* SAN SPIRITO.

SPORTING JACK. *See* LINGON, REVEREND JOHN.

SPOUNCER. A schoolmate with whom Tom Tulliver fights. *M. F.* Bk. 1, v–vi.

SPRAGUE, DR. The senior physician of Middlemarch, a hard-headed and dry-witted man who is averse to Lydgate and his newer ideas. *Mid.* xv–xvi, xviii, xxvi–xxvii, xlv–xlvi, lxxiv.

"The doctor was more than suspected of having no religion, but somehow Middlemarch tolerated this deficiency in him as if he had been a lord chancellor; indeed, it is probable that his professional weight was the more believed in, the world-old association of cleverness with the evil principle being still potent in the minds even of lady patients who had the strictest ideas of frilling and sentiment . . . Dr. Sprague was superfluously tall; his trousers got creased at the knees, and showed an excess of boot at a time when straps seemed necessary to any dignity of bearing; you heard him go in and out, and up and down, as if he had come to see after the roofing. In short, he had weight, and might be expected to grapple with a disease and throw it." Ch. xviii.

SPRAGUE, MRS. The doctor's wife, "elderly and old-fashioned in her opinions"; one of the women who sit in judgment on Mrs. Bulstrode. *Mid.* lxxiv.

SPRATT, MR. The hated manager of the Sproxton colliery. *F. H.* xi, xxx, xxxiii, xlvi.

On election day he falls into the hands of the Treby mob and is rescued from death by Felix Holt, who, while apparently sympathizing with the rioters, induces them to leave Spratt tied to a finger-post.

SPRATT, MR. Master of the Shepperton Workhouse. *Amos B.* ii.

Note.—In the lists of originals prepared in Nuneaton after the publication of the *Scenes of Clerical Life*, a Mr. Hackett was given as the original of Mr. Spratt. (*See* Olcott, *George Eliot*, p. 14.)

SPRAY, MR. Independent minister at St. Ogg's who preaches political sermons. *M. F.* Bk. 1, xii.

"SPRING COMES HITHER." One of Pablo's songs in the *Spanish Gypsy*. *Sp. G.* i.

SPROXTON. A mining hamlet near Treby Magna, where Felix Holt is in the habit of going to talk with the miners. *F. H.* iii, v, xi, xvi–xvii, xxiv, xxvii, xxx, xlvi.

STANDISH, MR. Lawyer in Middlemarch, a prosperous old man, "long concerned with the landed gentry," who had drawn up three wills for Mr. Featherstone. *Mid.* x, xiv, xxxv, xlix, li, lxii–lxiii, lxxxv.

"Mr. Standish was not a man who varied his manners; he behaved with the same deep-voiced, off-hand civility to everybody, as if he saw no difference in them, and talked chiefly of the hay crop, which would be 'Very fine, by God!' of the last bulletins concerning the King, and of the Duke of Clarence, who was a sailor every inch of him." Ch. xxxv.

STARTIN, MRS. Housekeeper at Offendene. *D. D.* iii.

STEENE, MR. Veterinary surgeon at Grimworth. *B. J.* ii–iii.

STEENE, MRS. The veterinary surgeon's wife, one of Edward

Freely's customers; she is not a good cook and starts the fashion of "buying at Freely's". *B. J.* ii–iii.

STEENE, WIDOW. *Adam B.* v.

STEFANO, SAN. *See* SAN STEFANO.

STELLING, LAURA. Mr. and Mrs. Stelling's little daughter, who is sometimes left in the care of Tom Tulliver. *M. F.* Bk. 2, i, iii.

STELLING, MRS. LOUISA. Wife of Mr. Stelling; a haughty little woman with pale blond ringlets, who imposes on Tom Tulliver's good nature. *M. F.* Bk. 1, iii; Bk. 2, i, iv, vii.

STELLING, REV. WALTER, M.A. Curate at King's Lorton; Tom Tulliver and Philip Wakem's schoolmaster who does not find his purse equal to his style of living. *M. F.* Bk. 1, iii, vii; Bk. 2, i, iii–vii.

"Mr. Stelling was a broad-chested healthy man, with the bearing of a gentleman, a conviction that a growing boy required a sufficiency of beef, and a certain hearty kindness in him that made him like to see Tom looking well and enjoying his dinner; not a man of refined conscience, or with any deep sense of the infinite issues belonging to everyday duties; not quite competent to his high offices; but incompetent gentlemen must live, and without private fortune it is difficult to see how they could all live genteelly if they had nothing to do with education or government." Bk. 2, iv.

STICKNEY, REV. MR. Independent minister in Milby, who failed at the Salem Chapel. *J. R.* ii–iii, viii, x–xi.

STILFOX. *D. D.* vii.

STINCHE (*Real*). The largest prison in Florence, in which, after the scene in the Rucellai Gardens, where he is denied by Tito, Baldassarre Calvo is imprisoned. *Rom.* xxxix, xlii.

Note. — The old prison of the Stinche, which was demolished in the nineteenth century, stood on the present site of the Accademia Filarmonica and the Teatro Pagliano. It was built at the end of the thirteenth century, and took its name from the fact that prisoners taken at the siege of Castello delle Stinche were confined there in 1304.

STODDART (*Hist.*). One of Mr. Brooke's acquaintances, who said that women were not thinkers. *Mid.* vi.

Note.—Sir John Stoddart (1773–1856).

STOKES, MASTER TOM. "A flippant town youth," Mr. Hackit's nephew. *Mr. G.'s L. S.* i.

STONE, MRS. SARAH. A widow; the shopkeeper in Stoniton, in whose house Hetty Sorrel's baby is born, and who gives evidence against Hetty at her trial. *Adam B.* xliii.

STONE COURT. Farm and residence of Peter Featherstone. *Mid.* xi–xii, xxv, xxvii, xxxi–xxxiii, xxxv, xli, liii, lxviii–lxx, lxxvi, lxxxv–lxxxvi, Finale.

"The house was already visible, looking as if it had been arrested in its growth toward a stone mansion by an unexpected budding of farm buildings on its left flank, which had hindered it from becoming anything more than the substantial dwelling of a gentleman farmer. It was not the less agreeable an object in the distance for the cluster of pinnacled corn ricks which balanced the fine row of walnuts on the right." Ch. xii.

After leading Fred Vincy to expect this property, old Featherstone leaves it to his illegitimate son, Rigg Featherstone. When the latter parts with it to Mr. Bulstrode, Fred Vincy and Mary Garth move into it and Fred gradually becomes owner of the stock and furniture.

STONE-PITS. The piece of ground on the outskirts of Raveloe where Silas Marner's cottage stands. *S. M.* i, iv–v, viii, x, xii–xiv, xvi–xviii, Conclusion.

"The lane . . . at its farther extremity, passed by the piece of unenclosed ground called the Stone-pit, where stood the cottage, once a stone-cutter's shed, now for fifteen years inhabited by Silas Marner. The spot looked very dreary at this season with the moist trodden clay about it, and the red muddy water high up in the deserted quarry." Ch. iv.

STONITON. A town in Stonyshire where Hetty Sorrel is tried for child-murder and convicted. *Adam B.* iv, xxii, xxxv–xxxvi, xxxviii, xl–xli, xlvi–xlvii.

Note.—The original of Stoniton is Derby, the county town of Derbyshire ("Stonyshire"). (*See* Mottram, *True Story of George Eliot*, p. 39.)

STONY STRATFORD (*Real*). One of the places at which Hetty Sorrel stops on her journey to Windsor in search of Arthur Donnithorne. *Adam B.* xxxvi.

Note.—An ancient market town in Buckinghamshire.

STONYSHIRE. One of the two counties in which the story of *Adam Bede* takes place; Snowfield, where Dinah Morris lives and Stoniton where Hetty Sorrel is tried for child-murder, are both in Stonyshire. *Adam B.* ii, and later chapters; *F. H.* mentioned xxix.

"That rich undulating district of Loamshire, to which Hayslope belonged, lies close to a grim outskirt of Stonyshire, overlooked by its barren hills . . . a bleak treeless region, intersected by lines of cold grey stone." Ch. ii.

Note.—The original of Stonyshire is Derbyshire.

STOPLEY, CANON. A friend of the Arrowpoint family. *D. D.* x.

STOREY, JACOB. A pupil in Bartle Massey's night school who turns all his z's the wrong way. *Adam B.* xxi.

STOTT. Formerly housekeeper for Mr. Tulliver's dead brother. *M. F.* Bk. 1, iii.

STOWE. An employee of Guest & Co. *M. F.* Bk. 5, iii.

STRADIVARIUS, ANTONIO (*Hist.*). The great violin maker who has the craftsman's delight in perfect work and defends his gospel of hard honest work against the jeers of Naldo the eclectic painter. *P.—Strad.*

"'Tis rare delight: I would not change my skill
To be the Emperor with bungling hands,
And lose my work, which comes as natural
As self at waking . . .
. . . 'Tis God gives skill,
But not without men's hands:
He could not make
Antonio Stradivari's violins
Without Antonio."

Note.—The central idea of the poem, the delight of the workman in perfect work, George Eliot took from the character of her father, Robert Evans. Antonio Stradivari, or Stradivarius (1644–1737) was a famous Italian maker of violins.

STRANGER ON HORSEBACK. *See* TOWNLEY, COLONEL.

STRATFORD-ON-AVON (*Real*). One of the places to which Hetty Sorrel goes on her journey back from Windsor. *Adam B.* xxxvi–xxxvii.

Note.—A town in Warwickshire, eight miles south-west of Warwick.

STROZZI, FIAMMETTA (*Hist.*). Young Tommaso Soderini's intended bride. *Rom.* xvi.

Note.—Daughter of Filippo di Matteo Strozzi and his wife, Fiammetta di Donato Adimari; she married Tommaso Soderini in 1494 and died 1497.

STRUTT, MR. Attorney at Rodham. *B. J.* ii.

STRYPE, MRS. Washerwoman, befriended by Mr. Bulstrode. *Mid.* xvi.

STUBBS. *Mid.* xvi.

STUBBS, DICK. *F. H.* xxiii.

SUCH, REVEREND MR. Theophrastus Such's father, a country clergyman in the Midlands. *T. S.* ii.

"My father was none the less beloved because he was understood to be of a saving disposition. . . . The sight of him was not unwelcome at any door, and he was remarkable among the clergy of his district for having no lasting feud with rich or poor in his parish . . . He was a pithy talker, and his sermons bore marks of his own composition."

SUCH, THEOPHRASTUS. An eccentric observer and humorist who analyses and comments upon the various types of people whom he meets in the "Nation of London". *T. S.* i–ii, and later.

"Yet I am a bachelor, and the person I love best has never loved me, or known that I loved her. Though continually in society, and caring about the joys and sorrows of my neighbours, I feel myself, so far as my personal lot is concerned, uncared for and alone . . . Why should I expect to be admired . . . I have done no services to my country beyond those of every peaceable orderly citizen; and as to intellectual contribution, my only published work was a failure so that I am spoken of to inquiring beholders as 'the author of a book you have probably not seen'... Then in some quarters my awkward feet are against me, the length of my upper lip, and an inveterate way I have of walking with my head foremost and my chin projecting." Ch. i.

"SUGAR LOAF." Chubb's public-house, Sproxton, where Felix Holt goes to talk to the miners. *F. H.* ix.

"SUPPER AT EMMAUS, BY GUIDO." A picture which Mr. Bulstrode asks Will Ladislaw to buy for him at the Larcher sale. *Mid.* lx.

SUTTON, MRS. An old lady who dies from the dropsy. *M. F.* Bk. 1, vii.

"SWEET ECHO" (*Real*). A song, which the boy Daniel Deronda sings beautifully. *D. D.* xvi.

Note.—" Sweet Echo," a favourite song in Milton's Comus, set to music by T. A. Arne.

SWING. Mr. Stelling impresses Mr. Tulliver by telling him several stories about "Swing". *M. F.* Bk. 2, i.

Note.—" Captain Swing" was the name signed to various threatening letters which in 1830 and shortly thereafter were written to farmers who were beginning to use agricultural machinery. The "Swing" letters preceded cases of incendiarism or other outrages, principally against users of agricultural machinery.

SWINTON. *D. D.* xxviii.

"SYNOPTICAL TABULATION." The outline, with directions for continuing his "Key to all Mythologies", which Mr. Casaubon leaves for Dorothea. *Mid.* xlix, l, liv.

T

TACCO, MAESTRO. A doctor from Padua, disliked by Nello the barber, upon whom Nello's assistant plays the practical joke described in the chapter in *Romola* entitled "A Florentine Joke". *Rom.* xvi.

"He's a doctor from Padua... his great trick is making rounds among the contadini. And do you note those great saddle-bags he carries? They are to hold the fat capons and eggs and meal he levies on silly clowns with whom coin is scarce. He vends his own secret medicines, so he keeps away from the doors of the druggists."

Note.—The story of Maestro Tacco and the joke which Nello plays on him is modelled after the kind of joke which is such a favourite in the *Novelle* of Sacchetti.

TADDEO. One of the Compagnacci. *Rom.* lxvi.

TAFT, MRS. An inhabitant of Middlemarch devoted to knitting. *Mid.* xxvi, xlv.

TAFT, BILLY. The idiot. *Adam B.* xxi.

TAFT, JACOB, *called* "FEYTHER" TAFT. The Hayslope patriarch "in his brown worsted nightcap, who was bent nearly double, but seemed tough enough to keep on his legs a long while." *Adam B.* ii, xxii.

TAFT, MUM. A silent carpenter. *Adam B.* i.

TANCRED. Stephen Guest's bay horse. *M. F.* Bk. 6, xi.

"TANKARD." Public-house in Middlemarch, the resort of a Benefit Club, which considers taking Doctor Lydgate as its medical man. *Mid.* xlv, lxxi.

TANTRIPP. Dorothea Brooke's lady's maid, who is much attached to her mistress. *Mid.* iv, x, xx–xxi, xxxvii, xlviii, liv, lix, lxxx.

TAPIR, LORD. A weak-minded young man. *Mid.* vi.

TARBETT, MR. Clergyman. *Mr. G.'s L. S.* i.

TARLEY. Parish near Raveloe. *S. M.* i–ii, vi, viii, x.

TEDD'S HOLE. A village two miles from Stoniton where John Olding, the labourer who finds Hetty's dead baby, lives. *Adam B.* xliii.

TEDMAN'S, DAME, SCHOOL. School to which Nancy Lammeter went. *S. M.* xi.

TEGG. Shoemaker. *Mid.* xvi.

"TEMPEST, THE" (*Real*). The music of "The Tempest" is among the songs sung by Stephen Guest, Philip Wakem, and Lucy Deane. *M. F.* Bk. 6, vii.

Note.—The incidental music of *The Tempest* was written by Thomas A. Arne (1710–78), when the play was revived at Drury Lane Theatre, 1746.

TEN, THE (*Hist.*). The Florentine Committee which managed external affairs and war. *Rom.* Proem, xlv, lvii, lxiv–lxv.

TENCH. One of Mr. Casaubon's critics. *Mid.* xxix.

TESSA. A pretty, stupid contadina who goes through a mock marriage ceremony with Tito Melema, and believes herself to be his wife. *Rom.* i–iii, viii–x, xiv, xviii, xx, xxxiii–xxxiv, l–li, lvi, lxvii, lxx, Epilogue.

"A young girl, apparently not more than sixteen, with a red hood surrounding her face, which was all the more baby-like in its prettiness from the entire concealment of her hair." Ch. ii.

"This creature who was without moral judgment that could condemn him, whose little loving ignorant soul made a world apart, where he might feel in freedom from suspicions and exacting demands, had a new attraction for him now. She seemed a refuge from the threatened isolation that would come with disgrace." Ch. xiv.

Tessa is the pretty contadina in the Mercato Vecchio from whom Tito Melema, a hungry stranger in Florence, begs a "breakfast for love". At the San Giovanni festa, Tito rescues her from annoyance, and later, at the Fierucola, goes through a mock marriage ceremony with her, which, as he is really in love with Romola, means nothing to him. After his marriage to Romola, finding that Tessa has taken the mock ceremony seriously, Tito establishes her in a house of his own, and two children, Lillo and Ninna, are born. Tito is really fond of the children, and, gradually, as he loses Romola's affection, he finds relief in Tessa's stupidity and her unquestioning devotion. When he plans to leave Florence he arranges to take Tessa and the children with him, but his death leaves Tessa stranded and in despair, until she is found by Romola, who looks after her and the children.

TETTERLEY. Place where Lord Watling's farm is located. *Amos B.* vi.

TETTO DE' PISANI (*Real*). *Rom.* lxv, lxxii.
 Note.—A projecting roof on the west side of Piazza della Signoria, Florence, built by prisoners from Pisa about 1364. It was torn down about 1865.

TEVEROY, MRS. Lord Grinsell's second wife. *Mid.* lv.

THAMES (*Real*). The river on which Daniel Deronda frequently rows, and from which he rescues Mirah Cohen when she tries to drown herself. *D. D.* xvii, xx, xl.
 Note.—The Thames, which is the most important river in England, divides London in two portions. A stretch of the river above London extending to Hampton Court is a favourite place for boating excursions.

THÉÂTRE FRANÇAIS, PARIS (*Real*). *D. D.* vi.
 Note.—The French national theatre, founded 1681, under the name Comédie française; the name Théâtre français dates from about 1791.

"THERE WAS A HOLY HERMIT." Song in the *Spanish Gypsy* sung by Arias, the page. *Sp. G.* ii.

THERON. A painstaking student whose condensed exposition is excluded to leave space for the copious brew of Adrastus, the too-ready writer. *T. S.* xiii.

THESIGER, MRS. The rector's wife. *Mid.* lxxiv.

THESIGER, REVEREND EDWARD. Rector of St. Peter's, Middlemarch, a moderate evangelical, "who never goes into extremes". *Mid.* xviii, lx, lxxi, lxxiv.

THESSALONICA (*Real*). One of the cities in which Tito Melema and Baldassarre Calvo had resided. *Rom.* vi.
 Note.—A city of ancient Greece, now Salonika.

THOLER, BOB. The dead man for whom Adam Bede makes a coffin that his father had neglected to make. *Adam B.* iv–v.

THOLER, TOM, *called* TOM SAFT. A half-witted labourer on Mr. Poyser's farm. *Adam B.* liii.

THOLOWAY, BEN. Labourer on Mr. Poyser's farm; a powerful thresher but not over-honest. *Adam B.* liii.

THOMAS. The Reverend Augustus Debarry's servant. *F. H.* xxiii.

THOMAS OF SARZANA. *See* NICHOLAS V, POPE.

THOMSON, LIZA. Servant. *J. R.* xxi.

THORWALDSEN (*Hist.*). An artist in Rome, to whose studio Will Ladislaw takes Mr. Casaubon and Dorothea. *Mid.* xxii.

Note.—Bertel Thorwaldsen (1770–1844), the well-known Danish sculptor, who lived in Rome for many years.

THREE BARNS. Meeting-place of the Wessex Hunt to which Gwendolen Harleth induces her cousin Rex to take her. *D. D.* vii.

"THREE CRANES." Hotel in Duffield, Garstin's headquarters. *F. H.* xxx.

THREE CROFTS. Part of Peter Featherstone's property. *Mid.* xxxii.

"THREE CROWNS." Inn, by Whitbridge. *S. M.* viii.

THRUPP, MR. Clerk at the Milby bank. *J. R.* iii.

THURLE, MR. The desirable prospective tenant of the Chase Farm. *Adam B.* xxxii–xxxiii.

THURSTON. Town. *J. R.* iii, xxv.

TIBBITS, MRS. Washerwoman. *B. J.* i.

TILIOT, MR. Rich spirit merchant in Treby Magna, whose church views become higher and higher as his gin becomes famous. *F. H.* iii, xxiv, xxxi, xxxiii.

TILIOT, MRS. MARY. The spirit merchant's wife. *F. H.* xxiv.

TILSTON. Place where Mr. Jerome used to live. *J. R.* viii.

TILT, MR. *M. F.* Bk. 6, xii.

TIM. The Poyser's ploughman and wagoner. *Adam B.* xx, xxii, xxxii, liii.

"TIMES" (*Real*). London newspaper. *D. D.* xxxiii, lxi; *F. H.* xvii; *Mid.* lxxxiv.

TIMOTHY'S BESS. *See* SALT, MRS. JIM.

TIMOTHY'S BESS'S BEN. Jim Salt's five-year-old son. *Adam B.* ii.

TIMPSON. Mr. Stelling's father-in-law. *M. F.* Bk. 1, iii; Bk. 2, i.

TIMPSON, LOUISA. *See* STELLING, MRS. LOUISA.

TINA. *See* SARTI, CATERINA.

TIPTON. The parish near Middlemarch where Mr. Brooke lives. *Mid.* i, iii–vi, x, xviii, xxvi, xxxiv, xxxviii, xl.

TIPTON GRANGE. Home of Mr. Brooke, where Dorothea and Celia Brooke live until they are married. *Mid.* i–ii, vi–x, xxx, xxxix, xlvi, l–li, liv, lxii, lxxi, Finale.

TITO MELEMA. *See* MELEMA, TITO.

TOBY. A mongrel dog. *M. F.* Bk. 4, iii.

TOD, JOSH. Landlord of the "Holly Bush". *Adam B.* i.

TOFTON. A village on the Floss, very near St. Ogg's, close to which Tom and Maggie Tulliver are drowned. *M. F.* Bk. 3, vii; Bk. 6, ii; Bk. 7, v.

Note.—The original of Tofton may have been Morton, a village on the Trent ("Floss") about one mile north of Gainsborough ("St. Ogg's"). (*See* article by John W. Fraser in *Bookman* (Lond.), vol. 9, p. 55.)

TOFTON FERRY. *M. F.* Bk. 5, vii.

TOFTON ROAD. The road leading out of St. Ogg's, toward which Mrs. Glegg's front windows look. *M. F.* Bk. 1, xii.

TOLLER, MR. A long-established medical practitioner in Middlemarch who disapproves of Dr.

Lydgate, and is hostile to Mr. Bulstrode. *Mid.* xv, xviii, xlv, lx, lxiii, lxxi.

"Mr. Toller shared the highest practice in the town, and belonged to an old Middlemarch family ... he had the easiest way in the world of taking things which might be supposed to annoy him, being a well-bred quietly facetious man, who kept a good house, was very fond of a little sporting when he could get it ... It may seem odd that with such pleasant habits he should have been given to the heroic treatment, bleeding, and blistering and starving his patients, with a dispassionate disregard to his personal example." Ch. xlv.

TOLLER, MR. HARRY. Brewer, a wealthy citizen of Middlemarch. *Mid.* lxiii–lxiv.

TOLLER, MISS SOPHY. The brewer's daughter who marries Ned Plymdale. *Mid.* lxiv.

TOLLER, MRS. TOM. One of the guests at Mrs. Hackbutt's small tea party, where Mrs. Bulstrode is discussed. *Mid.* lxxiv.

TOM SAFT. *See* THOLER, TOM.

TOMLINSON, MR. Rich miller at Milby; one of Lawyer Dempster's chief admirers. *J. R.* i–ii, iv, vi, viii, x, xvii, xxvi.

"Mr. Tomlinson ... often said his father had given him 'no eddication, and he didn't care who knowed it; he could buy up most o' th' eddicated men he'd ever come across'." Ch. i.

Note.—In the lists of originals prepared in Nuneaton, after the publication of *Scenes of Clerical Life*, a Mr. Hinks was given as the original of Mr. Tomlinson. (*See* Olcott, George Eliot, p. 16.)

TOMLINSON, THE THREE MISSES. *J. R.* ii.

TOMMS, MR. JACOB. A young tailor of Shepperton. *Amos B.* vii.

TOOKE, OLD MRS. *J. R.* xiii.

TOOKEY, MR. Deputy parish clerk at Raveloe, an unpopular young man whose musical gifts are criticized. *S. M.* vi, viii, x, Conclusion.

TOP MARKET, MIDDLEMARCH. *Mid.* xlv.

TOPPING ABBEY. Sir Hugo Mallinger's country place; "one of the finest in England, at once historical, romantic, and home-like; a picturesque architectural outgrowth from an abbey, which had still remnants of the old monastic trunk." *D. D.* xv–xvi, xxxv–xxxvi, lii, lxvii.

TOPPINGS. *See* KING'S TOPPING; MONK'S TOPPING.

TORBITS. A family in debt. *Mid.* lxiv.

TORBY. A town on the Floss, below St. Ogg's, at which Stephen Guest proposes to land when he and Maggie are carried down the river. *M. F.* Bk. 6, xiii.

TORNABUONI (*Hist.*). Relatives of Lorenzo Tornabuoni who avenge his execution by killing Francesco Valori. *Rom.* lxvi.

TORNABUONI, LORENZO (*Hist.*). An accomplished young member of the Medicean party, a guest at the supper in the Rucellai Gardens.

Rom. xxii–xxiii, xxvii, xxxviii–xxxix, xliv, lvi, lx.

He is one of those arrested and executed at the same time as Romola's godfather, Bernardo del Nero.

Note. — Lorenzo Tornabuoni, executed 1497 at the age of thirty-two, son of Giovanni Tornabuoni, who was Gonfalionere in 1482.

TORRINGTON, CAPTAIN. One of Grandcourt's guests at Diplow. *D. D.* xii, xxviii–xxix.

TORRINGTON, MRS. The Captain's wife; Mr. Grandcourt's cousin. *D. D.* xii–xiii, xv, xxviii–xxix.

TORRY, MISS. *M. F.* Bk. 6, vi.

TORRY, YOUNG. A conceited dandy of St. Ogg's. *M. F.* Bk. 5, iv; Bk. 6, ix; Bk. 7, ii.

TORRY, MRS. JAMES. An inhabitant of St. Ogg's who refuses to take Maggie Tulliver as a nursery governess. *M. F.* Bk. 7, iv.

TORRY'S MILL. Mill where Bob Jakin earns his first ten sovereigns by extinguishing a fire. *M. F.* Bk. 3, v–vi.

TORTOISE. The Garth's cat. *Mid.* xxiv.

TOUCAN, OF MAGDALEN. *T. S.* xi.

TOUCHWOOD. A bad-tempered man. *T. S.* vi.

"He is by turns insolent, quarrelsome, repulsively haughty to innocent people who approach him with respect, neglectful of his friends, angry in face of legitimate demands, procrastinating in the fulfilment of such demands, prompted to rude words and harsh looks by a moody disgust with his fellow men in general—and yet, as everybody will assure you, the soul of honour, a steadfast friend, a defender of the oppressed, an affectionate-hearted creature."

TOWERS, JOHN. A young dandy of Grimworth who finally wins the hand of Penny Palfrey. *B. J.* ii–iii.

TOWNLEY, COLONEL. The stranger on horseback who hears Dinah Morris preaching on the Green at Hayslope, and later, as a magistrate, gives her permission to visit Hetty Sorrel in prison at Stoniton, just before the time set for Hetty's execution. *Adam B.* ii, xlv.

TOWNLEY, MISS. Mistress of a girls' school in Milby. *J. R.* v.[1]

TOZER, MR. An old gardener in Shepperton. *Amos B.* x.

"TRACK" SOCIETY. *Amos B.* i.

TRADGETT. The name of Arthur Donnithorne's mother's family. *Adam B.* v.

TRADGETT. Arthur Donnithorne's cousin, who will have the estate in case of Arthur's death. *Adam B.* xlviii.

TRALLA. A Gypsy girl. *Sp. G.* iii.

TRANSOME, MR. Owner of Transome Court; a feeble-minded paralytic who lives in fear of his handsome, dominating wife. *F. H.* Introd., i–ii, vii–viii, xxxiv–xxxv, xl, xlii–xliii, xlix.

TRANSOME, MRS. ARABELLA. Harold Transome's mother; a handsome, imperious, disappointed woman

---

[1] A Nuneaton list gives Miss Towle as her prototype. (Manuscript notes.)

whose age is embittered by the unhappy consequences of a sin of her young married days. *F. H.* Introd., i–ii, vii–ix, xxxiv–xxxvi, xxxviii–xl, xlii–xlvi, xlviii–l, Epilogue.

"Her figure was slim and finely formed, though she was between fifty and sixty. She was a tall, proud-looking woman, with abundant grey hair, dark eyes and eyebrows, and a somewhat eagle-like, yet not unfeminine, face. Her tight-fitting black dress was much worn; the fine lace of her cuffs and collar, and of the small veil which fell backwards over her high comb, was visibly mended; but rare jewels flashed on her hands, which lay on her folded black-clad arms, like finely cut onyx cameos . . ."

"Crosses, mortifications, money cares, conscious blameworthiness, had changed the aspect of the world for her; there was anxiety in the morning sunlight; there was unkind triumph or disapproving pity in the glances of greeting neighbours . . . Mrs. Transome, whose imperious will had availed little to ward off the great evils of her life, found the opiate for her discontent in the exertion of her will about smaller things. She was not cruel, and could not enjoy thoroughly what she called the old woman's pleasure of tormenting; but she liked every little sign of power her lot had left her. She liked that a tenant should stand bareheaded below her as she sat on horseback. She liked to insist that work done without her orders should be undone from beginning to end . . . a woman's keen sensibility and dread . . . lay screened behind all her petty habits and narrow notions." Ch. i.

As a proud young beauty of good family but little money, she had made a loveless marriage with the feeble Mr. Transome. Feeling no fondness for either her husband or her half-idiot eldest son, she had responded to the attentions of the handsome young lawyer, Jermyn, and later had centred all her love and pride in her second son, Harold, a healthy handsome boy. Her dominating nature makes her enjoy managing the estate in place of her feeble husband, but lawsuits and the charges which the unscrupulous Jermyn has fastened on the estate have greatly reduced the income. On the death of her disreputable eldest son she eagerly anticipates Harold's return from the East, where he has gone to make his fortune, and expects to find in his devotion a solace for all her dissatisfactions. She is bitterly disappointed when, instead of this devotion, he gives her merely a good-humoured, condescending affection; feels the loss of authority when he does not defer to her about the management of the estate; and watches with helpless dread the growing antagonism between him and Jermyn. Finally, when Jermyn, in a public quarrel, tells Harold that he is his father, her unhappy secret is revealed to her son. After his first reaction to this shock, Harold treats her with gentleness, and takes her abroad, away from the associations of Transome Court.

TRANSOME, LADY BETTY. A beauty whom Sir Peter Lely painted. *F. H.* xl.

TRANSOME, BYCLIFFE *versus*. See BYCLIFFE *versus* TRANSOME.

TRANSOME, DURFEY. The vicious and imbecile son of the Transomes, whose death makes his younger brother, Harold, the heir to the estate. *F. H.* i–ii, viii.

TRANSOME, HAROLD. Mrs. Transome's younger son; a handsome, agreeable and selfish, but not dishonourable young man. *F. H.* i–iii, v, vii–ix, xi, xvi–xvii, xix–xxi, xxix–xxxi, xxxiv–l, Epilogue.

"This determined aiming at something not easy but clearly possible marked the direction in which Harold's nature was strong; he had the energetic will and muscle, the self-confidence, the quick perception, and the narrow imagination which make what is admiringly called the practical mind... He was addicted at once to rebellion and to conformity, and only an intimate personal knowledge could enable any one to predict where his conformity would begin... In fact, Harold Transome was a clever, frank, good-natured egoist; not stringently consistent, but without any disposition to falsity; proud, but with a pride that was moulded in an individual rather than an hereditary form; unspeculative, unsentimental, unsympathetic; fond of sensual pleasures, but disinclined to all vice, and attached as a healthy, clear-sighted person, to all conventional morality, construed with a certain freedom." Ch. viii.

In his youth he had gone to the East, where he married a Greek woman, originally a slave, and made a fortune. A widower of thirty-four, he returns to England when his brother's death makes him the heir to the Transome estates. Breaking with the family traditions of Toryism, he stands for Parliament as a Radical, and is defeated after an exciting campaign and election. In looking into the estate business management, he finds that Mr. Jermyn, the family lawyer, has taken advantage of his position to his own profit, and starts legal proceedings against him. When he learns that Esther Lyon is the rightful owner of the estate he becomes genuinely interested in her, wants to marry her, but fails to win her love. In a public quarrel Mr. Jermyn tells Harold that he, Jermyn, is his father, and, as a result Harold and his mother leave England for a time.

TRANSOME, HARRY. Harold Transome's little son; a black-eyed, tyrannical child of three. *F. H.* i, vii–viii, xix, xxxiv–xxxv, xl, xlii–xliii, xlviii.

TRANSOME, JOHN JUSTUS. The ancestor of the Transomes who, in 1729, entailed the estates on his son, Thomas, and his heirs-male, with remainder to the Bycliffes in fee. *F. H.* xxix, xxxvii.

TRANSOME, THOMAS. The prodigal son of John Justus Transome, who sold his own and his descendants' right to a cousin named Durfey. *F. H.* xxix.

TRANSOME, OR TROUNSEM, THOMAS. *See* TROUNSEM, TOMMY.

TRANSOME COURT. Home of the Transome family, near Treby Magna; "a place there had been a fine sight of lawsuits about." *F. H.* Introd., i–ii, vii–viii, xxxiv–xxxv, xxxviii–xl, xlii–xliii, xlviii–l, Epilogue.

TRANTER, GIL. A man who was laid up for a fortnight after a fight for fun with Adam Bede. *Adam B.* xvi.

TRASTAVERE (*Real*). *D. D.* xxxvii.
Note.—A quarter in Rome, now inhabited largely by the working classes; it includes the Janiculum.

TRAUNTER, DEB. A disreputable acquaintance of Mr. Budd. *J. R.* i, iv.¹

TRAWLEY. A friend of Lydgate's in his student days. *Mid.* xvii.

TREBY, LITTLE. *See* LITTLE TREBY.

TREBY MAGNA. Town in North Loamshire; the home of Felix Holt and the Lyons and the scene of an election riot. *F. H.* Introd., and following chapters.
"Treby Magna, on which the Reform Bill had thrust the new honour of being a polling-place, had been, at the beginning of the century, quite a typical old market-town, lying in pleasant sleepiness among green pastures, with a rush-fringed river meandering through them. Its principal street had various handsome and tall-windowed brick houses with walled gardens behind them; and at the end, where it widened into the market-place, there was the cheerful rough-stuccoed front of that excellent inn, the Marquis of Granby . . . And the church was one of those fine old English structures worth travelling to see, standing in a broad churchyard with a line of solemn yew-trees beside it, and lifting a majestic tower and spire far above the red- and-purple roofs of the town. . . Treby Magna gradually passed from being simply a respectable market-town—the heart of a great rural district, where the trade was only such as had close relations with the local landed interest— and took on the more complex life brought by mines and manufactures." Ch. iii.

Note.—It has been suggested that in the original of Treby Magna was the ancient town of Coventry, in Warwickshire, where George Eliot lived for some time, but beyond the fact that there was a Coventry original for Rufus Lyon's chapel, there seems to be nothing to support this suggestion. (Manuscript information; also Dryden, *Memorials of Old Warwickshire,* p. 125; Muirhead, *England,* p. 326.)

TREBY MANOR. Home of the Debarrys. *F. H.* vii, xii, xiv, xxxiii.

TRECCA, MONNA ("DAME GREEN-GROCER"). Dealer in the Mercato Vecchio. *Rom.* i.

---
¹ A Nuneaton list gives Poll Townend as the prototype. (Manuscript notes.)

TREDDLESTON. The market town about three miles from Hayslope. *Adam B.* ii, iv, vi, xi, xv–xvii, xxi, xxvi–xxvii, xxxiv–xxxv.

TRENT'S. The farm where Mrs. Poyser's maid, Betty, had once been dairymaid. *Adam B.* vi.

TRESPIANO (*Real*). A village where old Maso is to wait for Romola when she plans to leave Florence. *Rom.* xxxvi–xxxvii.

Note.—Trespiano, a village a few miles north of Florence, on the road to Bologna.

TRIAL BY FIRE (*Hist.*). The test of the truth of doctrines by walking through fire, to which Fra Francesco challenges Savonarola. It is staged with much ceremony, but it is eventually prevented by rain. *Rom.* lxiii–lxv.

Note.—The Trial, or Ordeal by Fire, was set for April 7, 1498. In her account of the preparations for the Ordeal, the various delays, and its final prevention by the coming of rain, George Eliot follows closely the historical account as given by Villari.

TRIESTE (*Real*). *D. D.* xliii, lx.

Note.—Trieste, an important seaport on the Adriatic, at the time of *Daniel Deronda* belonging to Austria, but ceded to Italy, 1919.

TRIP. The Poyser's black-and-tan terrier. *Adam B.* vi.

TRIPPLEGATE. Mr. Cleves' parish. *Amos B.* vi, ix.

Note.—In the lists of originals prepared in Nuneaton after the publication of the *Scenes of Clerical Life*, Higham is given as the original of Tripplegate. (*See* Olcott, George Eliot, p. 15.)

TRITON, LORD. A philanthropist, an acquaintance of Mrs. Cadwallader. *Mid.* liv, lxxxiv.

TROST. An optimist who believes that at some future period this will be the best of all possible worlds, and who does not agree with Theophrastus Such about the future of the human race. *T. S.* xvii.

TROT. A tiny spaniel. *Adam B.* xii.

TROUNSEM, OR TRANSOME, TOMMY. Bill-sticker; an old drunkard. *F. H.* xx, xxviii–xxix, xxxi, xxxiii–xxxiv.

Unknown to himself, he is the last descendant of the Thomas Transome who sold his and his descendants' rights in the Transome estate to the Durfeys. His death in the election riot makes Esther Lyon, the descendant of the Bycliffes, the legal owner of the estate.

TROWER. One of Lawyer Dempster's clients. *J. R.* i.

TRUBERRY. A politician who is ruled by his ambitious wife. *Mid.* lxxxiv.

TRUBERRY, MRS. Wife of the above; an acquaintance of the Dowager Lady Chettam. *Mid.* lxxxiv.

TRUFFORD, LORD. *J. R.* vi.

TRUMBULL, MR. BORTHROP. Auctioneer; second cousin to Peter Featherstone, who bequeathes him his gold-headed cane. *Mid.* xxxii, xxxv, xlv, lx, lxiv, lxxxvi.

"Mr. Borthrop Trumbull, a distinguished bachelor and auctioneer of those parts, much concerned in the sale of land and cattle ; a public character, indeed, whose name was seen on widely distributed placards, and who might reasonably be sorry for those who did not know of him ... There was no odious cupidity in Mr. Borthrop Trumbull — nothing more than a sincere sense of his own merit ... On the whole, in an auctioneering way, he was an honourable man, not ashamed of his business." Ch. xxxii.

TRUNCHEON, DR. A London physician. *F. H.* vii.

TRYAN, MISS. The curate's sister. *J. R.* xxvi.

TRYAN, REVEREND EDGAR. The evangelical curate at Paddiford Common, Milby, by whose influence Janet Dempster is rescued. *J. R.* i–xii, xvi, xviii–xxii, xxiv–xxviii.

"The strange light from the golden sky falling on his light brown hair, which is brushed high up round his head, makes it look almost like an aureole. His grey eyes, too, shine with unwonted brilliancy this evening. They were not remarkable eyes, but they accorded completely in their changing light with the changing expression of his person, which indicated the paradoxial character often observable in a large-limbed sanguine blond ; at once mild and irritable, gentle and overbearing, indolent and resolute, self-conscious and dreamy." Ch. iii.

"But Mr. Tryan was not cast in the mould of the gratuitous martyr. With a power of persistence which had been often blamed as obstinacy, he had an acute sensibility to the very hatred or ridicule he did not flinch from provoking. Every form of disapproval jarred him painfully ; and, though he fronted his opponents manfully, and often with considerable warmth of temper, he had no pugnacious pleasure in the contest. It was one of the weaknesses of his nature to be too keenly alive to every harsh wind of opinion." Ch. viii.

In his youth he had been wild, and the realization of his sins had caused him to enter the church and to devote his life to others. When he comes to Milby he has to struggle against the indifference of those whom he would help and the malevolent opposition of Lawyer Dempster. In the end his sympathy, faith, and high purpose give him the victory, for which, however, he pays with his life. He dies happy in the knowledge that, through his influence, Janet Dempster has been rescued from despair.

Note.—There was undoubtedly an original for the story of the persecution of Mr. Tryan. George Eliot, in 1857, said : "The story, as far as regards the persecution, is a real bit in the religious history of England that happened about eight and twenty years ago." The Reverend W. P. Jones wrote to William Blackwood that Mr. Tryan was drawn from his deceased brother but George Eliot disclaimed this, saying: "Mr. Tryan is not a portrait of any clergyman, living or dead." (*See* Cross, *George Eliot's Life*, vol. 1, pp. 458, 462.)

TUBAL-CAIN. *P.—L. J.*

TUCKER. A constable at Treby Magna. *F. H.* xxxiii, xxxvii, xlvi.

During the election riot he attacks Felix Holt, imagining him to be leading the riot. Felix unintentionally kills him, and as a result is tried for manslaughter.

TUCKER, MR. Mr. Casaubon's middle-aged curate. *Mid.* ix, xxviii, xxxiii, l.

"Mr. Tucker ... was just as old and musty looking as she would have expected Mr. Casaubon's curate to be; doubtless an excellent man who would go to heaven (for Celia wished not to be unprincipled), but the corners of his mouth were so unpleasant." Ch. ix.

TUCKER'S LANE, MILBY. *J. R.* iv.

TUDGE, MR. Job's grandfather; a stone-breaker. *F. H.* xxii.

TUDGE, JOB. A small *protégé* of Felix Holt's, to whom Mrs. Holt is very kind. *F. H.* xxii, xxvii, xxxii, xxxvii–xxxviii, xliii, Epilogue.

"Job was a small fellow about five, with a germinal nose, large round blue eyes, and red hair that curled close to his head like the wool on the back of an infantine lamb." Ch. xxii.

TULLIVER, EDWARD. Miller; Tom and Maggie's father; an honest, generous, quarrelsome man whose passion for lawsuits ruins him. *M. F.* Bk. 1, i–ix, xi, xiii; Bk. 2, i–ii, iv, vi–vii; Bk. 3, 1, iii–ix; Bk. 4, i–iii; Bk. 5, i, iii, v–vii.

"Mr. Tulliver was, on the whole, a man of safe traditional opinions; but on one or two points he had trusted to his unassisted intellect, and had arrived at several questionable conclusions; among the rest, that rats, weevils, and lawyers were created by Old Harry." Bk. 1, iii.

"Mr. Tulliver was a strictly honest man, and proud of being honest, but he considered that in law the ends of justice could only be achieved by employing a stronger knave to frustrate a weaker. Law was a sort of cockfight, in which it was the business of injured honesty to get a game bird with the best pluck and the strongest spurs." Bk. 2, ii.

He is devoted to Maggie, "the little wench," and generous to his less fortunate sister, Mrs. Moss, but his hot temper leads him into numerous lawsuits and eventually he loses Dorlcote Mill and becomes bankrupt. In order to save money for his creditors he manages the mill for his enemy, Lawyer Wakem, who has purchased it. When his debts are paid he gives way to his temper and hate, violently assaults Mr. Wakem, and dies from the shock to his enfeebled system.

Note.—It has been suggested that a certain Tom Hollick, a farmer and miller of Nuneaton, whose mill George Eliot used to pass on her way to school, may have been the original of Mr. Tulliver. Hollick was described by one who remembered him as a sanguine high-tempered man, impatient of any attempt to impose upon him, who was involved in a lawsuit. (Manuscript information; also article in *Great Thoughts*, March, 1901, p. 370.) Mr. Tulliver is not George Eliot's father, although the tender affection which Mr. Tulliver feels for Maggie may be drawn from the author's recollection of her own father.

TULLIVER, MRS. ELIZABETH (BESSY). Maggie and Tom Tulliver's mother; the handsomest and stupidest of the Dodson sisters, "a blonde, comely woman," utterly without any sense of humour. *M. F.* Bk. 1, i–x, xiii; Bk. 2, ii, vii; Bk. 3, i–ix; Bk. 4, ii–iii; Bk. 5, v–vii; Bk. 6, i–ii, vi–vii, x, xii–xiii; Bk. 1, i–v.

"Mrs. Tulliver was what is called a good-tempered person— never cried, when she was a baby, on any slighter ground than hunger and pins; and from the cradle upwards had been healthy, fair, plump, and dull-witted; in short, the flower of her family for beauty and amiability. But milk and mildness are not the best things for keeping." Bk. 1, ii.

"Mrs. Tulliver was a thorough Dodson, though a mild one, as small-beer, so long as it is anything, is only describable as very weak ale; and though she had groaned a little in her youth under the yoke of her elder sisters, and still shed occasional tears at their sisterly reproaches, it was not in Mrs. Tulliver to be an innovator on the family ideas. She was thankful to have been a Dodson, and to have one child who took after her own family." Bk. 1, vi.

She bemoans the fact that Maggie is not a Dodson like her cousin, Lucy, and when Mr. Tulliver fails and she loses her cherished household gods her little world is upset, and she does not know how to readjust herself. In spite of her preference for her son Tom, as "the child who took after her own family", she stands by Maggie when Tom turns against his sister.

TULLIVER, MAGGIE. A clever, imaginative, undisciplined girl, with an intense craving for love and a longing for happiness. *M. F.* Bk. 1, i–xi, xiii; Bk. 2, i–ii, v–vii; Bk. 3, i–ix; Bk. 4, ii–iii; Bk. 5, i–vii; Bk. 6, l–xiv; Bk. 7, i–v, Conclusion.

"Maggie, in her brown frock, with her eyes reddened and her heavy hair pushed back, looking from the bed where her father lay, to the dull walls of this sad chamber which was the centre of her world, was a creature full of eager, passionate longings for all that was beautiful and glad; thirsty for all knowledge; with an ear straining after dreamy music that died away and would not come near to her; with a blind unconscious yearning for something that would link together the wonderful impressions of this mysterious life, and give her soul a sense of home in it." Bk. 3, v.

"When Maggie was not angry, she was as dependent on kind or cold words as a daisy on the sunshine or the cloud; the need of being loved would always subdue her." Bk. 6, iv.

As a child she is devoted to her brother Tom and passionately fond of her father, who takes her part when she rebels against the traditions of her mother and all the Dodsons. She leads a life of ups and downs, happy with her brother and her books or miserable in her attic to which she flies for refuge. After her father fails she is inspired by her reading of Thomas à Kempis to lead a life of self-renunciation and repression. In the Red Deeps she renews her friendship with Philip Wakem, the cripple, who had been at school with Tom. When he declares his love for her she mistakes affection for him for love. After some time her brother Tom discovers that she and Philip are meeting and brutally forces Maggie to renounce Philip. When, at nineteen, she has developed into a beauty with wonderful dark eyes, she meets her cousin Lucy's lover, Stephen Guest, and he falls in love with her. In spite of the fact that she is still fond of Philip she ends by returning Stephen's love, although struggling against it. While boating on the Floss they are accidentally carried too far by the tide, and Maggie at first thinks that she will yield to Stephen's desire to continue the journey and be married, but her better nature triumphs, and she leaves him to return courageously to her family. Her brother refuses to forgive her and disowns her. They are united only when they lose their lives together in the flood, when Maggie attempts to rescue Tom. "Brother and sister had gone down in an embrace never to be parted; living through again in one supreme moment the days when they had clasped their hands in love, and roamed the daisied fields together."

Note.—The original of Maggie Tulliver, more particularly in childhood, was George Eliot herself, and the first part of the story is largely autobiographic. Mr. Cross says: "No doubt the early part of Maggie's portraiture is the best autobiographical representation we can have of George Eliot's own feelings in her childhood, and many of the incidents in the book are based on real experiences of family life—but ... mixed with fictitious elements and situations." (*See* Cross, *George Eliot's Life*, vol. 1, p. 31; *see also* Stephen, *George Eliot*, p. 87.)

TULLIVER, RALPH. Mr. Tulliver's ancestor, a clever fellow who had ruined himself. *M. F.* Bk. 4, i.

TULLIVER, TOM. Maggie's brother; a self-reliant, obstinate, clear-sighted young fellow, stupid with books, but possessing great common sense. *M. F.* Bk. 1, ii–vii, ix–xi, xiii; Bk. 2, i–vii; Bk. 3, i–ix ; Bk. 4, ii–iii ; Bk. 5, ii, v–vii ; Bk. 6, i–ii, iv–v, vii, xii ; Bk. 7, i–iii, v, Conclusion.

"He was one of those lads that grow everywhere in England, and, at twelve or thirteen years of age, look as much alike as goslings : a lad with light-brown hair, cheeks of cream and roses, full lips, indeterminate nose and eyebrows—a physiognomy in which it seems impossible to discern anything but the generic character of boyhood ; as different as possible from poor Maggie's phiz, which Nature seemed to have moulded and coloured with the most decided intention." Bk. l, v.

"Tom never did the same sort of foolish things as Maggie, having a wonderful, instinctive discernment of what would turn to his advantage or disadvantage ; and so it happened, that though he was much more wilful and inflexible than Maggie, his mother hardly ever called him naughty. But if Tom did make a mistake of that sort, he espoused it, and stood by it ; he 'didn't mind' . . . If Tom Tulliver whipped a gate, he was convinced, not that the whipping of gates by all boys was a justifiable act, but that he, Tom Tulliver was justifiable in whipping that particular gate, and he wasn't going to be sorry." Bk. 1, vii.

As a child he rules his young, loving sister with a firm and often hard hand. When Mr. Tulliver fails, Tom manfully goes to work with his Uncle Deane's firm and after a few years of hard work and self denial he is able to help his father pay his debts. He shares his father's hatred of Lawyer Wakem, and ruthlessly puts an end to the love affair between Maggie and Philip Wakem, his former schoolmate. He disowns Maggie after her flight with Stephen Guest, and is reconciled to her only when she rows to the Mill to rescue him and the two are drowned together in the flooded Floss.

Note.—The original of Tom Tulliver, in part at least, was George Eliot's elder brother, Isaac Evans, to whom she was much attached. The affectionate childhood relation between her and her brother is commemorated also in the poem *Brother and Sister*.

TULPIAN. A gentleman with considerable interest at his disposal to whom Hinze, the too deferential man, frequently appeals. *T. S.* v.

TURNBULL, DR. The Tullivers' physician. *M. F.* Bk. 1, ii, ix ; Bk. 3, i, iii–iv, vi–viii ; Bk. 5, vii.

TURNBULL, MRS. AND MISS. Old acquaintances who turn aside from Maggie Tulliver after her adventure with Stephen Guest. *M. F.* Bk. 7, ii.

TURVEY. Sir Hugo Mallinger's valet. *D. D.* xvi.

TWENTY, THE (*Hist.*). Twenty chief men of Florence, appointed after the departure of Charles VIII, with "dictatorial authority given them, by force of which they should for one year choose all magistrates, and set the frame of government in order." *Rom.* xxxv.

Note.—These were the twenty Accoppiatori, called the Venti, appointed in December, 1494. They served as the government of Florence for a short time, until after the formation of the Grand Council provided by the new constitution of 1494.

TWENTYLANDS. *M. F.* Bk. 1, vii.

"TWO TRAVELLERS." Public-house at Milby. *J. R.* ii.

TYKE, REV. WALTER. Curate in Middlemarch; a zealous man whose sermons are not popular and who is suspected of cant. *Mid.* xiii, xvi–xviii, 1, lxxiv.

Mr. Bulstrode favours him as Chaplain to the Infirmary and, with the assistance of Lydgate's vote, he is elected instead of Mr. Farebrother.

U

UBIQUE. A public speaker who is criticized by Semper for the very faults which Semper possesses. *T. S.* xiii.

V

VAIANO, MAESTRO. The mountebank, from whom Tito Melema rescues Tessa. *Rom.* viii, x, xiv, xvi.

He performs the mock marriage ceremony for Tessa and Tito, and later, disguised as a contadina, plays on the doctor, Maestro Tacco, the trick described in the chapter "The Florentine Joke".

VALLA, LORENZO (*Hist.*). A scholar on whose Latin translation of Thucydides Bardo de' Bardi had made many notes. *Rom.* xii.

Note.—Lorenzo Valla (*c.* 1406–57), Apostolic secretary under Nicholas V, for whom he made a Latin translation of Thucydides.

VALORI, FRANCESCO (*Hist.*). The "hot-tempered chieftain of the Piagnoni", a devoted adherent of Savonarola and a bitter enemy of Romola's godfather, Bernardo del Nero, upon whose execution he insists. *Rom.* xii, xxv, xxix, xlviii–xlix, lvii–lx, lxiii, lxvi, lxix.

Note.—Francesco Valori (1439–98), who was killed in the midst of the mob after the capture of Savonarola.

VANDERNOODT, MR. A visitor at Leubronn when Gwendolen Harleth gambles there; later a guest at Diplow and at Topping Abbey. *D. D.* i, xv, xxxv–xxxvi, xlviii.

"Mr. Vandernoodt, a man of the best Dutch blood imported at the revolution: for the rest, one of those commodious persons in society who are nothing in particular themselves, but are understood to be acquainted with the best in every department; close-clipped, pale-eyed, nonchalant." Ch. xxxv.

VANDYKE DUCHESS. Hans Meyrick's name for Gwendolen. *See* HARLETH, GWENDOLEN.

VATICAN (*Real*). Museum and Library which the Casaubons visit in Rome. *Mid.* x, xix–xxi.

Note.—The Vatican Palace, the residence of the popes and headquarters of the Papacy, contains many collections, including the collection of antiquities which Mrs. Casaubon visited, and a great library especially rich in manuscripts, where Mr. Casaubon carried on his researches.

VENICE (*Real*). *Rom.* i, v, viii–ix, xvi, xxxvi, xxxviii, xlii; *L. V.* mentioned i.

Note.—At the time of *Romola* the Republic of Venice was one of the five great powers of Italy. Its Great Council, created in 1189, furnished the model for the Great Council of Florence advocated by Savonarola.

VERDUN (*Real*). One of the French towns in which Maurice Christian Bycliffe and Henry Scaddon had been prisoners. *F. H.* xxi.

Note.—A fortress town in the *département* of the Meuse, in the north-eastern part of France.

VERNIO, COUNTS OF (*Hist.*). The branch of the Bardi family from which Bardo de' Bardi and his daughter are descended. *Rom.* v.

VESOUL (*Real*). The French town where Annette Ledru and Maurice Christian Bycliffe were married. *F. H.* xxi.

Note.—Vesoul, capital of the *département* of Haute-Saône.

VESPUCCI, GIOVANNI (*Hist.*). A Florentine who ordered from Piero di Cosimo a picture of Œdipus and Antigone, for which the artist wanted Romola and her father to sit. *Rom.* xviii.

Note.—According to **Vasari** Giovanni Vespucci really was a patron of Piero di Cosimo who painted various pictures for Vespucci's house in the Via de' Servi.

VESPUCCI, MESSER GUIDANTONIO (*Hist.*). A learned doctor of the law, one of the four syndics charged with effecting the treaty between Charles VIII and the people of Florence. *Rom.* xxix, xxxv.

Note.—Guidantonio Vespucci, a famous jurisconsult, and one of the most influential members of the Arrabbiati.

"VESTIGES." An anonymous work. *T. S.* xi.

VEVAY (*Real*). *L. V.* i.

Note.—A town in the canton of Vaud, Switzerland, on Lake Geneva.

VIA. For names of streets beginning with the word Via *see* the significant part of the name, e.g. Bardi, Via de'.

VIAREGGIO (*Real*). Little fishing village on the Mediterranean. *Rom.* lxi.

Note.—This is the present coast resort of Viareggio in Tuscany, 13 miles west of Lucca.

VIBRIO. The critic who writes in the *Medley Pie* praising Vorticella's book. *T. S.* xv.

VIENNA (*Real*). *D. D.* xx, xxxix; *L. V.* i; *Mid.* mentioned vii.

In the *Lifted Veil* Vienna is one of the cities in which Latimer has an experience of clairvoyance. In

Daniel Deronda it is one of the places where Mirah Cohen lived with her father, Lapidoth.

Note.—The capital of Austria; at the time of Latimer's visit there the city had not yet assumed its modern aspect, and the city walls around the Innere Stadt were still standing.

VIGO, MRS. An acquaintance of the Dowager Lady Chettam; an irreproachable woman who is proposed as a companion to Mrs. Casaubon. *Mid.* liv.

VINCY, BOB. Younger son of Mr. and Mrs. Vincy. *Mid.* xi.

VINCY, FRED. Eldest son of Mr. and Mrs. Vincy; a good-looking young man with an irrepressibly hopeful disposition who chooses farming instead of the Church for which he had been educated. *Mid.* xi–xiv, xvi, xxiii–xxvii, xxxi–xxxvi, xl, lii, lvi–lvii, lix, lxiii, lxvi, lxviii, lxxxv, Finale.

"Fred disliked bad weather within doors. He was too filial to be disrespectful to his father . . . it was disagreeable . . . to be obliged to look sulky instead of having fun; for Fred was so good-tempered that if he looked glum under scolding it was chiefly for propriety's sake . . . Fred piqued himself on keeping clear of lies, and even fibs . . . and rather than incur the accusation of falsehood he would even incur some trouble and self-restraint . . . Fred was not at all coarse . . . he rather looked down on the manners and speech of young men who had not been to the university." Ch. xxiii.

A favourite of his uncle, the rich Mr. Featherstone, he is regarded by himself and his family as the old man's heir, and he looks forward to an easy, pleasant life. When his uncle dies, leaving his money to a natural son, Fred receives nothing and finds it necessary to decide what he is to make of himself, as his father cannot support him in idleness. Since childhood he has loved Mary Garth, and it is mainly through her influence that he disappoints his family and gives up the Church, for which he has been educated. Through Fred's thoughtlessness Mr. Garth loses money which he can ill afford to spare, but in spite of that, for Mary's sake, takes Fred into his office as his assistant, and Fred applies himself to his new work in the hope of winning Mary. His generous rival, Mr. Farebrother, helps him at a critical period. Later he is made manager of Stone Court, the property which he had once expected to inherit, and he then marries Mary and becomes a successful and happy farmer, very steady and devoted to his wife and sons.

VINCY, HARRIET. Maiden name of Mrs. Bulstrode. *See* BULSTRODE, MRS. HARRIET.

VINCY, LOUISA. Little daughter of Mr. and Mrs. Vincy. *Mid.* xvi, lvi, lxiii.

VINCY, MRS. LUCY. The mayor's handsome, good-humoured wife, who sees no fault in her children; an innkeeper's daughter. *Mid.* xi–xii, xvi, xxiii, xxvi–xxvii, xxxi–

xxxvj, xl, lvi, lxiii, lxix, lxxv, Finale.

"She resigned no domestic function to her daughter ; and the matron's blooming good-natured face, with the too volatile pink strings floating from her fine throat, and her cheery manners to husband and children was certainly among the great attractions of the Vincy house . . . The tinge of unpretentious, inoffensive vulgarity in Mrs. Vincy gave more effect to Rosamond's refinement." Ch. xvi.

VINCY, ROSAMOND. The mayor's beautiful daughter, later Lydgate's wife. *Mid*. x–xii, xvi, xxvi–xxvii, xxix, xxxi, xxxv–xxxvi, xl, xliii, xlv–xlvi, lvi, lviii–lix, lxii–lxv, lxvii–lxviii, lxx, lxxiii–lxxxii, Finale.

"Rosamond Vincy, who had excellent taste in costume, with that nymph-like figure and pure blondeness which give the largest range to choice in the flow and color of drapery. But these things made only part of her charm. She was admitted to be the flower of Mrs. Lemon's school . . . Mrs. Lemon herself had always held up Miss Vincy as an example; no pupil, she said, exceeded that young lady for mental acquisition, and propriety of speech, while her musical execution was quite exceptional." Ch. xi.

"Rosamond was not one of those helpless girls who betray themselves unawares, and whose behavior is awkwardly driven by their impulses, instead of being steered by wary grace and propriety . . . Rosamond never showed any unbecoming knowledge, and was always that combination of correct sentiments, music, dancing, drawing, elegant note-writing, private album for extracted verse, and perfect blonde loveliness, which made the irresistible woman for the doomed man of that date . . . She was not in the habit of devising falsehoods, and if her statements were no direct clew to fact, why, they were not intended in that light—they were among her elegant accomplishments, intended to please. Nature had inspired many arts in finishing Mrs. Lemon's favourite pupil, who by general consent (Fred's excepted) was a rare compound of beauty, cleverness, and amiability." Ch. xxvii.

She holds herself above the young men of Middlemarch, but is attracted by Dr. Lydgate's superior breeding and connexions, falls as much in love with him as her self-centred nature will permit, and marries him without having the slightest understanding of his nobility of character and mind, and with no sympathy with his high aims in his profession. Worldly success measured in terms of income and social prestige is the only ambition which she can understand; she demands to be kept in luxury, refuses to yield to any of Lydgate's wishes, and to all of his attempts to explain to her his needs and his professional aims she opposes a gentle, inflexible obstinacy before which he is helpless. In the end he has to sacrifice his high ideals and scientific ambition and move to London in order to make the money necessary to give her the social position she craves. She never understands the ruin which she has made of his life, and continues to regard him as a person of mistaken ideas who needs the balance of her common sense.

VINCY, MR. WALTER. Mayor of Middlemarch; a manufacturer, a jolly, easy-going man, much given to hospitality and easily ruled by his wife and daughter. *Mid.* x–xiv, xvi, xxii–xxiv, xxvi–xxvii, xxxi, xxxiv–xxxvi, xl, li–lii, lvi, lviii–lix, lxiii, lxvii, lxix, lxxiv–lxxv, lxxvii, lxxxv. "Apart from his dinners and his coursing, Mr. Vincy, blustering as he was, had as little of his own way as if he had been a prime minister; the force of circumstances was easily too much for him, as it is for most pleasure-loving florid men." Ch. xxxvi.

VIXEN. Bartle Massey's dog, "a brown-and-tan coloured bitch, of that wise looking breed with short legs and long body, known to an unmechanical generation as turn-spits." *Adam B.* xxi, xl, xlii.

"VOI, CHE SAPETE" (*Real*). One of the songs which Rosamond Vincy sings. *Mid.* xvi. *Note.*—By Mozart.

VOLTIMAND. *P.—C. B. P.*

VOLVOX. The critic of the *Monitor*, who, according to Vorticella, contradicts himself in his review of her book. *T. S.* xv.

VORSTADT, THE. A suburban theatre in Vienna, where Mirah Cohen had sung. *D. D.* xx, lxii.

VORSTADT THEATRE, DRESDEN. *D. D.* lxii.

VORTICELLA. "A portly lady walking in silk attire," the authoress of a book entitled "The Channel Islands, with Notes and an Appendix", which she allows no one to forget. *T. S.* xv.

VULCANY, MRS. One of Mrs. Davilow's neighbours. *D. D.* iii, v–vi, xi.

VYAN. One of Fred Vincy's acquaintances. *Mid.* xii.

W

WACE, MR. Rich brewer in Treby Magna, a jolly, open-handed man. *F. H.* iii, vi, xx, xxiv, xxxi, xxxiii. Epilogue.

"WAGGON OVERTHROWN." Inn at Treddleston, patronized by Thias Bede. *Adam B.* iv, xxxviii.

WAGSTAFF, MRS. Mr. Tryan's landlady, noted for her dingy house and dubious cookery. *J. R.* iii, xi, xxv–xxvi.

WAKEFIELD, JIM, *called* GENTLEMAN WAKEFIELD. A farmer who used to make no difference between Sundays and week days. *Adam B.* xviii.

WAKEM, MRS. EMILY. Mr. Wakem's deceased wife. *M. F.* Bk. 3, vii; Bk. 6, vii.

WAKEM, JOHN. Philip's father; a shrewd, prosperous lawyer, fond of his son. *M. F.* Bk. 1, ii–iii, vii; Bk. 2, ii, vii; Bk. 3, vii–viii; Bk. 4, ii; Bk. 5, i, vi–vii; Bk. 6, v–ix, xii; Bk. 7, iii.

"Wakem was not a mere man of business: he was considered a pleasant fellow in the upper circles of St. Ogg's—chatted amusingly over his port-wine, did a little amateur farming, and had certainly been an excellent husband and father: at church, when he went there, he sat under the handsomest of mural monuments erected to the memory of his wife. Most men would have married again under his circumstances, but he was said to be more tender to his deformed son than most men were to their best-shapen off-spring." Bk. 3, vii.

In Mr. Tulliver's lawsuits, Mr. Wakem manages the cases for his opponents, hence Mr. Tulliver regards him as a creation of Old Harry. His vindictiveness towards Mr. Tulliver leads him to buy Dorlcote Mill when Mr. Tulliver fails.

WAKEM, PHILIP. Maggie Tulliver's lover, a shy and sensitive hump-back; a clever artist. *M. F.* Bk. 1, vii; Bk. 2, ii–vii; Bk. 3, vii; Bk. 5, i, iii–v; Bk. 6, i–iv, vi–x, xiii; Bk. 7, iii.

He and Tom Tulliver are at school together, and it is there that he meets Maggie and the two become friends. In spite of the enmity between the two families, he later prevails on Maggie to renew this friendship and they meet secretly in the Red Deeps to read and talk and he becomes her accepted lover. They are parted for a time but his love for her is his strongest feeling and he believes that he has overcome most of the obstacles in their way until Maggie and Stephen Guest fall in love.

Note.—M. d'Albert Durade, George Eliot's landlord during her stay at Geneva, is said to have been the original of some traits in the character of Philip Wakem. He was a man of great refinement, an artist and musician, small and with a humped back. (*See* Blind, *George Eliot*, p. 70; Browning, *Life of George Eliot*, p. 81.)

WAKLEY (*Hist.*). A medical reformer of whom Dr. Sprague disapproves. *Mid.* xvi.

Note.—Thomas Wakley (1795–1862), a surgeon and medical reformer, founder of the *Lancet*. He attacked hospital administration and agitated for the reform of the College of Surgeons.

WALL, MARY. Mrs. Holt's maiden name. *See* HOLT, MRS. MARY.

WALPURGA, FRÄULEIN. Armgart's humble and self-effacing cousin, who serves Armgart with uncomplaining affection in the days of her brilliant success, and after Armgart loses her voice rouses her from her despair by showing her the claims of others. *P.*—*Armg.* i, iii–v.

WALSH, MR. The curate who succeeds Mr. Tryan at Paddiford Common. *J. R.* xxvii–xxviii.

WALSINGHAM, MISS. *Mid.* lxxxiv.

WANCHESTER. Town in Wessex near the home of Gwendolen Harleth. *D. D.* iii–v, ix, xiii, xxvi, lxix.

WARBURTON. A scholar whose assertions on the Egyptian mysteries Mr. Casaubon intends to correct. *Mid.* xxix.

"WARM WHISPERING THROUGH THE SLENDER OLIVE LEAVES." One of Pablo's songs, in the *Spanish Gypsy. Sp. G.* i.

WARREN, MR. Sir Christopher Cheverel's valet. *Mr. G.'s L. S.* ii–iv, vii, xiv–xv, xix.

WARRENS, THE. The farm near Raveloe where the Lammeters live. *S. M.* vi, xv, xvii.

WARSON WAKE. Village five miles from Hayslope where Lisbeth Bede's sister had lived. *Adam B.* x.

WATLING, LORD. *Amos B.* vi.[1]

WAULE. Mrs. Waule's deceased husband, who had money. *Mid.* xii.

WAULE, ELIZABETH, JOANNA, AND REBECCA. Mrs. Waule's daughters; "all dark and ugly." *Mid.* xii.

WAULE, MRS. JANE. Mr. Featherstone's rich sister; a disagreeable, greedy woman, anxious for her brother's money. *Mid.* xii, xxxii–xxxv, liii, lvi.

WAULE, JOHN. Son of Mrs. Waule; a bore. *Mid.* xii, xiv.

WEBBE. Doctor from Crabsley. *Mid.* xlv.

"WEDDING PSALM" (*Real*). The psalm which caused a row when sung in Shepperton Church. *Amos B.* i.
Note.—W. Whittingham's version of the 133rd Psalm, in the old version of the Psalter.

"WEIGHTS AND SCALES." Public-house in Frick. *Mid.* lvi.

WENGSTEIN, PRINCESS. *Amos B.* iii.

WESLEY, MR. (*Hist.*). A great Methodist preacher whom Dinah Morris had seen and heard when she was a little girl. *Adam B.* ii, xxxviii; mentioned *M. F.* Bk. 1, xii (John Wesley).
Note.—John Wesley (1703–91).

WESSEX The part of England in which the principal scene of *Daniel Deronda* is laid, where the Gascoignes and Davilows and Gwendolen Harleth live. *D. D.* iii, and later.

WEST, MR. Factor at Rosseter. *Adam B.* vi.

WEST ORCHARDS. Constituency represented by Mr. Fenn. *D. D.* xxxv.

WHALE, SCRAG. An explorer; a Cetacean of unanswerable authority, whom Mr. Merman discovers to be at issue with Grampus. *T. S.* iii.

WHALE, PROFESSOR SPERM N. A distinguished Cetacean from whose spirited article in an American newspaper Grampus first learns of Mr. Merman's book. *T. S.* iii.

WHARF, THE. *Mr. G.'s L. S.* i.

"WHEN FIRST I SAW THY FACE." (*Real*). A song which Will Ladislaw hums. *Mid.* xlvi.
Note.—"Since first I saw your face," an old song, with music by Thomas Ford, dating from 1607, which has retained its popularity during three centuries.

---

[1] Some Nuneaton lists give Lord Aylesford as his prototype. (Manuscript notes.)

"When the Heart of a Man is Oppressed with Care" (*Real*). Arthur Donnithorne's favourite air from the "Beggar's Opera". *Adam B.* xii.

Note.—A song in Gay's *Beggar's Opera* beginning "If the heart of a man is depressed with cares".

Whispering Stones. A point in Cardell Chase. *D. D.* xiv.

White Hart." Inn at Loamford where Jermyn tells Harold Transome of their relationship. *F. H.* xlvii.

White Hart." Inn at Middlemarch, from the balcony of which Mr. Brooke addresses the electors of Middlemarch. *Mid.* li, lxxix.

White Hoss." Inn. Mr. *G.'s L. S.* xxi.

White House. Home of the Jeromes in Milby. *J. R.* xiii, xxvi.

"The garden was one of those old-fashioned paradises which hardly exist any longer except as memories of our childhood: no finical separation between flower and kitchen garden there; no monotony of enjoyment for one sense to the exclusion of another; but a charming paradisiacal mingling of all that was pleasant to the eyes and good for food." Ch. viii.

Whitefield, George, Bust of. An ornament of Mr. Lyon's study, which is covered with green gauze because Esther can not bear its squint. *F. H.* v.

Note.—George Whitefield (1714–70). Just such a bust of Whitefield stood in the stair-case window of the Misses Franklin's school in Coventry where George Eliot was a pupil. Mr. Franklin was the original of Rufus Lyon. (See article in *Our Times*, June, 1881.) This bust still is in existence, and is now the property of Mr. Bernard Franklin, a grandson of Francis Franklin.

Whitlow. Town near Milby. *J. R.* iv, xvii.

Whittlecombe. Parish near Shepperton, of which Mr. Pugh is curate. *Amos B.* vi.

Note.—In the lists of originals prepared at Nuneaton after the publication of *Scenes of Clerical Life*, the original of Whittlecombe was given as Stockingford. (See Olcott, *George Eliot*, p. 15.)

"Widgeon's Purifying Pills." A medicine much esteemed in Middlemarch. *Mid.* xlv.

Wiener, Mr. Jeweller at Leubronn, at whose shop Gwendolen Harleth sells her necklace after she has lost at the gambling table. *D. D.* ii.

Wilberforce (*Hist.*). One of Mr. Brooke's early acquaintances, who worked at negro emancipation. *Mid.* ii, xlvi.

Note.—William Wilberforce (1759–1833), philanthropist and statesman who had dedicated himself to the abolition of the slave trade.

Wildfire. Godfrey Cass's hunter. *S. M.* iii–iv, viii–x.

Godfrey, in order to obtain some needed money, agrees to let his brother Dunsey sell Wildfire, but the latter, while engaged in this task, joins the hunt and meets with an accident in which Wildfire is killed.

WILLIAMSON, SARAH. A Methodist preacher at Leeds, with whom Dinah Morris stays. *Adam B.* xl.

WILLIS. Game-keeper. *F. H.* xiv.

WILLOUGHBY, MISS. A schoolmate of Rosamond Vincy's. *Mid.* xxxvi.

WILLOW BROOK. The brook in front of the Bede cottage, in Hayslope, in which Thias Bede, Adam's father, is drowned. *Adam. B.* iv–v, viii, x, l.

Note.—At the bottom of a slope near the cottage where the Evans family lived in Ellastone ("Hayslope") there is a brook, very like the "Willow Brook" of *Adam Bede*. (See Parkinson, *Scenes*, p. 90.)

WIMPLE. An evangelical clergyman. *F. H.* xxiii.

WIMPLE, MRS. One of Dr. Minchin's patients. *Mid.* xviii.

WINDSOR (*Real*). The town to which Hetty Sorrel journeys to find Arthur Donnithorne, only to learn that his regiment has been moved from there to Ireland. *Adam B.* xxxv–xxxvi.

Note.—Windsor, on the Thames about twenty-one miles from London, has both infantry and cavalry barracks.

WINSHIP. Auctioneer. *M. F.* Bk. 3, vii.

WINTHROP, AARON. The wheelwright's little son, and, later, Eppie's lover; a sturdy, manly fellow; a gardener. *S. M.* vi, x–xi, xiv, xvi, xix–xxi, Conclusion.

WINTHROP, BEN. Wheelwright and leader of the choir at Raveloe; "a large jocose-looking man," fond of a joke and a drink. *S. M.* vi, x–xi, xiii, Conclusion.

WINTHROP, MRS. DOLLY. The wheelwright's good wife, who helps Silas Marner to care for the child Eppie. *S. M.* x, xiii–xiv, xvi, xix, xxi, Conclusion.

"She was in all respects a woman of scrupulous conscience, so eager for duties that life seemed to offer them too scantily unless she rose at half-past four, though this threw a scarcity of work over the more advanced hours of the morning, which it was a constant problem with her to remove. Yet she had not the vixenish temper which is sometimes supposed to be a necessary condition of such habits; she was a very mild, patient woman, whose nature it was to seek out all the sadder and more serious elements of life, and pasture her mind upon them . . . She was a 'comfortable woman'—good-looking, fresh-complexioned, having her lips always slightly screwed, as if she felt herself in a sick-room with the doctor or the clergyman present." Ch. x.

When Silas Marner decides to keep the child Eppie, Dolly Winthrop is the one who helps him to bring her up. By encouraging him to talk of his early life and troubles, she helps him to get back his lost faith.

WIRY BEN. *See* CRANAGE, BEN.

WISE WOMAN AT TARLEY. Dealer in charms. *S. M.* ii, x.

WITHERINGTON. Place where Mr. Sargent used to be curate. *Amos B.* vi.

WOODCOCK, MR. An admirer of the Countess Czerlaski. *Amos B.* iii.

WOODCOCK, MRS. A Milby hostess who, after one experience, refused to invite the Countess Czerlaski to dinner. *Amos B.* iii.

Note.—In lists of originals of characters which were made in Nuneaton ("Milby") after the publication of the *Scenes of Clerical Life* the prototype of Mrs. Woodcock was said to be Mrs. Craddock. (*See* Olcott, *George Eliot*, p. 14.)

WOODS, MR. Butcher in Shepperton. *Amos B.* ii.[1]

WOOL, MRS. An acquaintance of Mrs. Glegg's, who "wears her lace before it is paid for". *M. F.* Bk. 1, vii; Bk. 7, iii.

"WOOLPACK." Public-house at Grimworth. *B. J.* ii–iii.

WORDSWORTH (*Hist.*). The poet, with whom Mr. Brooke had once dined at Cartwright's. *Mid.* ii.

Note.—William Wordsworth (1770–1850).

"(THE) WORLD IS GREAT, THE BIRDS ALL FLY FROM ME." One of Pablo's songs. *Sp. G.* ii.

WRENCH, MR. Medical attendant to the Vincy family; an irritable man, who shows great hostility to Lydgate after the latter replaces him in the Vincy family. *Mid.* xi, xv, xviii, xxvi–xxvii, xxxvi, xlv, lxiv, lxxi.

"Mr. Wrench was a small, neat, bilious man, with a well-dressed wig; he had a laborious practice, an irascible temper, a lymphatic wife, and seven children." Ch. xxvi.

WRIGHT. One of Mr. Brooke's servants. *Mid.* vi.

WRIGHT, JACOB. A Dissenter who kept a night school. *J. R.* viii.

WYBROW, CAPTAIN ANTHONY. Sir Christopher Cheverel's nephew and heir; a handsome, irreproachable young dandy, incapable of any strong emotion. *Mr. G.'s L. S.* ii, iv–vi, viii–xvi, xix.

"If this young man had been less elegant in his person, he would have been remarked for the elegance of his dress. But the perfections of his slim, well-proportioned figure were so striking that no one but a tailor could notice the perfections of his velvet coat; and his small white hands, with their blue veins and taper fingers, quite eclipsed the beauty of his lace ruffles. The face, however—it was difficult to say why—was certainly not pleasing. Nothing could be more delicate than the blond complexion—its bloom set off by the powdered hair—than the veined overhanging eyelids, which gave an indolent expression to the hazel eyes; nothing more finely cut than the transparent nostril and the short upper-lip. Perhaps the chin

---

[1] A Nuneaton list gives George Moreton as his prototype. (MS. notes.)

and lower jaw were too small for an irreproachable profile, but the defect was on the side of that delicacy and *finesse* which was the distinctive characteristic of the whole person, and which was carried out in the clear brown arch of the eyebrows, and the marble smoothness of the sloping forehead." Ch. ii.

He deliberately wins the love of Caterina, his uncle's penniless *protégée*, without intending to marry her. In response to his uncle's wishes he becomes engaged to the beauty, Miss Assher, and gives no thought to the suffering he causes Caterina. When her jealousy annoys him, his weak heart causes his death.

Note.—Charles Parker, nephew and heir of Sir Roger Newdigate (" Sir Christopher Cheverel ") was, in the matter of his personal appearance, his relation to a rich and childless uncle and his sudden death, the original of Captain Wybrow. Captain Wybrow's love affair with Caterina is purely fictitious, however, as Sally Shilton (" Caterina ") was only a child at the time of Charles Parker's marriage to Miss Anstruther (" Miss Assher "). (*See* Newdigate, *The Cheverels*, p. 228.)

WYLDE. Counsellor. *M. F.* Bk. 2, i–ii.

WYVERN, LADY. Wife of Lord Wyvern. *F. H.* xl.

WYVERN, LORD. One of the Transomes' neighbours. *F. H.* xx.

X

" X-SHIRE GAZETTE." Newspaper. *B. J.* ii.

Y

YAP. The Tulliver's white and brown terrier. *M. F.* Bk. 1, i, iv, vi; Bk. 2, vi.

YARICO. Grandcourt's black horse. *D. D.* xxvii.

" YE BANKS AND BRAES " (*Real*). An air which Fred Vincy practises on his flute. *Mid.* xi.

Note.—" Ye banks and braes o' bonnie Doone," a song with words by Robert Burns set to an older tune of uncertain origin.

YELLOW COAT SCHOOL, GRIMWORTH. *B. J.* ii.

YEW-TREE WALK. Mr. Casaubon's favourite walk in the grounds of Lowick Manor; it is in a little summer house near this walk that Dorothea finds him dead. *Mid.* xlii, xlviii.

Note.—A Yew-tree walk in the garden of Griff House, George Eliot's early home, served as the original of the Yew-tree walk at Lowick Manor, and a round stone table, now preserved at Bedworth Rectory, the home of the Reverend Frederic R. Evans (George Eliot's nephew) is pointed out as the original of the table on which Mr. Casaubon was leaning when he died.

YODDRELL. Farmer. *Mid.* lvi.

YORK (*Real*). The town to which Maggie Tulliver goes after she leaves Stephen Guest. *M. F.* Bk. 6, xiv; Bk. 7, i; *Mid.* mentioned xl.

Note.—The ancient walled city of York, capital of Yorkshire, is about 42 miles north-west of Gainsborough (the "St. Ogg's" where Maggie Tulliver lived.)

Z

ZACHARY. Pew-opener at Mr. Lyon's chapel in Treby Magna. *F. H.* xv, xxvi, xxxviii.

ZAGAL, EL (*Hist.*). The Moorish king, with whom Zarca and his Gypsies are allied for the taking of Bedmár. *Sp. G.* i–ii.

Note.—Abdullah el Zagal, Moslem king of Granada, 1484–9.

ZAMAËL. Angel; "the terrible, the angel of fierce death, of agony that comes in battle and in pestilence." *P.—D. M.*

ZARCA. A Gypsy chief, Fedalma's father. *Sp. G.* i–vi.

A man of lofty and resolute purpose, capable of putting the claims of his people ahead of all personal considerations, he aspires to fuse together the scattered bands of Gypsies in Spain and lead them to found a Gypsy nation in Africa. At the opening of the poem he is held prisoner by the Spaniards in Bedmár, where he sees the beautiful Fedalma, the Duke's betrothed, and recognizes her as his long lost daughter, who had been stolen in childhood by marauding Spaniards. Revealing himself to her, he sets before her the claims of her race and so works upon her with his force and eloquence that she agrees to leave Duke Silva, whom she loves devotedly, and to escape with her father and devote herself to the welfare of her race. After Duke Silva, unable to bear the loss of Fedalma, follows her to the Gypsy camp and for her sake joins the Gypsy band, deserting his post at Bedmár, Zarca, and his Moorish ally, El Zagal, attack and capture Bedmár. Zarca shows some moderation in his victory, although he condemns the inquisitor, Father Isidor, to death, and when Silva, frantic at Father Isidor's death and the thought that the loss of the town is due to his desertion of his post, stabs Zarca, the Gypsy protects him and will not allow his people to harm Silva. Dying, Zarca lays upon Fedalma the solemn duty of taking his place in the leadership of his people.

Note.—Frederic Harrison has suggested that some traits in the character of Zarca were drawn from Dr. Richard Congreve, the Positivist leader. (*See* article in the *Positivist Review*, vol. 10, p. 160.) Congreve himself once declared that the Spanish Gypsy was a "mass of Positivism".

ZECCA, OR MINT. Its car figures in the San Giovanni procession in Florence. *Rom.* viii.

"Improved taste, with Cecca to help it, had devised for the magnificent Zecca a triumphal car like a pyramidal catafalque, with ingenious wheels warranted to turn all corners easily. Round the base were living figures of saints and angels arrayed in sculpturesque fashion; and on the summit, at the height of thirty feet, well bound to an iron rod and holding an iron cross also firmly infixed, stood a living representative of St. John the Baptist."

Note.—The Mint occupied the site of the present Post Office, and the old Mint, the Zecca Vecchia, was behind the church of Santa Croce, but this was given up in **1252** when the new Mint was built.

ZÍNCALI. The Spanish Gypsies, Zarca's men. *Sp. G.* i–v.

ZIND. Fedalma's Gypsy nurse, who lost her when she was a baby. *Sp. G.* i.

ZIPHIUS. A Cetacean of unanswerable authority, whom Mr. Merman finds to be at issue with the great Grampus. *T. S.* iii.

ZUZUMOTZIS. A subject of research on which Mr. Merman finds the great Grampus in error. *T. S.* iii.

BOOKS MENTIONED IN THE NOVELS AND STORIES

The following list contains the titles of the principal books read by George Eliot's characters or referred to in some way in the novels and stories. It does not claim to be absolutely complete, the main omissions being references so general in character as to indicate the author only and not some particular work, and all references to the Bible. As the interest of a list of the books mentioned by George Eliot lies principally in the use she makes of them to indicate character, local colour, etc., the books have been given here in just the way in which she refers to them, with no attempt to enter them in correct catalogue form, except that several works by one author have been brought together. In this latter case reference has been made from the form used in the novel. Sufficient information to identify the books is given in the notes.

Aeschylus (Foulis). *Adam B.* xvi.
    Aeschyli tragoediae quae extant septem, printed by R. Foulis in Glasgow in 1746. 2 v.

Aeschylus (Potter's). *L. V.* i.
    The *Tragedies* of Aeschylus, translated by Robert Potter, first published 1777.

Aesop's " Fables ". *M. F.* Bk. 1, iii.

Aldrich's " Logic ". *M. F.* Bk. 4, iii.
    The *Artis logicae compendium*, by Henry Aldrich, first published 1691.

Alleyne's " Alarm ". *F. H.* xxvi.
    An alarm to the unconverted, by Joseph Alleine, first published 1672, and frequently reprinted. Also published under the title: *Sure Guide to Heaven*.

" Animated nature." *M. F.* Bk. 1, iv.
    Animated nature; or Elements of the natural history of animals, by William Bingley, published 1814.

" Anne of Geierstein." *See* Scott, Sir Walter.

" Antigone." *D. D.* xxxii.
    Antigone, a play by Sophocles.

Bailey's "Dictionary". *Adam B.* xix; *Mid.* xv.
Universal etymological dictionary, by Nathan Bailey, first published 1721.

Baxter's "Saints' everlasting rest". *M. F.* Bk. 1, xii; Bk. 7, iii.
By Richard Baxter, first published 1649.

"Beauties of the Spectator." *M. F.* Bk. 4, iii.
This may be *Beauties of the Spectators, Tatlers, and Guardians connected and digested,* first published in London 1763. There was also a selection *Beauties of the Spectator, Tatler, and Guardian,* selected by G. Hamonière, published in Paris 1819.

Blair's "Rhetoric". *M. F.* Bk. 3, v.
Lectures on rhetoric and belles lettres, by Hugh Blair, first published 1783.

Boccaccio. "Decamerone." *Rom.* xlix, lxi; *P.—Lisa.*

"Bridgewater Treatises." *M. F.* Bk. 6, ii.
The Bridgewater Treatises on the power, wisdom, and goodness of God as manifested in the Creation, eight treatises written by various men, published 1833–6 from a fund given by the Earl of Bridgewater. Buckland's Treatise, which is mentioned, was *Geology and Mineralogy considered with reference to natural theology* (Treatise 6).

Brown, Robert. "Microscopic observations on the pollen of plants." *Mid.* xvii.
A brief account of microscopic observations . . . on the particles contained in the pollen of plants, by Robert Brown, published 1828.

Browne's "Pastorals". *D. D.* vi.
Britannia's pastorals, by William Browne, Book 1–2, first published 1613–16, Book 3 not published until 1852.

Bulwer. "Mr. Bulwer's Eugene Aram." *F. H.* vii.
Eugene Aram, by Sir Edward Bulwer-Lytton, first published 1832.

Bunyan's "Holy War". *Adam B.* xix.
By John Bunyan, published 1682.

Bunyan's "Pilgrim's Progress". *Adam B.* xiv, xix; *M. F.* Bk. 1, iii; Bk. 3, vi; *Mid.* iv, lxxxv.
Pilgrim's progress, by John Bunyan, was first published 1678.

Buondelmonte, Christoforo. "Isolario." *Rom.* vi.
His *Librum insularum archipelagi.*

Burke. "On the sublime and beautiful." *J. R.* iii.
The *Philosophical inquiry into the origin of our ideas on the sublime and the beautiful,* by Edmund Burke, first published 1756.

Byron's "Poems". *F. H.* v; *M. F.* Bk. 4, iii.

Byron. "Childe Harold." *F. H.* v.
> *Childe Harold's pilgrimage*, by Lord Byron, first published 1812–18.

Byron. "The Corsair." *B. J.* ii (title only).
> Written 1814.

Byron. "Siege of Corinth." *B. J.* ii (title only).
> Written 1815.

"**Catechism of geography.**" *See* Pinnock.

"**Christian Year.**" *See* Keble.

"**Chrysal, or the adventures of a guinea.**" *Mid.* xv.
> A novel by Charles Johnstone, first published 1768.

Ciriaco. "Itineraria." *Rom.* vi.
> The *Itinerarium* of Pizzicolli Ciriaco.

"**Corinne.**" *M. F.* Bk. 5, iv.
> *Corinne ; ou, l'Italie*, by Madame de Staël, first published 1807, and translated into English the same year.

"**The Corsair.**" *See* Byron.

Crayon, Geoffrey. "Sketch book." *M. F.* Bk. 6, ii.
> *The sketch book of Geoffrey Crayon, gent.*, by Washington Irving, first published 1820.

Culpepper. *Mid.* xii.
> Probably the *Works* of Nicholas Culpeper or Culpepper.

Davy's "Agricultural chemistry". *Mid.* ii.
> *Elements of agricultural chemistry*, by Sir Humphry Davy, published 1813.

Defoe, Daniel. "History of the Devil." *M. F.* Bk. 1, iii.
> *Political history of the Devil*, by Daniel Defoe, first 1726. The work passed through many editions, but the edition which Maggie Tulliver read was that of Exeter: Davies and Eldridge, 1815; new edition with engravings London, published by Thomas Kelly, 1817. This is the only edition containing the picture of the witch which Maggie points out to Mr. Riley, and it was, moreover, a book of George Eliot's own childhood. Her own copy of it is now owned by her nephew, the Rev. Frederic Rawlins Evans.

"**Delectus.**" *M. F.* Bk. 2, i; Bk. 6, iii.
> *Delectus sententiarum et historiarum*, by Richard Valpy.

"**De Senectute.**" *M. F.* Bk. 1, ii.
> One of Cicero's essays.

"**Don Carlos.**" *D. D.* lii.
> A tragedy by J. C. F. von Schiller, completed in **1787.**

"Don Quixote." *L. V.* i.
>   *Don Quixote de La Mancha*, by Cervantes, published 1605–15, translated into English 1612–20.

"Economy of human life." *M. F.* Bk. 4, iii.
>   *The œconomy of human life, translated from an Indian manuscript, written by an ancient Bramin*, by Robert Dodsley, first published 1751.

Erckmann-Chatrian's "Histoire d'un conscrit". *D. D.* xviii.
>   *Histoire d'un conscrit de 1813*, by E. Erckmann and P. A. Chatrian, published 1864.

"Essay of Elia, The praise of Chimney-sweeps." *D. D.* xxxix.
>   By Charles Lamb.

"Eton Grammar." *J. R.* ii ; *M. F.* Bk. 2, 1.
>   The *Eton Latin grammar*, a revision of Lilly and Colet's Latin grammar of 1577, which went through many editions.

Euclid. *M. F.* Bk. 2, i ; Bk. 4, iii.
>   *Elements of geometry*, of Euclid.

Euclid (Simson's). *D. D.* xxxiii.
>   *Elements* of Euclid, edited by Robert Simson, published 1756.

Eutropius. *M. F.* Bk. 4, iii.
>   The *Breviarium historiae Romanae* of Flavius Eutropius.

Falconer's "Shipwreck". *J. R.* iii.
>   *The Shipwreck*, a poem by William Falconer, first published 1762.

"Father Clement." *J. R.* iii.
>   A novel by Grace Kennedy, published 1823.

"Faublas." *Mr. G.'s L. S.* ii.
>   *Les amours du chevalier de Faublas*, by Louvet de Couvrai, first published 1787–90.

"Female Scripture characters." *Mid.* iii.
>   *Female Scripture characters ; exemplifying female virtues*, by Frances Elizabeth King, first published 1813.

Firenzuola. "Della bellezza delle donne." *Rom.* xix.
>   *Dialogo delle bellezze delle donne*, by Agnolo Firenzuolo, printed in 1548 in an edition of his Prose.

Gregory's "Letters". *M. F.* Bk. 4, iii.
>   *Letters to a friend on the evidences, doctrines, and duties of the Christian religion*, by Olinthus G. Gregory, published 1811.

"Gulliver." *Mid.* xv.
>   *Gulliver's travels*, by Jonathan Swift, first published 1726.

Herodotus. *Mid.* xlviii.
>   The *History* of Herodotus.

"**History of the decline and fall of the Roman Empire.**" *M. F.* Bk. 2, i.
    By Edward Gibbon, first published 1776–88.

Homer. " That fine Homer which was among the early glories of the Florentine Press." *Rom.* Proem.
    The famous Homer of 1488 in 2 v. was printed in Florence, December, 1488, at the expense of the brothers Nerli.

Homer. " Iliad." *M. F.* Bk. 2, iv (title only).

Homer. "**Odyssey.**" *M.F.* Bk. 2, iii (title only).

Hook. " One of Theodore Hook's novels." *M. F.* Bk. 2, iv.

Horace (Francis's). *L. V.* i.
    The translation by Philip Francis. *Odes, Epodes, and Carmen seculare*, issued 1742 ; *Satires, Epistles, and Art of poetry*, issued 1746 ; the whole re-issued 1747.

" **Horae Paulinae.**" *M. F.* Bk. 3, iv.
    By William Paley, first published 1790.

Howe's " **Living Temple.**" *F. H.* x.
    The living temple of God, by John Howe, first published 1675.

" **Iliad.**" *See* Homer.

" **Ivanhoe.**" *See* Scott, Sir Walter.

Jebb, Bishop. " **Memoirs.**" *Amos B.* iii.
    Probably *Thirty years correspondence between Bishop Jebb and Alexander Knox*, published 1834.

Johnson. " **The Rambler.**" *Mid.* li.
    The Rambler ; a periodical paper, March 20, 1750–March 14, 1752, edited by Samuel Johnson.

Josephus. *Mid.* xii.
    The Works of Flavius Josephus, including *Antiquities of the Jews* and *History of the Jewish war*.

Juvenal. *Rom.* iii.
    The *Satirae* of Juvenal.

Keble's " **Christian Year** ". *M. F.* Bk. 4, v (title only) ; *Mid.* xlviii.
    The Christian Year, religious poems by John Keble, first published 1827.

" **Keepsake.**" *M. F.* Bk. 4, iii ; *Mid.* xxvii.
    A literary annual published in London, 1827–57.

Klopstock's " **Messiah** ". *J. R.* iii ; *Mid.* xii.
    Das Messias, by F. G. Klopstock. There are various English translations.

" **Lalla Rookh.**" *B. J.* ii ; *Mid.* xvi.
    Lalla Rookh, an Oriental romance, poem by Thomas Moore, first published 1817.

" Life of Dr. Doddridge." *F. H.* x.
 Probably the *Correspondence and diary* of Philip Doddridge, published 1829–31. 5 v.

" Life of Henry Martyn." *J. R.* xxiii.
 Memoir of Rev. Henry Martyn, by John Sargent, first published 1819.

" Life of Legh Richmond." *J. R.* iii.
 Memoir of the Rev. Legh Richmond, by T. S. Grimshaw, first published 1828.

Louis' new book on Fever. *Mid.* xvi.
 Recherches anatomiques, pathologiques et thérapeutiques sur la maladie connue sous les noms de . . . *fièvre putride, typhoïde* . . . by Pierre C. A. Louis, published 1828.

" Lyrical ballads." *F. H.* i.
 Lyrical ballads, by William Wordsworth and S. T. Coleridge, first published 1798.

Maimon, Salomon. " Lebensgeschichte." *D. D.* xxxiii.

Mangnall's " Questions ". *B. J.* ii ; *Mid.* xxiii.
 Historical and miscellaneous questions, by Richmal Mangnall, first published 1800.

Mason " On self-knowledge ". *J. R.* iii.
 Self-knowledge, a treatise shewing the nature and benefit of that important science, by John Mason, published 1745.

Medici, Lorenzo de'. " Nencia da Barberino." *Rom.* x.
 A poem by Lorenzo the Magnificent containing descriptions of nature and rustic manners.

" Memoirs of Felix Neff." *J. R.* iii.
 Probably *A memoir of Felix Neff*, by William Stephen Gilley, published 1832, or *Memorials of Felix Neff*, by T. S. Ellerby, 1833.

Miller. " Anecdotes . . . to be procured only of Joe Miller." *J. R.* ii.
 Joe Miller's jests; or The wit's vade-mecum, compiled by J. Mottley, first published 1739, and frequently reprinted.

Moore. Dr. Moore's **" Zeluco ".** *Adam B.* xii.
 Zeluco. Various views of human nature, by John Moore, published 1789.

More, Hannah. " Sacred dramas." *J. R.* iii.
 Published 1782.

Murray, Lindley. *Mid.* xxiii–xxiv.
 English grammar, by Lindley Murray, published 1795, and many later editions.

Nonnus. "**Dionysiaca.**" *Rom.* v.
  A poem in forty-eight books on the history of Bacchus, by Nonnus of Panopolis, who lived in the fifth century.
"**Odyssey.**" *See* Homer.
Ovid, Story in. *Rom*, xviii; Ovid's works mentioned xlix.
  A story from the *Metamorphoses* of Ovid.
Pascal's "Pensées". *Mid.* i, xlviii.
  Pensées sur la religion et sur quelques autres sujets, by Blaise Pascal.
Pausanias. *Rom.* vi, xxxviii.
  Pausaniae Descriptio Graeciae.
"**Pickwick papers.**" *Amos. B.* vi.
  The posthumous papers of the Pickwick Club, by Charles Dickens, 1837.
"**Pilgrim's progress.**" *See* Bunyan.
Pinnock. *M. F.* Bk. 6, ii.
  William Pinnock's *Catechisms* on many subjects were published from 1821, and were used as school books.
Pinnock. "**Catechism of geography.**" *M. F.* Bk. 1, xi (title only).
  By William Pinnock.
Mrs. Piozzi's Recollections of Johnson. *Mid.* xxv.
  Anecdotes of the late Samuel Johnson, by Mrs. Hester Lynch Piozzi, first published 1786.
"**Pirate.**" *See* Scott, Sir Walter.
Plautus. "**Aulularia.**" *Rom.* v.
  A Latin comedy of Plautus.
Pliny's "Natural History". *D. D.* lviii; *Rom.* vi (no title).
Plutarch. *L. V.* i.
  The *Lives* by Plutarch.
Politian's "Miscellanea". *Rom.* v, vii.
  The *Miscellanea* of Angelo Ambrosini *known as* Poliziano or Politian, was published in 1489 in Florence.
Poliziano's [i.e. Politian] "**Orfeo**". *Rom.* xxxix.
  A lyrical drama by Poliziano or Politian.
Poliziano [i.e. Politian]. "**A commentator on the Pandects.**" *Rom.* v.
  The *Ragionamento istorico sopra la collazioni delle florentine pandette* of Politian.
"**Poor Richard's Almanac.**" *Adam B.* xix.
  Poor Richard's Almanac, by Benjamin Franklin, was published 1732–57.
Pope's "Essay on Man". *Mid.* xviii.

"Portrait Gallery." *M. F.* Bk. 4, iii.
    This may have been the *National Portrait Gallery of illustrious and eminent personages of the nineteenth century*, by William Jerdan, published 1830–4, which contains a portrait of George IV (mentioned in *Mill on the Floss*) in v. 2 (1830).

"Pug's tour of Europe." *M. F.* Bk. 1, iv.
    Pug's tour through Europe, published about 1824.

Pulci, Luigi. *Rom.* iii, vi, xlix, lvii.
    Il Morgante Maggiore, by Luigi Pulci. The first complete edition containing twenty-eight cantos was published 1482.

Rasselas. *J. R.* iii; *M. F.* Bk. 4, iii; *Mid.* xv.
    A novel by Dr. Samuel Johnson, first published 1759.

René. *F. H.* x.
    René, by Chateaubriand.

Rucellai, Bernardo. "An excellent, learned book of a new topographical sort, about ancient Rome." *Rom.* xxxviii.
    De urbe Roma, by Oricellarius (Bernardo Rucellai).

Sacchetti. "Franco Sacchetti's book." *Rom.* xii.
    The *Novelle*, by Franco Sacchetti.

Scott's "Force of truth". *J. R.* iii.
    By Thomas Scott, first published 1779.

Scott's "Novels". *M. F.* Bk. 4, iii.
    The novels of Sir Walter Scott.

Scott, Sir Walter. "Anne of Geierstein or The Maid of the mist, by the author of Waverley." *Mid.* xxxii.

Scott, Sir Walter. "Ivanhoe." *D. D.* xvii (title only); *Mid.* xxxii, lvii.

Scott, Sir Walter. "The Pirate." *M. F.* Bk. 5, i (title only).

Scott, Sir Walter. "Woodstock." *F. H.* xiv (title only).

"Siege of Corinth." *See* Byron.

Sismondi's "History of the Italian republics." *D. D.* xvi.
    Histoire des républiques italiennes au moyen âge, by Simonde di Sismondi, 1809–18.

Smollett. "Humphrey Clinker." *Mid.* xxx.
    The expedition of Humphrey Clinker, by Tobias George Smollett, first published 1771.

Smollett. "Roderick Random." *Mid.* xxx.
    The adventures of Roderick Random, by Tobias George Smollett, published 1748.

Southey's "Life of Cowper". *M. F.* Bk. 6, ii.
    Prefixed to Robert Southey's edition of William Cowper's Works, published 1836–7.

Southey's " Peninsular war ". *F. H.* vii (" the last great prose work of Mr. Southey ") ; *Mid.* ii.
    History of the Peninsular war, by Robert Southey, first published 1823–32.

Southey's " Thalaba ". *F. H.* i.
    Thalaba the destroyer, by Robert Southey, published 1801.

" Speaker." *M. F.* Bk. 2, iii.
    Probably *The juvenile speaker ; or Dialogues and miscellaneous pieces in prose and verse,* by Mary Weightman, first published 1787.

Tasso. **" Gerusalemme Liberata."** *D. D.* v.

Taylor's " Holy living and dying ". *Adam B.* xix ; *Mid.* i (no title) ; *M. F.* Bk. 1, iii (Jeremy Taylor's).
    The rule and exercises of holy living, by Jeremy Taylor, appeared in 1650, and *The rule and exercises of holy dying* in 1651.

" Télémaque." *M. F.* Bk. 4, iii.
    A novel by Fénelon, first published 1699.

Thomas à Kempis. *M. F.* Bk. 4, iii.
    His *Imitation of Christ* written in Latin and frequently translated into English.

Tillotson's " Sermons ". *Mr. G.'s L. S.* xi.
    Sermons of John Tillotson, published 1695–1704.

Traversari, Ambrogio. *Rom.* vi.
    The *Hodoeporicon* of Ambrogio Traversari ; his journal relating his travels visiting monasteries in Italy in 1430–4.

" Valentine and Orson." *Adam B.* xix.
    An old romance, authorship and date unknown.

Villani. " The honest pages of Giovanni Villani." *Rom.* v.
    The *Croniche* of Giovanni Villani (d. 1348), first published 1537.

Virgil. **" Aeneid."** *M. F.* Bk. 1, iii ; Bk. 4, iii ; *Rom.* v (" the great poem of Virgil ").

Virgil (Dryden's). *J. R.* iii.
    John Dryden's translation of Virgil was first published in 1697.

Wesley's abridgement of Madame Guyon's life. *Adam B.* l.
    Extract of the life of Madame Guion, by John Wesley, published 1776.

" Woodstock." *See* Scott, Sir Walter.

Young. " Arthur Young's books." *Adam B.* xvi.
    Arthur Young wrote numerous books on agricultural subjects, which are the books referred to.

Zunz. " Die synagogale poesie des mittelalters." *D. D.* xlii.
    By Leopold Zunz.

INDEX TO ORIGINALS

The names of real persons appearing in the novels and stories under their own names and characters are not included in this list.

Original	Character or Place
Albert-Durade, Monsieur d'	Wakem, Philip.
Allbutt, Sir T. Clifford	Lydgate, Tertius.
Anstruther, Lady	Assher, Lady.
Anstruther, Jane.	Assher, Beatrice.
Arbury Hall	Cheverel Manor.
Ashbourne.	Oakbourne.
Astley	Knebley.
Astley Castle	Knebley Abbey.
Astley Church	Knebley Church.
Aylesford, Lord	Watling, Lord.
Baines	Bates, Mr.
Baker (verger)	Fitchett, Mr.
Barnacle, Mr.	Gruby, Mr.
Barton, Mrs. Milly (name only)	Barton, Mrs. Milly.
Bellairs, Reverend Mr.	Fellowes, Mr.
Bond, Mr.	Pratt, Mr. Richard.
Bond Gate	Friar's Gate.
Bourne, Dr.	Madeley, Dr.
Bray, Mrs. Hennell, Sara	Meyrick sisters.
Briars	Camp Villa.
"Bromley-Davenport Arms"	"Donnithorne Arms."
Browning, Oscar	Lydgate, Tertius.
Buchanan, J. W.	Dempster, Robert.
Buchanan, Mrs. Nancy	Dempster, Janet.
Bucknill, Mr.	Pilgrim, Mr.
Bucknill, Rev. W. S.	Furness, Rev. Mr.
Bulkington, Warwickshire (suggested)	Raveloe.

Original	Character or Place
Bull, of Griff	Blacksmith, Popish.
Bull, Miss	Phipps, Miss.
Bull, Mr.	Phipps, Mr.
Bull, Mrs.	Phipps, Mrs.
"Bull Hotel," Nuneaton	"Red Lion," Milby.
Burchiello	Nello.
Burchiello's shop	"Apollo and the Razor."
Burton, Mr.	Budd, Mr.
Calwich Abbey (suggested only)	Donnithorne Chase.
Chilvers Coton	Shepperton.
Chilvers Coton Church	Shepperton Church.
Chilvers Coton Workhouse	The "College", Shepperton.
Church Street, Nuneaton	Orchard Street, Milby.
Club in Red Lion Square	"Philosophers," at Hand and Banner.
Cohn, or Kohn (watchmaker)	Cohen, Ezra Mordecai.
Congreve, Dr. Richard	Zarca.
Corley Hall	Hall Farm.
Coventry	Middlemarch.
Coventry (suggested only)	Treby Magna.
Cow Lane Chapel, Coventry	Malthouse Yard, Treby Magna.
Craddock, Mr.	Landor, Mr.
Craddock, Mrs.	Woodcock, Mrs.
Craddock, Mrs. (suggested)	Pettifer, Mrs.
Craddock, Mr. T. J.	Landor, Mr. Eustace.
"Crown and Anchor," Gainsborough	"Anchor Tavern," St. Ogg's.
Derby	Stoniton.
Derby Town Hall	Court Room, Stoniton.
Derbyshire	Stonyshire.
Dilke, Emilia Francis (Strong), Lady	Brooke, Dorothea.
Disraeli, Mrs.	Halm-Eberstein, Princess.
Docker, Mr.	Parry, Mr.
Dovedale	Eagledale.
"Eagre" or "Hygre", River Trent	"Eagre," The Floss.

ORIGINAL	CHARACTER OR PLACE
Ebdell, Reverend Bernard Gilpin	Gilfil, Reverend Maynard.
Eliot, George	Brooke, Dorothea.
Eliot, George	Lyon, Esther.
Eliot, George	"Sister."
Eliot, George	Tulliver, Maggie.
Ellastone, Staffordshire	Hayslope, Loamshire.
Ellastone Church.	Hayslope Church.
Ellastone Green	Hayslope Green.
Evans, Christiana	Brooke, Celia.
Evans, Christiana	Deane, Lucy.
Evans, Elizabeth.	Morris, Dinah.
Evans, George (suggested only)	Bede, Matthias.
Evans, Isaac	"Brother."
Evans, Isaac	Tulliver, Tom.
Evans, Mary (suggested only)	Bede, Lisbeth.
Evans, Mary Ann. *See* Eliot, George.	
Evans, Robert	Bede, Adam.
Evans, Robert	Garth, Caleb.
Evans, Robert	Hackit, Mr.
Evans, Robert	Stradivarius.
Evans, Mrs. Robert	Hackit, Mrs.
Evans, Mrs. Robert	Poyser, Mrs.
Evans, Samuel	Bede, Seth.
Everard, Mrs.	Glegg, Mrs. Jane.
Everhard, Mr.	Jerome, Mr.
Farn, John	Holt, Felix.
Fisher, Rev. John	Cleves, Rev. Martin.
Fitchett, Mrs.	Short, Mrs.
Franklin, Reverend Francis	Lyon, Reverend Rufus.
Gainsborough	St. Ogg's.
Garner, Mrs.	Deane, Mrs. Susan.
Greenway, Mr.	Pittman, Mr.
Griff Bottoms	Red Deeps.
Griff House	Dorlcote Mill (interior).
Griff House garden	Hall Farm garden.
Gurney, Edmund	Deronda, Daniel.

Original	Character or Place
Gwyther, Mrs. Emma	Barton, Milly.
Gwyther, Reverend John	Barton, Reverend Amos.
Hackett, Mr.	Spratt, Mr.
Hake, Reverend Henry	Gilfil, Reverend Maynard.
Harper, Mr.	Farquhar, Squire.
Harris, Mr.	Brand, Mr.
Hartnill, Mr.	Pickard, Mr.
Hennell, Sara. *See* Bray, Mrs.	
Higham	Tripplegate.
Hill, The Misses	Linnet, The Misses.
Hill, Mrs.	Linnet, Mrs.
Hinks, Mr.	Tomlinson, Mr.
Hoke, Reverend Mr.	Duke, Reverend Archibald.
Hollick, Mr. and Mrs.	Bond, Mr. and Mrs.
Hollick, Tom	Tulliver, Edward.
Homburg	Leubronn.
Hughes, Reverend Mr.	Crewe, Reverend Mr.
Hutchings (or Hutchins), Mrs.	Patten, Mrs.
Ibbetson, Miss	Gibbs, Miss Janet.
Isabel, Countess	Czerlaski, Countess.
Jaques, William	Jakin, Bob.
Johnson, Mrs.	Pullet, Mrs. Sophy.
Jones, Reverend Mr. (suggested only)	Tryan, Reverend Edgar.
King, Reverend Mr.	Ely, Mr.
Lewes, George Henry	Ladislaw, Will.
Lincoln	Lindum.
Liszt	Klesmer, Herr Julius.
Maskery (name only)	Maskery, Will.
Massey, Bartle	Massey, Bartle.
Massey, Gerald	Holt, Felix.
Milby Mill (name only)	Milby.
Mill near Griff	Dorlcote Mill.
Miller, Dr.	Madeley, Dr.
Moreton, George	Woods.
Morris, Mrs. George	Gibbs, Miss Janet.
Morton	Tofton.

Original	Character or Place
Motta, Dominic	Sarti.
Newdegate, Rt. Hon. Charles Newdigate	Oldinport, Mr.
Newdegate, Sir Richard, first baronet	Cheverel, Sir Anthony.
"Newdegate Arms"	"Oldinport Arms."
Newdigate, Francis Parker	Donnithorne, Squire.
Newdigate, Francis Parker	Oldinport, Mr.
Newdigate, Hester Margaretta (Mundy), Lady	Cheverel, Lady.
Newdigate, Sir Roger, fifth baronet	Cheverel, Sir Christopher.
Norbury	Norburne.
Nottingham	Laceham.
Nuneaton	Milby.
Nuneaton Vicarage	Milby Vicarage.
Old Hall, Gainsborough	Old Hall, St. Ogg's.
Overbeck, Johann Friedrich	Naumann, Adolf.
Parker, Charles	Wybrow, Captain Anthony.
Pattison, Mark	Casaubon, Reverend Edward.
Pattison, Mrs. Mark (later Lady Dilke)	Brooke, Dorothea.
Payne, Tom	Byler, Luke.
Pearsons, The	Dodsons, The.
Pool at Griff	Round Pool.
Poyser, Mrs. (name only)	Poyser, Mrs.
Robinson, Mrs.	Pettifer, Mrs.
Rocester	Rosseter.
Roston	Broxton.
Roston (suggested only)	Hayslope.
Saint Mary's Hall, Coventry	Court Room, Stoniton.
St. Nicholas, Church of, Nuneaton	Milby Church.
Sandford, Reverend Mr.	Baird, Reverend Mr.
Shilton, Sally	Sarti, Caterina.
Simms, Edward, jun.	Music Master at Mrs. Lemon's School.
Staffordshire	Loamshire.
Stockingford	Paddiford Common.

Original	Character or Place
Stockingford	Whittlecombe.
Stockwith	Luckreth.
Stopford, The Honourable and Reverend Mr.	Prendergast, The Honourable and Reverend Mr.
Stratton, Richard	Organist, Shepperton.
Tavern, Red Lion Square	"Hand and Banner."
Taylor, Mr.	Old Maxum.
Towle, Miss	Townely, Miss.
Towle, Mr.	Lowme, Mr.
Townend, Poll	Tranter, Deb.
Trent (river)	Floss (river).
Vicar's Lane, Coventry	Lantern Yard.
Voce, Mary.	Sorrel, Hester.
Waldron, Sir John	Bridmain, Mr.
Wallington, Mrs. Nancy	Raynor, Mrs.
Weaver Hills	Binton Hills.
Wheway, Mr.	Lamb, Jonathan.
Wicken, Miss	Jackson, Miss.
Wilkinson, Mrs.	Jennings, Mrs.
Wirksworth	Snowfield.
Wooten Hall	Donnithorne Chase.